W9-AWR-911

PRAISE FOR
A SHATTERED PEACE

"The failures of Versailles cast a long shadow. David A. Andelman provides a thoughtful assessment of the dilemmas of the Great War's victors, and Woodrow Wilson's noble and ill-fated quest to design a new international order."

—Henry A. Kissinger

"The peace settlements that followed World War I have recently come back into focus as one of the dominant factors shaping the modern world. The Balkans, the Middle East, Iraq, Turkey, and parts of Africa all owe their present-day problems, in part, to these negotiations. David Andelman brings it all back to life—the lofty ideals, the ugly compromises, the larger-than-life personalities who came to Paris in 1919. And he links that far-away diplomatic dance to present-day problems to illuminate our troubled times. A tremendous addition to this vitally important subject."

—Ambassador Richard Holbrooke

"The peace conference in Paris at the end of World War I was the first and last moment of pure hope for peace in the history of world affairs. Our president Woodrow Wilson was the sorcerer for this hope, and he kindled great expectations in people everywhere. David Andelman, a classic reporter and storyteller, tells this fascinating tale of hope falling finally and forever on the shoals of naivete and hard-headed cynicism."

—Leslie H. Gelb, former columnist for the *New York Times* and President Emeritus of the Council on Foreign Relations

"The failed peace settlement following the Great War of 1914–1918 has been the subject of many fine books. In many respects, David Andelman's *A Shattered Peace* is the best of these. It is compact and compellingly written. Moreover, it explains more clearly than any other work how the failure of peacemaking in 1919 shaped later history and, indeed, shapes our own era."

—Ernest R. May, Charles Warren Professor of American History, Harvard University

"It is the power and fascination of David Andelman's new book, *A Shattered Peace*, that he shows us—with the clarity of a first-rate reporter and the drama and detail at the command of a first-rate novelist—that we are all still enmeshed in the loose ends of the Treaty of Versailles. Andelman brings us to Korea, to Vietnam, to the Persian Gulf, and to Iraq in our own vexed era. His story is alive with color, conflict, and interesting people. We could not find a better guide to this time."

—Richard Snow, Editor in Chief, *American Heritage*

A
SHATTERED
PEACE

Also by David A. Andelman
The Peacemakers

*The Fourth World War: Diplomacy and
Espionage in the Age of Terrorism*
(with the Count de Marenches)

A
SHATTERED
PEACE

VERSAILLES 1919 AND THE PRICE
WE PAY TODAY

CENTENARY EDITION

David A. Andelman

WILEY

John Wiley & Sons, Inc.

Wiley General Trade, an imprint of Turner Publishing Company

www.turnerpublishing.com

A Shattered Peace: Versailles 1919 and the Price We Pay Today, Centenary Edition
Copyright © 2014 by David A. Andelman. All rights reserved

Illustration credits: Pages 2, 19, 137 courtesy of Brown Brothers; page 38 from Harold Nicolson, *Peacemaking, 1919*, Houghton Mifflin Company, 1933; page 51 courtesy of Culver Pictures; page 97 courtesy of Weizmann Institute Archives; page 127 courtesy of Vietnam News Agency, Hanoi; page 146 courtesy of Bettmann/Corbis; pages 199 and 251 courtesy of Corbis; page 232 from Marie, Queen of Roumania, *The Story of My Life*, Charles Scribner's Sons.

Design and composition by Navta Associates, Inc.
Centenary Edition jacket by Jason Smith

No part of this publication may be reproduced, stored in a retrieval system or transmitted in any form or by any means, electronic, mechanical, photocopying, recording, scanning or otherwise, except as permitted under Sections 107 or 108 of the 1976 United States Copyright Act, without either the prior written permission of the Publisher, or authorization through payment of the appropriate per-copy fee to the Copyright Clearance Center, 222 Rosewood Drive, Danvers, MA 01923, (978) 750-8400, fax (978) 750-4744. Requests to the Publisher for permission should be addressed to Turner Publishing Company, 424 Church Street, Suite 2240, Nashville, Tennessee, (615) 255-2665, fax (615) 255-5081, E-mail: submissions@turnerpublishing.com.

Limit of Liability/Disclaimer of Warranty: While the publisher and the author have used their best efforts in preparing this book, they make no representations or warranties with respect to the accuracy or completeness of the contents of this book and specifically disclaim any implied warranties of merchantability or fitness for a particular purpose. No warranty may be created or extended by sales representatives or written sales materials. The advice and strategies contained herein may not be suitable for your situation. You should consult with a professional where appropriate. Neither the publisher nor the author shall be liable for any loss of profit or any other commercial damages, including but not limited to special, incidental, consequential, or other damages.

Turner also publishes its books in a variety of electronic formats. Some content that appears in print may not be available in electronic books.

ISBN 978-1-63026-904-3 (hardcover), 978-1-62045-991-1 (paperback), 978-1-63026-905-0 (e-book)

Printed in the United States of America

14 13 12 11 10 9 8 7 6 5 4 3 2 1

To Pamela, my truly valorous woman

CONTENTS

FOREWORD

BY SIR HAROLD EVANS

"Magic Mirror on the wall, who is the fairest one of all?"
—The Queen, *Snow White and the Seven Dwarfs* (1937)

On January 18, 1919, there was but one answer from all 357 mirrors elegantly framed in the arches of the Hall of Mirrors at the Palace of Versailles in Paris: "Wilson! Wilson le juste! Wilson is the fairest one of all!"

Hundreds of thousands of people in Paris, London, and Rome came to look on Woodrow Wilson, the twenty-eighth president of the United States, to call his name and to bless him. He stepped ashore at the French port of Brest in December 1918 as the savior of mankind, the devout Presbyterian who would inspire the Versailles peace conference and bind the wounds of the seminal catastrophe of World War I (1914–1918). Candles were lit before poster portraits. British schoolgirls scattered white carnations where he walked. Men clasped hands with the simple bonding, "Wilson!"

America's entry into the war on April 2, 1917, had been decisive in terms of men and materials, tipping the balance against the Central Powers (Germany and its allies Austria-Hungary and Turkey), but the euphoria on his arrival was not only for victory nor was it confined to the winners. What made him a hero for the millions of war-sick civilians and soldiers on both sides of the trenches was his vision of a world without war. He had contained the United States in a fastidious neutrality for nearly three years while the Entente Powers (France, the British Empire, Russia, Japan, and Italy, belatedly) collectively shed the blood of millions of their citizens. Russia had nine million casualties, the French had six million, the British Empire three million, and Italy two million. Though Russia had suffered by far the most casualties, the Bolsheviks were not among the 27 Allied and associated powers at Versailles, their attendance having been vetoed by the French. Europeans feared the contagion of communism, and the Bolsheviks had already sued Germany for a separate peace in 1917, ceding Ukraine, the Baltic provinces, and Poland.

The French, British, and Italian leaders and their publics had convinced themselves that Kaiser Wilhelm II, the erratically headstrong leader of an imperial, resurgent Germany, had expansion in mind when he backed Austria-Hungary's eagerness to punish Serbia for the murder in Sarajevo of visiting Archduke Franz Ferdinand, heir to the throne. It was the "damned foolish thing" in the Balkans that in 1888 Otto von Bismarck had predicted could produce a great European war. The scholarship of blame had years to mature, but in the meantime the victorious French, British, and Italian leaders came to Versailles to punish the vanquished. They were determined not only to make sure that Germany never again had the capacity for aggression, but also to parcel out among themselves the "helpless parts"—Wilson's phrase—of the three sundered empires, Ottoman, German, and Austro-Hungarian. These remnants had fiercely complicated molecular structures of religion, culture, and language and prideful histories of their own. Paris seethed with lobbies of Arabs and Jews, Japanese and Chinese, Poles, Ukrainians, Kurds, Rumanians, Czechs, Skovaks, Lithuanians, Albanians, Koreans, Irish Sinn Feiners, Vietnamese, and Cossacks. It was, observed the British diplomat, Harold Nicolson, "a riot in a parrot house."

Wilson entered the negotiations at Versailles with a wholly different perspective from the Allies. American casualties were hardly insignificant—323,000—but atonement was alien to Wilson's mind. He was angered by the escalation of submarine warfare by the "madman" of Germany, but his decision to fight had been an epiphany rather than an exercise in realpolitik. He had for three years earnestly desired to be summoned as an arbitrator, a sublime referee. Now he realized that as a participant in the war he would have more leverage as a peacemaker when it ended. He used more than semantics when he went before Congress to announce that America would support the allies as an associate and not as an ally. His renunciation of self-interest sounded self-righteous but it was deep in his soul. "The world must be safe for democracy. . . . We have no selfish end to serve. We desire no conquest, no dominion. We seek no indemnities for ourselves, no material compensation for the sacrifices we shall freely make." Not content with rationalizing the immediate decision, he had proposed an unprecedented doctrine for relations between states. Moral principle, rather than military power, should be the governing force in a world organization of democracies dedicated to mutual security, a League of Nations. The universal interest in peace was to be superior to national interests. Wilson sought nothing less than replacing the principle of the balance of power, by principles of freedom, openness, and self-determination.

He had distilled the abstractions of his speeches into Fourteen Points, principles for the conduct of a brave new world with specific boundary changes. He unveiled them on January 8, 1918, and supplemented them with nine further principles of freedom: open covenants instead of secret treaties, free trade, subject peoples offered "self-determination," the chance to coalesce into new nations governed by their consent. The French president, Georges Clemenceau, the "Tiger of France," who presided at Versailles, did not conceal his disdain for Wilson's Fourteen Points: "God Almighty gave us only ten—and we broke those."

This timely new edition of David A. Andelman's classic work *A Shattered Peace*, first published in 2007, tells us how high principle got mugged on the way to the pulpit by raw anger, cynicism, colonial appetites, ignorance, and greed. Andelman, an experienced foreign correspondent and commentator, judges the outcome of Versailles a "colossal failure," without any of the elevating moral principles. The ideal of self-determination, he writes, was misapplied without taking heed of the strength of differences of religion, language, clan, tribe, and culture, ingrained by blood feuds, cemented by centuries of hatred and violence. And when Wilson had to choose his priorities, says Andelman, he was more ready to yield to the Allies on self-determination than on his beloved League of Nations.

Andelman takes us on a revealing journey, conflict by conflict, from 1919 to decades of wars and turmoil. He sees them as the flowering of obnoxious seeds sown at Versailles: the peace that stirred German resentment, the humiliation of the Chinese, the ethnic cleansing in the

Balkans, the creation of the unviable state of Iraq, and Islamic terrorism.

His compelling narrative resonates with our times. It is alive with the personalities who got ignored at Versailles but lived to make history: Nguyen Tat Thanh, in 1914 a dishwasher in the kitchen at the Carlton in London, who was inspired by Wilson's Fourteen Points to haunt the corridors of Versailles to ask that the people of Indochina have rights equal to their French colonizers. He was denied an audience but got the world's attention later as Ho Chi Minh. Most poignantly, there's the accord between the Bedouin prince of Arabia, Emir Faisal bin Hussein, a descendant of the Prophet, and the champion of Zionism, Chaim Weizmann, on establishing a "Jewish commonwealth" in Palestine. And it's maddening to read how the powers missed the opportunity to have a stab at rescuing the Middle East from imperialism, despotism, and today's terrorism. Andelman argues that had not the promises to Faisal been betrayed and had the French and British been even-handed, we might have had Syria and Lebanon in a Hashemite kingdom, like Jordan "a thus-far peaceful model of Arab governance." And out of the "pernicious stewpot" of Mesopotamia, we might have laid the ground for a new Arabia. Versailles could have created a loose federation of states each free to pursue its own religious and ethnic course. Instead we got Iraq, "9th-century imperialism barely covered with the fig leaf of self-determination." Only a despot could keep the lid on the combustible mixture of religions and the meddling of Shiite Iran next door. And then we had the ill-judged invasion by the United States. American sacrifices made it possible to envisage a triumph at last for democratic pluralism and the rule of law, but then all was swiftly wrecked by the vengefully partisan Shiite leader, Nouri al-Maliki. His victimization of the Sunnis opened the door for the Islamic State (ISIS), the detritus of Syria's civil war, barbaric corrupters of Islam with a medieval agenda.

Admirers of Wilson may think Andelman a little tough in his judgments of Wilson's attempts to fit the bits of jigsaw into a more heterogeneous map of states, constrained as he was by secret treaties and the principals' determination to hold fast to spheres of influence. But Andelman's judgments are not hindsight in hard covers. As a journalist commentator, he forecast the disintegration of Yugoslavia. As for Wilson, it can at least be said he was prophetic in warning of the dangers in the "peace after victory" that all the belligerents sought. "Victory would mean peace forced upon the loser," he said, "a victor's terms imposed upon the vanquished. It would be accepted in humiliation, under duress, at an intolerable sacrifice, and would leave a sting, a resentment, a bitter memory upon which terms of peace would rest, not permanently, but only as upon a quicksand. Only a peace between equals can last." After the "war to end all wars," the unequal peace contrived at Versailles lasted just twenty years.

A *Shattered Peace* was good history in its first edition and events have sharpened its relevance. It is essential reading because without an understanding of the history Andelman relates so well, the news today and tomorrow and tomorrow, lighting fools the way to dusty death, can only be a bewildering kaleidoscope of happenings.

Sir Harold Evans, Editor-at-Large for Reuters, is the author of The American Century.

Up to the Minute:
An Introduction

At nine o'clock on the evening of September 11, 2014, barely two years and four months before his second term would end, President Barack Obama's appearance was broadcast on every American television network as he strode confidently to the podium erected on the state floor of the White House, at the foot of the grand staircase. Looking as grave, as determined as most had seen him since early in his presidency, he told the world:

> I've insisted that additional U.S. [military] action depended upon Iraqis forming an inclusive government, which they have now done in recent days. So tonight, with a new Iraqi government in place, and following consultations with allies abroad and Congress at home, I can announce that America will lead a broad coalition to roll back this terrorist threat.

He was referring to the Islamic State of Iraq and the Levant, or ISIL. This band of terrorist thugs had already rolled through and assimilated vast swaths of northern Syria and Iraq en route to establishing a modern Caliphate. Now it was President Obama's announced intention to bring them to their knees. Ironic, because it was Obama's Democratic predecessor a century earlier who effectively brought an end to the last Caliphate.

Redrawing the map of the Middle East in such an ill-conceived manner back then has left today's self-styled Islamic State in a most tenable position to restore what the peacemakers of Versailles had dismembered and destroyed.

Seven years ago, as Sir Harold Evans so eloquently points out, I first published this work in an effort to help Western leaders and those from whom they derive their authority understand the errors committed by their forebears. In turn, our leaders today could avoid similar pitfalls that stem from an absence of understanding and a surfeit of hubris. Sadly, all have failed us—then and now. The cost in the most recent Iraq War has been high—the lives of at least 120,000 persons, soldiers and civilians, according to the Iraq body count project, though other surveys suggest numbers passing one million. The United Nations estimates another 190,000 have died in the ensuing Syrian Civil War. At the same time, these nations that the Treaty of Versailles so ignorantly conceived have made little progress toward establishing free and democratic societies. In the past seven years there have been dramatic political, social, and religious upheavals in this part of the world, directly or indirectly attributable to the shortcomings of the treaty and those who negotiated it for their own selfish or misguidedly principled purposes.

The world, or at least some parts of it, has changed dramatically in the intervening seven years since this book was first published. Many of the dynamics that laid the foundations for these latest transformations remain very much a reality frozen in historic time. Before we plunge directly into this maelstrom of history and the world whose leaders assembled in Paris in those early years of the twentieth century, it's worth a moment to sit back and reflect on where we are a century later and how we got here. Let's examine what has happened in each of these regions in the years since the first appearance of *A Shattered Peace,* and how much further each has fractured.

The Middle East

The most dramatically transformative events—the greatest fractures—have occurred in the Middle East, beginning with the second Iraq War. This war took a direction that should have been apparent but was hardly foreseen seven years ago when my book first appeared, even by the most pessimistic or prescient. The creation of a true quagmire all but unmatched in modern history sucked in American forces and cost the United States more than four thousand servicemen killed in action and more than thirty thousand wounded—many disabled for life. Though the United States departed from Iraq definitively more than a year ago, it left behind the legacy of a badly injured nation that successive events suggest may never be healed. Emerging with stunning, indeed frightening clarity were the deep divisions, the ancestral enmities of religions and nationalities—Sunnis, Shiites, Kurds—that have been feuding and warring across these sands for a millennium or more, hostilities never more than papered over by a succession of now-deposed regimes of strongmen and dictators. The putative democrats installed in their place have been ill equipped, ill-inclined, or too deeply sectarian themselves to have established the kind of transformative mechanisms that might have brought a degree of peace or at least metastability to these regions.

Indeed, the prediction contained in these original pages of a tripartite division of Iraq, the fundamentally artificial nation central to the Mesopotamian region or to the Levant, appears to be moving toward a frightening new reality. This new region, however it may finally evolve, is headed in the direction of an oil-rich Shiite nation in the south, closely allied with neighboring Shiite Iran; a prosperous, self-assured Kurdish nation in the north sustained by its own oil wealth and by a powerfully motivated business elite committed to building a country that could serve as a homeland to Kurds scattered across a half dozen other Middle East nations; and a rump Sunni nation surrounding Baghdad whose security and survival would be assured by the powerful Sunni petro-monarchy of Saudi Arabia just next door. Hastening, with lethal consequences, this inevitable breakup are the forces of ISIL, a band of violent Sunni bandits who have played on passions and venality across vast stretches of these lands. Their efforts to stitch together a twenty-first-century Caliphate have only laid bare the raw wounds that this earlier effort ignored or sidestepped.

The roots of today's violently disrupted world, as I predicted in these pages, were laid with the dissolution of the Ottoman Empire, the last Caliphate, that had persisted for half a millennium. Its Sunni ruling class at its peak dominated half the civilized world, alongside the powerful counterweight of Persia, the Shiite empire that became the mullahs' Iran. Replacing the Ottomans were a succession of artificial nation-states cobbled together by Westerners with little understanding of the peoples who lived there. The heart of this cancer that rapidly metastasized is of course Iraq, created by President Woodrow Wilson and his European allies and sustained today by American leaders across the political spectrum. The hopes or dreams of most of today's Western leaders, deeply anxious to ensure their legacy, are only reinforced by empty promises heaped on them by a succession of Shiite leaders in Baghdad desperate to preserve dominance over a region that was never fully theirs from the get-go, but in urgent need of Western steel to sustain a warped and historically perverted vision.

The emergence of the self-styled Islamic State has only served to highlight the more dramatic errors of the peacemakers at Versailles. None really understood the people whose lives they would change forever—and hardly for the better. Yet this is the nature of the region that has emerged from years of bloodshed and that has been plunged again into a horror barely envisioned when this book was first written. With a reach that stretches across Syria through northern Iraq and with even broader ambitions far beyond these expansive boundaries, these latter-day warriors of jihad that the West calls ISIL have a capacity of spreading terror and bloodshed on a scale barely envisioned by the conservative Wahhabis whom I describe as the creators of modern Saudi Arabia.

Establishing even a coalition of the barely willing to dismantle ISIL's nascent Caliphate before it is fully created will hardly be easy. But any power that succeeds in redrawing the boundaries of the Middle East on a more rational basis with a broader and fuller understanding of the deeply felt religious and ethnic forces that is more readily at hand today than a century ago will be taking a major step toward returning peace to a region that has known little but war, conflict, or repression for too long.

Land of Jews and Arabs

The other, still deeply traumatized area of the Middle East is the nation of Israel—carved from the region of Palestine that was both a legacy of the British Empire and integral to its designs on a vast and strategic territory that stretched from the shores of the Mediterranean to India. For a host of reasons I explain in these pages, the British wanted a nation for and by the Jews that might serve as an anchor for broad and expansionist ambitions—an empire on which the sun would never set. What they left behind at the end of the colonial area was a legacy as deeply fractured and filled with ancestral religious and ethnic enmity as any other region where Western leaders laid their hands.

British officials assumed that Palestinians and Jews could learn to coexist, sharing the lands that each considered its birthright. Initially, this worked nicely. Jewish settlers began buying from Palestinian landowners their farms and territories for what seemed at the time a fair market value. There was no effort by the British or their allies assembled in Paris to alter the partition terms delineated years before in the Balfour Declaration or divide these territories further into two lands—one for Palestinians, another for Jews. The two-state solution that today, nearly a century later, still eludes those who inhabit this territory, might then have proved far less disruptive than the partition of the Indian subcontinent into India and Pakistan when British colonials packed up and departed the Raj.

In the years since I first discussed this dilemma, the positions of Israelis and Palestinians have become more hardened, their confrontations even more lethal. The recent warfare between Israel and Palestinians in Gaza appears to be but the latest in a string of skirmishes that will stretch interminably into the future, with the truce that brought the immediate fighting to an end proffering only a momentary respite in the continuum of that region. Equally, the new communities of Jews that still spring up in Israel's New Territories (or Occupied Territories, depending on which side your allegiance may fall) claimed by Palestinians, only serve to enflame passions that are in desperate need of soothing.

Clearly, a century ago Britain believed that if Scots, Welsh, and Irish could all live with degrees of amity under the umbrella of the United Kingdom, then Arabs and Jews could share the Holy Land. But the British Isles are all Christian lands with a shared, if not common, heritage. Even so, there have been decades of bloodshed in Northern Ireland, freedom for the Republic of Ireland, and a passion for independence held by nearly half the people of Scotland. Imagine the lengths to which Palestinians and Jews might be prepared to go to achieve their dreams of a homeland. Sadly, today we are not close even to a superficial understanding of the power of such aspirations. Moreover, the divisions over the past seven years even within Israel, the rise of potent new right-wing religious parties with a single-minded goal of a greater Holy Land, and demographic shifts that promise even deeper divisions in the future threaten to derail Israel's position as the one real democracy between Greece and India. Across an ever-widening divide, the even more pressing demographic imperative within the shrinking territory the Palestinians legitimately call their own has only expanded the recruiting base for extremist groups anxious to impose their own radical, confrontational stamp on this region. Understanding the roots of these problems could go a long way toward resolving them. But without people of good faith on both sides, it is difficult to see any path to the future that is not strewn with bombs and bodies.

Remade in Their Image

Fortunately, other parts of this world the peacemakers of a century ago sought to remake in their own image have fared better over the past seven years—but largely by transcending the vision of the Versailles Treaty's drafters and returning to their roots. Poland, Hungary, the finally separated Czech and Slovak Republics, and the prosperous and now-peaceful new nations created from the breakup of an artificial Yugoslavia have all joined the European Union. Most are growing today more rapidly than the nations whose leaders created them in the Versailles Treaty.

Notwithstanding the best efforts of the Western Allies to reduce the nation they conquered in World War I to a permanently second-rank power in 1919, Germany has a potent economy that has proven to be the engine sustaining much of a united Europe—a reality never appreciated by the peacemakers of Versailles. Indeed, were it not for the German economic miracle, the entire mechanism of the Euro as a currency uniting eighteen disparate nations (plus Lithuania joining in January 2015) appeared unsustainable over the past seven years of economic collapse and turmoil.

At the same time, there have been innumerable challenges to the coherence of a united Europe. The peacemakers assembled in Paris hardly imagined such a structure emerging from the ashes of the First World War, let alone from the vast destruction left from a second continent-wide conflict barely a generation later. But having surmounted a series of tests—economic, political, diplomatic, even military—this united entity has managed to confound both critics and skeptics, expanding to the fringes of the old Soviet empire and embracing a broad spectrum of political leadership that in recent years has skewed increasingly to the right.

It is still Russia that seems to pose the most direct and virulent challenges to the European heartland whose leaders came to Paris in 1919 as either victors or victims. Russia, then as now, however, was on the out-side looking in, its nose pressed threateningly against the glass. A century apart, two Vladimirs have proved to be Europe's greatest adversaries. In 1919, it was the newly minted Bolshevik leadership of Vladimir Ilyich Lenin and his coterie who shunned the Versailles process, pledging that communism would, before long, stretch from the Atlantic to the Urals and sending shivers of fear across Europe—a shadow overhanging the entire negotiations. Now, Vladimir Putin, the communist leader's suc-cessor as master of the Russian colossus, presents the continent's greatest challenge. But the roots of today's confrontations can certainly be seen in those events a century in the past, and are ignored only at our own peril and that of our leaders. The fears and passions of Russia that were motivating forces then have hardly abated or even changed dramatically.

Today, both halves of Europe are capitalist to the core. And that is, perhaps, their greatest strength—and the greatest prospect for future peace and prosperity. Germany could no more be restrained in its capac-ity for ingenuity and diligence than could Russia with its passion for recognition and respect. These are the lessons of Versailles that today we must all understand and absorb.

Asia Rising

At the Paris conference in 1919, Asia was little more than a side issue. A surging Japan did its best to restrain a fading and demoralized China. Today the positions are directly reversed. Japan has embarked on what appears to be an inevitable and unrestrained long period of decline, while China has become the economic engine of the Orient and Occident alike. Part of this shift in circumstances was a tribute, again to decisions of the peacemakers of Paris.

But in the past seven years, an all but unforeseen series of demographic imperatives have bestowed on China the human and natural resources to overwhelm the rest of humanity. That some of the foundations of this strength were laid in Paris a century ago is all but forgotten, though explored in some depth in Chapter Nine. Today, a Chinese company, Alibaba, and its slight, cheerful founder Jack Ma, a simple English teacher from Hangzhou, made the largest corporate debut in history on the New York Stock Exchange. My new iPhone 6 Plus, ordered from Apple in Palo Alto, California, was shipped via UPS from Zhengzhou,

China, where it had been assembled and packaged. As the years pass, this leadership shift becomes increasingly apparent, only highlighting the shortsightedness of the peacemakers in Paris. Might a more even-handed approach to Japan and China a century ago have set each nation on a different path? Today, there are new, even more challenging realities to which we must adjust.

Hopes and Dreams

Woodrow Wilson came to Paris to create a peace that would end what he earnestly believed would be the last world war. His goal? To bring the concept of self-determination to all people. It was a goal shared only in words, not deeds, by his allies. Today's Western leaders profess similar solidarity, but with as little functional understanding of fundamental realities as their predecessors a century ago. Self-determination, enabled perhaps from the outside, but growing organically from within, has been and remains the key to peace in every corner of the globe. Yet true self-determination often implies a homogeneity that we who have long embraced this concept and the democracy that accompanies it are reluctant to accept. The lessons of Versailles, since this volume first appeared, have been only marginally heeded.

In fifty years of traveling through and reporting on more than eighty countries, but especially after spending the last seven years observing the path the peacemakers of Versailles carved out of ancestral empires, I have arrived at one hope: That this work may yet help Western leaders to avoid the same errors that have perpetuated ever-widening cycles of violence. My life as a journalist and a historian has been devoted to what I hope may be my legacy—an understanding of what motivates many of those whose dreams I have chronicled. The past seven years have offered little evidence that we are moving in the right direction, only that my conclusions were not misguided. President Obama has already warned of more turns in this lethal spiral, stretching beyond his own presidency. It is a sad legacy he was bequeathed and that he is now poised to bequeath again. It is a cycle Woodrow Wilson and his aide Colonel Edward M. House launched with consequences neither could ever have foreseen or imagined. Yet today's leaders of America and the West must pledge themselves to complete this process their predecessors set so terribly awry.

This pledge must go far beyond simply serving as the world's policeman, identifying our friends and enemies, and supporting the former while attacking the latter. We also must develop a deep understanding of what truly motivates these friends and enemies, their origins, hopes, fears, and aspirations, and how likely they are to prove transformative to their regions and their cultures. Such an understanding may not inoculate us from pledging our own lives and our fortunes, not to mention our sacred honor. But at least we may be prevented from squandering our most valuable possession—our good name. Now, if we have even a hope of success, we must bend to the task resolutely—with honor and diligence, and above all with some degree of intelligence. As President Obama insisted, "It is not America's fight alone." But recall the words of Woodrow Wilson as he was taking his nation into war:

> The world [must] be made fit and safe to live in; and particularly it [must] be made safe for every peace-loving nation which, like our own, wishes to live its own life, determine its own institutions, be assured of justice and fair dealing by the other peoples of the world as against force and selfish aggression. All the peoples of the world are in effect partners in this interest, and for our own part we see very clearly that unless justice be done to others it will not be done to us.

We now pick up our story with the young British diplomat Harold Nicholson opening the door to the study of Woodrow Wilson in Paris. It is May 1919, and the world is about to change, irrevocably.

—David A. Andelman
Paris, October 6, 2014

ACKNOWLEDGMENTS

The origins of *A Shattered Peace* go back more than forty years to research I undertook for my senior honors thesis at Harvard, inspired by Professor Ernest May, now the Charles Warren Professor of American History, the leading diplomatic historian of our time. My choice back in 1965 was between studying and writing about diplomatic history or, by contrast, reporting on such history as it was being made. I chose the latter and embarked on an endlessly fascinating career as a journalist, which has taken me to more than fifty countries. In every case, my reporting was enriched by my studies of events and personalities of the past. It was when I came to the preparation of this volume, that I was finally able to call on some of those individuals and their writings which appear in the bibliography at the end of this volume. Here, however, I would like to acknowledge some of those who played important roles in the making of this book.

First, there are the diligent archivists of Columbia University's Rare Book and Manuscript Library who helped uncover some of the manuscript diaries that proved so valuable. Archivist Spencer Howard at the Herbert Hoover Presidential Library in West Branch, Iowa, and archivist Tom Hyry at the Colonel Edward House papers of the Manuscripts & Archives division of the Yale University Library each helped me uncover some key documents. At the Weizmann Institute in Israel, a special thanks to Orna Zeltzer and Merav Segal; and at the Vietnam News Agency in Hanoi, I am particularly indebted to Ban Thuy Ky for providing early photographs of a young Ho Chi Minh in France. In Paris, Madame Lise Devinat, the grandniece of Georges Clemenceau, was an extraordinary guide and font of knowledge of the archives of her great uncle in the same Rue Benjamin Franklin *hôtel particulier* where he lived and was shot during the peace talks. Another congenial and informative guide to the atmosphere of the time was the veteran New York fund manager Louis Auchincloss, whose father Gordon served as aide and confidant to Louis's grandfather Colonel Edward House. Then there are those who read part or all of this manuscript, providing excellent advice and counsel—Russell Flannery, *Forbes*'s brilliant Shanghai bureau chief and Chinese expert; Jenny Krasner; and Jerry Silver, a truly meticulous researcher whose encyclopedic mind snagged more faux pas than should be in the capacity of any single human being. Skip Stephens did yeoman service getting the word out in Washington.

This author has also had the good fortune that everyone connected with this work from its conception has been an extraordinary professional and congenial companion. First there was my agent, Alexis Hurley of Inkwell Management, who believed in me and the project from the start, even finding the energy and time in her frantic schedule to read and counsel me on every page. Then there was Hana Lane at John Wiley & Sons, a truly gifted editor whose personal interest in this project was an enormous support as she helped shape and form this work. Also at Wiley, Rachel Meyers, Matt Kaye, and Mike Onorato believed passionately in the project. D. L. McElhannon drew the illuminating maps. Nina Gould designed a deft and engaging Web site. I am deeply indebted to my diligent copy editor, Dolores Dwyer. At Turner Publishing, which has done me the honor of issuing this Centenary Edition, my deepest thanks to my accomplished editor, Christina Roth, to Kelsey Reiman, and of course to Turner's president and publisher, Todd Bottorff, who recognized the deep value this volume would have in these parlous times. Finally, of course, there was my wife, Pamela Title, who relinquished countless weekends and untold fishing trips to read each draft with loving care and skillful attention, urging me on in sleepless predawn hours when so many of the best words and phrases were crafted.

PROLOGUE

INFLECTION POINTS

SPRING IN PARIS, A BRILLIANT TUESDAY, MAY 13, 1919. AT FOUR o'clock
the city is still bathed in that crystal light that washes every building
clean, even the aging but elegant town houses in the city's fashionable
sixteenth arrondissement. There, on the Rue Nitot, President Woodrow
Wilson has gathered the leaders of the four victorious Allies. World War
I is over. And now these statesmen are remaking the world—in their
own image. The issue today is Iraq—carving what will become a new
nation out of the sands of Mesopotamia. The brilliant young British
diplomat Harold Nicolson has been cooling his heels in the anteroom,
engrossed in *The Picture of Dorian Gray*, when suddenly a door flies
open and he is summoned into the presence of the leaders. He picks up
the story in his diary:

> A heavily furnished study with my huge map on the carpet. Bend-
> ing over it (bubble, bubble toil and trouble) are Clemenceau,
> Lloyd George and PW. They have pulled up armchairs and crouch
> low over the map. . . . They are cutting the Baghdad railway.
> Clemenceau says nothing during all of this. He sits at the edge of
> his chair and leans his two blue-gloved hands down upon the map.
> More than ever does he look like a gorilla of yellow ivory. . . . It
> is appalling that these ignorant and irresponsible men should be

1

cutting Asia Minor to bits as if they were dividing a cake. . . . Isn't it terrible, the happiness of millions being discarded in that way? Their decisions are immoral and impracticable. . . . These three ignorant men with a child to lead them. . . . The child, I suppose, is me. Anyhow, it is an anxious child.

This self-deprecating Nicolson was perhaps the only truly prescient individual in the room—one who understood that those who fail to learn from history are condemned to repeat it. And repeat it we certainly have.

It all began in this fashion in Paris. If there was a single moment in the twentieth century when it all might have been different, this was the moment: Paris, 1919. The end of the Great War, which in perfect hindsight we call World War I, changed everything. Certainly the peace imposed at Versailles by the Western powers—Britain, France, Italy,

The Big Four Allied leaders at the Paris peace talks: Italy's Prime Minister Vittorio Emmanuele Orlando being lectured by British Prime Minister David Lloyd George, with French Prime Minister Georges Clemenceau and U.S. President Woodrow Wilson standing by.

and the United States—on the vanquished, not to mention the weak, the powerless, the orphaned, and the friendless, determined much of what went wrong for the balance of the century and beyond.

For the sins of omission at that crossroads of history were in many cases as important or more important than the sins of commission. Those who were ignored and disdained at Versailles, for whatever multitude of reasons, were those whose heirs and descendants would return and wreak their vengeance on us all. Countless books have been written dealing with the failures of the Great Powers—the single-minded goal of the French and the British being to destroy or emasculate Germany, their historic military foe and economic rival, and its allies Austria-Hungary and the Ottoman Empire, to make certain that they had neither the means nor the will ever to challenge French hegemony on Continental Europe or British control over the high seas. And then there was the inability of the Americans to impose their own moral values on allies and enemies alike—a failure whose seeds were sown in those distant days but whose results resonate loudly today. Far less attention has been paid to those marginalized individuals and peoples who huddled around the fringe of the plenary sessions for that epiphanal year in Paris, whose needs and desires received only the most passing attention.

Yet their oversights, errors in judgment, or outright refusals to deal with many of the most pressing imperatives in far-off regions, where politicians and diplomats with a Eurocentric shortsightedness perceived little real or immediate threat to world peace and the established order, have led directly to many of the most catastrophic events of our own time. The lapses of that brief period in Paris in 1919 were driven by a chain of diplomatic DNA that has become imbedded, with often the most pernicious results, in our own world order.

Over the course of two decades, I traveled vast reaches of Europe, Asia, and the Middle East as a foreign correspondent, speaking with the powerful and the disenfranchised, kings and commoners, on four continents. Wherever I went I was confronted with the same questions, in various forms, posed by people who thought deeply about what had gone wrong, sometimes horribly wrong, with their system of government, their way of life. How did we get here and where did things go off the rail?

I've never been a believer in single-causation theories; history is far too complex for such a simplistic approach. Yet I am a deep believer in inflection points. And the more I reflected on this question—asked by people as distantly removed as a Thai princess, the last surviving granddaughter of the littlest prince of Anna's King Mongkut; a Hungarian professor of American studies, the son-in-law of the nation's revered poet laureate; an Israeli diplomat in the court of Golda Meir; an Austrian cardinal; a bodyguard of Yasir Arafat; and a host of others—the more I came to believe that there may indeed have been a single moment in modern times when all their worlds did intersect, collide, then spin off again out of control.

This was a truly rare occasion when such disparate cultures and peoples, such diverse systems of political and social organization came together in one place to shape the future of the civilized world. Certainly there have been other summits of world leaders. There was the creation of the United Nations at Lake Success and its recurrent annual fall ritual of the opening of its General Assembly. There was Bretton Woods, where the world's modern monetary system was launched. There were superpower conferences throughout the history of the cold war. There were multinational peace conferences from Vietnam to the Middle East. I've been present for many of them. Each of these events was shaped—indeed, predestined in its own peculiar way—by the events of those months in Paris. As winter gave way to spring, summer, and fall of 1919, leaders of a handful of nations presumed to take over as a global government and impose their will—effectively to transform the world and history into their own image.

It was not, in its own way, dissimilar to our own troubled time when a small group of powers, again led by the United States with its own form of self-styled moral authority, also sought to impose its will on a large part of the world that neither chose nor invited this presumptive imperative. The paramount difference is that in that far simpler world, it was indeed possible for a handful of nations to stop time, effectively, and change the nature and direction of history, albeit with an impact with which we are still coping. The lines they drew of the nations they were creating, the peoples they assembled within these artificial boundaries, the powerful forces of ethnicity, religion, and nationality they unleashed, and the economies they set up that were destined to fail created many of the troubles we have inherited today.

What exactly went wrong in Paris that was later to cost us so dearly, especially in parts of the world to which those great statesmen, powerful politicians, and towering diplomatic thinkers never gave much more than passing attention? That is the question we'll try to answer in these pages, focusing our attention on the bit players who hovered on the edges of the Great Powers, hoping that some small droppings from their table would improve their lot and guarantee the freedom and prosperity of their people—only to be sadly disappointed. For these bit players were the ones whose small needs, dismissed often with a disdainful wave of the hand in 1919, would translate into cataclysmic events a half-century or more later. The seeds of today's terrorist wars were planted in the halls of the Paris peace talks—by those who were there and by those who were not.

Listen to a frustrated Woodrow Wilson, who came to Paris with the intention of bringing a new era of moral responsibility to the management of international affairs and an end to global conflict, but who within weeks found himself mired in a swamp of intra-European intrigue and colonial profiteering: "The world will say that the Great Powers first parceled out the helpless parts of the world, and then formed the League of Nations. The crude fact will be that each of these parts of the world had been assigned to one of the Great Powers."

These helpless parts of the world nevertheless had their voices in Paris. Their frustration was in how rarely and faintly those voices were heard by those who were remaking the world. Who were some of these people? There was Nguyen Tat Thanh, a part-time photofinisher and full-time busboy at the Ritz Hotel, who longed passionately for freedom for his people in a far-off French colony called Cochin China. Feisal ibn Hussein, a Bedouin prince of Arabia, descendant of the Prophet, member of the ancient Hashemite clan, sought unity for the Arab people and affirmation of his rule over vast reaches of the Arabian Peninsula, from the Gulf of Aqaba across Iraq and the endless sands of the Empty Quarter to the Mediterranean. A Jewish patriot, Chaim Weizmann, dreamed of returning his people to the Holy Land he believed God had promised them. And there were scores of others: Asian princes from Japan; freedom fighters from Poland; musicians, writers, knaves, and revolutionaries from the Balkans across the plains of the Hungarian *puszta* and the coal mines of Czechoslovakia to the steppes of Russia and the doors of the Kremlin. All were part of the brilliant, but in the final analysis failed, tableau of interests that led to a treaty that was painfully ill-designed to establish the lasting peace that at least some of its drafters so desperately desired.

Each came to Paris with his or her particular, at times peculiar, even quixotic, needs, desires, and agendas that fell on the ears of at best deaf, at worst arrogant, men, filled with hubris, who shrugged off their pleas, dismissing them with disdain, resorting all too quickly and too often to mockery and derision. These men, and the occasional woman, were so supremely confident of their ability to manipulate the controls of power because they were playing on their home turf. It was a playground they had designed, built, and manicured each morning—using their own rules in a game they had designed with a particular outcome they had scripted even before their arrival in Europe in the weeks that followed the Armistice. This is not to say these were the only rules, or even the best. They were merely the ones these players had decided would be observed.

Imagine what might have happened had the Allied powers been forced to negotiate terms of the future of humanity under the rules and organization of the Bedouin Arabs of the Empty Quarter or the Cochin Chinese of Annam. All were surely civilizations no less advanced and sophisticated in every sense than ours—culturally, politically, even militarily. Instead, all were made to play under rules that for them were all but impenetrable, dooming their goals to defeat.

These bit players spent much of those months in Paris, with their noses pressed against the glass as their nations were divided up. Very quickly they found dashed the dreams of their people for the kinds of self-government promised by the lofty Fourteen Points. These had been drafted by Wilson as the principles on which the United States entered the war that was to establish an enduring peace. Instead, while the great statesmen played games of realpolitik, the future of scores of these smaller nations was entrusted to a handful of academics and junior diplomats—a tall order, though each did his best to navigate the shoals of global diplomacy where, as we shall see, the shape of the peace and the realignment of the world began to emerge. In the end, they left behind a failed peace in the form of an eighty thousand–word document, the longest such treaty in history. But their legacy consisted of much more—a wreckage of national hopes that led to a second world war and the domination of half of Europe by a communist despotism for the rest of the century.

All this played out against a vivid tableau peopled by a host of petty despots and thieves, not to mention charlatans, pimps, partygoers, literati, journalists, and artists of every stripe. This broad kaleidoscope of individuals gave those months in Paris their texture and helped form the backdrop of the stage where the Treaty of Versailles was negotiated. Society's party-giver Elsa Maxwell came as a young lady and organized the first of her great soirees in the town house of Boni de Castellane at 71 Rue de Lille for the young American heiress she was accompanying. The great actress Sarah Bernhardt appeared in galas for French charities. The celebrity designer Elsie de Wolfe offered her renowned teas. Megan, the young daughter of Britain's David Lloyd George, danced the night away in the basement of the Hotel Majestic, at times in the arms of the young diplomat Harold Nicolson. Allen Dulles, a junior U.S. official, prowled the boîtes and the corridors of Paris, learning the tradecraft of espionage around which he would build an organization that three decades later came to be known as the Central Intelligence Agency. His jealous older brother, John Foster Dulles, also managed to maneuver his way to Paris, where his hubris turned into a painful interlude in efforts to establish a new economic order for Europe.

A glamorous French army colonel headed a fact-finding mission into Poland amid rumors of fighting that reached the ears of the delegations in Paris. That colonel was Charles de Gaulle. A young assistant navy secretary named Franklin Delano Roosevelt brought his wife, Eleanor, who found him far too attentive to the many unattached Parisian women whose husbands had been lost in the war. There were evenings when Jean Cocteau read aloud his "Cap de Bonne Espérance" and André Gide mingled with Marcel Proust. There were Japanese barons and viscounts, Rumanian kings and Transylvanian poets, even Wellington Koo, the thirty-two-year-old Chinese ambassador to Washington, fresh from an education at Columbia, who still delighted in singing his college fight songs.

On each of the major delegations, bit players often turned out to be the real keepers of the flame of liberty and justice that much of the civilized world desired—but failed to achieve. On the U.S. delegation, Stephen Bonsal, an army major, had stumbled on Wilson's principal aide and the éminence grise of his presidency, Colonel Edward House, by chance in Berlin in March 1915, helping him as a German translator when the war was just getting under way. Three and half years later, Bonsal, plucked from the front lines, was given a mandate by the principal American negotiator in his first meeting at House's quarters in the

Rue de l'Université. It was just before the armistice that brought the war to an end in November 1918, and House was preparing for the difficult negotiations to come. Bonsal described what House had in mind for him:

> I will follow the President's example and give you no definite instructions, but just a hazy idea of what I expect from you. I think I can handle Lloyd George and the "Tiger" [Georges Clemenceau] without much help. But into your hands I commit all the mighty men of the rest of the world. I shall expect you to call at least once a day and my door will always be open to you. From time to time, if inconvenient to call, send me a memo—or better still, leave it with the sailors who will guard my gate. . . . The war that has destroyed cities has puffed up some little men until they find their hats and their boots too small, much too small for them. I shall count on you to present them to me in their original proportions. . . . [Especially] I want you to keep in touch with the strange peoples from southeastern Europe who are assembling in such numbers in Paris in expectation, I fear, of the millennium—which may not be so near at hand as we all hope.

Bonsal himself was flabbergasted: "I went out of the room gasping. It was certainly quite a job I had fallen into by 'picking up' Colonel House on the streets of Berlin in March 1915."

Most representatives of the Great Powers did their best to ignore all those like Wilson who aimed for higher values or higher ends. So among the Allies in Paris there was often strife and ill will. The British saw the French as competitors for Ottoman territories in the Middle East and Russian lands in Central Asia. And both feared these regions were falling prey to the onslaught of communism, which threatened to snatch these colonies from their grasp. At the same time, the French—an enormously proud people on whose territory the Great War was largely fought and won—found the conflict had left their economy in a shambles. They were forced to go hat in hand to the British for a handout while the Americans seemed to be selling their birthright for cash.

All that bitterness emerged in so many petty ways in Paris. The welcoming cheers with which the French crowds first greeted Wilson gave way to a stony silence after a few months. These same crowds sat on their hands when the president's face appeared on the newsreel screens in their cinemas. And French bureaucrats overbilled the Americans for the plush accommodations at the Hotel Crillon they used for offices during the peace talks. All of these personal and geopolitical forces, large and small, played a critical role in setting the course of the world for the next century during those months crammed into the pressure cooker that was Paris after a debilitating war. The pressure had been released, and in what had always been the Continent's gayest city, it all came spilling out in those early months of 1919.

In his diaries, the young Harold Nicolson wrote emotionally of his trip from London across the channel to Calais and on to Paris, and of his thoughts as he was traveling by train and ferry to this new and exciting adventure. He was determined not to replay the Congress of Vienna which, more than a century earlier, had brought to a conclusion the last pan-European war. His goal was to make certain this would be a conference that emphasized the establishment of a much desired era of permanent peace, rather than a conference to divide spoils and exact retribution at all costs even from the innocent populations on the losing side. These people had already paid so dearly with the lives of their families and loved ones and their own ability to live rewarding and productive lives in the future. "As I lunched that morning between Calais and the Gare du Nord, I was aware of the differences with the last great conference, the Congress of Vienna in 1814," Nicolson wrote. "They'd worked in secret, we were committed to 'open covenants openly arrived at.' We were preparing not only Peace, but Eternal Peace."

It's impossible to say with any certainty what might have happened if the world leaders gathered in Paris in 1919 had behaved or reacted differently. What if they had paid closer attention to the Nicolsons of the world? What if they had more carefully considered their every action, reined in their emotions, educated their colleagues back home, and prepared their electorates as well? History is not a science, at least not in the conventional sense of the natural or physical sciences, where carefully controlled experiments with varying parameters can ascertain what outcome can be expected, and replicated, again and again. Still, imagine if the partition of Iraq had been treated with a bit more care than the manner in which Harold Nicolson described in his diary.

Many of the minor players in Paris who came out on the losing end in the Treaty of Versailles learned much from their contacts with the Great Powers and their military, political, and diplomatic tactics. Did we unwittingly provide the Arab states with the necessary political, and eventually military, techniques that would ultimately be turned back on us half a century later and half a world away? The seeds of the 1970s' Iranian hostage crisis and the Islamic-inspired terrorism of the twenty-first century were planted in Paris long before the mullahs and their followers ever reached for, let alone succeeded in grasping, political power. Which of our many weaknesses did we teach an aristocratic Japanese diplomat who, a generation later, dared to take his nation into war with the United States as his country's prime minister?

Even among the victorious Allies in Paris, there were two opposing views of the optimal organization of the postwar world. The Americans and President Wilson tried to force on their European allies the concept of a unified world under a global government called the League of Nations. This would have removed much of the ability of the victors to impose their will on the colonial nations they had conquered at considerable effort and expense and from which they still expected to extract the kind of wealth their own aging economies no longer were able to supply. The Europeans, still mired in their fragmented organization of small nations—England, France, Belgium, Italy—saw the world in their own image. Their advantage lay in accelerating the fragmentation of the defeated Central Powers. So the Austro-Hungarian Empire gave way to independent mini-states of Austria, Hungary, Czechoslovakia, and the nation of the south Slavs—Yugoslavia. A reborn Poland was carved out of Germany and Russia. The boundaries of all southeastern Europe were reconfigured. And the League of Nations, designed to enforce the frontiers of these new nations and nourish their development, became a watered-down club for diplomats beside an isolated Swiss lake.

Moreover, the major Western powers were able to exert all but unfettered control over their mandate states or colonies. Rather than assist their gradual transition toward independence and self government, the League simply became a depository for decisions taken elsewhere. The failure of the League has been laid at the feet of the Americans' refusal to ratify the Treaty of Versailles and assume control as the leading force behind world unity. But resistance from the other Allied powers played at least an equal role in the League's untimely demise. As a result, the smaller nations and colonies remained under the boot heels of the West with ultimately explosive consequences that accelerated and multiplied into such wars as Vietnam and Iraq, and the ultimate conflict between the haves and have-nots: terrorism.

Indeed, much of the rhetoric of the crises of Europe that marked the year 1919 resonates vividly with everyone who listens to those leaders of today's world struggling to cope with a new form of global unrest and terrorism. While we look at the actions of the players, we must also look at their words, and it is here that we find the most striking, and at times frightening, parallels with those of our own leaders in our own times. Indeed, no matter how closely we study history, we still seem inevitably to be repeating it or, at the very least, echoing it.

There were terrorists, perceived and at times very real, in 1919. They just came in different colors (red and white), flying a different banner (the hammer and sickle), and worshiping a different religion (Marxism rather than Islam). But Bolsheviks were the terrorists of that era—frequently described in such a fashion, though there had really been no terrorist incidents aimed at the West—at least not yet. Any real violence was still confined to Greater Russia, where the post-czarist war between the Reds and the Whites still raged; and parts of Eastern Europe, such as Hungary, where Soviet-style governments managed to seize power, at least briefly, in the vacuum that reigned after the war. So if we suspend disbelief for a moment, and make a few rhetorical substitutions in some pronouncements of that time, we can see some truly frightening portents for our own troubled era. Listen, for instance, to Colonel House, and swap "al-Qaeda" for "Bolshevism," "Iraq" for "Hungary":

> From the look of things the crisis will soon be here. I hear rumblings of discontent every day. The people want peace. Bolshevism [al-Qaeda] is gaining ground everywhere. Hungary [Iraq] has just succumbed. We are sitting on an open powder magazine and someday a spark may ignite it. . . . It is not that we are taking too much for normal conditions, but since the world is crumbling about us, it is necessary to act with a celerity commensurate with the dangers that confront us.

Indeed, many of Wilson's advisers in 1919—like those in the White House in the weeks preceding the 2003 invasion of Iraq—were urging some strong, definitive action. There was, for instance, the cable Wilson received on March 25, 1919, from Joseph Tumulty. His private secretary was holding down the fort in Washington while the president fought for what he believed was the future of a free and peaceful world in Paris. It was a crusade that many believed was becoming a quixotic and ill-conceived battle in which the United States had little if anything to gain. Again, substitute "al-Qaeda" for "Bolshevism," "Iraq and Afghanistan" for "Hungary and the Balkans": "There is a great danger to you in the present situation. I can see signs that our enemies here and abroad would try to make it appear that you are responsible for delay in peace settlement and that delay has increased momentum of Bolshevism [al-Qaeda] and anarchy in Hungary [Iraq] and the Balkans [Afghanistan]."

These were perceived threats to the natural order as profound in their own way at that time as the menace today's terrorists pose to the world. And clearly we have learned little from the mistakes of the past. In 1919 many of Europe's statesmen descended on Paris to formulate the peace with a misplaced sense of paternalism that overlaid some very strong self-interests that frequently became indistinguishable. In their months together at the conference tables, they considered themselves, as they often expressed it, the world's government. This applied equally to the great powers they represented and the smaller powers as well. The Big Four suffered the real and elected leaders of these lesser players to make cameo appearances in their negotiations—after the real work of determining their future was finished.

Even those among the major powers with the best of intentions believed they controlled the keys to prosperity. So it would be a failure on their part, or at least an abdication of their responsibilities to those less endowed with wealth or power, to turn the resources and vast populations of the underdeveloped world over to homegrown Third World leaders. With perfect hindsight, some of these fears proved to be well-founded—with the rise of such petty, though vicious, dictators as Haile Selassie in Ethiopia, Alfredo Stroessner in Paraguay, the self-proclaimed "emperor" of Central Africa, Jean-Bédel Bokassa, or Haiti's Papa Doc Duvalier, and a host of unstable, repressive, and violent regimes in the Middle East and across Asia. But had these nations been placed under the mandate of a strong League of Nations, endowed with real powers to ease their path to independence and statehood under a democratic system, might their histories also have been different? Might different forces from those that brought to power these tyrants have come to the fore, just as different forces might very well have left an Austrian housepainter and his megalomaniac followers ranting to themselves in a remote Bavarian beer hall?

The aim of most of the victors who began arriving in Paris after the armistice in November 1918 was to create an imperial peace. This was tailor-made to maintain British hegemony on the high seas, thereby protecting its global empire. It helped France dust itself off and reestablish its claim as the preeminent Continental power. And it mandated the rest of the world—especially those less powerful but no less endowed with natural or material wealth—to dispatch their tribute to the victors in the form of commodities, cheap labor, and expanding markets. We are still paying the price today for all those diplomats and politicians who, with great insouciance, dismembered nations and divided peoples carelessly and thoughtlessly according to a simple whim, or worse. Listen to how Harold Nicolson describes the fate of the Austro-Hungarian Empire:

Another cloudless day . . . Down with [Foreign Secretary Sir Arthur J. Balfour] to the Quai d'Orsay. There (in that heavily tapestried room, under the simper of Marie de Medici, with the windows open upon the garden and the sound of water sprinkling from a fountain and from a lawn hose) the fate of the Austro-Hungarian Empire is finally settled. Hungary is partitioned by these . . . distinguished gentlemen—indolently, irresponsibly partitioned—while the water sprinkles on the lilacs outside—while the experts watch anxiously—while AJB, in the intervals of dialectics on secondary points, relapsed into somnolence, while [U.S. Secretary of State Robert] Lansing draws hobgoblins upon his writing pad—while [French Foreign Minister Stéphen] Pichon, crouching in his large chair, blinks owlishly as decision after decision is actually recorded. . . .While the flies drone in and out of open windows, Hungary loses her North and East. Then the frontier with Austria, which is maintained intact. Then the Jugo-Slav frontier. Then tea and macaroons. . . . AJB makes all of Paris seem vulgar.

From nearly a century away, much of the vulgarity of these times has come to seem almost civil—especially in the face of the barbarity that has engulfed so much of a world that the signers of Versailles sliced and diced in what they saw as their own most important self-interests. While President Wilson came to Paris armed with a set of moral principles founded on his profound Presbyterianism, nurtured by his theologian father, he found this worldview shared by few among the leadership of his allies, who paid little more than lip service to any religious morality. Though France and Italy were closely aligned with the Roman Catholic Church, and the British monarchy was the guarantor of the Church of England, their leaders in Paris found no religion to guide their hands during their deliberations in 1919. There was little of the moralism, often bordering on zealotry, that so engulfs our twenty-first-century world—forming the fundamental underpinnings of such extremes as Islamic terrorism on the one hand and theocracy of the Christian right on the other. Equally there was little sensitivity to the urgent needs of the sick, the hungry, and the homeless, except as they influenced the political fortunes of leaders of the Western world, which was picking itself up and restoring itself after a debilitating war.

My goal is to expose the small vulgarities and larger forces that have morphed into the barbarities of our own time nearly a century later. We will look much farther into the future, with our gift of twenty-twenty hindsight, than would ever have been possible for these negotiators—to understand and acknowledge the consequences five, even ten moves ahead. Part of their dilemma was an inability to appreciate that the world had already begun to change with a speed that they, still mired in the nineteenth century, could not begin to understand. That this change would accelerate, gathering speed and energy from unforeseen forces that they had set in motion, was something they neither needed nor wanted to know.

When Europe emerged from the Great War, it was still a schizo-phrenic place. On one side of the divide were the old forces that had brought on the conflict in the first place—a realpolitik of monumental clashes to recoup small slivers of territory. On the other side of that divide, however, were new forces. Radio, the telegraph, and the airplane were already shrinking vast distances. Elsa Maxwell arrived in a Paris "swept by a dance craze as people went wild over the new school of jazz that had been developing in America during the war." While Georges Clemenceau retired each evening to his tiny garden apartment on the Rue Franklin, other younger delegates found their way to the Ritz bar or the new nightclub of Paul Poiret, where they rubbed shoulders with the four corners of the world.

My intention here is to lift the curtain on the undersides of Paris 1919—a crossroads of history. All the old assumptions of stability and security—the way we made war and guaranteed peace—began going out the window as we plunged pell-mell from the signing of the Treaty of Versailles through the rest of the twentieth century.

1

ONWARD TO PARIS

Aᴌᴌᴇɴ ᴅᴜᴌᴌᴇs ᴡᴀs ᴌᴀᴛᴇ ꜰᴏʀ ᴀ ᴛᴇɴɴɪs ɢᴀᴍᴇ ɪɴ ᴛʜᴇ sᴡɪss capital of Bern. The twenty-four-year-old who would one day become America's master spy, the patriarch of the Central Intelligence Agency, had just arrived by train from the U.S. mission in Vienna to take up his new post, and he'd run into an old friend from his school days—a buxom Swiss lass who played quite a passable game of tennis. Now he was at the U.S. legation in the Hirschengraben seeing to his luggage and was just closing up the office when the phone rang. The caller identified himself as a Russian revolutionary who needed to speak immediately with someone at the legation. Dulles insisted it was quite impossible and to ring back on Monday. The caller insisted, urgency in his voice. Dulles refused, hung up abruptly, and went off to his tennis match. The next night, the Russian was sealed into a Swiss train with his comrades for the trip across Germany to the Finland Station in the Russian capital of Petrograd. The caller was Vladimir Ilyich Lenin.

How different might the world have been had he answered the call of the revolutionary rather than the call of the blonde, Dulles wondered barely two years later as he began packing his bags again, this time for Paris and the peace talks that were to mark his true debut on the world stage. Though Dulles never learned what was on Lenin's mind—he may simply have hoped to open a dialogue with the West—it's entirely

possible such an overture might have led to the young American staying
in Switzerland. The venue of the talks had been moved to Paris from
Lausanne after worker demonstrations, sparked by Lenin and his Bolshevik followers, erupted in Lausanne and across Switzerland.

Though Dulles was disappointed to be leaving Switzerland and a post
where at his tender age he had managed to acquire some considerable
responsibilities for a young diplomat, he was especially excited by this
opportunity to play a role in shaping the future of the world—while
at the same time serving alongside his beloved uncle, who happened to
be the secretary of state of the United States—Robert Lansing. Still, he
knew that he would not be alone since many young diplomats would be
joining him, helping to establish the new world order.

A brilliant fifty-three-year-old army officer, Ralph Van Deman, had
already built a unique intelligence service for the United States in the
final years of the war. His next mission, as delegated by his boss, Army
Chief of Staff General Tasker Howard Bliss, was simpler: to make certain that the American mission in Paris could do its work without any
interference from the strange foreign manipulators who were arriving all
around them with agendas far different from that of Woodrow Wilson.
Or as Van Deman wrote in a memorandum to General Bliss:

> Persons known to hold disloyal sentiments and those of anarchist
> or terrorist tendencies should be denied admission to the buildings
> and constant and close supervision should be kept on all persons
> entering the buildings whose sentiments and affiliations were not
> known. . . . We must know what persons were admitted to the
> buildings, where they went in the buildings and when they left. Also,
> due to the unusual conditions following the long war, it was neces-
> sary to assure ourselves as far as possible that no evil intended [sic]
> persons were allowed to loaf about the entrances of the buildings.

Nearly seventy intelligence police were assigned to assure Van Deman
that his direct orders would be carried out to the letter. The profound
mistrust of foreigners, friends and foes alike, was but a foretaste of the
kind of reception the new world order—and America's place in it—
would receive back home. Ultimately, this national attitude would keep
the U.S. isolated with little understanding of the forces set so powerfully
in motion—until it was too late.

The senior U.S. delegation in Paris (from left to right): Wilson adviser Colonel Edward M. House, Secretary of State Robert Lansing, President Woodrow Wilson, Henry D. White (a retired diplomat and the only Republican), and General Tasker H. Bliss, U.S. Army chief of staff.

By the time the first American delegates began arriving at the posh Hotel Crillon, platoons of marines were already unpacking cases beneath the brilliant chandeliers of the building requisitioned by Van Deman as the headquarters, caravansary, cafeteria, and social gathering place of the U.S. delegation. An army lieutenant, once manager of New York's Vanderbilt Hotel, had been assigned to run the accommodations under the intelligence chief's supervision.

Van Deman, a Harvard graduate of the nineteenth century, was fully prepared for the arrival in Paris of the next generation of Ivy Leaguers whom Wilson and his top aide Colonel Edward House had organized to prepare the U.S. delegation for its role, as they saw it, of reshaping the world. This largely patrician bunch of researchers, historians, economists, and all varieties of political thinkers, was called the Inquiry. It included a twenty-eight-year-old Harvard-trained journalist and political philosopher named Walter Lippmann; the Harvard historian Samuel Eliot Morrison, to redraw Slavic Eastern Europe; Charles Seymour, the thirty-three-year-old alumnus of Choate and Harvard, to parcel out the remnants of the Hapsburg Empire; and the cartographer Isaiah Bowman to draw the maps that would ultimately define the nature of the postwar world.

This super-secret group, which ultimately numbered 126 researchers drawn largely from Harvard, Yale, Princeton, Columbia, and the University of Chicago, produced more than a thousand reports of problems that these academics believed might be encountered by the peacemakers in Paris. The early meetings took place at the New York Public Library. Yet apart from its masterful maps, most of its work was decidedly amateurish. Its ten-member Middle Eastern group, operating out of Princeton, contained no specialists in contemporary affairs in the region. It was chaired by a scholar of the Crusades whose son, also a member, was a specialist in Latin American studies—a subject far removed from Arabia. The Arab group's members included experts on the American Indian, an engineer, and two Persian-language instructors. Often the reports did little more than repeat summaries from encyclopedias the Inquiry members found in the public library. The Middle Eastern report failed even to mention that there might be any deposits of the petroleum which, with the era of mechanized warfare already dawning, would be of enormous strategic value to any nation that controlled them.

So it was not too surprising that by the time the group arrived in Paris, Lippmann, who ran the Inquiry with Bowman, wanted more. He had already uncovered the brilliant intelligence reports of Allen Dulles that were being passed back through diplomatic channels to the State Department. Dulles had been quickly sucked up into the mix—crossing, mostly deftly, the artificial boundaries between diplomacy, intelligence, and academe. He was already installed in Paris when Wilson's private train, carrying him from the harbor of Brest where his ship had docked to great fanfare, arrived in Paris to a hero's welcome. The young American diplomat had been involved in many of the arrival arrangements—from the red carpet welcome by Prime Minister Georges Clemenceau to the ride in an open carriage down the Champs-Élysées to the Place de la Concorde and the doors of the Crillon. Crowds swarmed the streets, all but choking the grand plaza in front of the hotel, youths hanging off lampposts, waving American flags. The savior of Europe, and especially of France, had arrived to remake a new world. And the French, of course, expected to be at its epicenter. These moments, as Dulles was to discover, were the peak of the excitement. For Wilson and the rest of the U.S. delegation, it was only downhill from there.

At first Dulles was delegated to his uncle, who would be increasingly marginalized but, by virtue of his official position as secretary of state, occupied a palatial suite with twelve-foot ceilings at the end of a corridor guarded by two marine sergeants and looking out over the Place de la Concorde. The less fortunate found themselves in more ramshackle rooms in an adjacent wing that stretched out toward Maxim's restaurant on the backside. Some of the younger and more carefree of the diplomats and support personnel quickly discovered one advantage to these quarters. It seemed the building was connected through a trap door at the rear to the second floor of Maxim's, whose gilded front entrance was around the corner on the Rue Royale. This celebrated restaurant boasted several private rooms on the second floor long used for trysts by the wealthy and famous.

Van Deman spotted this obvious security loophole on December 4, 1918, before the bulk of the U.S. delegation began to arrive, and would have none of it. "I ordered a padlock placed on the trap door and the keys thereof placed in the charge of a sergeant reported to be entirely reliable," Van Deman reported to his commanding officer, General Bliss. But two weeks later, he discovered that the trap door "which had been padlocked was open. This made it necessary, of course, to again padlock the door and remove the keys from the custody of the sergeant, which was done." As Harold Nicolson observed to his smug delight, however, somehow Van Deman's most valiant and persistent efforts failed to prevent traffic, which eventually proceeded quite regularly between the U.S. delegation and the evening entertainment on the other side.

Dulles was quick to discover that the real work of the conference and the U.S. mission was proceeding not in his uncle's palatial suite but in the more modest quarters of Colonel House and members of the Inquiry. Eventually Dulles and Seymour, two young patricians, gravitated toward each other. Seymour appreciated the pedigree and intelligence, as well as the accomplishments, of the young Princeton-educated diplomat who had already managed to acquire a deep understanding of the complex politics and diplomacy of the regions he was delegated to oversee. Dulles understood the power that together they could wield, both in the negotiations that were just getting under way and in the fledgling nations they were effectively to rule—at least for their months in Paris—and to shape for a century. Dulles and Seymour played key roles in redrawing the map of central Europe and the Balkans, a map that was to cause untold problems from World War II through the bitter ethnic battles of Kosovo. But they were not to operate alone. Alongside them in their endeavors was a young Brit of equally impeccable academic credentials—and bloodlines. His name was Harold Nicolson.

When the armistice was announced on November 11, 1918, Nicolson was already preparing for the Peace Conference in the basement of the British Foreign Office in Whitehall. He had an impeccable diplomatic background. He was born in Tehran, where his father, Sir Arthur Nicolson, was serving as British ambassador. With the outbreak of the war, Sir Arthur and family had returned to London, where he had taken up his post as permanent undersecretary of the Foreign Office—the principal British officer of the nation's diplomatic corps. By the time of the armistice, his son was already well up the ladder of his own success.

Young Harold's immediate focus was on the Strumnitza enclave—an obscure corner of Serbia that had been in dispute throughout a series of Balkan wars. Nicolson was en route to the map room in the tower when he heard a loud commotion on the sidewalks below, looked down on Number 10 Downing Street, and saw a beaming David Lloyd George emerge to toast the crowds. "So the Germans had signed after all," Nicolson mused, returning, maps in hand, to his basement office and the Strumnitza dilemma. "When I again emerged, the whole of London had gone mad," he recalled in his memoirs.

A month later, Nicolson was strolling past the Academy of St. Martin in the Fields with the redoubtable editor of the *Observer*, James L. Garvin, and expounding as the cynical and worldly Garvin listened kindly. "We had no revengeful desire to subjugate and penalize our late enemies, but a fervent aspiration to create and fortify the new nations whom we regarded, with maternal instinct, as the justification of our sufferings and our victory," Nicolson explained, only a trifle condescending perhaps. Still, Garvin smiled indulgently. "Well, if that is the spirit in which you are all leaving for Paris, I am glad at heart," he replied.

Just a few days later, Nicolson was loading himself and his maps onto the eleven o'clock train, bound for Paris from the Charing Cross Station in company with another old college chum, Eustace Percy, and his beautiful young bride of one month, Stella Drummond. At Calais they boarded the train to Paris and lunched lavishly in the dining car, thinking grand thoughts. After an extensive delay en route due to an accident on the rail line, where trains just crawled through the regions of northern France still devastated by the ravages of war, Nicolson and his entourage arrived finally at eleven o'clock at night in a brilliantly lit and, after the grim days of the war, newly gay Paris. Nicolson took a motorcar directly to the Avenue Kléber, dropping Percy and his bride at the sprawling ground-floor flat they had rented not far away at 72 Avenue d'Iéna. Arriving at the British compound, he found the delegation ensconced in two lavish hotels: the Majestic, fronting on the Avenue Kléber, and just behind, the Astoria—both a few blocks from the Étoile and the Arc de Triomphe.

The Majestic, festooned with onyx to the delight of the wealthy Brazilian women who had camped there on their regular prewar shopping trips to Paris, and the Astoria have had a checkered and ironic history in the days since Nicolson and the British and Commonwealth delegations arrived to negotiate the peace. A quarter century later, the Majestic was to become a headquarters of the feared Gestapo; as one French diplomat once whispered to me, screams could often be heard in the 1940s from the basement torture chambers where enemies of the Reich were worked over. The irony was that in this same basement, the British delegation had held their weekly soirées and Nicolson had invited some of his colleagues and best friends, Dulles included.

For these brilliant young swells, Paris 1919 was really little more than a continuation of life in the common rooms and the colleges of Oxford or Harvard, Cambridge or Yale. There were 207 British and Commonwealth personnel divided between the two buildings—a far cry from the 17 whom Lord Castlereagh had brought to the Congress of Vienna, which had set the course of the civilized world for the balance of the nineteenth century, as Versailles was to do for the twentieth century. In the dining room, female staff from some of the better English provincial hotels, "under the direction of a chaperone," Nicolson pointed out, served up the same sort of Anglo-Swiss swill that was available in some of the better Pall Mall men's clubs, "while coffee was British to the core."

Scotland Yard's Sir Basil Thompson organized security along the lines of Van Deman's plans at the Crillon—to the extent that it was quite easy to leave the Majestic compound though all but impossible to get in, even for rulers of the new nation-states of Central Europe, not to mention the detritus of the Hapsburg Empire, the petty diplomats and scheming politicians of the Balkans, and the exotic potentates of Arabia, India, China, and Japan. Many were subjected to unspeakable indignities, often detained by force of arms for daring to cross the doorstep, even on invitation of British diplomats. The attitude quickly became apparent. Such delegates were little more than curiosities—lab experiments or curious butterflies to be captured, pinned to a velvet cushion, then carefully examined and finally filed away and catalogued with little thought to the consequences for the environment left behind. All this despite the best of intentions of Nicolson and his young Oxbridge chums and their parallel numbers they found on the U.S. delegation. "We were hampered by the atmosphere of Paris," young Charles Seymour recalled to Nicolson. Nicolson himself took an even more antiseptic view of it all, though: "We felt like surgeons operating in the ballroom with the aunts of the patient gathered all around."

The fact is that Paris, indeed much of France, was still licking its wounds, as were many peoples in the most remote corners of the world for which the peace conference was a powerful attraction—promising freedom and new beginnings. It seems they all descended on the French capital.

One of these was an obscure Indochinese busboy and photo retoucher named Nguyen Tat Thanh. A young man of fierce determination and passion for his homeland, Thanh had been in the French capital for nearly a year when Paris went wild for the armistice. While Dulles was moving into the plush Crillon and Nicolson was installing himself in the Majestic, Thanh was living in a run-down residential hotel in Montmartre. Indeed, much of his life in the West had paralleled that of Nicolson, Dulles, and their crowd—but very much in a curious upstairs-downstairs fashion. While Nicolson was finishing his schooling at Balliol College, Oxford, and Dulles was winding up his days at Harvard, Thanh was leaving behind the mandarinate into which he had been born in Annam, son of a brilliant scholar in the service of the emperor. At the time Annam, or Cochin China, was engaged in a frantic intellectual struggle to maintain its independence—physical, cultural, and political—from its enormous neighbor to the north, China, and at the same time from the colonial French overlords who wanted little more from this strange, lush, far-off land than the riches they could extract in rubber and rice, of which it was the world's third largest exporter. Like many of those gathering in Paris, Thanh was deeply

committed to the independence and self-determination of his homeland, later to be known as Vietnam.

Thanh was not alone in believing that the contributions his
people had made to the Allied victory, and Wilson's pledge of self-
determination for all the world's oppressed or enslaved, entitled them
to special consideration as the West gathered in Paris. Feisal ibn Hussein—son of Emir Ali ibn Hussein, the powerful sherif of Mecca, king
of the Hejaz—commanded Bedouin legions that had been placed at the
disposal of the Allies against the Ottoman allies of Germany. At his side
was Colonel T. E. Lawrence, the official liaison between Feisal and General Sir Edmund Allenby, commander in chief of British forces in the
Middle East—but unofficially Feisal's self-styled "guide, philosopher
and friend." Lawrence of Arabia, as he came to be known, if not Feisal,
recognized the difficult path that lay before them. First there was the
military issue of just how central Lawrence and Feisal had really been
to the Allied victory. Then there was a host of political and diplomatic
reasons tied to a division of the spoils of the region among the Western
powers. Feisal and Lawrence both were products of the aristocracy of
their own nations—as schooled in the patrician manners of the well-
born as Dulles, Nicolson, or any of the young Ivy or Oxbridge swells
who would face them across the conference tables in Paris. The two
battle-tested leaders from Arabia came to these tables braced with a
background of steel, shot, and powder that none of their opposite numbers could boast. Yet absent the veneer of diplomatic refinement their
demands were no less insistent, their needs no less imperative, and the
consequences of their failures no less profound.

From Central and Eastern Europe and the Balkans, other equally
insistent national leaders also converged on the Peace Conference.
Edvard Beneš, the brilliant thirty-four-year-old foreign minister of the
would-be nation of Czechoslovakia, was entrusted by President Tomáš
Masaryk to represent a free Czechoslovak state in Paris. Poland was
blessed with a national treasure. Ignace Paderewski, perhaps the world's
greatest living pianist, spent the war years thrilling audiences throughout
the United States, building a reservoir of goodwill that was reinforced by
four million expatriate Poles who formed the largest single Polish community outside Warsaw. By the time the delegates began assembling in
Paris, vast numbers of this multitude had also decided to gather there,
each pressing his own personal agenda. These included such disparate

individuals as a doctor from the ski resort of Zakopane in the Tatra Mountains that straddle the Czech frontier along with a dozen of his advisers, and Roman Dmowski, a brilliant Polish chemist who relinquished the life of a scientist in an effort to shape the future of a free Poland. Dmowski wound up in perpetual confrontation with Józef Pilsudski, a revolutionary and field marshal who happened to be installed at the moment in Warsaw as the self-appointed president of the nation.

And from the Balkans, that remote and violent stew pot of southeastern Europe, came a host of dark political figures. The intrigues of this region, indeed, had launched the world into war five years earlier in the city of Sarajevo where the Hapsburg crown prince had been assassinated, providing just the excuse the Central Powers needed to open hostilities. Each wanted peace on his own terms, the populations of their neighbors be hanged—perhaps literally. As the American negotiator Stephen Bonsal put it, "They came as suppliants, it is true, but not on bended knee."

Though the focus of the large nations remained firmly on the new shape of Europe, the fate of the smaller members proved often to be a mere afterthought. But there were still many other delegates gathering from the four corners of the world—especially Asia. From Japan came Foreign Minister Baron Nobuaki Makino and ambassador to Britain Viscount Sutemi Chinda, and both ultimately kowtowed to the dark eminence, Prince Kimmochi Saionji, member of the ruling royal family. Known as the last genro, one of the great lords who westernized Japan during the Meiji Restoration, Saionji pulled all the strings yet rarely emerged from a self-imposed hermetic existence deep within a sumptuous apartment near the Parc Monceau. The rest of the delegation installed themselves comfortably in the Hotel Bristol on the fashionable Faubourg Saint-Honoré, just blocks from the Hotel Crillon. Their goal was a simple one: to preserve and expand Japanese hegemony in Asia, to continue its political, military, and economic dominance in the region. And all this would have to be done with the least cost to the purse or the resources of the nation.

But they ran up against a formidable opponent in Paris. For China, too, had sent a remarkable collection of negotiators who had spent the war years cultivating relationships and goodwill in Washington that were to serve them well. The public faces of the delegation were Alfred Sze, ambassador to London, and V. K. Wellington Koo, the thirty-two-year-old ambassador to Washington who had so ingratiated himself with Wilson that the American president invited him along on the *George Washington* on the trip to Paris. Koo and his sixty fellow members of the Chinese delegation moved in across the river at the plush Hotel Lutetia Concorde on the Boulevard Raspail, just steps from the French ministries where the fate of their nation was debated during those months of negotiations. Their goals were equally ambitious—to contain the spread of Japan that had begun with its victory over China in 1895, and to win back control of vast areas of their own country that had been stolen by Western nations at the time they were carving it up into "spheres of influence" in the last century.

Korea was another nation with a big beef to pick with Japan, whose overwhelming military force had annexed the poor mainland country, forcing the emperor of Korea, also a vassal of the Qing rulers of China, to cede his country to the Japanese. They had been ruling it with an iron fist for a decade before the delegates began gathering in Paris. Now the sorry little delegation it managed to assemble in Paris sought its freedom, to the chagrin of much of the West, which appeared to be doing its best to appease Japan—Asia's most powerful, and at least not overtly anti-European, nation.

Ahead of all of these diplomats who made their way to Paris, each accompanied by hundreds of advisers, aides, and assorted hangers-on, lay months of frenetic bargaining, manipulation, and inevitably pleasure and abandon. The result for most was disappointing failure and decades of unrest and turmoil as they scrambled, battled, and manipulated to remake their corner of the world to their own liking. Some yearned for what the new world order might do for them, while others feared what the new order might hold for millions of their countrymen. Many of these men, and occasionally women, were to play an enormous role in the history of the twentieth century that was to be written—a future shaped, as we shall see, by disappointment and disillusionment, dismissals and denials that met them from their first days in Paris.

2

LE DÉBUT

SATURDAY, JANUARY 18, 1919, DAWNED GRAY AND COLD, WITH scattered flakes of snow cascading onto the near-frozen cobblestones. For days Paris had been all but vibrating, pointing toward this much-anticipated day when the leaders of the world, or at least the victorious world, would gather to begin their task of drafting a peace to be imposed on the vanquished. At the Quai d'Orsay, France's ornate foreign ministry building overlooking the Seine, preparations for the first plenary session of the peace talks had been under way from before the late dawn on that frigid morning. The building, surrounded by its heavy wrought-iron picket fence, each tall black pole topped with a gilded spike, was ablaze with lights. Inside the grand Salle de la Paix with its twenty-foot-tall windows, workers had built a huge U-shaped table where each of the delegates would find his seat. At the head would sit the French prime minister Georges Clemenceau and President Raymond Poincaré, to be flanked on their right by President Woodrow Wilson and the U.S. delegates and on their left by British prime minister David Lloyd George and his delegation. Shortly after the traditional long lunch of the French capital, the delegates began to gather, their black motorcars swinging in through the gates to deposit the world's leaders at the foot of the grand staircase.

One observer, the Associated Press correspondent Charles Thompson, noted a critical peculiarity. "While there were two presidents—Poincaré and Wilson, nine premiers and numberless foreign ministers," he wrote, "in this it was in marked contrast with the Vienna congress, where emperors, kings, princes, and lords shaped the destinies of Europe, whereas today among the scores of European statesmen, there was not one bearing the title of nobility with the single exception of Baron Sonnino" of Italy. Reflecting a much-changed world and a broader stage, the delegates filing into the grand Salle were a far more diverse group than any previously gathered for such an international undertaking— Siamese, Chinese, and Japanese, an emir from Arabia, a maharajah of India. And President Wilson, in his opening remarks, paid tribute to the extraordinary nature of the assembled delegates: "In a sense, this is the supreme conference in the history of mankind, for more nations are represented here than were ever represented in such a Conference before, and the fortunes of the entire world are involved."

This was true in both senses, for better or for worse. The fortunes of much of the world would be made by the delegates in the coming months. But already, even as the proceedings were opened with such grand statements from the leading statesmen, some very bad precedents were being set.

This scene was little more than a somewhat hollow ceremonial gesture. The real work of the conference had already begun, by a far smaller, more elite, and far less disparate set of individuals. All were white Westerners of elite backgrounds with more congruent temperaments and, as it turned out, goals. The first unofficial meetings between the leaders of the Big Four peacemakers—dubbed the Supreme Council—and their aides had been taking place for a week in a smaller chamber in the same building, and the maneuverings were afoot.

It was nine weeks since the armistice had been signed. Six of them had been wasted on deciding who was worthy of being heard by the peace conference. The small nations found themselves decidedly below the salt at the negotiating table. There were some bitter rows, especially from Serbia and Belgium, over how many delegates each would be allotted. When the dust settled, the Great Powers—the United States, Britain, France, Italy, and Japan—had five apiece; there were three apiece for Belgium, Brazil, and Serbia; two delegates each for China, Greece,

Arabia, Poland, Portugal, Rumania, Siam (Thailand, as it is known today), and Czechoslovakia. There was one each for just about any other country that found its way to Paris and was recognized as a nation—Bolivia, Cuba, Ecuador, Guatemala, Haiti, Honduras, Liberia, Nicaragua, Panama, Peru, and Uruguay. Britain's colonies also won seats at the table—two each for Australia, Canada, South Africa, and India, with one seat to New Zealand—which embittered some delegations who calculated that this effectively gave the British Empire some fourteen seats. Of course, none of this mattered one jot, as it turned out.

The entire backbone of the conference, the major Allied powers, minus Japan—Britain, France, Italy, and the United States—simply moved into the private offices of Foreign Minister Stéphen Pichon, relaxed into his regency chairs, and continued to set the world's agenda. It was certainly a congenial setting, as Harold Nicolson later described it: "A high room: domed ceiling, heavy chandelier, dado of modern oak, Doric paneling, electric light, Catherine de Medici tapestries all round the room, fine Aubusson carpet with a magnificent swan border and regency tables."

The proceedings were similar to the way the United Nations works today. The entire world is seated each fall at the General Assembly and listens to interminable speeches from heads of state and government from every power that wants to send its leader. Then, at the slightest suggestion of a crisis, the real power convenes—the Security Council. But wait, not just the Security Council—the five permanent members: Britain, France, Russia, China, and the United States, whose powers of the veto have so often shaped the body's ineffectual responses to a host of world conflicts.

So in January 1919, with a monopoly of power in Paris effectively delegated to the four major Allied victors, it was clear that pressure on their efforts to shape the future of the world would come from other, outside forces. While the Supreme Council was organizing itself within the walls of the Quai d'Orsay and Pichon's office suite, the staffs and the delegations, large and small, were preparing for the challenges they would confront.

In the Hotel Crillon, a short walk across the Pont de la Concorde from the Quai d'Orsay, Allen Dulles found himself at the top of a list of 250 foreign service officers who knew the languages of Central Europe. He seemed a natural recruit for Colonel Ralph Van Deman's most critical mission—one that was to have repercussions far beyond the narrow confines of Paris and the Peace Conference. By mid-November, Van Deman had been designated chief intelligence officer of the U.S. delegation, responsible not only for counterintelligence against his counterparts among the other Allied services, but in charge of gathering information on what was going on more broadly in the rest of Europe. Colonel Edward House recognized that the peace was likely to be won by the power that had the best understanding of the situation on the ground in each of the territories that the delegates were about to carve up and remodel. So in mid-November House and Van Deman hit on an original approach to the rapid establishment of an effective spy network throughout Europe. Van Deman described it in his own words: "It will be remembered at the time Herbert Hoover had been given charge of providing food and relief for certain devastated sections of Europe. We desired to send with Mr. Hoover's workers going into those areas certain intelligence agents who were familiar with the country, but to this Mr. Hoover violently objected."

It was a brilliant system of the utmost simplicity. Herbert Hoover, who would become the thirty-first president of the United States, then headed a network of private relief workers in the defeated nations. They could move with total freedom and without a scintilla of suspicion among all the subject people of Europe. Indeed, as the dispensers of life-giving food and water, they would be welcomed as saviors. The only remaining problem was to persuade Hoover himself. House enlisted as his ally Hugh Gibson, a gifted young American diplomat. While serving as principal aide to Hoover in his relief efforts in Belgium during the war, Gibson had also managed to distinguish himself in gathering battlefield intelligence by wriggling through German lines. House now promised Gibson a cushy post as coordinator of the intelligence effort at the U.S. legation in Vienna if he would persuade Hoover to go along with the plan. "There is some talking [sic] of having me settle down inside the Central Empires to have general oversight of the various agents who are to be sent there to gather information," Gibson confided to his diary on November 16, 1918. Things moved quickly. Two days later, "at noon [Gibson] went over to see Colonel House who said the [State] Dept. has approved the idea of establishing an intelligence service in the Central Empires. He wants to suggest now that Hoover and I lay the basis for the system and that I remain at the end of the trip with HQ in Vienna to oversee the work of the various agents sent in to gather information."

Gibson was surpassingly discreet, but he and House prevailed. In a face-to-face showdown in Paris with Colonel House, Hoover, who never really managed to overcome his roots as a simple mining engineer from Iowa, was forced to give in. The coordinator of the largest international relief effort ever mounted was persuaded to agree to the use of his pan-European organization as a cover for the first network of spies the United States ever fielded in a coordinated fashion across the continent. Secretary of State Robert Lansing was also reluctant to cooperate with such an adventure. He refused to allow any State Department officer to participate in what he viewed as a squirrelly undertaking—one calculated to place any American diplomat seen to be cooperating in the gathering of illicit intelligence in a most difficult and embarrassing position. So it took a bit of maneuvering for Dulles, Lansing's diplomat nephew, to place himself on the receiving end of a host of cryptic messages from agents whose dispatches helped the United States redraw the map of Europe.

Dulles's officially designated role was principal aide to Charles Seymour of the Inquiry. His mission was to parcel out the remains of the Austro-Hungarian Empire and much of the Balkans—the region of Europe perhaps least understood by the Americans and most subject to the kind of intrigue and obfuscation that firsthand intelligence was designed to penetrate. For Dulles, serving as the principal coordinator and interpreter of the dispatches from the field and of the interesting and inventive bits of tradecraft being relayed by Gibson and his crew across Europe, was an especially useful exercise since he ultimately was to build the Central Intelligence Agency after the structure he supervised in Paris. Hoover had demanded that the espionage agents imbedded within his relief organization report only "in clear" (in plain English), not code, to deflect suspicion that they were serving a double function of intelligence agents and relief workers. Eventually, Hoover became proud of the accomplishments of the intelligence operatives he had harbored, and especially how they'd played the game, developing their own code that sounded very much like American vernacular. As he wrote in his memoirs, "Slang that had been dead for fifty years came to life. Slang of armies, baseball, football, colleges, stock markets and service clubs spread over the wires."

There was, for instance, the case of Captain Thomas T. C. Gregory, operating under cover of Hoover's relief operation in Budapest. Captain Gregory was told to convey to the Archduke Josef that he would never return to power, never be recognized by the United States or any of the Western powers, and that he would have to abdicate. Reporting on these events, effectively the final chapter in the downfall of the Hapsburgs, Captain Gregory translated them into this cable: ARCHIE ON THE CARPET 7 P.M. WENT THROUGH THE HOOP AT 7:05.

Sixty years later, U.S. intelligence agents in communist nations like Yugoslavia were still using such transparent cover as "labor attaché" to conceal their activities from America's enemies during the cold war. In 1977, shortly before I left Washington to take up my post in Belgrade as the *New York Times* correspondent, and anxious to learn who the CIA station chief might be, I asked an old friend, Dusko Doder, recently returned from the Yugoslav capital for the *Washington Post*. Doder called me back the next morning. "Just think baby food," was all he would say. A week or so after my arrival in Belgrade, the U.S. ambassador, Lawrence S. Eagleburger, invited me to a reception at his residence in the suburb of Dedinje, just down the block from the residence of Josip Broz Tito, the communist president of Yugoslavia. As I wandered from room to room in the cavernous mansion, I spotted a thin, solitary man with black-rimmed eyeglasses leaning against a mantel and walked up to him. I introduced myself as the new *New York Times* correspondent. He smiled, stuck out his hand, and said, "Hi, I'm the labor attaché at the Embassy. Burt Gerber." As I came to know him there, and later in Moscow, I came to recognize that there was no one—ambassador, diplomat, counselor—better informed about the country, its people, and its leadership than this simple labor attaché.

So in Paris in 1919, no one was better informed about events across Europe than the Americans with an access to the network established by Van Deman and House and run by Dulles and his colleagues. With the enormous gaps in the somewhat amateurish research turned out by the inquiry's academics, this kind of basic, operational intelligence became essential as the rapidly changing landscape began to move events more quickly than the delegates could keep up with as they drafted the peace document. The last thing the Allies wanted, especially the Americans with their own moralistic priorities, was for the treaties and the frontiers of Europe to be driven by military or political changes that they would become powerless to alter or shape.

It turned out to be unfortunate that Hoover's intelligence network did not extend past the Balkans and failed to encompass the Middle East or any part of Asia. Still, it served to point out the advantages of what came to be known as "humint," or human intelligence. What can be obtained by savvy men and women on the scene, talking with sources, or "assets" as they are known, sensing nuances of the twitch of an eyebrow or the lilt of an imperative, is far superior in the long run over "sigint," or signal intelligence—what can be obtained by electronic means, plucked from the airwaves or glimpsed from a powerful satellite thousands of miles from the event being monitored. Dulles and his network had little access to signal intelligence. They had only their own minds and the experience that came with personal knowledge of the societies they needed to understand and appreciate.

In 1919 the U.S. delegation's operational intelligence did, of course, function independently of the Peace Conference bureaucracy, the Western allies, or any of the other delegations. The goal of the U.S. delegation was to outflank the Europeans with extensive on-the-ground resources of its own, since House knew that information was the ultimate source of power. The network was established and the intelligence began to flow. How accurate it proved to be was perpetually a matter of debate. This debate continued far past the end of the Peace Conference and required personal visits by Dulles and Gibson to some of the most dangerous and obscure corners of Europe.

For throughout these small nations, powerful events were stirring that would have a more profound influence over the deliberations in Paris than most of the participants were aware of. Only those observing them close up would have even a prayer of understanding these forces as they were brought into play. Scores of spinmeisters in Paris were prepared to whisper their own personal interpretations of these events into the ears of any available Western diplomat, hoping against hope that their interpretation might be the one that would tilt the balance toward their particular goal of remaking a county, a nation, a region, or their own personal fortunes.

Dulles, one of whose closest friends had become his young British counterpart, Harold Nicolson, made it his business to be in touch directly with many of the leading behind-the-scenes figures of East European politics and diplomacy. But he had considerable trouble bringing his profound understanding and detailed information to the attention of the leaders of the Allied delegations. It was a dilemma that he and a host of successors among America's intelligence leadership were to confront, down to the present day, and that only intensified as the intelligence bureaucracy multiplied and became ever more byzantine.

In the postwar Europe of 1919 the situation was already demonstrating many of the same elements of polarization and paralysis that would characterize the depths of the cold war a half century later. Indeed, at that very moment many of the dynamics of the conflict that was to dominate the entire last half of the twentieth century were first emerging. Poles, Hungarians, Lithuanians, even Czechs and Austrians were deeply afraid that their own feeble, newly independent governments would be unable to survive as buffers between the forces of Lenin in Russia and a Germany that was being impelled increasingly toward Bolshevism. In December 1918, even before the conference opened, Dulles paid a quick return visit to Bern and made contact with some sources. He pleaded in a secret dispatch:

> During the past few days I've had the occasion in Berne to talk with a number of Lithuanians, Poles, Hungarians and Austrians. Their own internal, political and economic difficulties appear to be forced into the background as a result of their dread of the Bolshevik invasion. In pleading for immediate military assistance, two leading Lithuanians stated that the present feeble but anti-Bolshevik government in Lithuania and the Pilsudski government in Poland were the last line of defense between a Germany that was tending more and more toward Bolshevism and the forces of Lenin in Russia. . . . Polish and Lithuanian informants in Switzerland agree that the Allies should not be deterred from a military expedition because of the fear that it would require hundreds of thousands of men. All they ask is a small army as a nucleus for their own forces. They affirm that the growth of the Bolshevist power is due to the fact that they have never met a serious military defeat. . . . According to the statements of Austrians and Hungarians, they are watching with fear and trembling the approach of the Bolsheviks and with the ever increasing tendency towards Bolshevism

which is especially making itself felt in Hungary they do not believe that either Austria or Hungary would act as a barrier to its advance but rather as fertile soil in case Poland and Lithuania are eliminated.

What Dulles may not have recognized at the moment he filed that highly prescient, though in the end ignored, note was that he had sounded what would become the tocsin for a central theme of the entire Peace Conference: the creation of the first cordon sanitaire of small, newly minted countries around a fledgling yet powerful Bolshevik Russia. How the conferees would deal with these small nations being ground between great powers was to have a central role in shaping the balance of the century in Europe. Moreover, Dulles's memo was only the first of numerous occasions over the next eighty-five years when a senior U.S. intelligence official believed that military force could actually tilt the balance in the direction of the forces of good over evil in a serious political confrontation. As it turned out, the delegates in Paris didn't buy the value of a military strike against Bolshevik Russia, but for none of the most obvious reasons, as we shall discover.

But there was a further disconnect as well between the younger members of each of the major delegations and their more seasoned elders. It had some curious manifestations. On one side of the divide was Woodrow Wilson, son and grandson of theologians, a determined Presbyterian and a man of enormous self-righteousness who, in 1915, had written in a letter to Nancy Toy, a long-time personal friend: "My life would not be worth living if it were not for the driving power of religion, for *faith*, pure and simple. I have seen all my life the arguments against it without ever having been moved by them . . . never for a moment have I had one doubt about my religious beliefs. There are people who *believe* only so far as they *understand*."

He had brought his nation, so he thought, into the war to defend a series of abstract and as it turned out unrealistic but thoroughly moral principles called the Fourteen Points. They would, he hoped, create a world in his own image and that of his Maker. By contrast, many of the junior members of the U.S. delegation, including a host of pragmatists, both academic members of the Inquiry such as Charles Seymour and young diplomats such as Dulles, all the way up to Colonel House himself, were far more closely connected with realities on the ground. They quickly became disillusioned, then horrified, as Wilson vetoed again and again the kinds of practical measures they knew were essential to building the kind of world that would survive and where a permanent peace might be a more realistic alternative. All sought to create a world that would work, while their leader seemed to answer only to a higher power.

On the British delegation there were equally profound disconnects. Here, the likes of Nicolson, who was persuaded that this conference of world leaders would be able to avoid the pitfalls of the Congress of Vienna and establish a truly just and equitable world of individual rights, came flush against the bullheaded Welshman David Lloyd George, who would never allow principle to trump expediency. Unlike Lloyd George, who'd battled his way to the top from an impoverished childhood in the tiny Welsh village of Llanystumdwy, Nicolson was a bisexual aesthete, to the manner born. He had been married to Vita Sackville-West in the chapel of a 365-room estate at Knole in Kent, a sixteenth-century present from Queen Elizabeth I to Thomas Sackville, earl of Dorset, that belonged to Vita's father, Lord Sackville. The handsome young couple traveled among the Bloomsbury crowd of Virginia Woolf. Young Nicolson wrote a profile of Paul Verlaine, the first of six literary biographies he turned out. Nicolson was also a determined globalist.

Nicolson and his fellow young Oxbridge mates in Paris were to clash repeatedly throughout the winter and into the spring of 1919 with the old-line leaders of their own and other Allied delegations. The elder diplomats were seeking desperately to hang on to a world that they had created in the last century and that they understood, while all around them everything was changing. In the end, of course, the youths found they had little real impact. The result was a series of most disastrous and ill-conceived moves in every region that the Allies sought to shape, and especially in every region these leaders so cavalierly ignored or dismissed out of hand.

Somehow, though, the practical Dulles and the effete intellectual Nicolson managed to find a certain common appreciation that derived from a shared community of interests. "My liking for the Americans is becoming a vice," Nicolson wrote. "I like the scholarly sort, such as Coolidge, Seymour, Day and Allen Dulles, because they are quiet and scholarly and because they like the truth." The fact that he was writing these words in 1933 may have contributed to his perceptions through a

Young British diplomat Harold Nicolson
during the Paris Peace Conference.

rose-colored rearview mirror of a world barreling toward the horrors of Nazism that was about to sweep across Europe.

In 1919 Nicolson had his own way of gathering intelligence of this rapidly changing world. While Dulles was helping to establish his on-the-ground network across Europe under the aegis of Hoover and his relief operation, his British colleague was dining out across Paris. Without the American's vast network, Nicolson, like many of the delegates at the Peace Conference, was forced to rely on a stream of more or less informed opinion from a host of interested parties who had found their way to the French capital. Indeed, most of the work of the conference and most exchanges of information were done at breakfasts, lunches, and dinners. Even on the train to Paris on January 4, Nicolson took the opportunity to dine with some Italians headed for the Peace Conference—the Marchese Camillo Casati, a young Milanese nobleman and husband of one of the most scandalous women of her day, Marchesa Luisa Casati; and the Baron Giacomo di Martino, permanent undersecretary of the Italian Foreign Ministry, a "querulous, precise little man" who insisted on paying for Nicolson's dinner since his "first postwar meal in France should be at the expense of Italy."

On his arrival in Paris, Nicolson found the main hall of the British delegation at the Hotel Majestic to be gay every evening with the clatter of teacups. But Nicolson didn't waste much time there. Within a matter of hours he had plunged into gathering intelligence in his own peculiar manner, through a vast network of the right stuff. This ranged from old Oxbridge types to contacts from the four corners of the empire. Many of them he'd met during his previous diplomatic posting in Constantinople as well as his father's diplomatic parties of his youth in a host of world capitals from the Balkans to the Middle East, Morocco, Madrid, and St. Petersburg.

Two days after his arrival, Nicolson was calling on Take Ionescu, the Rumanian foreign minister, at his suite at the Hotel Meurice. The young Brit found himself in a hot, stuffy bedroom just off a passage lined with Turkish carpets and guarded by the *fustanella*-clad bodyguards of Montenegro's King Nikita, who had also taken up residence in the hotel for the duration of the Peace Conference. Ionescu, a rotund, dapper gentleman sporting a lush though neatly trimmed beard, had just passed his sixtieth birthday. Nicolson was patient as Ionescu struggled to speak English, then lapsed into the French he had spoken since his youth. Within minutes, Nicolson began to understand some of the quicksand of Balkan politics into which he was dipping his toe. Ionescu, it seems, was particularly bitter about his treatment by Prime Minister Ion Brătianu, the official leader of the delegation, and was seriously thinking of pushing off to the more congenial winter climate of Cannes. But he switched quickly to a detailed description of the weak and impulsive King Ferdinand and his subordination to the glamorous and strong-willed Queen Marie, who would shortly arrive in Paris herself to take charge of Rumania's demands from the peace delegates. Ionescu was bitter and vengeful—a useful bit of intelligence as Nicolson began considering the long, difficult process that lay ahead to redraw the complex, potentially explosive map of the Balkans.

By Tuesday Nicolson was reaching even deeper into the Rumanian delegation to Viorel Virgil Tilea, a young diplomat and later ambassador to Britain, who was particularly interested in defining the Hungarian-Rumanian frontier. Much blood was to be spilled in the next year or so as diplomats struggled to resolve this question, which the Rumanians hoped would bring in major new territories from Hungary and Bessarabia. Over lunch at the Griffon, Nicolson pressed him, with little success, on guarantees of autonomy for the host of new peoples who might be brought within the newly expanded Rumanian borders. On Wednesday Nicolson lunched with the English doctor to the Rumanian court. Then he debriefed another English traveler who'd just returned from a swing through Transylvania and believed that Budapest was turning toward Bolshevism under the leadership of Count Mihály Károlyi von Nagykároly. Thursday saw him lunching with Czech Foreign Minister Edvard Beneš.

Throughout, Nicolson made good use of his early—especially old school—contacts. Lunch on Thursday with Beneš was followed by a chat with William Beveridge, a fellow Balliol College alum at Oxford, though seven years his senior. The English baronet, lawyer, economist, and social reformer had recently passed through Prague, Vienna, and Budapest. He'd been on a relief mission as permanent secretary to the Ministry of Food and was returning to London to take up the post of director of the London School of Economics and Political Science. Nicolson sniffed that he was "very pro-Magyar." His nose was serving him well.

Friday brought Nicolson's first meeting with Nicholas Mişu. The veteran Rumanian ambassador to London was serving as the deputy chief of mission behind Brătianu and often as his interpreter, with the unenviable task of smoothing some of his foreign minister's more extreme rants. Nicolson found Mişu most indignant that the young Brit had been placed in charge of the Balkan section. "Un fort gentil garçon—mais enfin il n'est qu'un troisième secrétaire!" (A terribly nice boy, but in the end he is nothing but a third secretary!) The Rumanian had stumbled early upon one of the hard realities of the Paris peace talks—that the final shape of Europe and much of the rest of the world was being entrusted to youths with little deep diplomatic or political experience. Still, most were already most adept at gathering the kind of intelligence they needed.

Indeed, decades later, in most parts of the world, there is often no better intelligence on the ground in scores of capitals than the British ambassador and his immediate entourage, though they still lag their American cousins badly in terms of technology or financial resources. In the final days of the war in Indochina, in the spring of 1975, I arrived in Laos to cover what would prove to be the fall of the Laotian monarchy and the takeover by the communist Pathet Lao. It was a Saturday afternoon. I had never before been to Laos and in the next twelve hours I had to file what would end up as a page one story in the *New York Times*. My first stop was the residence of the British ambassador, Alan Davidson. There was a leisurely lunch of Mekong River fish, since the ambassador was one of the world's leading authorities, having recently penned the definitive book on the subject, *The Fish and Fish Dishes of Laos*. Within three hours I had been given a crash course in Laotian politics, history, and culture, and the future outlook for the nation where he had traveled widely, meeting huge numbers of its people and leaders. His insights proved accurate down to the final comma. Meanwhile, the Americans were hiring private guards to encircle their compound, where they'd retreated to monitor radio broadcasts of the Pathet Lao.

In Paris more than a half century earlier, while the diplomats were establishing their positions and studying the political landscape, others were bringing their own unique and individual sensibilities to the new Europe that was already beginning to emerge after the World War I. A young Elsa Maxwell traveled to Paris as companion to a twenty-nine-year-old Philadephia Main Line society divorcée, Henrietta Louise Cromwell Brooks, fresh from an affair with General John J. Pershing. Mrs. Brooks's goal was to land an eligible second husband. She came home with a dashing brigadier general, at thirty-nine the U.S. army's youngest. His name was Douglas MacArthur. But Miss Maxwell's goal was an even broader one: to bring a new America to Europe. As she wrote later:

> The exhilarating atmosphere of Paris during the peace talks. Every day was like a sparkling holiday. There was an aroma in the air as though a thousand girls wearing a wonderful perfume had just passed. The city echoed to the music of bands welcoming returning soldiers. Shops, theatres & cafés were jammed with people who'd lived under the drab shadows of war for four years. Every where, every hour of the day & night, there were parties.

Many of the most glittering soirees took place at the home of Mrs. Brooks's mother, where the gay young flapper and Miss Maxwell installed themselves. They quickly turned this elegant town house into a headquarters for the American military delegation and other young foreign army officers attached to the various embassies. They came for the Saturday night dances, but they took away the music performed on the piano by the inimitable Elsa:

> If I say so myself I was a damned good pianist. Europe was swept by a dance craze after World War I and in those days it wasn't possible to hear the latest recordings by flicking a radio or a phonograph switch. People went wild over the new school of jazz that had been developed in America during the war and I was among the first to import it to Paris and London. I was in constant demand to play for dancing and to sing numbers from new Broadway shows.

And so she did—enrapturing hosts of invited and uninvited guests from Bernard Baruch, later an adviser to seven presidents but then a young aide on the U.S. mission, to Arthur Balfour, the British foreign secretary whom, one evening, Elsa captivated with Cole Porter's latest hits. "Balfour's eyebrows became an extension of his hairline when he first heard the irreverent lyrics, but his reserve soon cracked and he laughed uproariously as I dipped deeper into Cole's private stock," Miss Maxwell observed.

At the dinner party at the Ritz that followed, Miss Maxwell mixed Balfour with Lord d'Abernon, former financial adviser to the Egyptian government and shortly to become the first postwar British ambassador to Berlin; Mrs. George Keppel, the avowed mistress of King Edward VII, and whose daughter Violet was just winding up a notorious love affair with Harold Nicolson's Vita Sackville-West; the celebrated Edwardian beauty Lady Ripon; her great friend the Grand Duke Alexander of Russia, who'd been hoping (in vain, of course) that the Peace Conference might help restore to the Russian throne the remnants of his just-deposed and executed family; and thirty-eight-year-old Sir Ronald Storrs, who ran Britain's disastrous Middle East policy. Harold Nicolson was not among the invited.

It was an extraordinary evening, which wound up very late at night in the newly opened nightclub of Paul Poiret, where Elsa's guests gazed on "undressed French chorus girls" and were privy to "ribald jokes which probably never before had assaulted the ears of one of His Majesty's elder statesmen, but (who) chortled like a schoolboy." When Balfour bade a fond farewell to Miss Maxwell before dawn the next morning, he enthused that this was "the most delightful and degrading evening I have ever spent."

The guest list was most opportune. The author of the famed Balfour Declaration, which set the Jews on a path to a homeland in the Middle East, was dining cheek by jowl—literally, it would appear—with young Storrs, military governor of Jerusalem, who had his own issues with how the Middle East should be divided, the role of the Jews and of Britain. They were thrown together for that one evening, but they were ultimately to provide some of the most explosive moments of the Peace Conference itself and many decades that followed.

And into this heady mix were to arrive the ultimate catalysts—Sheikh Feisal ibn al-Hussein and Lawrence of Arabia—self-styled power brokers who brokered little, in the very long run, but their own interests. Sad that few were perceptive enough to see this at the time.

3

LE MISTRAL

IN LATE NOVEMBER 1918, A SHORT, HANDSOME, DARK-HAIRED prince with flashing black eyes accompanied by a phalanx of Bedouin warriors boarded the British naval vessel HMS *Gloucester* in the harbor of Beirut, bound for Europe. The goal of the Emir Feisal ibn al-Hussein was to speak for his Arab warriors who had just defeated the hated Turks, rulers of the Middle East and one of the defeated Central Powers. The Arab rebels now sought what they thought was their just reward. But Feisal's goal was to speak even more broadly—for the vast and ultimately diverse mass of the peoples of Arabia from the shores of the Mediterranean to the Persian Gulf, from the mountains of Anatolia to the pyramids of Egypt.

His was, he believed, a mission that was entirely congruent with what he had been reading and hearing of the mission of Woodrow Wilson, the self-styled voice of the voiceless who believed in self-determination for all those people who had been effectively liberated by the Allied victory on the battlefields. But he was wrong. For the leaders of Britain, France, and to a degree, Italy, were persuaded instead that the Arabs were ill-prepared to make their own way in an increasingly complex and dangerous world. The view of Allied statesmen was that the Arabs wanted, indeed needed, to be ruled by Europeans for their own benefit—and for the benefit of the victors in the Great War, to whom, they believed, belonged all the spoils.

For most of the regions whose futures would be determined and borders redrawn by the peacemakers gathering in Paris—the future lands of
Syria, Jordan, Israel, Saudi Arabia, Iraq, and beyond—the predominant
issues were power and territory. The Middle East added a third, and
what turned out to be prime, determinant—religion. Unfortunately,
few of even the most astute peacemakers recognized this overwhelming constant. And those who did appreciate the power of faith saw it as
simply another lever to control the territory and peoples they needed for
their blinkered geopolitical purposes. Indeed, throughout the history of
Europe in the Middle East, few recognized this ultimate reality. Yet this
dynamic was to continue to the present day. With our failure to recognize and deal with the power of religion—and especially the Islam that
its adherents are now seeking to export to the rest of the world at the
point of guns, bombs, and terror—we are faced with our biggest challenges. Few of today's Western leaders recognize that the origins lie in
the failures of their own predecessors.

As Feisal made his way to Paris, he fully expected that the allies
of his family and their warriors would receive the hearing they and
their Bedouin warriors had bought with their loyalty and their arms
throughout the war. But others were preparing an entirely different
sort of reception. It was a script carefully prepared by the Europeans long before the Central Powers and the Allies began facing
off in Europe—indeed, whose outlines had first been drawn even
before Columbus set sail to discover America.

Since 1299 the Sublime Porte, the sultan's court, had ruled the vast
Ottoman Empire, which over the course of five hundred years had conquered more of the known world than even the ancient Roman Empire.
The sultan's reach at one time extended from Gibraltar, across North
Africa and the Middle East, and back up into Europe nearly to the gates
of Vienna. Early on, Europe recognized the value of dealing with the
enormous wealth and power the Ottomans represented. In 1453 the
Porte granted the first of the major economic and tariff concessions
known as Capitulations to a Christian state, the Genoese, and their traders. In 1536 French emissaries approached Sultan Suleyman I, demanding the right to protect Christians. The outcome was the sultan awarding
France vast extraterritorial rights and economic, tariff, and political concessions. Similar Capitulations were awarded to the British in 1580,
long before the oil of the Middle East became a global currency. Still,

for England, whose East India Company was chartered by the British Crown in 1600, the Middle East was even more important. As the small island nation began growing a vast series of overseas outposts of imperial conquests across India and into Asia, the empire on which the sun never set needed a secure route to each of its valuable colonies.

The problem, of course, was that none of the European powers that moved their military forces and government operatives into the Middle East ever made any real effort to understand these regions or their people in any more than geographical, economic, or strategic terms. Since the Ottoman sultan and his entourage represented the only real contact that European nations ever had with the people and powers of the Middle East, most Westerners were unaware that a host of powerful religious and ethnic forces were developing that even the sultan proved unable to control. There was, for instance, the battle between the Ottoman Sunnis and the Iranian Shiites for control of Iraq, which contained shrines profoundly sacred to both of the principal Moslem sects. Even while the French and British were building their diplomatic and economic relations with the Sublime Porte and protecting their routes to Asia, the shah of Iran was seizing Baghdad in 1508 for the Shiites while Sultan Murat IV was reconquering it in 1638 for the Sunnis.

And this was not the only region of the Ottoman Empire where the foundations of deep future conflicts were being laid. In 1703 Muhammad ibn Abd al-Wahhab was born; after a religious education in the twin Islamic capitals of Mecca and Medina, he developed his own strictly fundamentalist form of Islam with an emphasis on one God. By the time of his death in 1792, he had managed to attract the support of a powerful local chieftain from the Arabian city of Najd—Muhammad ibn Saud. This leader of a band of accomplished Bedouin warriors launched his forces in the name of Wahhab across the northern Arabian peninsula, finally capturing the sacred city of Medina in 1802. His descendant, Abdul Aziz ibn Saud, known simply as Ibn Saud, was to establish the House of Saud and the Kingdom of Saudi Arabia.

But it was another Bedouin prince who managed to capture the attention of the British: Hussein ibn Ali, named by the Ottoman sultan as sherif of Mecca and the Hejaz. For years the English, and the French as well, had sought counterweights in the Middle East for the sultans and their grand viziers, who they saw becoming increasingly aloof and independent in their dealings with the West. At the same time, there were powerful forces in Arabia who were seeking allies—some means of neutralizing the potent religious and military might wielded by the followers of Wahhab and assuring as much autonomy as possible for their own regions and their own families. Meanwhile, in London, many military officials had come to fear the ultimate catastrophe of a jihad: a Moslem holy war against British interests in the Middle East. Indeed, the sultan was to proclaim just such a jihad at the opening of World War I. But by then, it had become an all but empty threat.

For centuries, the Ottoman sultans had ruled their far-flung empire through a broad network of appointed, often anointed, officials such as Sherif Hussein. Some, like this ruler of the Hejaz, boasted bloodlines that traced back to Mohammed, the Prophet himself. Hussein's lands covered one hundred thousand square miles of the world's most desolate territory with fewer than three persons per square mile, mostly Bedouin tribesmen, and an occasional small town. The Hejaz—in the northwestern portion of what is today Saudi Arabia, whose largest city is the port of Jeddah—was of vital importance to the sultan largely because it contained Mecca, where millions of pilgrims journeyed under the watchful eye of Hussein and his military forces.

By the months leading up to the outbreak of war in Europe in 1914, Hussein was already feeling insecure. Ibn Saud and his Wahhabi tribesmen were flexing their muscles. And the Ottoman sultan was talking of a new rail link into the Hejaz, looking to cement his own control over the region. At the same time, Hussein was lusting after the powerful position of caliph, successor to the Prophet Mohammed and therefore leader of the *umma*—the broad Islamic community. Hussein believed that his right to the position seemed preordained by blood as well as steel. The caliph was to Islam what the pope was to Catholicism—successor to Allah, representative of the one God on earth. Since Hussein already considered himself a direct descendant of the Prophet, such a designation would merely cement his family's rule over much of the Middle East. His goal was to unite Moslem Arabia under a single powerful religious figure—himself and eventually one of his sons.

Hussein's archrival, Ibn Saud, had no interest in allowing Hussein to assume this mantle when it was, he believed, the more intensely observant Wahhabis who deserved to determine the fate and direction of the Arab world. His religious shock troops, the Ikhwan, were determined to turn back the clock in these lands to the seventh century and the time of the Prophet Mohammed.

The West, especially Britain, picked the wrong horse. They chose Hussein, the individual who reached out to them, offering his fealty, a currency that they could understand and that they believed they needed. His sons, especially his middle son, Feisal, ultimately would play the greatest role in the colossal errors of judgment that were to emerge from Paris and the Peace Conference, eventually turning the Middle East into the breeding ground for regional and global violence it has become today.

In the first years of the twentieth century, Britain already had established in the Middle East a substantial intelligence operation headquartered in Cairo and overseen by Sir Henry McMahon, newly arrived from India as Britain's high commissioner in Egypt. McMahon replaced Field Marshal Horatio Herbert Kitchener, first earl of Khartoum, who had won Sudan for the British and then, as war was about to break out in Europe, was summoned home to become war minister. Lord Kitchener, however, considered himself not just war minister but master of the Middle East, to him a far grander and ultimately more satisfying position. So it was Kitchener whom Hussein first approached for assistance in maintaining and expanding his position in Arabia. The Sherif of Mecca dispatched his favorite son, Abdullah, to Cairo at least two years before the world war broke out and suggested, in meetings with Kitchener and his staff, that powerful forces in Arabia might just be ripe for revolt against the Ottoman Turks. Finally, on October 1, 1914, Kitchener sent a seminal message through Abdullah for his father:

Salaams to the Sherif. That which we foresaw has come to pass, Germany has bought the Turkish Government with gold, notwithstanding that Great Britain, France and Russia guaranteed the integrity of the Ottoman Turks if Turkey remained neutral in this war. . . . If the Emir and the Arabs in general agree to assist Great Britain in this conflict that has been forced upon us by Turkey, Great Britain will promise not to intervene in any manner whatsoever, whether in things religious or otherwise. Moreover, recognizing and respecting the sacred and unique office of the Emir Hussein, Great Britain will guarantee the independence, rights and privileges of the Sherifate against all external foreign aggression, in particular that of the Ottomans. Till now we have defended and befriended Islam in the person of the Turks; henceforward it shall be in that of the noble Arab. . . . It would be well if Your Highness could convey to your followers and devotees, who are found throughout the world, in every country, the good tidings of the freedom of the Arabs, and the rising of the sun over Arabia.

Hussein and his sons took to the bank this pledge of "independence, rights and privileges." It was a cynical commitment from both sides, but certainly from the British, with one top British intelligence officer in Cairo writing to McMahon less than two years later that "luckily we have been very careful indeed to commit ourselves to nothing whatsoever." Except guns and money. These were two promises that were kept. Throughout the war, huge quantities of gold and weapons made their way from the British government to the coffers of the Hussein family. And the man who carried most of it was a young intelligence officer—Thomas Edward Lawrence.

The depths of this cynicism can be fully grasped only if we look at just how the British were playing all sides of the Arabian equation for their own benefit. At the same moment Kitchener was messaging Hussein and Lawrence was en route to Hussein's tents bearing vast quantities of gold, Britain's India Office was dispatching another special emissary to reassure Hussein's mortal enemy Ibn Saud of London's good intentions and unqualified support. The man dispatched on this mission was to prove in so many ways a very special emissary—Harry St. John Bridger Philby. This British explorer and expert on Arabia was the first European to cross the Rub' al-Khali, or Empty Quarter, from east to west in what is now Saudi Arabia. His journey to Jeddah bearing pledges of support and friendship to Ibn Saud appeared to be purely routine—cementing relations with another of the principal players and would-be belligerents in a volatile and strategically important region. But Philby, Lawrence, and a host of other British officials and special agents were setting in motion a train of events that ultimately would lead the peacemakers of Paris to break faith on countless levels. Had a modicum of these pledges been kept, the Middle East would look far different today.

It's difficult from our perspective, nine decades in the future, to visualize the composition of the Middle East in those years before, during, and immediately after World War I. There were no nations then, no national boundaries, yet there were scores of fragmented associations and alliances that were as shifting as the sands of the territories where they were based. Tribes of nomadic Bedouins migrated throughout the year across trackless desert and rugged, rocky territory. Few ventured at all into the vast Empty Quarter, the size of France, Belgium, and Holland combined, with sand dunes as tall as a ten-story building. The only reliable transport was the camel. Westerners such T. E. Lawrence, St. John Philby, or Gertrude Bell who wanted to establish a foothold in the region needed to acquire skills unlike any they had learned in their previous experiences.

What the West was seeking was far from the top priority of leaders of the region itself. The British government in Whitehall and French diplomats from the Quai d'Orsay wanted some certainty in how to divide up the spoils of these territories which, as the war developed between the Central Powers and the Allies, took on increasing strategic importance. There was the geographical significance astride the trade routes that linked Europe and the East, overland and through the Suez Canal. And then there was oil. As the war wore on, it developed into the first conflict to highlight the strategic importance of oil. It was the fuel for trucks, tanks, ships, and aircraft—all powered by distilled derivatives of the commodity that was just coming to be discovered in the Middle East. For Britain and France there were a host of other interests as well, ranging from a missionary zeal for Christianizing the heathens to simple greed for land and subjects.

So on November 23, 1915, François Georges Picot arrived in London and began talks with Sir Ronald Sykes for an agreement that was to prove an enormous stumbling block for those in Paris three years later who sought to do the right thing in the Middle East. Picot, a politician committed to France's stewardship of Syria, was born to his task. One of six brothers, each well over six feet tall, he was a devoted Catholic and the latest in a line of French colonial masters that included his father and brothers. On the other side of the table was Sykes, a Yorkshire baronet, raised by a father who was fascinated by the Middle East. By the time he'd entered Cambridge, the younger Sykes had already traveled extensively in the region. He believed equally strongly that Britain had its own entitlements there.

Within days after the two began their negotiations in London, they had reached an agreement. Picot won for France the region to which it had already committed substantial resources and effort. Greater Lebanon had ties with the French stretching back to the Crusades. Now France's exclusive rule was confirmed over Syria as well—a territory stretching from the Mediterranean inland as far as Mosul, with its large Kurdish population in what is now Iraq, and north to the point where Russian forces had moved south and west onto the frontiers of the Ottoman Empire. Effectively, France was to serve in the Middle East the role it envisioned playing in Europe—blocking Russian, eventually Soviet, expansion. For England, Sykes acquired the rest of the Middle East—the provinces of Basra and Baghdad in Iraq and, by default, the rest of Arabia down to the Persian Gulf where British forces had already held sway for two centuries among its sheikdoms and emirates.

Palestine was the biggest problem, as it would be later in Paris and still later before the League of Nations that was to emerge from the peace talks. Sykes and Picot each wanted control of Palestine. In a less-than-Solomonic compromise (where they each agreed to divide the baby), the Brits got the ports of Acre and Haifa and a swath of territory that would allow construction of a rail line into Mesopotamia. Everything else was left to some sort of ill-defined international administration. The Sykes-Picot Agreement was followed, as we shall see, by the Balfour Declaration, which was designed to turn over at least a portion of the Palestinian territory to the Jews for their first homeland in Israel in a millennium. Still, the focus of Britain in the Middle East was for the moment a mad dash for territory at the point of a gun—indeed thousands of guns.

This dash for territory began the moment hostilities broke out and the Ottoman Empire linked itself with Germany and Austria-Hungary. At the time, T. E. Lawrence, the illegitimate great-grandson of an Irish baronet, had been recruited into the British intelligence establishment by his old university professor. At Jesus College at Oxford, just across town, and a year behind Harold Nicolson at Balliol College, Lawrence had read history and become all but fluent in French. His obsession with his own heraldic past led him to extensive firsthand research into crusader castles in the Middle East and to the attention of the distinguished Arabist and Keeper of Oxford's Ashmolean Museum, David George Hogarth. At the behest of British intelligence, Hogarth had organized the Arab Bureau—the principal Western espionage operation in the Middle East. It was inevitable that Lawrence would become one of his recruits.

By the outbreak of the war, Lawrence was scraping by in Cairo's Savoy Hotel on £400 a year from which ten shillings were deducted daily for room and board. He was already developing a reputation for the unorthodox, in his unkempt grooming and frequent outbursts that flouted the British party line in the Middle East. He had what were becoming increasingly clear tendencies to support the Arabs wherever their interests collided with British priorities—particularly his complaints that the western front in Europe was being favored in terms of military resources and strategic attention over any needs of the Ottoman region. Still, his extraordinary command of the Arab language and his deep understanding of the subtleties of the Arab mind had admitted him

T. E. Lawrence (of Arabia) in the native Arab costume he often favored, complete with scimitar at his waist.

to the inner circle of the small band of intelligence mandarins known as the "Intrusives"—a code name that was very well suited to this group that was determined to shape the Arab world to fit the needs of the Empire. They called themselves a "brotherhood of visionaries," which, as it turned out, was not so far from the truth. This Arab Bureau's stock in trade turned out to be not dissimilar from what was to take place in Paris just a few years hence—backstairs trafficking in territory, concessions, and bribes in the form of stipends, arms, and ammunition. Indeed, by 1916 Hussein had managed to wring from the British a monthly stipend of £125,000 and promises of Royal Navy assistance and arms.

This came about for two reasons—both of them foreseen and forewarned by the Intrusives. First was the proclamation by the Ottoman sultan of a jihad against the British. The mandarins of Whitehall feared, wrongly as it turned out, that such a religious commandment could seriously compromise their position in large portions of their Indian empire. The Arab Bureau suggested that an alliance with Hussein, the self-styled direct descendant of Mohammed, could go a long way toward neutralizing any of the sultan's fatwas or religious proclamations. The second reason the British put their money on Hussein and the Hejaz was an impression, courtesy of some defectors, of the possibility of an Arab revolt—an impression only encouraged by Hussein himself and his sons. Such a populist rebellion against the sultan would distract and tie down substantial military resources of this key German ally.

So in the fall of 1916, Lawrence set out to make contact with the leaders of the Hejaz. Lawrence had already achieved some renown for having rescued a British force from India that had been ambushed in central Iraq. Late in 1914 these troops had landed at the port city of Basra and begun advancing toward Baghdad, only to be surprised and surrounded by native Ottoman forces—an ominous foretaste of military life in central Iraq nine decades later.

Since then, Lawrence had watched impatiently from his rooms at the Savoy Hotel as the much-vaunted Arab revolt, led by Sherif Hussein and his forces, fizzled and neared extinction. Now it was time for Lawrence to see for himself just what these Hashemites were all about. When Lawrence arrived in the Hejaz, he found Arab armies commanded by Hussein's sons. Lawrence quickly sized up three of his four offspring and concluded that none of them would do. Instead, he set off in search of the fourth son, encamped with his Bedouin forces deep in the interior of the Hejaz. Leaving behind his French counterpart, Colonel Edouard Brémond, who had also turned up in Hussein's camp, much to Lawrence's dismay, the young British officer set off on an eighty-mile trip by camel through the desert. His destination was the camp at al-Hamra where Emir Feisal was billeted with four thousand Arab irregulars. This was the Arab leader England needed. As Lawrence wrote later:

> I felt at first glance that this was the man I had come to Arabia to seek—the leader who would bring the Arab revolt to full glory. Feisal looked very tall and pillar-like, very slender, in his long white silk robes and his brown head-cloth bound with brilliant scarlet and gold cord. His eyelids were drooped; and his black beard and colorless face were like a mask against the strange watchfulness of his body. His hands were crossed in front of him on his dagger.

This was the individual on whom the British were to build their hopes, dreams, and plans for the Middle East.

Back in Cairo, Lawrence began to assemble what Feisal's forces in the desert needed—artillery, ammunition, six aircraft—and returned to spend the next two years by his side. It was during this critical period that Lawrence went fully native, doffing the mufti of the British army officer in favor of richly embroidered Arab robes with a gold dagger at his side. Moreover, each month, he served as paymaster of rapidly growing subsidies—distributing to Feisal some £75,000 in gold sovereigns, as well as £200,000 to his father, Sherif Hussein.

But while the British continued to back Hussein, tolerating his self-proclamation as king of the Arabs in November 1917, other forces were becoming increasingly infuriated by the sherif's hubris. Hussein continued to boast of his claim to the caliphate, of hegemony over all Arab peoples and lands, yet failed to produce even a semblance of an Arab revolt. At the same time, Hussein's archenemy Ibn Saud in Riyadh was preparing, with the help of Philby, to mount his own efforts to dominate Arabia.

Philby, who served for decades as Ibn Saud's principal political and military adviser, was at once a creature of the Raj and a bitter opponent of everything British rule stood for. A brilliant career at Westminster and Cambridge's Trinity College led to his entry into the British Indian service when it was at the peak of its power in the heart of the Punjab. But Philby found it impossible to accept the central lesson of his commanding officer that cut to the heart of the British attitude across the Middle East and the Indian subcontinent: "We rule over these races which would do their best to exterminate each other if it were not for us. . . . There is no compromise between our personal rule and chaos."

Philby's rejection of such concepts led to a rocky, and brief, stay in India. Still, his extraordinary capacity for languages led to a continued role in the British Indian service and his next posting, to Iraq. It was to be the start of an extraordinary career in central Arabia—one filled with bitterness against the imperial system. Philby had already correctly perceived the Raj as designed solely to perpetuate itself—a way of life that was profoundly out of step with the contemporary realities of the people it ruled.

In the Middle East, these regions had struggled mightily to rid themselves of foreign oversight in the form of the Ottoman Turks and had little interest in substituting the rule of Europeans, or any infidels. Philby fancied himself as neither. Indeed, he became the unwavering champion of Ibn Saud, who embraced him like a son. The Bedouin ruler stood by Philby's side as he kissed the stone of the Kaaba, converting to Islam and pledging his energies to secure the supremacy of the House of Saud in Arabia. Despite Philby's deep prejudices against Britain's overseas presence, however, Whitehall on its own was coming to appreciate Ibn Saud as a leader to reckon with.

By the time hostilities erupted in Europe, Britain had signed a treaty outlining the boundaries of Ibn Saud's territories and accepting his pledge not to be "antagonistic to the British government in any respect," while recognizing Britain's interest in any treasure that lay beneath the sands he controlled. The pact was an acknowledgment, on the British side, of some ancestral yarns—that Arabia held within its frontiers King Solomon's gold mines. There might even be some trace amounts of oil in the province of Hasa. As for Ibn Saud, he acknowledged to Philby that, while he would continue to rail at the insulting discrepancy of Hussein's £200,000 a month subsidy and his £5,000, he still had a simple and pragmatic reason for signing up with the British: "I have nothing in common with the English. They are strangers to us, and Christians. But I need the help of a Great Power and the British are better than the other Powers like France and Italy."

With all the twisting alliances and commitments, the British faced some critical dynamics that would have to be resolved, in some manner, after the armistice. First, there was the bitter rivalry between Lawrence, Feisal, and the Hashemites of the Hejaz on the one side and Philby and Ibn Saud of Arabia on the other. At the same time, there was the equally critical rivalry between Britain and France that had been only thinly papered over by the Sykes-Picot Agreement.

By the time of the armistice, the far-off lonely voices of Philby and Ibn Saud had been all but totally overwhelmed by the carefully cultivated celebrity of Lawrence and the Emir Feisal, whom his British adviser supported and guided through the thickets of global diplomacy. Though some substantial questions remained as to just how material Lawrence was to the Allied victory in the Middle East, there were several exploits that cemented his reputation and earned him a hearing in the high councils of state. Lawrence, so it was said, had led a force of Bedouin Arabs across hundreds of miles of burning desert to surprise and overwhelm the Turkish guns guarding the narrow entrance to the Red Sea at the port of Aqaba. It was Lawrence who then rode hundreds more miles north through the Sinai to emerge from the deep desert, haggard though triumphant, to announce to an astonished and worshipful crowd of British military leaders in Cairo that the straits were cleared and General Allenby's forces could land at Aqaba to take on the Turks and their German allies.

Finally, Lawrence, Feisal, and their camelry of Arab irregulars were credited with riding first into Damascus, seizing the Ottoman-controlled Syrian capital for the Allies. In reality it was all a colossal hoax—designed to cement British claims to the heart of Syria and neutralize the French territorial position that was a central element of the Sykes-Picot Agreement. After all, David Lloyd George observed, territorial possession would count for far more at the Paris Peace Conference than any piece of paper negotiated in the heat of a world war. Certainly it would mean far more than any moralistic pronouncements in favor of self-determination. Syria actually had been conquered in a blitzkrieg-style operation led by the formidable British tactician General Edmund Allenby. His campaign for Damascus began with a monumental victory over Ottoman forces and their German advisers on the Plain of Megiddo on September 18, 1918. Feisal's Hashemite irregulars blew up a few bridges and rail lines. But Allenby and the political bosses back in Whitehall were all anxious to have Feisal, with Lawrence at his side, enter the city of Damascus and take possession in the name of the Arab people. They believed an Arab victory would be of enormous help in Paris, where the British were bracing to deal with President Wilson's demands of autonomy for the native populations of the Ottoman Empire. Furthermore, with Feisal in control of Damascus and a British officer in control of Feisal, the French would be at an enormous disadvantage in pressing their claims to this territory. Moreover, the first of Wilson's Fourteen Points, open covenants, openly arrived at, scarcely described the secret Sykes-Picot Pact.

However, the problem for Allenby in Syria was enormous. His forces were at the gates of Damascus on September 29. Feisal and his men were three days away. So Allenby called a halt. Finally, on October 3, Feisal arrived at the head of more than three hundred Arab troops. At three in the afternoon, Allenby sent word for Lawrence and Feisal to meet him at the Hotel Victoria, where he had set up his headquarters. Still under orders to respect the letter, if not the spirit, of Sykes-Picot, Allenby announced to the pair that the French would be "the protecting power over Syria." Feisal demurred, wanting a continuation of British assistance and funding. He knew how stingy French overseas administrators could be. So Feisal rejected the French liaison officer, Colonel Brémond, and any French guidance or partnership. Allenby was furious, at least for the record, and asked Lawrence whether he had advised Feisal of the realities of Sykes-Picot. Lawrence feigned ignorance of what was supposed to be a secret treaty. Allenby said the treaty stood—at least until the issue was settled in Paris after the war.

A few days later, Lawrence boarded the *Kaiser-i-Hind* in Port Said, Egypt, bound for the Italian port of Taranto, thence by train to Le Havre, and across the Channel to England. On October 28, 1918, two weeks before the armistice, he arrived in London. By then a genuine Arabian hero on both sides of the Atlantic, Lawrence pitched right in to lay the groundwork for a Hashemite diplomatic victory in Paris two months hence. His first step: to present the Cabinet with a series of demands that fell on apparently receptive ears. The young British officer believed deeply in a unified Arab nation, if not self-determination. It was equally clear in his mind that Arab unity could keep the hated French at bay and cement his own position as the predominant British presence in the Middle East. Though he kept such feelings to himself, he did assert boldly that Feisal had earned the right to reject the French as his overlords. After all, he proclaimed, the emir had led a column of some four thousand mounted tribesmen into Damascus, conquering the Syrian capital for Allenby after slipping courageously into the city in the dead of night.

In less than a month, the size of Feisal's forces had officially grown more than tenfold from the motley crew of barely three hundred he had actually led into the already conquered and secured city in broad daylight. Allenby, hero of the Second Battle of Ypres and commander of the Middle East Expeditionary Force, had become a minor supporting character in an Arab military triumph. Lawrence was fulfilling the role he so deeply desired, while Allenby and most of the Cabinet appeared to be willing accomplices. France's claims to vast territory in Syria and Lebanon would be throttled—the rights of military conquest effectively trumping the Sykes-Picot Agreement.

The next day Lawrence was off to Buckingham Palace. At a private audience with King George V, the young officer told an astonished monarch that he was refusing a knighthood since he feared the government might break faith with the Arabs. Lawrence was right to feel this way, of course. Up to the moment of his departure for Paris—and indeed throughout the negotiations—he remained nervous about the peace settlement and the intentions, particularly of the British and French.

When Feisal boarded the HMS *Gloucester* to make his way to Europe, the British appeared to have decided that, for the moment, they would play along with Lawrence's game—Sherif Hussein's son was the great Arab conqueror of the Ottoman Middle East and the British were merely there to support his aspirations and applaud his victories. Privately, British officials up to and including Prime Minister Lloyd George were claiming that Feisal was doing the bidding of the Cabinet as conveyed by his British advisers.

Indeed, by early December, the winds had shifted. Lawrence received the news he had feared when he expressed his skepticism over British actions to King George. The Cabinet would continue to respect the Sykes-Picot accord in Paris that turned over to France much of the territory Feisal and Lawrence had won. A few days later, Feisal arrived in London for a series of meetings that only cemented his private belief that he was dealing with individuals who, while having all the wealth and power in the world, were totally out of their depth when it came to determining the future of the Middle East. To British newspaper magnate Lord George Riddell, Feisal likened the British and French governments to a string of camels in the desert: "The camels travel in a long train, the head-rope of each being tied to the tail of the one in front. When you have overtaken fifty or sixty camels moving along in this fashion and you come to the head of the train, you find that the leader is a clever little donkey."

Behind the scenes, however, there were still forces, within the U.S. and even the British delegations who were campaigning vigorously to help Lawrence and Feisal achieve their goals. These forces placed their faith in President Wilson, who seemed impressed by Feisal's apparent willingness to cooperate in achieving a lasting settlement that would give to the Arabs a nation they could call their own. But Feisal, and even Lawrence, appeared unaware that one of the foundations of Wilson's determination to achieve a lasting peace in the Middle East was his concern for the Protestant mission schools that had sprung up across the region—teaching Christianity, hoping to convert Moslems. At least in this respect, Wilson's concerns were identical with those of Lloyd George, whose fundamentalist upbringing also led him to believe that Britain was doing the Lord's work in that region. Of course, the Lord's work also happened to be precisely consonant with British imperial ambitions.

Somehow, Wilson, at the outset, seemed able to ignore the latter and embrace the former. Above all, Wilson recognized that the Western powers, even though they might be in a position at the moment to dominate the region by force of arms, would never be able to interpret the will of the Arab people as effectively as their own leaders—no matter how despotic or how insensitive they might prove to be in satisfying the needs of their least advantaged subjects. Unfortunately, the other Western leaders gathering in Paris failed to grasp this one immutable reality, though there were certainly many on their delegations who sought gamely, but ultimately unsuccessfully, to press this point of view.

Wilson's own views of the Middle East, and particularly those of Colonel Edward House, were shaped heavily by the report of the ten-member Middle Eastern commission of the Inquiry. This was most unfortunate since many of its members turned out to be desperately ill-informed. Of 127 reports the unit prepared on the Middle East, just five dealt with religion. The principal source for several of the drafters was the *Encyclopædia Britannica*. This is how Arthur I. Andrews, one Middle East committee member, described the critical Kurdish minority that straddled, then as it does now, the explosive frontiers of Iraq, Iran, and Turkey:

> In some respects the Koords [*sic*] remind one of the North American Indians. They have a tawny skin, high cheek bones, broad mouth and black straight hair. Their mien too is rather quiet, morose, dull. Their temper is passionate, resentful, revengeful, intriguing, and treacherous. They make good soldiers, but poor leaders. They are avaricious, utterly selfish, shameless beggars, and have a great propensity to steal. They are fond of the chase and of raising their rivals, are adept in the exercise of frightfulness. Mentally they are slow.

Not surprisingly, many of the Inquiry's reports contained pleas for a single, unified Arab nation to be carved out of the remains of the sprawling Ottoman Empire—the same demand that Feisal and Lawrence were pressing in London at that moment. Howard Crosby Butler, a Princeton professor of archaeology and the history of architecture, proposed in his "Report on the Proposals for an Independent Arab State" that Arabia be united under an Arab caliphate located in Mecca. Although Butler was one of the rare members of the Inquiry whose archaeological research had actually taken him to the region, his conclusion was based on the extraordinary assertion that Arab society had regressed to an era some seven hundred years in the past. Moreover, since Mecca was shortly to be in the hands of Ibn Saud, and Feisal's father laid principal claim to the title of caliph by virtue of his claimed linear descent from the Prophet, Butler's "proposal" would have required some accommodation between these two bitterly hostile powers. This was a reality that Butler never acknowledged, though he did concede that a free and unified Arabia would have to maintain friendly relations with Britain. The Inquiry's final report came around to the position that when dealing with the twenty or more tribes that inhabited the interior of Arabia, no Western nation would be in any position to control them.

The leader of the Inquiry's Middle East unit, as he boarded the *George Washington* with President Wilson, was as filled with optimism about what the United States and the Western alliance could do for the peoples of the Ottoman Empire as Harold Nicolson was for what the Peace Conference could do to build a strong and independent Europe. Both regions, the two acolytes believed, should be filled with nations whose citizens chose their own leaders and their own governments. But forty-five-year-old William Westermann was an odd choice as a regional adviser for a diplomatic conference. This was no Lawrence or Philby. This was a University of Wisconsin classicist whose specialty was the pre-Ottoman Middle East. His academic expertise ended with the era of the Greeks and the Romans. Still, he was filled with a youthful exuberance. And he had come to believe with a passion that self-determination, not subjugation to any of the victorious Allied powers, was the only proper course for the diverse people of the region. As he wrote in his private diary: "If the British were put into control of any portion of the Turkish Empire, I want them to be forced to sign an agreement to leave at some future date and to sign in letters so big that they can be seen from one end of the British Empire to the other."

Westermann also believed—quite rightly, as subsequent events were

to prove—that religion was the only viable determination of where
boundaries should be drawn. Within the Ottoman Empire, the concepts
of ethnicity and nationhood were as vague and shifting as the sands
where tribes roamed hundreds of miles of territory on the whims of their
leaders. Indeed, the best solution for Arabia, Westermann wrote in his
diary, was "to allow the independent desert tribes to work out their own
destiny along the lines of the patriarchal tribunal government traditional
among them." Westermann never suggested, nor believed in, a mandate
for any of these territories, so it was clear that he shared many of the
views of Lawrence, Feisal, and even Ibn Saud back in Arabia.

Notably absent from most of the Inquiry's principal reports on the
Middle East was any mention of oil—an astonishing omission, given its
already growing strategic importance. Indeed, several other U.S. agen-
cies, particularly the Navy Department, were urging the U.S. delegation
to make efforts to preserve American access to Middle Eastern oil fields,
notably in Mesopotamia (present-day Iraq). Navy Secretary Josephus
Daniels emphasized "the extreme importance to the American nation of
maintaining a strong position in the petroleum trade of the world," and
worried about "the exploitation of the oil resources of [Mesopotamia]
for the sole benefit of Great Britain." As it turned out, however, this
was all merely another token to be traded away when necessary for the
broader diplomatic and political agenda of President Wilson.

By early January all the principal players, great and small, were converging on Paris, while others—potentially central individuals in the
complex equation of a peaceful postwar Middle East—were not in
attendance. Back in Riyadh, Ibn Saud and his British confidant Philby
were feeling themselves deeply betrayed. No invitation to Paris had been
received; they were being kept very much at arm's length. Not that this
should have come as any great shock. In September 1918, while Allenby
was at the gates of Damascus awaiting the arrival of Feisal and Lawrence,
Philby was in Cairo at the Arab Bureau being told by Sir Ronald Wing-
ate that His Majesty's government considered Ibn Saud to be a "black-
mailer" and that Whitehall was no longer interested in doing business
with him. This had something to do with a large batch of high-tech
Lee-Enfield rifles. Ibn Saud had demanded them as a price for his support of the Arab revolt and, incidentally, for restraining his redoubtable
Ikhwan warriors from attacking Hussein's forces, which they most certainly would have overwhelmed. Philby brought this news of a profound

British betrayal back to Ibn Saud, who promptly snarled, "Who after this will put their trust in you?" He was referring to the British government, since he could not stay angry for long with Philby.

By this time, however, Ibn Saud's attitude scarcely mattered to the mandarins of Whitehall. The voices of Lawrence, a great warrior hero, and Emir Feisal, descendant of the Prophet and potential heir to his father's self-proclaimed caliphate, were drowning out those of Philby and Ibn Saud. But there was more. For as Philby later learned, the Cabinet, to which Lawrence had presented his case for Feisal's leadership of a united Arab nation, was persuaded that Ibn Saud had no oil. If there was any oil in the Middle East, it was in the Hejaz on the Red Sea, and possibly in Mosul—present-day Iraq, which Britain believed it could control through Hussein and his family.

On January 19, Feisal and Lawrence arrived in Paris. Lawrence joined the British delegation at the Majestic, while Feisal moved into the Hotel Continental, from which the Germans later were to run Paris during World War II. His rooms overlooked the Tuileries Gardens and were just down the block from the U.S. delegation at the Crillon. Eventually Feisal moved to a small private hotel, actually a former Louis XVI mansion, which he leased in its entirety on the posh Avenue du Bois in the sixteenth arrondissement. With draperies and rugs, he transformed his quarters into the tent of a desert Arab where he, Lawrence, and Gertrude Bell all felt most at home and where they were likely to turn up at any hour of the day or night. Beneath a canopy of silk and embroidered velvet, Feisal held court in a black robe and tight-fitting trousers. But unlike in the formal halls of diplomacy where he was the supplicant, at home in his suite, where he received visitors, he was very clearly in charge. It was this Feisal to whom President Wilson became so deeply attached. "Listening to the Emir," he told Colonel House, "I think to hear the voice of liberty, a strange and, I fear, a stray voice, coming from Asia."

Lawrence and Feisal plunged immediately into the diplomatic frenzy that gripped the French capital. In this high-pressure lobbying circuit, they found themselves able to present their views unfiltered and unchallenged by the likes of the French or other opponents—of whom there were many. The very first night after their arrival, they dined at the Hotel Crillon with William Westermann, who was accompanied by fellow Inquiry leaders, Columbia University professors George Louis Beer, the group's chief expert on colonial questions whose academic specialty was the British colonial system before 1765, and world history specialist James Shotwell. Also at the table was Isaiah Bowman, a cartographer and president of the American Geographical Society, who would draw the new map of the Middle East. Westermann's account in his private diary is a unique insight into the arguments Feisal was making to those he thought might help his case.

Westermann reported that Lawrence wore a Meccan headdress of gray cloth that fell to his shoulders and was held in place by a white coil traced with gold thread and pink balls of cloth hanging off it. The emir wore a black robe of fine broadcloth with seams down the front of gold embroidery—all shrouding a loose black vest with a gold-threaded girdle. He carried a large curved dagger with a gold handle. Feisal began by describing his pedigree as the fifty-fifth generation of direct descent from Mohammed. In his diary, Westermann quoted Feisal as noting that under the Turks, Mesopotamia had suffered the most of all Arab lands—its "great water system was broken up and Iraq reverted almost to savagery. The real Arab spirit was beaten back into the desert where the Turks could not get at it. But it could not progress there. Now, with airplanes and automobiles, the desert was no longer closed to the outside world." That was, of course, good and bad. It opened up these vast territories to new alliances, and new betrayals.

Then Westermann reported on perhaps the most startling of Feisal's revelations. A network of "secret societies" had grown up to oppose Turkish and eventually Western aims in the region, the most prominent of which was known as al-Fatah—"a society which any Arab could join." Members were bound by oaths to give their lives for Arab freedom, a half century before its explosive re-emergence in public as the military arm of Arab Palestine and Yasir Arafat. This society of Fatah, Westermann asserted, had never been mentioned before outside of Arab circles. Even Lawrence didn't know much about it. Yet it was gaining members by the thousands in Mesopotamia, in Syria, even in the Hejaz. Still, for their own security, for arms and munitions, it became necessary for the Hejaz to choose among the various foreign forces that were attempting to gain a foothold among his people, Feisal told his American listeners. He'd rejected the French, who had sent no soldiers into Syria, yet claimed it over the Arabs, who had driven out the Turks. Instead, Feisal chose Britain. In fact, Westermann concluded, Feisal "wanted no ruler over his country, British or French, he wanted independence. . . . He had not freed Syria to make it French."

In a few hours that evening, Feisal won a roomful of allies. "Voilà!" Westermann concluded in his diary. "Great is Lawrence and great is Feisal. I am a convert."

But Lawrence and Feisal did not stop there. Within hours of their arrival, the pair had also called on Colonel House's aide Stephen Bonsal, who had first met Lawrence four years earlier when the young British officer saved Bonsal's life by insisting that the French ship on which he was transiting the Suez Canal be sandbagged against Ottoman guns. Bonsal was most impressed with the Hashemite prince, while recognizing some of the futility of his task, which Feisal described as Lawrence translated:

> I hope you will try to disabuse the minds of many of our Allies that we Arabs are an uncivilized people. I venture to point out that much of our culture has been incorporated into the civilization of the Western World. . . . We entered the war not to improve our own position but to liberate our brothers in blood and in religion who have been throughout the centuries less fortunate. Above all else we did not enter the war to have our brothers and their lands apportioned among the Allies, although, of course, we recognize that this new servitude would be quite different from the yoke of the Turks. We are not asking for a favored position, but merely for justice and the fulfillment of solemn promises. . . . Our lands should not be regarded as war booty by the conquerors. Our provinces should not be allocated to this or that power. We have paid a heavy price for our liberty, but we are not exhausted. We are ready to fight on, and I cannot believe that the great rulers here assembled will treat us as did our former oppressors. I think they will act from higher, nobler motives, but—if not—they should remember how badly it has turned out for our former oppressors.

This was vintage Feisal—pouring out all the frustrations, all the aspirations of his family and his people—their long history of struggle for independence, their loyalty to friends and allies that they hoped would be rewarded in Paris with freedom and self-determination, but they feared would not. In the end there was that edge of steel, a warning of what might happen in the future, if his words were not heeded.

Feisal and Lawrence weren't the only proponents of a unified Arabia who were working the corridors of Paris, however. Gertrude Bell, a brilliant, blue-eyed, and utterly fearless beauty, was using her vast contacts as a woman of firsts—first to win first-class honors in history from Oxford, first to work for British military intelligence, first to cross Mesopotamia on a camel. Her background as the daughter of a wealthy and powerful industrialist and the fact that she had been dispatched by the Arab Bureau and Arnold Wilson, who ran Mesopotamia for Britain out of Baghdad, won Bell a room at British headquarters in the Majestic. It also won her audiences with everyone from Arthur Balfour to David Lloyd George. She plunged into the social and diplomatic whirlwind that had enveloped Feisal and Lawrence. She pressed their views on all who would listen. As she wrote to her parents: "I'm lunching tomorrow with Mr. Balfour (Foreign Secretary) who, I fancy, really doesn't care. Ultimately I hope to catch Mr. Lloyd George by the coat tails, and if I can manage to do so I believe I can enlist his sympathies. Meanwhile, we've sent for Colonel Wilson from Baghdad."

Bell, joined by David Hogarth, Lawrence's old Oxford archaeology professor and still head of British intelligence in Cairo, launched her own, often quirky, proposals into the increasingly turbulent fray. On March 23 she lunched with two of Westermann's Inquiry colleagues, George Louis Beer and James Shotwell. Beer later recorded in his diary that Bell "wants Senator Lodge to be the American Commissioner in the Near East." Had anyone taken that suggestion seriously, the virulently anti-Wilson, Republican Senator Henry Cabot Lodge, a bitter and effective opponent of the League of Nations and all it represented, might have been removed as an obstacle to ratification of the Treaty of Versailles. Much of the history of Europe and the Middle East would have been altered.

Feisal, Lawrence, and Bell did manage to win over large numbers of delegates, advisers, and experts on their early rounds in Paris. Alas, most would turn out to have little impact on the character of the settlement and the shape of the Middle East. From the get-go, though, Feisal found himself slighted by the principal delegates to the Peace Conference, especially the French. The first insult came when he found that his name had been omitted from the list of official representatives and hence deprived of a seat at the opening assembly at the Quai d'Orsay—a symbolic, but to an Arab, a deeply cutting slight. It was only the opening salvo of France's campaign to carve out an empire from the territories of the defeated powers—especially the Ottomans. But on this issue the British and the Americans intervened. The Hejaz was admitted as a delegation, with Feisal as its representative. And on February 6 he had his first formal presentation before the Supreme Council of the Entente Powers.

Feisal chose to look every inch a Middle East warrior-potentate dressing carefully in a flowing white robe with gold embroidery, a jewel-encrusted revolver added to his nasty-looking gold-handled scimitar, both barely concealed as he swept into the hall, with Lawrence at his side. The young officer had bowed to his government's pressure and exchanged his preferred robes of an Arabian sheikh for the uniform of a British lieutenant-colonel with Sam Browne belt. Feisal, flanked by his principal military aide, General Nouri Pasha, and with Lawrence translating, began:

> The aim of the Arab nationalist movement is to unite the Arabs eventually into one nation. We believe that our ideal of Arab unity in Asia is justified beyond the need of argument. If argument is required, we would point to the general principles accepted by the Allies when the U.S. joined them, to our splendid past, to the tenacity with which our race has for 600 years resisted Turkish attempts to absorb us and in a lesser degree to what we tried our best to do in this war as one of the Allies. My father has a privileged place among Arabs as the head of their greatest family and as Sherif of Mecca. He is convinced of the ultimate triumph of the ideal of unity, if no attempt is made now to thwart it or hinder it by dividing the area as spoils of war among the Great Powers. I came to Europe on behalf of my father and the Arabs of Asia to say that they are expecting the powers at the Conference not to attach undue importance to superficial differences of condition among us and not to consider them only from the low ground of existing European material interests and supposed spheres of influence. They expect the Powers to think of them as one potential people, jealous of their language and liberty, and they ask that no step be taken inconsistent with the prospect of an eventual union of these areas under one sovereign government.

It may have been among the most important statements of fundamental Arab belief ever formulated before an international gathering of statesmen—presaging a century of turmoil and factionalism, violence and ultimately terrorism. Feisal's pronouncement was equally a warning. It would be ignored by his listeners at their own peril and to the detriment of generations of their successors, who would appear to have no knowledge that these words had ever been spoken. Yet from the moment they were uttered, they caused enormous consternation among the Big Four, who sat spellbound and horrified before Feisal and Lawrence. Indeed, Stephen Bonsal later approached Lawrence with a request to temper the emir's language a bit in his translation. Lawrence refused: "I am an interpreter. I merely translate. The Emir is speaking for the horsemen who carried the Arab flag across the great desert from the holy city of Mecca to the holy city of Jerusalem and to Damascus beyond. He is speaking for the thousands who died in that long struggle. He is the bearer of their words. He cannot alter them. I cannot soften them."

And indeed he never did.

Overshadowing Lawrence, Feisal, Bell, Hogarth, and the other proponents of a free, unified, and self-determined Middle East were the proponents of a different shape for the region. Under this vision, the Middle East had been carefully parceled out among the Western powers during the depths of the Great War. These victorious nations, with enormous debts, would now be repaid. Chief among the visionaries of this new world was Sir Mark Sykes, an immensely popular British diplomat and world traveler. It was now his time to defend the document he had drafted with his French counterpart Picot. From the Druse region of Lebanon to the palaces of Monte Carlo, the drawing rooms of Brussels and Weimar, Sykes, a product of great wealth and the best of schooling, had charmed his way across Europe and the Middle East. Now as January gave way to February in 1919, he had been summoned to Paris to render an accounting of the no longer secret agreement he had drafted with the French—and to confront those whose dreams it would destroy.

On February 9, the delegation of the Hejaz—its diplomats and warriors—was gathered in all their desert finery before the enlarged Council of Ten assembled around the U-shaped table covered in green baize in the elaborate Salon de l'Horloge (the Clock Room) of the Quai d'Orsay. Lord Balfour called the meeting to order beneath the clock and summoned Sykes to the podium. Bonsal whispered to Lawrence that "Sir Mark must be a brave man to face that phalanx" of Arab warriors who sat stone-faced before their inquisitors. Lawrence replied, "He is a brave man and, worse luck, a stubborn one." But Sykes was nowhere to be found; he was laid low by the flu. Two days later, all were assembled again, but this time the news was catastrophic. "His servant has just brought me sad news," said Balfour's aide, Sir Maurice Hankey, secretary of the delegation. "Sykes is dead. He died this morning at daybreak—septic pneumonia following on flu." Despite what Sykes had sought to do to Feisal, his family, and his people, the Arab ruler placed a carpet of rare flowers on his casket before it was returned to his native Yorkshire for burial.

The very next day, they returned to the Clock Room. Feisal, still accompanied by Nouri Pasha and Lawrence, again was prepared to face down those he still saw as his adversaries. Lord Balfour represented an England that the Arabs believed was about to deal them profoundly wrong by upholding the Sykes-Picot pact. "We are told," Bonsal quoted Feisal as sneering at Balfour, "that this secret arrangement cancels the promises that were made to us openly before all the world."

"How extraordinary," sniffed Balfour, who promptly added, "owing to the tragic death of our expert, the review of these complicated negotiations, so generally misunderstood, will have to go over to another day."

It was the last public hearing that Feisal would have before the tribunal of the Paris Peace Conference. Still, that scarcely prevented the Allied nations from divvying up these territories among them according to their own particular whims or necessities. For Britain these included a desperate fear about other events that were happening in the Empire. On April 13, a British officer in India ordered his troops to fire on unarmed civilian demonstrators. The Amritsar massacre gave new life to Mahatma Gandhi's anti-British campaign of civil disobedience in his own search for independence. This back story played a profound role in the views of Britain and its stubborn intent to hang on to its territories in the Middle East—the gateway to India. At the same time these events on the subcontinent failed to turn Feisal and Lawrence from their goal of reshaping Arab lands according to their own mold. With this goal in mind, they had not come alone to Paris. They had brought with them a host of witnesses and lobbyists, who now fanned out across the city. An aging Daniel Bliss, founder of the American College in Beirut, and his son, hung out with Stephen Bonsal and the U.S. delegation, describing in lurid detail the Turks' desecration of the Tomb of the Prophet in

Medina, the slaughter of 350,000 Syrians, plus grisly battles in Iraq and Mesopotamia where 30,000 more were massacred.

Bonsal called on Feisal at least twice a week in his town house, providing the most regular liaison between the Hejaz and the U.S. delegation. Afterward he would describe Feisal's demands: Wilson and the Americans must assume a direct mandate over Greater Syria, then appoint the emir as their representative there. Bonsal consulted with Colonel House on Feisal's proposals, then brought back the not unexpected news that this was out of the question. At this point Feisal shot back that he wanted an American army officer attached to his personal entourage. That, at least, was within the realm of the possible. House ordered General John J. Pershing, commander of U.S. forces in Europe, to make it happen. Still, Feisal's pleas did not fall entirely on deaf ears in the American delegation. Despite his realization that the United States was unlikely to play any managerial or imperial role in the Middle East, Wilson was reported to have exclaimed to some aides that "listening to the Emir, I think to hear the voice of liberty, a strange and, I fear, a stray voice, coming from Asia."

In the end, though, it became increasingly obvious that other, more powerful dynamics were at work. Wilson was prepared to trade away self-determination in Arabia for other, more pressing, and what appeared to be more globally significant measures on the table in Paris that the American people might embrace. Above all, he wanted a League of Nations that could assure peace and self-determination in every corner of the world—particularly the Middle East, and without the need for a direct U.S. presence in the region as guarantor of a mandate. Even many of the most devoted and passionate lobbyists for the Arab cause, including the Blisses, father and son, who had devoted their lives to the region, recognized that Congress and the nation, having just concluded an enormously draining conflict, were unlikely to assume the burden of running a major portion of the Ottoman Empire.

All kinds of cocked-up concepts for a new Middle East were broached at the endless series of lunches and interminable dinners that marked off the days and weeks of the Peace Conference. There was a constant ebb and flow of diplomats, experts, and journalists who aspired to the rank of statesman. Most were attempting to raise their own standing and further their future prospects. One French journalist, Philippe Millet, managed to ingratiate himself with everyone from Frances Stevenson, Lloyd

George's secretary and lover, to Beer of the Inquiry. Millet was floating an idea endorsed by Jean Herbette, another journalist, who five years later was to become the first French ambassador to Bolshevik Russia. As Beer noted in his diary: "Millet's idea is to preserve unity of Anatolia and Constantinople under [the] Sultan with a French mandate. France would then give up all of Syria. If France got only northern Anatolia and Constantinople, then she would want [a] Syrian coastal strip excluding Damascus and Aleppo from mandate. . . . Millet would give [the Italians] the French Congo, if they gave up Anatolia."

Of course, none of these half-baked schemes ever went anywhere. Still, they took up considerable time and attention from a host of professional diplomats who were distracted from figuring out something that might really have worked.

Not surprisingly, meanwhile, senior French officials were playing a role in moving the Peace Conference in their own self-centered direction. While others around the fringe were floating trial balloons and watching them drift off into the sky, the official delegation from Georges Clemenceau on down was speaking with a near-unified voice. Arabia must be sliced and diced just as Sykes and Picot had divided it up in secret three years earlier. By the end of February, virtually all who had campaigned for a free Arabia were fed up with the French. "Of course these people are short-sighted and incredibly stupid," sniffed Gertrude Bell. Lloyd George himself shared many of her feelings about France's desires for an ownership stake in the region. By mid-March, Allenby himself had followed his protégée, Miss Bell, to Paris. The general, described by Frances Stevenson as "a fine looking man, and one I imagine who would stand no nonsense," came to lunch with the prime minister. Stevenson reported: "D [David Lloyd George] was urging him to give the French the facts about Syria, that the French would not be tolerated there. I believe he did at a subsequent meeting between the P.M. [Lloyd George], Clemenceau & Wilson. The French are very obstinate about Syria & trying to take the line that the English want it for themselves & are stirring up the Arabs against the French."

But Feisal continued to stand firm. As George Louis Beer confided in his diary, "Lawrence tells me that there is no chance whatsoever of Feisal agreeing to a French mandate as he fears they will convert Syria into a French colony and make Syrians half-baked Frenchmen." At this point, the Americans hit on a short-term solution that would at least allow the

Peace Conference to move past the Middle East to more immediately pressing issues. It was a solution that U.S. diplomats would try many times over the next century—and with equivalent levels of success in the region. They proposed a fact-finding mission. The facts they were seeking were simple—did the people of the Middle East, especially Syria and Mesopotamia, want the French or the British as their overlords? Heading the commission were Oberlin College president Henry Churchill King and Chicago businessman and Democratic Party contributor Charles R. Crane, a noted Arabophile who would achieve some degree of notoriety in future years by opening up Ibn Saud's Arabia to the first U.S. oil interests on the invitation of Philby. It was supposed to be a joint American-French-British commission, but the French refused to name a member and the British never got around to it. They spent weeks traveling through Syria and Palestine, preceded by British officials who carefully chose whom they would see, while the French seethed on the sidelines. The commission took its time, finally reporting the obvious in July 1919. Weeks after the treaty with Germany had been signed and the leaders had left Paris, the commission concluded the French were not wanted in Syria.

By that time, Feisal had returned to the Middle East to declare himself ruler of Syria, but not before a last, bitter private confrontation with Clemenceau. The two met on April 29 in the prime minister's private office in the Ministry of the Interior. It was a brief and explosive session. And the issues raised by Sykes and Picot all came to a boil.

"We Arabs would rather die than accept the supremacy of the French—although it be sugar-coated as a mandate subject to the control of the League," Feisal thundered.

Clemenceau, by the account of his own principal aide, General Jean Jules Henri Mordacq, turned on Feisal and shouted, his face turning almost purple, "We must have the French flag over Damascus."

Feisal glared at him, shouted, "Never!" and turned on his heels.

Two days later, Feisal packed up and left for Rome, seeking an alliance with the Pope, before continuing on toward his home in the Hejaz. He left Lawrence behind to salvage whatever might be possible from the train wreck the Peace Conference was in the process of creating in the Middle East. Lawrence saw Bonsal for one last time, and offered a prophecy that was only too quickly to come true: "There will be hell to pay, and that will continue until we get together and honor our war-time pledges."

.   .   .

By the time the Peace Conference had adjourned and the delegations and their entourages headed home, the Middle East had become little more than another bargaining chip for the Americans. Self-determination was traded away in a vain effort to salvage Wilson's precious League of Nations. The British and French both realized, separately, that they could prey on the president's desire for an international body that he believed would be capable of salving any wound, correcting any injustice that diplomats had foisted on innocent people at a distant conference table. The result was a broad series of failures. The Paris Peace Conference effectively awarded 80 million new Arab subjects to Britain. But it failed to resolve the principal outstanding issues troubling the region. Feisal and Lawrence had been doing their best to impress on the world's leaders that such a resolution was of vital urgency if conflict was not to be assured throughout the Middle East immediately and for generations to come. The only parties who really came out winners in Paris were the Zionists. With Britain assuming control over Palestine, and Lloyd George determined to stand firmly behind the Balfour Declaration, Jewish immigration to what would eventually become the land of Israel was effectively assured. Such guarantees, however, would carry a high price—levels of bloodshed comparable to the wars that were to sweep the rest of the region.

Bloodshed began while the plenipotentiaries were still meeting in Paris and should have provided advance warning of the dangers ahead—if the delegates had been able to see beyond their most immediate economic and geopolitical needs and desires. On May 19, 1919, at the Khurma Oasis, Ibn Saud's Ikhwan cavalry attacked the British-armed forces of Hussein, led by his son Abdullah, and routed them. The Ikhwan threatened to seize the Moslem holy cities of Mecca and Medina. Wahhabism was on the march. The British promptly ordered Lawrence and Philby to the region in a desperate attempt to broker a cease-fire. Lawrence succeeded, after a perilous trip via Crete where his plane crashed, killing two crewmembers. But his success left a jealous Philby even more embittered and the region no more stable.

A year later, at the Congress of San Remo in Italy, the Ottoman Empire was formally divided between Britain and France in a fashion not fundamentally different from the partition envisioned by Sykes and Picot four years, and a different world, earlier. The British and French

promptly assumed control of their mandates under the League of
Nations, which already had opened its doors in Geneva. But by then,
the U.S. Senate had dealt the entire process a mortal blow. It rejected
the Treaty of Versailles and declined U.S. membership in the League.
In fact, the whole mandate system proved to be a thinly veiled device
to assure British and French control over the portions of the world that
each claimed by right of victory in the Great War. At the same time, it
served as an empty gesture to the concept of self-determination that was
so important to their American ally. And none of these gestures took
into consideration the realities of the postwar Middle East.

Even before the Congress of San Remo, the collapse of what was left
of the order that the Ottoman Empire had brought to these conquered
regions sent each nationality on its own, often highly destructive, way.
For the British, the officially enunciated goal of the empire was to
"bring order out of chaos." They failed miserably for a host of reasons.
First, few of the small nations into which the region was being divided
had the economic heft or military muscle to remain independent or
self-sufficient without the heavy hand of a Western overlord. Neither
Britain nor France was particularly inclined to nurture the necessary
skills among the indigenous people. So most of these territories remained
ill-prepared for the period of outright independence that eventually followed—in most cases after World War II. Moreover, the nations the
Paris peacemakers created were engineered with little understanding or
acceptance of the realities of their ethnic and religious composition. Not
surprisingly, most were artificial in conception and inherently unstable,
not unlike Yugoslavia, which, as we will explore, was also created out of
the rubble of the war by the same peace delegates. Each new Arab state
was itself a potpourri of various tribal, ethnic, or religious entities—
Syria, Lebanon, Palestine, Iraq, and Transjordan, plus Saudi Arabia,
Yemen, and the Persian Gulf sheikdoms that were already, in their own
fashion, independent.

Take Syria—scene of the first true Arab government, apparently
self-determined and the product of a freely constituted congress, which
selected Feisal as king. But not for long. The French saw Feisal as a
mere tool of Britain, which had ceded Syria to France in the Sykes-Picot
treaty and again in the Treaty of Versailles. Feisal tried gamely to open
talks with the French. Instead the local commander, General Henri
Gouraud, in no mood for compromise, quickly overwhelmed Feisal's

troops and drove him into exile in Europe. Syria promptly became a French vassal, any pretense of self-government crushed beneath the heels of the colonial administrators who arrived from Paris. In March 1921, Winston Churchill, then serving as colonial secretary, summoned a conference in Cairo on the future of the Arab world, and installed Feisal on the throne of Mesopotamia—what today we call Iraq.

This kingdom of Mesopotamia, its tight boundaries also drawn by the Peace Conference, comprised a pernicious stewpot of hostile religions and conflicting nationalities. Kurds, Sunnis, Shiites, and Jews—each group sought to preserve at all costs its religion and its way of life. This was far from the grand, loose pan-Arab federation Feisal had envisioned. Yet within the borders of Mesopotamia were the holiest sites for the practice of the religious beliefs that were as important to each Moslem as life itself. For Shiites, the city of Samarra is the place where their last and greatest leader, the mystical Twelfth Imam, disappeared as a child but where he reputedly will come again to save the world. Pilgrims pray for the return of this "Hidden Imam." Karbala, site of the massacre of Husayn ibn Ali, the Prophet Muhammad's grandson, is another of the Shiites' holiest shrines. At Najaf, site of the tomb of the man Shiites believe is the righteous caliph and first imam, many Moslems begin the hajd—the pilgrimage to Mecca. For the Sunnis, who dominated the Ottoman Empire, Baghdad served as the sacred Abbasid capital from which caliphs ruled for more than five centuries. But with the arrival of British overlords, suddenly all these religions felt threatened. The Ottomans, though Turkish foreigners, at least were not infidels. Now infidels were at the gates of their shrines—and, whether British or American, they would stay there until the present, despite every violent effort to expel them.

Like the other mandates, Iraq was little more than nineteenth century imperialism barely covered with the fig leaf of Wilsonian self-determination. Geographically it was an amalgam of three Ottoman provinces. Basra, Baghdad, and Mosul had little in common. Much like the similarly artificial nation of Yugoslavia, with multiple religions and ethnicities, Iraq was destined for internal conflict and bloodshed from its birth. From the beginning, even its Arab majority was divided along religious lines. Over half were Shiites, concentrated in the oil-rich southern sectors, more closely aligned with the populace of neighboring Iran than with the Sunni tribes who dominated the countryside. This was a reality that no Western occupier has ever understood. In the north and center were large Sunni Kurdish populations along with Assyrian Christians and large numbers of Jews in Baghdad, many of them businessmen and tradesmen. Most ultimately fled to Israel, leaving behind an economic vacuum. Yet the Sunni leadership was born to rule—inheriting political and military skills from the once all-powerful Ottoman establishment.

The first explosion was not long in coming. In June 1920, the tribes of the Euphrates rose up against their British masters—a rebellion that cost Britain £40 million and 450 troops, leaving 10,000 Iraqis dead. That's when Winston Churchill finally realized that direct rule would never work and he sought a ruler he could control. Enter Feisal. The Hashemite prince, stateless since the French deposed him in Syria, was the perfect puppet. Though a foreigner to the people of Mesopotamia, he was quickly "elected" in a stage-managed national referendum, paraded into Baghdad, and crowned in a comic-opera ceremony that might have been produced by Gilbert and Sullivan, complete with a small military band playing "God Save the King."

Britain's gamble quickly appeared to pay off. By 1925 it had signed a seventy-five-year "contract" with the Iraq Petroleum Company by which the state received some modest royalties, while Britain owned the oil. Seven years later, Iraq was granted full independence and was promptly admitted to the League of Nations as a member. But British forces remained in the country, and the pressures beneath the surface were building sharply. The next year, just turned fifty years old, Feisal died suddenly of a heart attack in Bern, Switzerland. With his untimely death, his son Ghazi assumed the throne. An inept, weak-chinned, uninterested youth who was rumored to harbor Nazi sympathies and at one point sought to annex Kuwait (how history seems to repeat itself so insistently in the Middle East), Ghazi was staunchly opposed to the British presence in the region. Still, it was his powerful prime minister, Nuri al-Said, who ran the chaotic nation through a succession of six military coups in eight years. In 1939, after Ghazi's death in a mysterious accident while driving his sports car, his son Feisal was crowned king at the age of three. Al-Said continued to pull the strings.

Finally, in 1958, the monarchy was overthrown, paving the way for the arrival of Saddam Hussein at the helm of the Baath party a decade later. Ironically, even the Baaths were a relic of colonialism—founded in the 1940s by an Orthodox Christian from Damascus, Michel Aflaq, and a Sunni Moslem, Salah al-Din al-Bitar, who met when they embraced socialism as students in Paris. Though both were Syrians, their belief in a single Arab nation attracted to their cause a number of Iraqis, including Saddam Hussein. The military coup that brought them to power in Iraq had widespread popular support, especially in the Sunni-dominated north, where Saddam had been born into a family of landless peasants in the impoverished village of Tikrit, north of Baghdad. His roots in the socialist, pan-Arab Baathist dogma continue to resonate among Iraqis even today after decades of repression and terror under his leadership. Indeed Saddam made many of the right gestures toward ridding his nation of the infidel West. In 1972 he ordered the nationalization of the British-owned Iraq Petroleum Company and voided the seventy-five-year lease the British had foisted on King Feisal, though it still had twenty-eight years to run. By then, Iraq had become the second-largest oil producer in the Persian Gulf after Saudi Arabia. For a while, Saddam endeared himself to the West, keeping at bay the ayatollahs of Iran, who, if they had succeeded in taking over the Shiite regions of the Gulf as they apparently are still seeking to do, would control half the world's oil supply.

Certainly Iraq was not alone in the region in its troubled, often bloody, struggle toward independence. Despite Wilson's Fourteen Points and his expressed belief in self-determination for every nation, few corners of the Middle East have ever known democracy. In many cases, real self-determination from the beginning could have meant the right to choose an Islamic state, which might have obviated a resort to terrorism to achieve the objectives of the people. Might such an Islamic nation not have wound up as antidemocratic anyway? We will probably never have the opportunity to know, although that certainly was the case in Iran and Afghanistan under the Taliban.

There was another alternative: a real mandate system run by the powers gathered in Paris in 1919 and policed by a well-fortified League of Nations. Functioning as intended, such a system could have prepared each of these nations for independence, if not democracy in a Western sense. But the United States opted out, leaving the world to its own devices. As a result, the Middle East has become a patchwork of religious, military, and political leaderships that have called the shots and continue to do so without a gesture toward real democracy. Throughout these decades of chaos, in Iraq the minority Sunnis retained power. All top Iraqi military officers had been carefully selected and trained in the Sunni-dominated Ottoman Empire, which saw Mesopotamia as a counterweight to its archenemy—the Shiite theocracy of Iran.

Iran was the one portion of the Middle East that never fell prey to the peacemakers in Paris. In part this was a tribute to its success in remaining independent through the centuries, never being swept into the Ottoman Empire, and maintaining its neutrality during World War I. But while it was never a colony, a mandate, or a protectorate, it was still effectively denied its sovereignty for much of the twentieth century. Iran's entire economic development—its very ability to survive as a viable nation in the modern era—was almost entirely dependent on Western entrepreneurs. First came the British, then the Americans. And as in much of the rest of the Middle East, especially the Islam-dominated regions, Iranians at every level of society resented the role played by foreigners in their development. Eventually, Iran became divided between two powerful forces. On one side there was the religious community run by the Shiite clerics led by the ayatollahs. Then there was the Anglo-American Oil Company, which by World War II had effectively become a state within a state, with its own roads, airports, security, and municipal services and economic infrastructure. The collision of these two powerful forces eventually led to the toxic mix of a nation run by the ayatollahs and the wealth of a global oil power that was increasingly in a position to project its religious imperatives far beyond its borders.

So while Iran was never on the Paris agenda, the principles established in 1919 by the Allied conferees, designed to cement their power and influence in the Middle East, certainly played a major role in determining the future course of Iran as well—and relations with its Shiite neighbor, Iraq. Today the artificial nation of Iraq is still divided effectively into the same three sections, as it would have been had the Paris peacemakers actually redrawn the boundaries of the Middle East along religious lines.

The Shiite-dominated region of Basra in oil-rich southern Iraq is today effectively ruled from Tehran. Its ayatollahs have decreed, and are enforcing through their local militias, many of the fundamentalist religious beliefs and practices that enslave their own Iranian people. This is a fear of Saudi Arabia right next door—that its own fundamentalist Wahhabis and the Shiites in the oil-rich eastern territories are simply biding their time before rising up to seize control of their own destiny.

The ultimate nightmare? A huge Shiite crescent from Iran across south-ern Iraq and into eastern Saudi Arabia—combined, the largest single oil reserve in the world. At the same time the Kurds, who continue to dominate northern Iraq, are desperate to determine their fate in unity with Kurds in neighboring Turkey. The third region, around Baghdad, was and remains a natural Sunni territory.

Few British officials then or Americans today have understood these realities of religion and power, or the enormous frustrations these forces have generated since Mesopotamia was first created as a mandate in Paris. The precursors of those who seek to rule Iraq from Washington today were the British, who sought to rule it from Whitehall in 1919. Today's terrorism is another manifestation of the frustration of the peo-ple of the Middle East that they remain unable to take control of their own affairs. The one difference today is the ability of these disenfran-chised to take their frustration, often violently, to the very doors of those they see as their oppressors. Since these nations managed, not so very long ago, to cast aside the oppressive past of the British and the French, the last thing they want is a new oppressor arriving from the West.

Still, there is enough blame for everyone. While the British were cementing their rule over Mesopotamia, France was committing its own, terribly French, bêtises in neighboring Syria. Unlike the British, who strove to project at least a veneer of self-rule on their mandate subjects, the French moved in with full military and administrative muscle. France's Greater Syria comprised an enlarged Lebanon—from Druze and Alawis to Maronite Christians to Sunni and Shiite Moslems. Their French overlords were ill-disposed to allow them any substantial freedom or move them toward the self-government that they would ulti-mately attain with little preparation from their masters. France believed it had won the right to these colonies at a terrible cost of French lives on the World War I battlefields of Europe. They managed to find ways of justifying this all but tyrannical rule: French missionaries needed to be protected while they continued the Lord's work of turning heathen Moslems into good Catholics. Which of course merely intensified the hostility and alienation of the native Arabs.

The French only compounded the problem by choosing a particular subset of these Arabs to deal with on a regular basis. French bureaucrats were most comfortable with the urban, conservative propertied class of Sunnis. As in neighboring Iraq, these were remnants of the Ottoman

Empire's bureaucracy. All were monitored and patrolled at every step by 15,000 troops of the Armée du Levant and a High Commissioner's office. The top posts were all reserved for French overseas functionaries – the most narrow-minded of their class, who insisted on checking every obscure document produced by the lowliest Syrian clerk. So it was scarcely surprising that there were regular, often violent explosions, beginning with a July 1925 Druze rebellion. This spread to Damascus itself, leveling the city and leaving more than 5,000 Syrians dead in its wake. The French legacy to Syria and Lebanon over the next three decades was an almost certain guarantee of chaos and violence.

If anything, the Lebanese portions of Greater Syria were an even more intractable problem. There, the French found conflicts not only among Moslem sects but between Moslems and a powerful indigenous Christian community that was a legacy of the earliest efforts by French missionaries. These Maronite Christian politicians were led by an extraordinary figure—Émile Eddé. Decades later, I came to know his son Raymond in Paris, where he lived an extremely comfortable, yet he insisted merely temporary, exile in the luxurious Hotel George V. Though the entire family was thoroughly Francophile, the Eddés, father and son, worked and prayed until their deaths for the only truly multireligious nation in the Middle East. "Coexistence is the only route that will work in our nation," Raymond once told me. "We must find a way." He reacted bitterly to Henry Kissinger's deep involvement in the affairs of the Middle East and his country. Eddé believed the goal of the then secretary of state was simply to make Lebanon grateful to, even dependent on, yet another major power—the United States. But in our long conversations in Paris twenty years ago over endless cups of thick Lebanese coffee, Raymond Eddé was, in his own way, saying something far more profound than a simple rant against Dr. Kissinger. Eddé, like his father before him, was just the latest in a long line of prescient minor players in the fields of international politics and diplomacy, dating at least back to Paris in 1919. All recognized the errors of their colonial masters—not to mention the motives of political, social, and economic profit springing from the depths of self-aggrandizement. In the end, however, these far-sighted Middle East leaders were powerless to correct the errors of the West. The result for Eddé in his beloved Lebanon was personal tragedy. Decades of internecine bloodshed led to the death of his sister at the hands of a sniper in Beirut, the invasion of his nation by

Israel from the south and Syria from the east, and ultimately its transformation into a haven for terrorist cells of Hezbollah and a host of other extremist groups.

But while France left its mandates Syria and Lebanon in shambles, another Arab entity carved out of Palestine by the peac makers of Paris turned out to be at once the most ethnically homogeneous and stable nation in the Middle East. This one experiment demonstrated graphically that a nation built on ethnic and religious homogeneity can work. The dynasty that began with the coronation of Feisal's brother, Abdullah, continues today to rule the Hashemite Kingdom of Jordan, which throughout its history has enjoyed minimal interference from the outside world. A large part of this is a tribute to the hard reality that it possesses little the outside world has coveted since 1919—no vast oil wealth and little strategic or geopolitical significance. At the same time, it has been blessed with a succession of savvy rulers who have understood with enormous precision how to thread their nation's way through the thickets of international geopolitics in the Middle East.

Nowhere was the patrimony carved up by the Peace Conference more valuable than in the Arabian Peninsula—the bulk of it ruled by Ibn Saud and his descendants. Together with his Wahhabi followers, by the time of the Paris Peace Conference Ibn Saud had managed to seize and retain control over the cities of Jeddah and Riyadh, the vast, soon to be discovered oil and mineral riches as well as the sands of the Empty Quarter. Ruling not as a dictator, but as simply the first among equals among the tribal sheikhs who had roamed these stretches for centuries, Ibn Saud rode to power behind his band of fierce, profoundly religious warriors.

The armistice and the events in Paris—given the exclusion of Ibn Saud and the cold shoulder turned to his British adviser, St. John Philby—were followed by violence as the Ikhwan (the Brethren) were turned loose. Ibn Saud feared, quite rightly as it turned out, that the Peace Conference was intent on a process that would leave him surrounded by hostile powers. Hashemite rule was established in Jordan and Iraq as Hussein's son Ali became king of the Hejaz and Feisal mounted the throne of Mesopotamia. At the same time, the French were seizing Greater Syria. So, especially after Sherif Hussein suddenly and unilaterally declared himself caliph, supreme religious ruler for all of Islam, it was not a difficult decision for Saud to send the Ikhwan on their mission. Unleashed, they rode out of central Arabia to extend their fierce brand of Wahhabi Islam to the entire region. By the mid-1920s, some eighteen thousand camel-mounted Ikhwan warriors had driven into the Hejaz, seizing Mecca and Medina, forcing Sherif Hussein into exile. By that time, the British had gotten fed up with both Arab leaders—Hussein and Ibn Saud. They had decided by then to cut them loose. And Philby was hung out to dry along with them. As Philby wrote in his memoirs, the rage he was so assiduously nursing against the British government was a "simple dualism in which the powers of darkness are represented by H.M.G. [His Majesty's Government]."

But Philby also had a son, Kim, born during his father's earlier service with the government of the Raj in India. Growing up in the shadow of his father and the Ibn Saud family of Arabia, he was a personal witness to the indignities perpetrated by the mandarins of Whitehall. As a friend wrote during that period, the young Kim had become "enraptured by his father's voice, his accomplishments, his thoughts on society and his unending denunciation of some of the more famous of his colleagues in the Middle East during the war." By the time Kim had followed his father's footsteps into Trinity College, Cambridge, he was ripe for conversion to another religion—communism. Already, he had met and become fascinated by his father's best friend in Jeddah. Hassim Haki-moff Khan, the Soviet representative in Arabia, was also closely allied with Ibn Saud and was staunchly opposed to Western penetration in the Middle East. And so we have more fallout of the failures of Paris and British policy: Kim Philby became one of the Soviet Union's most valuable and pernicious spies, wreaking incalculable damage on the Western Allies who'd spurned his father and casually dismissed the Arab peoples to whom they had made what both Philbys believed were inviolable promises.

Ironically, by effectively ignoring Ibn Saud at the Peace Conference, the delegates, particularly the British, had unwittingly delivered to the Arabian leader an enormous gift. He alone among Middle East rulers had been freed from the horrors of Western mandates, and effectively rewarded a carte blanche to profit from the Croesian wealth of oil that would be found beneath his soil by U.S. prospectors of his own choosing. Until this oil wealth began to arrive, the principal income of the Kingdom of Hejaz and Sultanate of Najd had been the annual pilgrimage to Mecca, known as the hajj, which every able-bodied Moslem who can afford to do so is obligated to make at least once in his life. In 1932, Ibn Saud united his two regions into a single nation and called it Saudi Arabia. And shortly thereafter, Philby, operating on Ibn Saud's instructions and independently of his onetime British masters, invited Charles R. Crane to Jeddah with the intention of opening the resources of Arabia to his oil prospectors.

This was the same Charles Crane whom Wilson had dispatched from Paris to explore the true feelings of the people of the Middle East toward French or British hegemony. With his conclusions, Crane had endeared himself to those who had followed his mission. As Crane's report observed: "Eloquent Arab orators appealed to America, having freed them, to uphold their independence before the Peace Conference." This, of course, never happened. But by the time Ibn Saud, his treasury severely depleted, had come to agree with his adviser Philby that he desperately needed to exploit any natural resources beneath his lands, Crane had cemented his position as the Westerner to call upon. Crane in turn summoned a Vermont geological engineer named Karl S. Twitchell, who found oil and brought the Standard Oil Company of California to Arabia. Aramco was born. The United States replaced Britain as the dominant power in the Arabian peninsula.

With the arrival of the Americans came some profound changes in Saudi Arabia. Roads, trucks, automobiles, telephones, and complex machinery appeared. The Wahhabi desire to maintain a strict seventh-century Islamic nationhood began to founder on the needs and desires of Ibn Saud. While his split with the Wahhabis began to evolve shortly after the Ikhwans' conquest of Medina in 1925, by the arrival of the American oil developers, the break had become all but complete. Over the next decades, the first U.S. air bases sprang up during World War II. The United States became the principal guarantor of Saudi independence and modernization. For those devout Moslems who remained actively practicing their adherence to centuries-old fundamental Islamic beliefs, the United States had replaced Britain as the imperial power to be detested and reviled.

Though the Ikhwan have given way to al-Qaeda as the shock troops of militant Islam, there are still Wahhabis in Saudi Arabia, among a host of fundamentalist elements throughout the Middle East. And they are growing in strength. But there is a broader question: Would there have been an Osama bin Laden, or even an excuse for one, had there been a

united Islamic world, one that might have learned to tolerate a pluralism among Sunni and Shiite or at least one that did not have a common enemy to defy with a jihad? At his dinner at the Hotel Crillon on
January 20, 1919, Feisal asked Westermann of the Inquiry, "America
has twenty-eight [*sic*] states and yet is one nation. Why can not Arabia,
which includes Mesopotamia . . . have many states and yet [exist] in one
confederation?" None of the parties in Paris in 1919 or their successors
for the remainder of the century did much to prepare the Islamic world
for even a modicum of the democracy that might have allowed religious
and secular civilizations to coexist peacefully.

All the British managed to accomplish in this portion of the Middle
East was to impose the modern territorial boundaries of Saudi Arabia.
And this was merely an incidental by-product of guaranteeing the sovereignty of the Persian Gulf sheikdoms from Kuwait down through Qatar,
Abu Dhabi, Dubai, and Oman. In Paris the peacemakers drew a frontier
separating Kuwait from the new artificial mandate state of Iraq. Fifteen
years later, Sheikh Ahmad al-Jabir al-Sabah signed an agreement with
British Petroleum as coequal owner of Kuwait Oil Company. Four years
later, British engineers discovered one of the world's largest reservoirs
of petroleum—by then out of the reach of King Ibn Saud. So it should
scarcely prove surprising that the embittered Saudis ultimately embraced
U.S. oil interests over the British when it came time to choose their own
partner.

The French and the British, beginning in Paris, sought to replace
Arab political structures with their own European designs, creating
nations after their own Western models. It was hardly a recipe for peace
and prosperity. This template had, after all, led to a succession of bloody
wars in Europe over the previous millennium. Still, Europe became the
central power in the Middle East. Western-style nations appeared to the
peacemakers in Paris to be far more convenient political organizations
with which to negotiate and do business than a host of feuding tribes.
The result is a legacy that continues to plague the region.

Today the United States is the region's dominant power. But do the
Iraqi people really want America's type of democracy or, like the British
and French before, does the United States simply want to create nations
that resemble itself? In any case, it's probably too late. The ethnic amal-
gams created in Paris in 1919 make any democratic nation as now constituted in a region such as the Middle East problematic, as the West has

already discovered in Yugoslavia. There, as we will see in a later chapter, peace could be assured today only by disassembling the creation of the peacemakers in Paris nearly a century ago.

So what might we have been left with had Feisal had his way and had the British and the French proved more flexible, or at least more even-handed, in dealing with the principal powers of the post-Ottoman Middle East? First, in Syria and Lebanon we might have had a Hashemite Arab kingdom like Jordan, which has been a thus-far peaceful model of Arab governance. Instead, we have two all but dysfunctional nations—an anti-Western Syria, ruled by a dictator and his family, hospitable to terror and disorder, and a Christian-Moslem Lebanon torn apart by decades of civil war and instability. Second, we might have had a Mesopotamia consisting of a loose federation of states, each free to pursue its own religious and ethnic course. Instead, we find ourselves saddled with Iraq—a nation assembled by European diplomats in Paris that became all but ungovernable in the hands of anyone but a despot.

Most Arabs wound up with a deep bitterness toward Britain and France, with most unable, or unwilling, to distinguish one from the other. The United States inherited this enmity toward foreign overlords that began with America's colonial predecessor in the region, the Ottoman Turks. In Paris, the British and French sought to serve their own economic and geopolitical interests. Now, in the post–cold war period, the United States appears to be doing the same—shaping the region to serve its own global interests. And Americans wonder why they face such implacable hostility. The United States may have become the dominant outside force in the region, but as the British and French discovered post–Paris 1919, it is in maintaining this dominance that America's role there has come unglued. The troops the United States sent and who remain, the boundaries the United States has inherited and is seeking to guarantee, the rulers it is supporting, or subverting, are all a constant, never-ending reminder of the imperialism the region thought it had shed when the Ottoman Empire was dismantled in Paris so long ago. Today's terrorism is merely another manifestation of yesterday's Arab revolt.

4

THE STATE
OF THE JEWS

ON JANUARY 4, 1919, CHAIM WEIZMANN ARRIVED IN PARIS TO head the Zionist delegation to the Peace Conference. It was a triumphal moment for a Jew born in a remote East European shtetl. The day before his departure from London, he had signed a monumental agreement with Emir Feisal. For Weizmann, this accord climaxed years of negotiations and ceaseless shuttles between the Middle East and the capitals of Western Europe. It promised to usher in an era of peace and cooperation between the two principal ethnic groups of Palestine: Arabs and Jews. This meeting was by no means the first contact between the two men of such disparate backgrounds and aspirations, united only by a common goal of coexistence with the great powers that for years had been busily dividing up the region they both hoped to make their home. Both Weizmann and Feisal believed they desperately needed this agreement to work as a foundation for building strong and prosperous nations that could coexist in a hostile world.

For the Zionist leader, this need was especially acute and painfully immediate. Chaim Weizmann was born November 27, 1874, in the shtetl of Motal about twenty miles west of Pinsk in a region that has, over the past century or so, been successively a part of Poland, Lithuania, Russia, the Soviet Union, and today the nation of Belarus. Through the centuries, a host of wars and pogroms had washed across its few hundred families. When young Chaim was a child, there were two wooden synagogues in the tiny village, but the most notable characteristic was its location—as Weizmann later described it—"in one of the darkest and most forlorn corners of the Pale of Settlement, that prison house created by czarist Russia for the largest part of its Jewish population." It is difficult to describe the profound poverty and even more profound isolation of shtetls like Motal, which make the emergence of individuals like Chaim Weizmann, who changed the world, so truly extraordinary. When a rare newspaper arrived in the village, it came from Warsaw and was often a month or more old. Though Weizmann's family was among the more privileged in the village, their annual income rarely surpassed $300 and there were a dozen children in the family to be fed, clothed, and educated. His father was a timber merchant, and when it came time for the eleven-year-old to continue his education, the family found the means to send him to the provincial capital of Pinsk. It was there that Weizmann, the future first president of the State of Israel, developed the two passions that would change the course of his life: chemistry and Zionism.

Zionism in those days was nothing like the political and economic force it would become in the years after the Paris Peace Conference, or even the moral force it had become in the years immediately preceding it. Outlawed as a movement by the czars, Zionism was a powerful aspiration among Jews, and little more. The occasional brave pioneer would take off to settle in the swamps and deserts of the Holy Land. The synagogues of Pinsk would raise some small funds to support the cause. Most of the resources for the first kibbutzim in fact came from the West, especially from the wealthy French Jew Baron Edmond de Rothschild. His largesse spawned the first such settlements, like Petah Tikva in the Achor Valley near Jericho in the early 1880s.

Young Chaim was very much captivated by the romance of Zionism and the faith that it could help his fellow Jews escape their virtual prison in the Pale of Settlement. But it was his academic prowess that paved the way for his own escape. At the age of eighteen, a high school diploma in hand, the teenager fled Russia by jumping ship off a river raft en route to Danzig with no passport and a few coins in his pocket. A brief passage teaching in a German-Jewish academy in the village of Pfiugnstadt near Darmstadt (about forty miles southeast of Frankfurt) led him eventually to Berlin. There, in 1896, in his second year at university, he had his first contact with Theodor Herzl, author of *Der Judenstaat* (The Jewish State), the bible of Zionism. "The effect produced by *The Jewish State* was profound," Weizmann recalled later. "Not the ideas, but the personality which stood behind them appealed to us. Here was daring, clarity and energy." In that year, he committed himself to the lifelong propagation of these ideas—of a nation for the Jews in the homeland of their ancestors.

Meanwhile, Weizmann was pursuing his secular studies. He had found a particular talent in the field of chemistry, and after his earlier education in Berlin, he headed for Freiburg on the western edge of the Black Forest to pursue a doctorate based on research in dyestuffs that he had begun in Berlin, receiving his degree with the highest honors. He managed to sell one of his discoveries to the German industrial complex of I.G. Farbenindustrie, which in a horrible irony much later became a leader among German manufacturers that used slave labor from Auschwitz and manufactured the Zyklon B for Hitler's gas chambers. In July 1904 Weizmann decided to leave for England, "a deliberate and desperate step," as he described it, but one fraught with meaning for the future course of the Zionist movement. At the time, however, he thought it was simply a protective move that kept the young scientist from being "eaten up by Zionism, with no benefit either to my scientific career or to Zionism." Still, he chose England, prophetically, as "the one country which seemed likely to show a genuine sympathy for a movement like ours." The young chemist settled in Manchester, the northern English center of the nation's chemical industry. There he stumbled on two key godfathers. Charles Dreyfus was managing director of the Clayton Aniline Works and chairman of the Manchester Zionist Society. Dreyfus introduced Weizmann to a fifty-seven-year-old former prime minister of England who had lost his parliamentary seat and in North Manchester was going after a new constituency to return to the House of Commons. In early 1906 the thirty-one-year-old Zionist chemist met Arthur James Balfour. Weizmann recalled their first meeting vividly:

I had been less than two years in the country, and my English was still not easy to listen to. I remember how Balfour sat in his usual pose, his legs stretched out in front of him, an imperturbable expression on his face. The British Government was really anxious to do something to relieve the misery of the Jews; and the problem was a practical one, calling for a practical approach. . . . I pointed out that nothing but a deep religious conviction expressed in modern political terms could keep the movement alive, and that this conviction had to be based on Palestine and on Palestine alone. Any deflection from Palestine was—well, a form of idolatry.

Balfour was clearly taken aback, and impressed. "Are there many Jews who think like you?" he asked.

"I believe I speak the mind of millions of Jews whom you will never see and who cannot speak for themselves," Weizmann replied.

Balfour paused thoughtfully. "If that is so, you will one day be a force."

At the moment, neither truly understood just what a force. Ba four won his seat in 1906 and returned to Parliament. When war broke out in 1914, he was a member of the cabinet as first sea lord, then eventually as foreign secretary. Weizmann, meanwhile, continued on his own route, building a reputation among international Zionists, working feverishly in his chemistry lab, developing a revolutionary process of fermentation. Properly positioned, Weizmann came to realize, Zionism could have as powerful an impact as any scientific advance.

The catalyst was C. P. Scott, renowned editor of the *Manchester Guardian*, one of Britain's most powerful and respected papers, who brought Balfour and Weizmann together again at a party in the home of some prominent German-Jewish Zionists. Already Weizmann had formulated a pitch that Scott found most compelling: "Should Palestine fall within the British sphere of influence and should Britain encourage a Jewish settlement there, as a British dependency, we could have in twenty to thirty years a million Jews out there, perhaps more; they would develop the country, bring back civilization to it, form a very effective guard for the Suez Canal."

Contained in this simple statement were three critical geopolitical issues: Palestine for the British, development and civilization of a desert wasteland, and a loyal and powerful ally prepared to do battle in defense of the Suez Canal—the fastest and most direct route to India and the East. By now it was December 1914, war had just broken out, and Scott thought it would be a good idea for Weizmann to meet David Lloyd George, the Welsh statesman who was serving at the time as chancellor of the Exchequer. In addition to the chancellor, Scott, and Weizmann, others were present at what would turn out to be an historic encounter: Josiah Wedgwood, a member of Parliament and great-great-grandson of the potter; and Herbert Samuel, the first practicing Jew ever appointed to the British cabinet, as home secretary. (Disraeli, the nineteenth-century prime minister, while born of Jewish parents, was baptized in the Anglican Church.) Later, Samuel was to become the first high commissioner of Palestine. Lloyd George was as impressed by Weizmann as had been Scott and Balfour before him, and passed him along to the prime minister, Herbert Asquith. In his diary, Asquith admitted he had some reservations about Weizmann's Zionist arguments, but he laid out a cogent case for the support that Lloyd George, a devout Christian, was prepared to lend the Zionist cause: "I need not say he does not care a damn for the Jews or their past or their future, but thinks it will be an outrage to let the Holy Places pass into the possession or under the protectorate of 'agnostic and atheistic' France."

At the same time that Weizmann was lining up support among the British political establishment, he was also doing battle on his own flanks. The Jewish leadership of Britain, and on the Continent as well, was deeply divided over the issue of Palestine. Many of the wealthiest and most powerful of what Weizmann called "secular Jews" were bitterly opposed to a Jewish national homeland in the Middle East, or indeed anywhere else. Among them was Sir Edwin Montagu, a leading British member of Parliament, whose views stood in sharp contrast to those of his cousin, the confirmed Zionist Herbert Samuel. Montagu, as Weizmann put it, "saw the specter of anti-Semitism in every country if its Jews permitted themselves to dream of a territorial center or a national political existence outside their present citizenship."

Even the Rothschilds—perhaps the single most powerful and wealthy Jewish family in Europe, with members scattered across England, France, and Germany—held sharply divergent views on the prospects of a Jewish homeland. In Paris, Baron Edmond de Rothschild had been a benefactor of a Jewish Palestine for decades since his earliest assistance to kibbutz settlements in the nineteenth century. His son James, an eccentric and arrogant young man who affected a monocle, had joined the army and, during the war, was stationed with Allied forces in Palestine. England was home to two Rothschild branches: Lord Lionel Walter Rothschild, the British patron of Zionism; and Leopold de Rothschild, furiously anti-Zionist together with his wife, Lady Leopold, who was pathologically opposed to the creation of a Jewish state. Weizmann needed to separate the two families if he was to win his goal of public British support for a homeland in Palestine.

Fortuitously, other events were playing directly into his hands. At the outbreak of the war in August 1914, Weizmann had received a flyer that had been sent by the War Office to all working scientists in England asking if they were in possession of any discoveries that might have even the most remote military application. Weizmann offered his fermentation process. Nearly two years passed before suddenly there appeared in his Manchester laboratory the chief research scientist of Nobel's Explosives Company, one of Britain's largest munitions makers. Within days, in March 1916, Weizmann was summoned to the office of Sir Frederick L. Nathan, head of the navy's powder department, who ushered him into the presence of the first lord of the Admiralty, the forty-one-year-old Winston Churchill. "Well, Dr. Weizmann," Churchill began, "we need 30,000 tons of acetone. Can you make it?" Weizmann confessed he had never used his process to make more than a few ounces of acetone—an essential component of munitions—but that it might be scaled up. It was. For the next two years, Weizmann devoted himself to this process, which led to the wealth and power he needed to pursue his dream and the political ambitions for his people. Indeed, there were reports that Lloyd George told friends that he had "rewarded" Weizmann with a Jewish homeland in Palestine for his donation of the acetone process during the war. In fact, the whole issue was far more complex.

By mid-October in 1916, Weizmann and his growing family were comfortably ensconced in a sprawling fifteen-room London mansion at 67 Addison Road, a broad, tree-lined street in Kensington that quickly became the center of the Zionist movement in Britain. Weizmann continued to widen his circle of secular support, adding a network of newspapers from the *Manchester Guardian* to the venerable *Times* of London, and well-placed individuals, including Colonel Richard Meinertzhagen. Son of a distinguished English banker of German origin, Meinertzhagen had become a leading member of British military intelligence, as well as a colleague and later a Paris neighbor of T. E. Lawrence. Meinertzhagen had been converted from anti-Semitism by another member of the Zionist inner circle, Aaron Aaronson, a valiant Jewish fighter and intelligence officer who had impressed the young British officer with his bravery and resourcefulness.

But Weizmann's greatest find as an ally was Sir Mark Sykes, chief secretary of the War Cabinet and, unbeknownst to the Zionists until later, cosigner of the initially secret Sykes-Picot Agreement. Weizmann and Sykes had been brought together by another Zionist leader—Dr. Moses Gaster, a Rumanian Jewish scholar. Expelled from his homeland for his Zionist activities, Gaster had settled in England, where he'd risen to the post of chief rabbi of the Sephardic community and had become a distinguished lecturer at Oxford. Sykes, himself won over to Zionism by Gaster, would be the critical individual guiding the quest for a Jewish homeland through the War Cabinet and on to the Peace Conference in Paris.

With the backing of Sykes, events now began to move more quickly at top levels of the government. In January 1917, with the British eager to win the support of the Jewish populations of the Middle East and Russia, Sykes presented to the cabinet a memo that Weizmann had drafted. The document sought recognition of the Jewish population of Palestine as a Jewish nation, its people granted the full right to immigrate and purchase land, with a government, under British protection, that would rule the territory. But the Zionist program faced two principal obstacles, one known to Weizmann and one unknown. First, there was the opposition of the group of powerful secular Jews led by Montagu and now known as the Conjoint Committee; second, there was the Sykes-Picot pact, which remained largely under wraps until Lenin's Bolsheviks seized power in Russia and published all the czar's secret files.

Sykes-Picot, it will be recalled, awarded a large swath of Palestine to the French. The first obstacle posed by Britain's homegrown Jewish anti-Zionists was a matter for compromise; the second turned out to be an opportunity. Sykes, and much of the War Cabinet, never cared very much for the agreement with Picot in the first place. There was a widespread belief in top government circles that Britain had every right to much of Palestine, Greater Syria, and Iraq, which the pact had effectively awarded to France; indeed, the British forces were already in the process of seizing much of that region from the Ottoman Turks, who had entered the war in October 1914. Weizmann had little difficulty selling C. P. Scott with a persuasive argument against a French presence in the Holy Land:

I don't think that she should claim more than Syria, as far as Beyrouth. The so-called French influence which is merely spiritual and religious, is predominant in Syria. In Palestine there is very little of it—a few monastic establishments. The only work which may be termed civilizing pioneer work has been carried out by the Jews. From the point of view of justice, therefore, France cannot lay claim to a country with which it has no connection whatsoever.

On March 22, 1917, Weizmann met with Balfour, now the foreign secretary, to press this same point. One month later the Zionist leader learned of the Sykes-Picot Agreement for the first time from Scott, who had stumbled on its existence in Paris even before Lenin published it more widely. "This was startling information indeed!" Weizmann wrote later. "It seemed to me that the proposal was devoid of rhyme or reason. It was unjust to England, fatal to us, and not helpful to the Arabs. I could easily understand why Sykes had not been averse to the abrogation of the treaty and why Picot had not been able to defend it with any particular energy." Nine days later, Weizmann pressed the point with Lord Robert Cecil, deputy to Balfour, who in 1937 would win the Nobel Peace Prize for his activities on behalf of the League of Nations. Jews everywhere, Weizmann pointed out, trusted England, but the French as colonizers "had always interfered with the population and tried to impose on it the *esprit Français*," a sentiment that French colonial subjects would unanimously, though ineffectually, second at the Peace Conference two years later.

Behind the scenes, the wheels were grinding with painful slowness, at least as far as Weizmann was concerned. The Zionist leader believed—with what turned out to be extraordinary prescience—that the British, as we have seen, were attempting to juggle a host of priorities in the Middle East. They wanted a homeland for the Jews, and at least for the moment they also needed the Arabs as allies on the region's desert battlefields. But Weizmann was to acquire one more powerful ally. The United States had entered the war in April 1917. A month later, Balfour arrived in Washington for his first visit as an Allied representative. At the White House, he was greeted by Louis Dembitz Brandeis, nominated less than a year before by Woodrow Wilson as the first Jewish justice of the Supreme Court. Brandeis was not only a Jew, but a committed

Zionist, and he spent much of his first meeting with Balfour pressing the view of the American Zionist community that they wanted to see a British administration of a Jewish Palestine. Balfour agreed, pledging, as he had to Weizmann, his commitment to such a plan. Back in England, Balfour received Lord Rothschild, who handed the foreign secretary a statement that, in somewhat watered-down form, would serve as the definitive commitment to a Jewish state in the Middle East. Lord Rothschild asked the War Cabinet to "accept the principle of recognizing Palestine as the National Home of the Jewish people and the right of the Jewish people to build up its national life in Palestine under a protection to be established at the conclusion of peace."

On October 4, the War Cabinet met to debate the issue, only to hear an impassioned diatribe by Montagu. Weizmann sat waiting anxiously in an adjacent office, but could not be found for a rebuttal when messengers who had been sent frantically seeking the Zionist leader failed to look right next door. In his absence, an amended formula was drafted pledging "establishment in Palestine of a National Home for the Jewish race . . . [while] nothing shall be done which may prejudice the civil and religious rights of the existing non-Jewish communities." It was, as Weizmann observed, "a painful recession" from what he thought the government was prepared to offer—to the Jewish people (a religion, not a race) who were clearly put on an equal footing with all others who happened to be found in Palestine at the time. Brandeis, equally horrified, managed to persuade Colonel Edward House to intervene with Balfour. Finally, on November 18, following a second, equally fraught cabinet meeting, Sykes emerged, waving the approved text. Embracing the Zionist leader, he proclaimed, "Dr. Weizmann, it's a boy." That night, Balfour sent the agreement to Lord Rothschild in the form of a letter. This was the Balfour Declaration:

> His Majesty's Government view with favour the establishment in Palestine of a National Home for the Jewish people, and will use their best endeavors to facilitate the achievement of this object, it being clearly understood that nothing shall be done which may prejudice the civil and religious rights of the existing non-Jewish communities in Palestine or the rights and political status enjoyed by Jews in any other country.

It was a game attempt to satisfy every interest group—and in the end, of course, it satisfied none completely. It presumed that the Jews should be happy with a National Home for their people (not a race), while the Arabs should be satisfied to retain some slim guarantee that their rights would be observed; and for the secular Jews of the Conjoint Committee, their rights in England would be preserved as well.

With the agreement ratified by the Cabinet, it was now time to begin testing it on the ground. So in January 1918, the British government dispatched a multinational Zionist Commission to the Holy Land. The goal? To survey the situation and prepare the terrain for implementation of the Balfour Declaration. The commission was just barely multilateral. The United States was not yet officially at war with the Ottoman Turks, so it bowed out. Italy sent Commendatore Angelo Levi-Bianchini, a thirty-year-old Venetian-born straight-backed mustachioed naval officer, one of the few Jews to have risen to such a post and at such a tender age. Levi-Bianchini eventually would find his way to Paris as an advocate of the Zionist position during the Peace Conference. After winning the friendship of the British, Arabs, and Jews, he would help organize the self-defense of the Palestinian Jewish community, ultimately dying in 1920 during a Bedouin attack on a train he was guarding, barely two years after embracing the Zionist cause. France sent Sylvain Lévi, an avowed anti-Zionist but president of the powerful Alliance Israélite.

In London, before his departure, Weizmann was given an audience with King George V—nearly a year before he received Colonel T. E. Lawrence. This time, no knighthood was even proffered. During the audience, the monarch rambled on about the Bolshevik Revolution, telling Weizmann, "I always warned Nicky [his first cousin, Czar Nicholas II, who'd been executed with his entire family by the Bolsheviks] about the risks he ran in maintaining that regime, but he would not listen." Finally the king wished Weizmann "success in your endeavors."

The commission set off on a long and dangerous trip across war torn Europe to the port of Taranto in southern Italy. Then, when the Italians were unable to come up with a naval escort across the German submarine–infested waters of the Mediterranean, a Japanese destroyer escorted the commission's transport ship on a nine-day zigzagging voyage to the British port of Alexandria in Egypt. Weizmann promptly plunged into his study of the Arab mentality with which he would have to cope for the next thirty-four years. As he put it later: "The Arab is a very subtle debater and controversialist—much more so than the average educated European—and until one has acquired the technique, one is at a great disadvantage. . . . Conversations and negotiations with Arabs are not unlike chasing a mirage in the desert: full of promise and good to look at, but likely to lead you to death by thirst."

The commission members installed themselves near Tel Aviv, then a small seaside town of a hundred houses and a few hundred residents sandwiched between sand dunes and the Mediterranean. Weizmann set out to win over the British military, particularly General Edmund Allenby, but in the process snubbed one of his aides, the young James de Rothschild. It was a move that would come back to haunt Weizmann at a critical moment barely a year later. Weizmann found the British officer corps particularly difficult—their minds having been poisoned, he learned, by a virulently anti-Semitic tract called *The Protocols of the Elders of Zion*, which some officers had brought to the Middle East from the Caucasus. The native Arabs were even more difficult—having proclaimed, from the moment the delegation set foot in Palestine, that "the British have sent for the Jews to take over the country."

Finally, frustrated at his glacial progress and the scant acceptance of the principles of the Balfour Declaration, "the genuine skepticism [by Allenby] as to the intrinsic practicality of the plan for the Jewish Homeland," Weizmann sat down with the British commander and tried to explain the situation in terms he could understand:

> You have conquered a great part of Palestine, and you can measure your conquest by one of two yardsticks: either in square kilometers—and in that sense your victory, though great, is not unique: the Germans have overrun vaster areas—or else by the yardstick of history. If this conquest of yours be measured by the centuries of hallowed tradition which attach to every square kilometer of this ground, then yours is one of the greatest victories in history. And the traditions which make it so are largely bound up with the history of my people. The day may come when we shall make good your victory, so that it may remain graven in something more enduring than rock in the lives of men and nations. It would be a great pity if anything were done now—for instance by a few officials or administrators—to mar this victory.

Allenby was visibly moved. So, three months after Weizmann's arrival in Palestine, the British commander suggested it was time for him to see the most important Arab leader in the Middle East. In May 1918, Weizmann set off for the Arabian Desert to meet Feisal.

Weizmann was already ill-disposed toward the Arabs he had met personally, including those in a series of meetings with Palestinian Arabs in early May and one epiphanal session, chronicled by Weizmann's biographer Jehuda Reinharz. This meeting, which included the mufti of Jerusalem, Kamel Bey al-Husseini, and the mayor of Jaffa, Abdul Rauf Bitar, got off to a bad start when Musa Kazem, former governor of Yemen and later major of Jerusalem, flourished a copy of the *Protocols*, which had been slipped to him by a British officer. He demanded to know if they reflected the true Zionist intention to seize all of Palestine from the Arabs for their own use. Weizmann denied any such plan, but it was painfully clear none of his interlocutors really believed him. Still, the Zionist leader had high hopes for his meeting with Feisal. The session was arranged by Alan Dawnay, an aide to Allenby and a close friend of T. E. Lawrence.

At the highest levels, the British wanted desperately for this first meeting between Feisal and Weizmann to go well. Accordingly, they had already dispatched David Hogarth, head of British intelligence in Cairo, to pave the way. His message, well received by Feisal, was a simple one: Jewish friendship toward the Arabs in Palestine would translate into political pressure on behalf of Arab interests wherever Jews had influence around the world, and especially at the Peace Conference that would convene in Paris after the Allies won the war. There the Arabs would need all the support, from whatever quarter, they could muster.

For his part, Weizmann was prepared to go the extra mile indeed, many extra miles. He traveled by rail to Suez, on to Aqaba via a grimy, vermin-infested tramp steamer circumnavigating the German-held Sinai Peninsula, then north via car, then on camel when the car broke down," and finally on foot through "a wilderness of burning sand and rock," as Weizmann described it, to the heights of the Transjordanian plateau, where Feisal and his Arab legions had made their camp. That night, before the fateful meeting the next morning, Weizmann wandered out of his tent, gazed up at the brilliant moonlit night, then looked down on the Jordan Valley, the Dead Sea, and the Judean hills beyond: "I suddenly had the feeling that three thousand years had vanished, had become as nothing. Here I was on the identical ground, on the identical errand, of my ancestors in the dawn of my people's history, when they came to negotiate with the ruler of the country for a right of way that they might return to their home."

The next morning, Weizmann was ushered into the presence of Feisal, who was surrounded by a group of forbidding-looking Bedouin warriors. Lawrence moved casually among them "making arrangements for that night to blow up a few more kilometers of the Hejaz railway," and distributing gold English sovereigns, which had come down on Weizmann's boat to Aqaba. Over the next two hours, the Zionist leader explained his mission: "to do everything in our power to allay Arab fears and susceptibilities, and our hope that he would lend us his powerful moral support." Over sickly-sweet coffee and tea, there was an immediate meeting of minds. As it turned out, Feisal and Lawrence both believed that the Jews, particularly the Zionists, could be a great help in furthering the Arabs' own agenda in the Middle East. Afterward Feisal insisted on a photograph with Weizmann; the result was a near-comic portrait outside the emir's tent, Feisal staring grimly into the camera clad in the robes of a Bedouin warrior, Weizmann in a white three-piece suit and dark tie, sporting a floral Arab headdress with just the hint of a smirk playing across his face. "This first meeting in the desert laid the foundations of a lifelong friendship," Weizmann recalled later. "The Emir was in earnest when he said he was eager to see the Jews and Arabs working in harmony during the Peace Conference which was to come and that in his view the destiny of the two peoples was linked with the Middle East and must depend on the good will of the Great Powers."

Weizmann recognized that he had accomplished as much as he could in Palestine for the moment and that it was imperative he return to Europe to cement the goodwill of the Great Powers, or at a minimum of Britain and the United States. Still, he made certain to take a long route home, via Rome and Paris, to smooth over issues that had arisen while he was traveling in Palestine. By October 1918, the war all but won, the Zionist leader was back in London and laying plans for the Peace Conference to come. Shortly after his return, Lloyd George booked a lunch with him at the prime minister's residence, Number 10 Downing Street, for November 11, 1918. When the morning dawned with the surprise announcement that war had ended, Weizmann phoned the prime minister's private secretary, Philip Kerr, assuming that the lunch was off.

After the historic meeting with Zionist leader Chaim Weizmann deep in the desert near Aqaba, the Arab leader Feisal ibn Hussein insisted on this remarkable photograph outside his tent—Feisal clad in the robes of a Bedouin warrior, Weizmann in a white three-piece suit and dark tie, sporting a traditional Arab headdress.

By no means, said Kerr, "it is still on." Weizmann managed to make his way through the enormous throngs around Downing Street (which Harold Nicolson was watching from his perch in the Foreign Ministry). The Zionist leader found the prime minister alone in his study, reading the Psalms, "moved to the depths of his soul, and was indeed near to tears." A hurried and confused lunch followed. Weizmann reported on his trip to Palestine. Eventually Lloyd George excused himself, as he was due for a three o'clock thanksgiving service in Westminster Abbey, emerging from his doorway only to be met by "a cheering crowd and borne, shoulder high," Weizmann recalled.

It was now time for the Zionists to prepare for the Peace Conference that would determine the future of a Jewish homeland in Palestine. Unlike many of his fellow Zionists, Weizmann recognized that the Balfour Declaration was little more than the pledge of a single government at that table and only one of a host of wartime treaties or agreements that would shape the nature of deliberations in Paris—"a framework that had to be filled in by our own efforts." Twelve years later, Weizmann told a Zionist Congress that "like all people and groups without the traditional political responsibility, the Jews are apt to see in the printed text of a document the sole and sufficient guarantee of political rights." Even such savvy public figures as Justice Brandeis and other American Zionist leaders "shared the illusions of our Continental friends; they too assumed that all political problems had been settled once and for all, and the only important task before Zionists was the economic upbuilding of the Jewish National Home. This misunderstanding was to haunt us for many years." Weizmann recognized that there was a broad range of immediate issues to deal with. The specter of pogroms still hung over Jewish communities across Eastern and Central Europe and Palestine; and Britain needed to be ratified formally as the mandatory power over Palestine when the Middle East and the Ottoman Empire were divided among the Allies in Paris.

The first step was the drafting of a Zionist presentation to the Peace Conference. A distinguished committee was assembled, including Herbert Samuel; Sir Alfred Mond, founding chairman of Imperial Chemical Industries; Sir Robert Waley-Cohen, chairman of British Shell Oil; Sir Lionel Abrahams, a leading British financial official; and even the brilliant economist John Maynard Keynes, who was to play a central role in the debate over the structure of German reparations and postwar Europe's economy. The starting point was the Balfour Declaration, but the Zionist submission required a detailed blueprint for establishing a Jewish homeland in Palestine, under British tutelage, of course. It was completed by the time Feisal showed up in London in mid-December, en route to Paris. Feisal had just learned, to his horror, of the Sykes-Picot pact, and told Weizmann in London that he believed it was "dangerous to Arabs and Jews alike." Lord Rothschild hosted both of them at a lavish dinner at his residence. On January 3, 1919, Feisal and Weizmann signed their own pact. They agreed that an independent Jewish state of Palestine would be equivalent in all ways to a coexisting and independent Arab state, Feisal adding a handwritten condition that Britain adhere strictly to his own demands. With Weizmann set to embark the next day to Paris, followed quickly by Feisal, this document was designed to serve a multitude of ends. But most immediately it would deprive France of the territorial and political goals it had sought to cement in the Sykes-Picot Agreement.

At the Peace Conference, however, the ends of both of these leaders were vastly overshadowed by what the Allied powers saw as more pressing issues. So Feisal was forced to wait until February 9 for his first audience before the Peace Conference. Weizmann and the Zionists waited two weeks more. Throughout this period, the Zionists and the Arabs were far from idle. There was much lobbying to be done on multiple agendas. The Zionists were concerned with widespread reports of pogroms against Jewish communities in Poland and hostility by British forces in the Middle East to the thousands of Jews arriving in Palestine in fulfillment of the promises of the Balfour Declaration. The need to cope with these events helped strengthen the Zionist backbone, as did the arrival with Wilson on board the *George Washington* of Brandeis's thirty-six-year-old protégé, Viennese-born Felix Frankfurter, whom President Franklin D. Roosevelt would name twenty years later as the third Jewish justice of the Supreme Court.

The Zionist agenda now evolving was far more ambitious than any envisioned by Balfour—including the transformation of all of Palestine into a self-governing Jewish commonwealth under a British mandate, with Hebrew as the official language. Weizmann was meeting with anyone who would see him. On January 14, C. P. Scott managed to win him a forty-minute audience with President Wilson. The president asked the Zionist leader whether he got along with the French. "I speak French fluently," Weizmann said. "But the French and I speak a different language." Wilson smiled and agreed that, alas, he had the same problem.

At the same time, Feisal and Lawrence were having their own meeting with American Zionists. In a tense session, Felix Frankfurter was won over by the young emir and later reported to Brandeis that "the Arab question has ceased to exist as a difficulty to the realization of our program before the Peace Conference." Feisal confirmed his pledge in a letter addressed to "Mr. Frankfurter":

> We feel that the Arabs and Jews are cousins in having suffered similar oppressions at the hands of powers stronger than themselves, and by a happy coincidence have been able to take the first step towards the attainment of their national ideals together.

We Arabs, especially the educated among us look with the deepest sympathy on the Zionist movement. Our deputation here in Paris is fully acquainted with the proposals submitted yesterday by the Zionist Organization to the Peace Conference, and we regard them as moderate and proper. We will do our best, in so far as we are concerned, to help them through: we will wish the Jews a most hearty welcome home.

We are working together for a reformed and revived Near East, and our two movements complete one another. The Jewish movement is national and not imperialist. Our movement is national and not imperialist, and there is room in Syria [sic] for us both. Indeed I think that neither can be a real success without the other.

Basically, Feisal was telling the American Jewish delegation what he had pledged—with his handwritten caveat—to Weizmann on January 3: that he would honor the Balfour Declaration and exclude Palestine from the area he was claiming for Arab independence. Now all that remained was for all these parties to persuade the Allied leaders to go along.

The chance for the Zionists came at three-thirty on Thursday afternoon, February 27, 1919, when the doors swung open to the conference room at the Quai d'Orsay and the Zionist delegation was ushered in. Somehow, all of the leaders—Wilson, Lloyd George, and Italy's Vittorio Emmanuele Orlando—were absent; only Clemenceau managed to slip in for a portion of the session. For Britain there was Balfour and Lord Alfred Milner, Britain's colonial secretary and South African expert; France was represented by Clemenceau aide André Tardieu and Foreign Minister Stéphen Pichon; Foreign Minister Baron Sidney Sonnino sat in for Italy; while the United States sent Secretary of State Robert Lansing and Henry White, former ambassador to France and Italy.

Nahum Sokolow, a Polish-born editor and London Jewish leader to whom had been delegated during the war the apparently hopeless task of winning French and Italian support for the cause of a Jewish homeland, opened the Zionists' presentation. It was a brief but deeply moving examination of the role Jews had played among the Allied powers in winning the war, accompanied by an historical claim of the Jewish people to the Holy Land, dating back a millennium, to Eretz Yisrael—

the Land of Israel. "Without being sentimental," Weizmann recalled, "it was as if two thousand years of Jewish suffering rested on his shoulders."

Weizmann went next. His mission was to describe the great sacrifices of the Jews during the war, the privations and abuse they had suffered, and their "frighteningly weakened condition." All this could be resolved by removing them from the territories where they were subjected to repeated pogroms and discrimination to a land of their own where they could develop and prosper through their own skills and efforts. It was a powerful social and economic case and was reinforced by the next speaker, Menachem Ussishkin, a Russian-born Zionist, speaking in Hebrew on behalf of three million Jews in Russia. Ussishkin was followed by the French-Jewish poet André Spire, who had written lyrically of suffering during the war. His mission that afternoon was to persuade the Allied representatives that France and Europe had nothing to fear from the Zionist cause.

Then it was time for the final speaker: Sylvain Lévi, a distinguished French academic expert in Sanskrit and Middle Eastern studies, who had spent considerable time in the region. He proclaimed himself satisfied with the fashion in which Jews had already settled in their own communities in Palestine, coexisting with Moslem or Christian communities that had been there for centuries. Indeed, Lévi was a close friend and confidant of Baron Edmond de Rothschild. The aristocratic French Jew had funded many of these very communities and supported Lévi for leadership of the Paris-based Alliance Israélite. It was at this moment, however, that Lévi turned on the Zionists. A cool and crafty figure, Rothschild had known what he was doing when he used his power at the highest levels of French officialdom to have Lévi placed on the delegation. Despite his early friendship and support of Weizmann, Rothschild had become disenchanted with the style of the Zionist leader, and particularly with the way he had treated his son, the young James de Rothschild, when he was stationed in Palestine. Now the elder Rothschild would have his revenge on an individual he had privately termed "a fanatic, even a dangerous man." Lévi was to be his instrument of revenge.

Palestine, Lévi reminded the delegates, was an impoverished territory with 600,000 Arabs. Immigrant Jews with a higher standard of living were already dispossessing the native Moslem population. Moreover, playing on the fears of a surging Bolshevik menace that was gripping the Allied delegations, Lévi observed that the vast bulk of those Jews who were arriving in increasing numbers were from Eastern Europe. These were mainly Russian Jews of "explosive" temperament who could touch off serious trouble in a pressure cooker that would become effectively a concentration camp. Finally, and speaking directly to the French delegates, he concluded by predicting that a Jewish National Homeland in Palestine would introduce a dangerous precedent of divided loyalties that could imperil broader interests the Allies might have in this region.

Weizmann and his fellow Zionists were stunned into a shocked silence as Lévi wound up a presentation that was already as long as the combined speeches by all his fellow delegates. We were "profoundly embarrassed," Weizmann reported. "The astoundingly unexpected character of his utterance—it was not for this purpose that he had been invited as a *Jewish* representative—constituted a chillul ha-shem, a public desecration." Moreover, there was no mechanism of rebuttal, least of all for a member of their own delegation.

But Lansing came quickly to the rescue. Turning to Weizmann, the U.S. secretary of state asked, "What do you mean by a Jewish National Home?"

The Zionist leader was able to reassure the Allies that Lévi's spin reflected neither the reality nor the intentions of the mainstream movement for a Jewish homeland. Its government, Weizmann said, "would arise out of the natural conditions of the country—always safeguarding the interests of non-Jews—with the hope that by Jewish immigration Palestine would ultimately become as Jewish as England is English." Moreover—and here Weizmann turned to the French delegates whom Lévi had also addressed—he added, "what the French could do in Tunisia, the Jews would be able to do in Palestine, with Jewish will, Jewish money, Jewish enthusiasm."

The rebuttal, Balfour remarked, was "the swish of a sword," and he sent out his secretary to congratulate the delegation as they filed out of the chamber.

In the anteroom, there was a final, bitter confrontation. As Weizmann recalled, "M. Lévi came up to me and held out his hand. Instinctively I withdrew my own and said: 'You have sought to betray us.' That was the last time I saw Sylvain Lévi."

That evening, Tardieu issued an official French statement summarizing the proceedings and proclaiming for the first time that France "would not oppose the placing of Palestine under British trusteeship and formation of a Jewish state." The words "Jewish state" threw the Zionists into a momentary paroxysm of joy since, as Weizmann observed, "even we had refrained from using them."

For all practical purposes, this single episode was the last time Zionism would make its appearance on the main stage of the Paris Peace Conference. The Allies had enough else on their plate. The central focus was on the treaty with Germany. Palestine was an Ottoman issue and would be dealt with when the victors had dispensed with the central players and could turn to the Turks. Meanwhile France, Tardieu's statement notwithstanding, was seeking to retain something from the Sykes-Picot Agreement, now apparently in tatters—hopefully, some substantive colonial presence in the Middle East.

All Weizmann and the Zionists wanted was British control over the region of Palestine where they'd been pledged a Jewish homeland. So in 1920, when Allied representatives gathered in San Remo, Italy, to conclude the final peace treaty of the war with the Ottoman Empire, the Zionists were there.

Weizmann had spent the intervening months in Palestine, returning twice between the signing of the Versailles Treaty in June 1919 and the launch of the San Remo Conference in the late spring of 1920. What he found in the Holy Land was profoundly disturbing. Already the Balfour Declaration was starting to come apart. It had become the victim of a hostile British officer corps, the lack of any functioning civilian regime, and especially the one all but unforeseen reality—that Feisal, despite all his good intentions, had little real clout in the Middle East regions where the Jews were planning their homeland. There the Arabs were of a different stripe—Palestinians to the core. They had no history in the Hejaz; indeed, they had a profound distrust of Bedouin Arabs and their leaders. At the same time, behind the scenes the French were doing little to discourage this perspective.

All this became patently clear even before Weizmann and his party landed in Egypt en route to Palestine. During the group's ten-day Mediterranean passage from Marseille to Alexandria, General Walter

Congreve, British military commander and acting high commissioner in Egypt, was told that a "Zionist named Weizmann would shortly be arriving in Egypt and as his coming would certainly make trouble, he should be barred from landing." The fact that Weizmann was carrying personal letters from General Allenby and Lloyd George himself made no difference. It was only when Colonel Meinertzhagen, the senior British intelligence office and friend of Lawrence, back in Egypt from the Paris conference, appealed, at great peril to his own career, over Congreve's head to Whitehall, that direct orders were issued to the high commissioner to let the Zionist delegation land. This proved to be only the first of a host of problems the Jews would face in dealing with the British government, the same one that had supported their goals from the beginning.

By early 1920, the Zionists had come to realize they would have to raise substantial funds to buy every acre of land they needed to settle new immigrants—they could expect not a single square foot of territory from government-controlled tracts. Moreover, as the Jews improved the lands they did settle on—with vast irrigation schemes that turned the desert into fertile agricultural regions—the price of every successive purchase from Arab landlords rose. "We found we had to cover the soil of Palestine with Jewish gold," Weizmann remarked bitterly. "And that gold, for many, many years, came out of the pockets, not of the Jewish millionaires, but of the poor."

At the same time, there were the first violent clashes between Arabs and Jews. Even before the final demarcation lines between French and British territory in the Middle East were drawn at San Remo, the British had already ceded Damascus and the Upper Galilee to the French. And the French were in the process of easing Feisal out of their Syrian regions. All this emboldened bands of Arab marauders, who began looting and murdering Jews in more remote settlements along the demarcation lines—shades of Hezbollah and their lethal rocket attacks eighty-five years later. Moreover, in the British efforts to support Feisal, it appeared to Weizmann that Whitehall had lost interest in furthering Zionism or protecting the rights or even the lives of Jews.

Shortly before Passover in 1920, a large group of Arabs assembled in Jerusalem's Mosque of Omar, listening to speeches from Arab leaders—including several whom Weizmann himself had met before the Peace Conference. With stem-winding speeches warning that the British were already encouraging the rule of Feisal over Palestine, it took little to whip a receptive audience into action. On April 4, 1920, riots broke out that quickly turned into pogroms. Arab mobs tore through the streets and alleys of Jerusalem "fired with fanatic zeal . . . attacking any Jews they happened to meet," as Weizmann later described it. He cabled Lloyd George that British authorities barely lifted a finger to halt the violence, a conclusion later confirmed by a British investigating commission.

Days later, Weizmann headed for San Remo, but not before telling Allenby that he hoped the conference would install a civil administration in the British territories.

"You don't seem to have much faith in the military administration," Allenby replied.

"That's putting it mildly," Weizmann shot back. "In fact I have none whatsoever. The sooner they leave, the better for everyone concerned."

Weizmann arrived at the Hotel Royal in San Remo on April 20, two days after the San Remo conference had convened. The first person he saw in the lobby was Philip Kerr, still private secretary to Lloyd George. He congratulated Kerr on the first pogrom ever conducted under the British flag, taking Kerr by surprise and leading to the British official's suggestion that he take a day or so to calm down before meeting with the prime minister.

Indeed, the Zionist leader had some critical goals for which he desperately needed the support of Lloyd George and Balfour, both of whom were at San Remo. Weizmann's agenda this time was even more specific than in Paris. Now, with the peace process winding to a close, he needed to win concrete commitments from the Allies. Jews must assume control of their own destiny in Palestine. The British must make good on the pledges in the Balfour Declaration, which was still a living document for the Zionists.

In a private session on April 22, Weizmann pressed Balfour and Lloyd George for a civil administration in Palestine, run by the British under a League of Nations mandate.

"We have no time to waste," Lloyd George agreed. "Today the world is like the Baltic before a frost. For the moment it is still in motion. But if it gets set, you will have to batter your heads against ice blocks and wait for a second thaw."

The French, however, had their own agenda. Clemenceau's successor as prime minister, Alexandre Millerand, and Foreign Secretary Philippe

Berthelot were determined to keep the text of the Balfour Declaration out of the Ottoman treaty. Not surprisingly, the Italian delegation, headed by Francesco Saverio Nitti, which was having a host of other problems with France, particularly over the portion of Europe dearest to them—namely, Fiume and the Adriatic littoral of Yugoslavia—refused to support the French.

The question of Palestine came near the end of the proceedings. On April 25, the conference agreed that Britain would be awarded the mandate over Palestine. Moreover, "the mandatory would be responsible for putting into effect the declaration originally made on the 8th November 1917 by the British government." The Balfour Declaration was affirmed in an international treaty. That night Jewish and Arab delegations dined together in the Hotel Royal, toasting each other as the British looked on benevolently at the next table.

A few days later, Weizmann arrived back in London, met at Victoria Station by representatives of England's Jewish community bearing a Torah. On August 17, 1920, the Ottoman Empire and the Allies would formally sign the San Remo agreement, known as the Treaty of Sèvres—the last of the peace treaties ending the war. Zionism had become an officially sanctioned reality in the Middle East. It was, however, as Lloyd George recognized, not an end, indeed barely a beginning.

On June 30, 1920, Herbert Samuel arrived in Palestine as the first civilian high commissioner for Palestine. General Louis Bols handed over the reins after presenting a receipt for "one Palestine taken over in good condition," Sir Herbert adding in his own hand, "E.O.E.—Errors and Omissions Excepted." There were certainly enough of those from the first days.

Feisal, fighting for his throne in the face of bitter French opposition, was already suggesting that there was room for at most one million Jews in Palestine—but only if an equal number of Moslems and Christians were deported. This, Feisal observed sarcastically, he doubted would ever happen. Indeed, the one million mark was reached by 1950, and without a single deportation. At the same time, the French had succeeded in shrinking the territory of the actual Palestine mandate into a far smaller area than the Zionists had at one time envisioned. Now it was confined to the region west of the Jordan River and south of a border fixed by a joint Anglo-French accord dating from December 1920, nineteen months before the mandate was officially assigned to Britain by a League of Nations decree. The eastern frontier became a reality during the recognition of an independent government in Transjordan. That left the Jews, almost literally, with their backs to the wall of the Mediterranean.

All the fine sentiments of Weizmann and Feisal ratified in the glow of the Paris Peace Conference were drowning in the tsunami of Jewish immigration once the mandate became law. While the peacemakers in Paris had been arbitrarily redrawing the map of Europe on ethnic grounds and paying lip service to the rights of self-determination under Wilson's Fourteen Points, they were equally ignoring powerful demographic imperatives they had set in motion in Palestine. Wilson's King-Crane Commission was the first to point out the perils in its official report of August 28, 1919, opposing unlimited Jewish immigration. By then, however, the Versailles Treaty signed, the senior delegates had already left Paris. The commission's report was not widely published until the League of Nations approved the British mandate over Palestine. Initially, the rate of immigration was fixed at 12,000 Jews per year at a time when Arabs constituted 90 percent of the population of the territory. Weizmann said at the time that he believed the territory could absorb triple that number as "such immigrants could be brought into the country without in the slightest degree infringing the rights of the present population."

The population growth—a result of legal and illegal immigration—was already dramatic, probably far surpassing the official limits. In 1800 there had been 5,000 Jews and 250,000 Arabs in Palestine. More than a century later, in 1917, there were 50,000 Jews in Palestine and 610,000 Arabs. By 1922 the Jewish population had edged up to 84,000 thousand, constituting 11 percent of the population. In 1935, even before the Nazi Holocaust had begun in Europe, there were 320,000 Jews, a quarter of the population. By the end of the British mandate and the independence of the State of Israel in 1948, there were 650,000 Jews. With all limits removed from immigration, the Jewish population more than doubled again in the next three years, making Jews a majority in the territories they controlled.

Meanwhile, other aspects of the Balfour Declaration and the Feisal-Weizmann agreement were coming seriously unstuck. When the French deposed Feisal from his throne in Transjordan on July 27, 1920, the emir fled to Palestine seeking refuge and help from the British. That was when they placed him on the throne of Iraq—far removed from any influence over the Arab populations of Palestine, who had always distrusted him and his Bedouin brethren from the Hejaz. That failed to ease tensions that were building rapidly. Violent disturbances also erupted—a reflection of the demographic stresses between Arabs and Jews and the failure of the British or the other Allies to recognize that the demands of the Palestinian Arabs for their own homeland were as compelling in their own right as those of the Jews. Between Arab violence and British suppression, Jews and Arabs were being killed and wounded in equal proportions. The immediate result was the debut of the Jews' own paramilitary forces. By 1921 Weizmann was prepared to support initiatives to create the Haganah and buy arms for self-defense, since clearly the British were unable to maintain order and protect the Jewish settlers.

The Palestinians were also flexing their muscles—in diplomatic terms as well as in the streets. In 1921 they dispatched a high-level delegation to the Vatican. They were warmly received by Pope Benedict XV, who expressed his support and his fear that the Holy Places were not adequately protected by the British Mandate. Weizmann also made a fairly fruitless trip to Rome and the Vatican. By June 1922 the Zionist leader, frustrated by the apparent accumulation of enemies in every quarter, wrote to one of his leading international supporters, Albert Einstein: "All the shady characters of the world are at work, against us. Rich servile Jews, dark fanatic Jewish obscurantists, in combination with the Vatican, with Arab assassins, English imperialist anti-Semitic reactionaries—in short, all the dogs are howling. Never in my life have I felt so alone—and yet so certain and confident."

Indeed, the Zionists were winning some important diplomatic battles. On June 30, 1922, a joint resolution of Congress, backed by the same Senator Henry Cabot Lodge who had managed to torpedo the Treaty of Versailles and U.S. participation in the League of Nations, endorsed the concept of the Jewish National Homeland. It was the beginning of eight decades of U.S. support for a Jewish Palestine and State of Israel that was to so inflame passions across the entire region. Three weeks later, the League of Nations, meeting at St. James's Palace in London, unanimously approved the British mandate for Palestine. It was a pyrrhic victory. The mandate was quickly rejected by an Arab Congress, meeting with no legal but with substantial moral authority in Nablus, the historic West Bank city where, reputedly, Abraham first entered Canaan. The battle lines for the rest of the century were drawn.

It took nearly two more decades, punctuated by repeated and growing civil unrest, but by July 1937, the British, who held the Mandate over an increasingly fractious and violent region, realized that the entire premise of the Balfour Declaration was untenable. A commission headed by Lord William Robert Wellesley Peel, dispatched when the costs to Britain of public security in Palestine passed the two million pound mark, concluded that "Arab nationalism is as intense a force as Jewish. . . . The gulf between the races is thus already wide and will continue to widen if the present Mandate is maintained." In language that echoes today's debates at Camp David and the United Nations, Lord Peel added, "an irrepressible conflict has arisen between two national communities within the narrow bounds of one small country. There is no common ground between them. Their national aspirations are incompatible." The Palestinians and the Jews quite simply could not coexist, the report concluded. The commission suggested that Britain could no longer adhere to the pledges Lord Balfour had made two decades earlier. The final recommendation of the commission—partition of Palestine into separate Arab and Jewish states—would have meant the fulfillment of the Wilsonian concept of self-determination. But it was a Hobson's choice—indeed, no choice at all.

By this time, however, the Jews were armed and ready. Beyond the Haganah main force army, the Zionists had also built some fearsome guerrilla forces—the Irgun and the Stern Gang—which spent at least a part of their energy harassing British interests in an effort to win full independence. But this goal would take another decade, a second world war, and the Holocaust, all of which drove tens of thousands more Jews to Palestine. They were fleeing extermination in Europe and the deprivations of the postwar world on both sides of the Iron Curtain. Eventually, in 1948, the British threw up their hands, terminated the Mandate, and pulled out.

At midnight on May 14, 1948, the last British high commissioner left from the port of Haifa. The State of Israel, with Chaim Weizmann as its first president and David Ben-Gurion as prime minister, was proclaimed with the playing of the national anthem, "Hatikvah," on a radio broadcast heard around the world. The United States immediately became the first country to recognize the new nation. Within hours, combined Arab armies totaling 25,000 men poured across the Israeli frontiers. They met stiff resistance from 35,000 Israeli troops. By January 1949, Israeli forces had pushed the Arab legions out of the country and secured borders that were larger than those recognized by the United Nations but which were to last for eighteen years.

The results are well known—decades of virtually uninterrupted violence and civil unrest and a deep well of resentment throughout the region directed at the Western nations that left this legacy in the Holy Land. It was not until 1964 that the Palestinians managed to organize themselves sufficiently to form the Palestine Liberation Organization and its militant wing, al-Fatah—both outgrowths of the search for power and influence by a people who had turned first to Islamic organizations. When religion failed to improve their lives amid the secular modernism around them, the Palestinians took to the streets. They were egged on by rabid anti-Zionists, including a succession of grand muftis of Jerusalem who blamed their continued oppression on their Israeli neighbors. Over the ensuing decades, these Palestinians became, for most of their fellow Arabs throughout the Middle East, a persistent reminder of the Western infidel presence that sought to profit at every turn from the lands that had been snatched from them.

Indeed, with the advent of independence, the Israelis were now in a position to place their mark on a territory that they controlled with none of the restrictions of the mandate or the Balfour Declaration. Between 1945 and 1970, the number of Arab villages in the territory that constituted Palestine shrank to 433 from 807. Some 374 simply disappeared, according to Oxford historian Noah Lucas, along with a quarter of a million acres of land owned by Israeli Arabs that was expropriated by the government. Little has changed in the past three decades. Even today, Israel continues to appropriate territories claimed by Palestinians in a number of areas. Palestinians are little closer to independence. The Jewish National Homeland is little closer to the security Chaim Weizmann and Arthur Balfour had both sought for their own purposes nearly a century ago.

The peacemakers of Paris failed the Jews and the Palestinians in equal measure as profoundly as they failed the Bedouin Arabs—Shiites and Sunnis alike. The Western leaders were simply unable or unwilling to appreciate that each of these groups had its own very specific characteristics. They might very well have found a means of coexisting as separate, independent neighbors. But each was unable to exist in any fashion commingled in diverse, heterogeneous nations that only intensified their mutual antipathies and broke into violence at the slightest provocation. The Middle East remains as unstable as and perhaps even more unstable than its advocates had envisioned when they met with the Allies in Paris in 1919. The West is still unable to appreciate that small, homogeneous states in such volatile regions are inherently more stable than large, heterogeneous groupings. Still, there were many other peoples in far-off corners of the world who would be disappointed by these same leaders who were gathered in Paris in 1919, producing equally catastrophic results.

5

A Wicked Wind from the East

EARLY IN 1914, AUGUSTE ESCOFFIER, THE RENOWNED CHEF OF London's Carlton Hotel, noticed a young dishwasher who very carefully separated the leftover food on diners' discarded plates—a quarter chicken, a huge piece of steak—keeping them clean, then returning them to the kitchen. "Why don't you throw the remains into the rubbish as the others do?" Escoffier asked.

"These things shouldn't be thrown away, they should be given to the poor," the young man replied.

"My dear young friend." Escoffier smiled. "Leave your revolutionary ideas outside for a moment and I will teach you the art of cooking which will bring you a lot of money."

So Nguyen Tat Thanh, "Nguyen Who Will Succeed," was plucked from the ranks of dishwashers and promoted to trainee pastry chef. That meant more money, far better prospects. But within a year, Thanh was finished with London. This was not the destiny he had envisioned for himself—the first Annamese three-star chef. His destiny was a different one. He wanted independence for his own people—freedom from rule by a foreign nation that understood little about his roots, needs, and desires and those of his countrymen. And those who continued to enslave the Annamese were across the English Channel in France. Paris was his final destination. That was where he must make his ultimate impact.

Already his journey had been a long one. He was born on May 19, 1890, the second son of a mandarin father in the jungle village of Kim Lien just north of Da Nang in central Vietnam. By the age of eleven, when he began his formal instruction with the celebrated scholar and Annamese nationalist Phan Boi Chau, his father had given him the name he would take with him to France, Nguyen Tat Thanh. Four years later, the brilliant young scholar was already learning French at one of the handful of schools set up by Governor-General Paul Doumer. By that time, several thousand colonists had settled in the nation whose imperial government had been conquered and subordinated by the French military.

The first French arrived in Indochina as early as the sixteenth century. The early traders and missionaries all had their own goals. The merchants sought to establish a beachhead in Asia to rival Britain, whose successful colonization of India at the expense of the French had proved so profitable as the crowning jewel of a global empire. The missionaries who followed would attend to the souls of the natives and convert the heathens to Christianity. By the last quarter of the nineteenth century, the Annamese emperors had been forced at gunpoint to cede first the southern provinces, then the entire nation, to the French.

Attracted by the lush rubber plantations and fertile rice paddies, the early settlers had fanned out from the port of Saigon into the countryside, turning peasants into slaves for the vast profits available from the rice and rubber that quickly made Cochin China, as they called it, one of the world's largest exporters of these valuable products. The cash from these enterprises led to manufacturing—as textile mills, cement factories, and food processing plants quickly followed. Increasingly wealthy French entrepreneurs competed with local Chinese and a growing class of urban Annamese for wealth and power. The Vietnamese labor, attracted or dragooned from the provinces, in turn became ripe customers for the government-run opium and alcohol trades that the French administration also encouraged. Forcing these products on the population, they began raking in enormous profit for the colonial treasury.

By the time young Thanh found his way to Saigon, the city was already established as an overseas French capital. Its broad boulevards were lined with elegant provincial-style houses with wrought-iron terraces. Down the street, cafés teemed with chic parasoled women and attentive, mustachioed planters. The young provincial student was at

once fascinated and horrified by what he saw. But he was more intent
on the mission that had brought him to Saigon—to go abroad and see
the world, but especially France. It was the only way, he believed, to
understand those who had overrun his nation and to persuade them to
relinquish their hold over his people.

As the man who would later become Ho Chi Minh told the American left-wing journalist Anna Louise Strong:

> The people of Vietnam, including my own father, often wondered
> who would help them remove the yoke of French control. Some
> said Japan, others Great Britain, and some said the United States. I
> saw that I must go abroad to see for myself. After I had found out
> how they lived, I would return to help my countrymen. . . . When
> I was about 13 years old, for the first time I heard the French
> words 'liberté, égalité, fraternité.' At the time I thought all white
> people were French. Since a Frenchman had written those words, I
> wanted to become acquainted with French civilization to see what
> meaning lay in those words.

This was no doubt true in part. But at that very moment, Thanh had
two other motives. First, his father had been dismissed from his teaching
post by the imperial government of Cochin China, which still existed,
though under French control. So the young Thanh was hoping he might
persuade the French to reverse this action. And he was anxious to study
at the prestigious Colonial School, to which admission was possible only
by special appointment. Nguyen Tat Thanh had already begun to grasp
that the French had put down broad and deep roots in Indochina.

Vietnam was no mere colonial outpost. It had been transformed into
an integral part of the French economy and way of life. While it was geographically far from the "metropole," it was carefully controlled at every
turn from Paris. A member of the prime minister's cabinet, the minister
of colonies, controlled every aspect of life through the governor-general
in Hanoi and the police and military in every city and province.

Thanh had already managed to acquire a good grounding in the
French language—enough to persuade Captain Louis Eduard Maisen,
captain of the Chargeurs Réunis liner *Amiral Latouche-Tréville*, to
employ him as a waiter and kitchen helper, though he had no experience in either restaurants or boats. So in 1911 Thanh shipped out for

Europe, spending most of his days belowdecks scrubbing in the kitchen, toting coal for the stoves, dragging supplies up from the hold.

After stops in Singapore, Ceylon, and Egypt, the *Amiral Latouche-Tréville* docked in the harbor of Marseille. With his small wages, he disembarked. The first time he sat down in a café on the Rue Cannabière and was promptly addressed by a waiter as "Monsieur," he was struck by how polite the metropolitan French were to foreigners compared with the way the colonial French dealt with his sort back home. Thanh quickly decided to appeal directly to the president of France for entrance to the Colonial School. In a perfectly framed letter, Thanh described his employment in the French merchant marine and his "eagerness to receive an education" that would enable him "to become useful to France with regard to my compatriots." Thanh's application was rejected, so he decided to continue his tour of the world. Algeria, Tunisia, Morocco, India, Saudi Arabia, Senegal, Sudan, Dahomey (now Benin), and Madagascar were among his ports of call. At each stop, when the crew was allowed ashore, he visited the town and observed carefully the people, their customs, how they lived, and especially their interactions with their colonial masters.

By 1913 Thanh had made his way to New York. The United States was one of the nations, he believed, that might help his people throw off the yoke of French imperialism. Indeed, he wrote much later that he marveled at the equality enjoyed by Asian immigrants in Chinatown and elsewhere as he strolled through the city, awestruck by the huge skyscrapers and the wealth that surrounded him. He found his way to meetings of such black activists as Marcus Garvey, who lectured widely in Harlem. In Boston, another stop on his travels, he worked briefly at the Parker House Hotel as pastry chef before finally shipping out to Britain, convinced he could improve his command of English more effectively in England than in New England. He was also closing in on his ultimate objective: Paris.

But London was no walk in the park. Before he ended up at Escoffier's lavish restaurant, he held jobs as a snow shoveler at a British school and as a boiler operator, which was even more physically demanding, finally finding work in the kitchen of the Carlton. All this time he was perfecting his English, paying out of his meager wages for a private tutor. It was around this time that Thanh began to correspond with a colleague of his father—Phan Chu Trinh, a scholar, lawyer, and ardent

Annamese nationalist who had emigrated to Paris in an effort that would parallel Thanh's to win independence for his nation. It was also the first time, though certainly not the last, that Thanh came to the notice of French authorities. It seems that Trinh and a close friend, the Annamese attorney Phan Van Truong, had been arrested and briefly detained by the French government, which suspected them of meeting with German agents. Police of the Sûreté found, in a search of Trinh's apartment, letters and postcards from London written by a certain Nguyen Tat Thanh who was complaining bitterly about conditions in their native land.

Thanh spent the early years of the war in London, but sometime in late 1917, he finally decided the moment had arrived to head to Paris. Thousands of his compatriots had been conscripted and they began to arrive in France to replace French factory workers who had gone to the front. Eventually at least one hundred thousand Indochinese would be ordered to take up arms in defense of the empire. While the precise date is unclear, Thanh is believed to have arrived in France after the United States had decided to enter the war, and quite possibly right after the October Revolution that brought Lenin and the Bolsheviks to power in Russia. While his countrymen were living in truly appalling conditions in Paris and at the front, Thanh moved immediately into the spartan, yet comfortable, quarters of his father's friend. Phan Chu Trinh's apartment was located in the Villa des Gobelins, a small cul-de-sac around the corner from the Gobelins tapestry factory two blocks from the Place d'Italie in the thirteenth arrondissement.

Thanh plunged right into his work. First, there was his day job. He became an accomplished photo retoucher. It was semiskilled work that put a small amount of change in his pocket and still allowed him sufficient free time to begin building a network of like-minded political activists who would inaugurate him into the world of socialist agitation. Most of this activism was centered around the French Socialist Party, which in those days still included a broad spectrum of radicals ranging from anarchists to Bolsheviks to moderate socialists. Thanh became close to many of them as they adopted this young man who became known as the "mute of Montmartre"—a tribute to his all but unique self-effacement amid a group known for their outspokenness. At first blush, he appeared "timid, almost humble, very gentle, avid for learning," as Léo Poldès, founder of the leftist speaking group Club du

Faubourg, described him. Talking with the American writer Stanley Karnow decades later, Poldès recalled that when he first met Thanh at a Club du Faubourg meeting, he had "a Chaplinesque aura about him—at once sad and comic."

This did not last long. As Thanh became more familiar with his surroundings, more comfortable and fluent in the French language, he began moving himself forward increasingly into the public arena. His refrain was a simple one: the suffering of his people at the hands of the repressive French colonial administration that was, often literally, raping and pillaging his native land. About this time, Thanh took on a new name, Nguyen Ai Quoc, or "Nguyen the Patriot." This name followed him to the point when, decades later, he would become, finally, Ho Chi Minh. Under his new pseudonym, he acquired a more compelling air as a speaker, often keeping his swelling left-wing audiences spellbound with descriptions of life in Vietnam. He expanded his reach by frequent contributions to leading left-wing periodicals, especially *L'Humanité*, the great journal of the socialist left that ultimately became the mouthpiece of the French Communist Party. For instance, there was his frightening description of the arrival of French troops in a remote Annamese village:

> The colonial sadism is of an incredible frequency and cruelty. At the arrival of soldiers, all the population fled; there remained only two old men and two women—a virgin and a mother nursing her new-born and holding by her hand a little girl of eight years old. The soldiers asked for money, brandy and opium. When they weren't understood, they became furious and began beating one of the grandfathers. And then for long hours, two of them, already drunk when they arrived, amused themselves by cooking the other old man on a fire of branches. Meanwhile the others raped the two women and the little girl and ended by massacring the little girl. The mother, having taken flight with her infant, hid in a bush, watching while her little girl was martyred. For what reason, she didn't know, but the little girl, lying on her back, was gagged, tied, and one of these men, numerous times, bit by bit, gently forced his bayonet into her vagina and very slowly pulled it out. Then he cut off the finger of the dead girl to take her ring and cut off her head to steal a necklace. Then they left on the ground the three cadavers: the little half-naked girl, the disemboweled woman, her left arm

straight toward an indifferent sky, and the body of the old man, horrible, naked like the others, disfigured by the cooking, his skin crisp and golden like a grilled pig.

But Quoc was concerned with more than personal abuses of his countrymen. He was especially troubled by the policy of France that treated the resources of his native land—human and material—as commodities that could be owned by a foreign government and its citizens who had nothing but their own security, well-being, and prosperity as their goals. A correspondent of the Chinese newspaper *Yi Che Pao*, who had arrived in Paris to cover the Peace Conference, published a long interview with Quoc, which brought him to the attention of the French authorities. It wasn't hard to understand why:

Question: To what end did you come to France?

Answer: To reclaim the liberties that are our right.

Question: What is your program [at the Peace Conference]?

Answer: France wants to perpetuate the inequalities between the French and the Annamites so that she may profit from the work of the Annamites, continue indefinitely to milk the products of all sorts from Indochina and so enrich themselves and keep the Annamites from creating an independent economic situation. The broad nature of taxes as well as the restrictive nature of the regime of public instruction have been inspired by these considerations. In placing obstacles to civilization and progress of the Annamite race, the French are assured of maintaining them forever on the margins of world civilization and keeping them indefinitely subordinate without any chance of being raised up. In these recent years, the state of life in Indochina has become as deplorable as it has ever been.

Question: What have you been doing since your arrival in France?

Answer: I've sought everywhere to raise sympathy. Among other places, the Socialist Party has shown itself little satisfied with government procedures and has given us freely of their support. That, in France, is where we find our only hope. As for our actions in other countries, it's there in America that we have had our greatest successes. Everywhere else, however, we have encountered nothing but difficulties.

Needless to say, such vivid speeches, writings, and interviews did not go unnoticed by the French intellectual elite, especially the left, which was a growing power in the streets, if not in influence within the government. The redoubtable founding editor of *L'Humanité*, Marcel Cachin, took him under his wing and Quoc was soon a regular contributor to his pages. This in turn brought the young Vietnamese to the attention of the likes of Paul Vaillant-Couturier, the great French antiwar writer, journalist, and politician, later a founder of the French Communist Party and briefly editor of *L'Humanité*, after whom an avenue on Montparnasse is named and who became one of Quoc's closest friends among the left-wing intelligentsia; Léon Blum, parliamentarian and leader of the French Socialist Party, who later became prime minister under the Front Populaire; Edouard Herriot, another socialist politician who, after Quoc had left France, became prime minister and was among the first to offer diplomatic recognition to Stalin's Soviet Union; brilliant novelists, dramatists, and entertainers from Colette to Maurice Chevalier, Romain Rolland to Anatole France, winners of the Nobel Prize in Literature in 1915 and 1921 respectively; and Charles Longuet, grandson of Karl Marx, who persuaded young Quoc to read *Das Kapital*, which he found on the shelves of the Bibliothèque Sainte-Genevieve around the corner from the Sorbonne.

But Quoc was not yet a full-blown communist. While he believed deeply in the ideals of socialism, he also knew that in his largely peasant-agrarian nation there was not much of the urban proletariat under which communism was supposed to thrive and expand. Still, from the first days of his arrival in France, Quoc recognized where he would find the most sympathetic allies, and he sought them out. Unfortunately, few of these individuals, most of whom would eventually take strong positions against the Treaty of Versailles and the League of Nations, had much clout with the Western diplomats who were arriving in Paris in the winter of 1918–1919. Most of these world leaders feared, and many hated, the rise of Bolshevism in Russia and its implications for their own nations in Western Europe, even the United States. They were equally ill-equipped emotionally or intellectually to distinguish between the socialist form of leftism that was sweeping the Continent after the war and the radical revolutionary Bolshevism that had taken over in Moscow and St. Petersburg and was attempting to sway some quarters of the more radical leftists abroad.

By the end of 1918, Quoc had become an officer of the Association of Annamite Patriots, founded by Phan Chu Trinh and Phan Van Truong, whose activities had gotten this pair arrested before Quoc even arrived in France. Quoc's rise to the leadership of what the French administration clearly considered a subversive organization, together with his growing ties to the French left and the interviews and speeches that were drawing increasing comment, brought him to the attention of the Ministry of Colonies and the powerful Sûreté, the French secret police. At least two agents were permanently assigned to monitor him. They began to watch his activities and follow his movements. One of them, identified in intelligence reports only as Agent Désiré, managed to become a confidant of Quoc; every word was reported back to senior levels of the French government, especially the minister of colonies, who had become especially interested in the young Annamese.

Désiré and his colleague Agent Jean had a lot to follow. For Quoc recognized that with the attention of the world focused on Paris, this was his moment to act. His early allies included not only politicians and intellectuals of the French left, but also immigrants from other French colonies—Algeria, Tunisia, Morocco, and black Africa—as well as Asians, particularly Koreans and Chinese, both of whom, ironically, would get hearings at the Peace Conference that Quoc never managed. He hung out often at the Bureau of Information of the Republic of Korea that was set up at 38 Rue Châteaudun, four blocks from the Opéra—enthralled by the rapid activity and the volume of all the circulars, books, and magazines, including the impressive *Korea Review*, published in Philadelphia by Korean students. Quoc was especially fascinated by the devotion of the Koreans to emancipation, in their case from the hated Japanese, who appeared no less oppressive than the colonial French. He saw the Koreans as a similarly enslaved race, strongly marked by Chinese civilization and thus with many of the same historical and cultural affinities.

By the time the Peace Conference was under way, Quoc had become as well positioned as possible for a poor young man from a distant colony with no diplomatic status and no hope of official recognition. He became a busboy at the Hotel Ritz, hovering at the fringes of the tables of many wealthy and powerful men and women who were pushing around the chess pieces of the world and redrawing its boundaries. While there is, of course, no real record, it is not unreasonable to ponder whether Quoc might have been clearing the tables after the dinner party Elsa Maxwell gave for Arthur Balfour, or when Marcel Proust demanded that Harold Nicolson describe every nuance of the Peace Conference deliberations.

But for the most part, Quoc was an outsider, though a passionate one, his nose pressed against the glass. He did, however, have large hopes—especially for the Americans and Woodrow Wilson, whose Fourteen Points seemed to embody so many of his own deeply felt aspirations for his own nation. But a simple Vietnamese peasant—no matter how accomplished his French and English—would not get past the marine guards at the Hotel Crillon by himself for a tête-à-tête. Quoc realized that he needed a document of his own that would mirror Wilson's and raise the kind of sympathy for his points that Feisal and a host of other regional rulers were eliciting from people who might be able to influence the outcome of the Peace Conference. The result was an extraordinary manifesto, "Eight Claims of the Annamite People" ("Huit Revendications du Peuple Annamite"), which even today is cited as the fundamental basis of all Vietnamese law by the nation's rulers in Hanoi.

The document was quite moderate in tone, making none of the demands for full independence that had punctuated many of Quoc's most inflammatory speeches and that had appeared so threatening to the French colonial administration and the police who monitored his activities. The claims did, however, range from political autonomy to freedom of assembly, association, religion, press, and movement. Much of it was drawn from America's Declaration of Independence and Bill of Rights, both of which Quoc had studied and professed to admire:

Since the victory of the Allies, all the enslaved people of the world shivered with hope for an era of rights and justice open to them as a result of the solemn and formal promises, made before the entire world, by each of the Entente powers during their struggle for Civilization against Barbarity.

While awaiting the passage of these nations' principles from the domain of the ideal to the reality of the sacred right of all people for self-determination, the People of the former Empire of Annam, today French Indochina, present to the Noble Governments of the Entente in general, and specifically to the Honorable Government of France in particular, the humble demands as follows:

1st General amnesty for all political prisoners.

2nd Reform of Indochinese justice by granting to natives the same judicial guarantees as Europeans, and the complete and final elimination of the Special Tribunals which are instruments of terrorism and oppression against the most honest of the Annamite people.

3rd Freedom of Press and Opinion.

4th Freedom of association and assembly.

5th Freedom to emigrate and travel abroad.

6th Freedom of teaching and creation in all provinces of schools to teach techniques and professions of use to natives.

7th Replacement of rule by decree with rule by law,

8th A permanent delegation of natives elected to the French Parliament.

The Annamite People, in presenting its demands above, count on the global justice of all the Powers and in particular the good will of the Noble French People who hold our future in their hands.

As soon as they were drafted—and probably edited by several of Quoc's friends and colleagues whose written French was far more eloquent than his as a second language—the eager young rebel began knocking on the door of anyone he could locate who he thought might have some tangible impact. Quoc's Soviet biographer, Yevgeny Kobelev, described the scene when he arrived early one morning at the door of Jules Cambon, a distinguished French diplomat and one of the delegates to the Peace Conference:

The door was opened by a young woman named Geneviève Tabouis. The future famous woman journalist was her ambassador uncle's secretary. He spoke with a strong accent:

"I want to hand the ambassador a document."

Geneviève let in the early visitor, seated him at a long richly adorned table that still stands in the drawing room of the Tabouis home and began questioning him.

"Mademoiselle, my name is Nguyen Ai Quoc. I should like to see Monsieur Cambon."

The young man opened a file, and handed it to Geneviève.

"This is an appeal from the people of Indochina. I want to give it to the Ambassador."

The writing, Geneviève saw, was clear and orderly. There was also a letter to "Esteemed Mr. Ambassador Cambon, plenipotentiary representative of France at the Paris Conference."

Kobelev offers no suggestion of what happened to this document or whether Cambon ever actually saw it. But Quoc did deliver the petition by hand to many leading members of the Assemblée Nationale (the French parliament). He had the Confédération Générale du Travail, the left-wing trade union, print thousands of copies of the Claims, and he circulated them on the streets of Paris. Eventually they found their way to Saigon, touching off protests and demonstrations, which again attracted the attention of the French colonial administration and the police.

Unfortunately, none of these actions or the individuals Quoc and his friends succeeded in contacting had the least impact on the proceedings that were unfolding at the Quai d'Orsay. Quoc eventually came to realize that the future of neither Vietnam nor any of France's colonies would ever be on the table of the Allies in Paris. Indeed, there is no record that any representative of Vietnam made his way to the doorstep of any leading American in Paris, many of whose days were filled by sessions with importuning delegations from a host of foreign regions. Take, for example, President Wilson's calendar for the single day of April 17, 1919, as issued officially by the White House: meetings with the Assyrian-Chaldean delegation, the Dalmatian delegation, the San Marino chargé d'affaires Monsieur Bucquet, the Patriarch of Constantinople, Albanian delegate Essad Pacha, Swiss Foreign Minister Colonder, Greece's ambassador to Rome M. L. Coromilas, the Rumanian delegate Bratiănu, Albanian leader Boghos Nubar and his Serbian counterpart. On that same day there was another list of those who were documented to have tried but failed to make it into Wilson's suite—the Egyptian delegation, M. Ytchez of Lithuania, delegates of Persia and

Mount Lebanon in the Holy Land, I. Kusic Soho Kim of the Korean delegation, and Sean T. O'Ceallaigh of the Irish provisional government. So it's not surprising that Quoc never got very far with the Americans. Still, in the archives of Colonel Edward House on deposit in Yale's Manuscript Library, there is a record that the U.S. delegation did receive Quoc's document. On June 18, 1919—six weeks after the Germans received the completed Treaty of Versailles and ten days after it was signed—the young Vietnamese finally succeeded in delivering a brief note, drafted in impeccable, diplomatic French, addressed to Colonel House at the Crillon. It read:

> Monsieur le Colonel,
>
> We take the liberty of sending to you the enclosed note of the Claim of the Annamite people on the occasion of the Allies' victory.
>
> We are counting on your great kindness to honor it with your support before the proper authorities.
>
> We beg you, Monsieur le Colonel, to accept our most pr found respect,
>
> > For the Group of Annamite Patriots.
> > Nguyen ai Quoc
> > 56, Rue Monsieur le Prince, Paris

There is no record in House's files or indeed in any of the official records of the U.S. delegation to the Peace Conference that the demands even made it as far as House's desk, let alone to the eyes of President Wilson, who had already left for Washington. The next day, however, Arthur Hugh Frazier, a fifty-one-year-old career foreign service officer who'd been secretary of the U.S. embassies in Vienna and Paris and who, with Stephen Bonsal and House's son-in-law Gordon Auchincloss, was one of the three principal aides of Colonel House, sent a coldly correct reply to Quoc, also in French, that read:

> Monsieur,
>
> Colonel House has charged me with acknowledging reception of your letter of 18 June, 1919, and to thank you for the copy that

you enclosed of the Note of Claims of the annamite [*sic*] people on the occasion of the Allies' victory.

Sincerely yours,
Arthur Hugh Frazier
Embassy Counselor

Decades later, the collected papers of Ho Chi Minh, published in Vietnamese in Hanoi, suggested there was a third letter—from House himself, promising to pass along the Annamite claims to Wilson. However, there is no record that this ever happened. In any event, it was all far too little, too late. Ironically, the Koreans and the Irish, who did receive more than passing attention by the Peace Conference, as well as the Tunisians, Senegalese, and several other African nationalities, became allies of Quoc during those days in Paris. Among the militant left in France in 1919, it was the Irish, Koreans, and Arabs who received the most attention, especially in the pages of such major French dailies as *L'Humanité*. Many prepared their own manifestos, though few were quite as eloquent as Quoc's. Still, for a host of undoubtedly selfish reasons, none of these groups seemed prepared to present Quoc's cause in the few moments they had to lobby for their own self-determination and freedom from colonial rule.

If the United States delegation had agreed to examine the status of the French colonies, a colossally pernicious Pandora's box would have been opened, and a principal edict of diplomacy violated, having to do with those living in glass houses. The war, after all, had been fought to defeat the enemy and ultimately deprive them of their colonies. So the Austro-Hungarian Empire stretching from Central Europe down through the Balkans, the Ottomans in the Middle East, and the German colonies from China to Africa were on the table. But the colonies of no one else. After all, who were the Americans to cast stones over Vietnam when they had their own possessions—from the Philippines to the Caribbean? If the Peace Conference were to open the issue of places like Cochin China, why not Hawaii or Puerto Rico for that matter? Still, Quoc, even if he understood these political niceties, was undeterred. Wilson had his Fourteen Points. Quoc would have just eight. All of which caused considerable concern among senior French officials, who reacted accordingly.

.   .   .

After the "Claims" first appeared on the streets of Saigon, the governor general of Indochina demanded that Paris investigate Quoc's actions. An agent of the Ministry of Colonies, Pierre Guesde, opened a formal inquiry. The local Prefecture de Police hauled him in to be photographed and fingerprinted, and a few days later, he received a formal summons to see the minister himself. Albert Sarraut had just returned at the age of forty-seven from a tour of duty as governor general of Indochina. He would eventually serve twice as prime minister of France during the Third Republic until the Germans invaded in 1940. And while he was later a member of the Radical Socialist Party, he firmly believed in France's colonial destiny. The exchange between Quoc and Sarraut was, therefore, brief and to the point.

"I want nothing except the eight claims I presented to the Peace Conference," Quoc later said he had told Sarraut. "If you can help intervene with the French government to accept our demands, we would be infinitely grateful."

"If France gave you back Indochina," Sarraut replied, "you couldn't rule yourselves because you are not well enough armed."

"But, Monsieur le Ministre," Quoc shot back, "look at Siam and Japan. These two countries do not have an older civilization than ours; they are, however, among the great nations of the world. If France gave us back our country, she would see without any doubt that we would know how to govern ourselves." Sarraut changed the subject and the interview terminated shortly thereafter.

There gradually began to dawn on Quoc a host of reasons confirming that his quest for independence and self-determination would have to be undertaken by other means. His reasoning seems to have divided along two lines: ideological and practical. In practical terms, Quoc was getting nowhere in his efforts to enlist the United States or any other delegates to the Peace Conference to embrace his plea for self-determination for his homeland. As the leaders dispersed after the signing of the Treaty of Versailles at the end of June, he saw his chances receding as well. Another avenue was necessary. Here, ideology provided the answer. In his years in France, Quoc had gradually come to accept Marxism-Leninism as the only real hope for the oppressed people of the Third World. Lenin had launched the Communist International (Comintern) in March 1919, effectively throwing down the gauntlet, as we shall see, to the Western delegates meeting in Paris. As Quoc told the journalist and scholar Bernard Fall decades later: "What emotion, enthusiasm, clear-sightedness and confidence it instilled in me! I was overjoyed to tears. Though sitting alone in my room, I shouted aloud as if addressing large crowds: Dear martyrs, compatriots! That is what we need, this is the path to our liberation."

The Peace Conference, Lenin proclaimed at the Second Congress of the Comintern in Moscow, had been simply a clever ruse by the West to divide the territorial spoils of an imperialist war while covering their rapacious actions with a veneer of Wilsonian democracy. Quoc did not attend this Comintern Congress, but the French Socialist Party was represented by its general secretary, Louis Frossard, and by Quoc's friend Marcel Cachin of *L'Humanité*.

At the landmark congress of the French Socialist Party in Tours in December 1920, thirty-year-old Nguyen Ai Quoc, rebuffed the year before by the Allied delegations in Paris, rose to pledge his fealty to Lenin. It was a prelude to his departure for Moscow and assumption of the nom de guerre Ho Chi Minh. At the bottom right, his radical patron, Paul Vaillant-Couturier, listens raptly.

On their return, the Socialist Party called a watershed congress of its own. Hundreds of delegates massed in a large riding school next to the St. Julian Church on the south bank of the Loire River in the provincial capital of Tours in December 1920. Nearly three hundred delegates seated themselves at long wooden tables, divided according to their political persuasions. Quoc was placed near Cachin, who was by then a committed communist. There was one principal item on the agenda— whether the French Socialist Party should join the Comintern, become the French Communist Party, and work toward the global revolution of the proletariat. Quoc was given twelve minutes, as the president of the congress called "Indochina to the podium":

> Comrades, it is with the greatest sadness and most profound desolation that I come before you today, as a socialist [sic], to protest against the abominable crimes committed in my native land. You know that for a half century French capitalism has come to Indochina—conquering us at the point of bayonets and in the name of capitalism . . . and since then, not only have we been shamefully oppressed and exploited, but still more atrociously martyred and poisoned (I underline the word poisoned, by opium, alcohol etc). It is impossible for me in just a few minutes to demonstrate to you all the atrocities committed in Indochina by the bandits of capitalism. There are more prisons than schools and the prisons are always terribly overpopulated. . . . Freedom of the press and opinion does not exist for us, no more than the freedom to unite or associate. We don't have the right to emigrate or travel abroad. We live in the blackest ignorance because we don't have the freedom of instruction. In Indochina, they do their best to intoxicate us with opium and brutalize us with alcohol. They kill many thousands of Annamites and massacre thousands of others to defend interests that are not theirs. That, comrades, is how twenty million Annamites, who represent more than half the population of France, are treated. And moreover, these Annamites are the protégés of France. (applause) The Socialist Party must lead an efficient action in favor of these terribly oppressed. (Bravos) In the name of all humanity, in the name of all socialists, those of the right and those of the left, I say to you: Comrades, save us. (Applause)

PRESIDENT: The representative of Indochina can see by the applause that meets his words that the entire Socialist Party is with him to protest against the crimes of the bourgeoisie.

They were plaintive words, "comrades, save us," but with little practical impact, drowned out within hours by a bitter split in France's socialist ranks. The radical majority of the Congress of Tours, among them Quoc himself, voted three to one to join the Comintern and form the PCF, the French Communist Party. The minority of more moderate socialists walked out in disgust. Among the latter were Quoc's Annamese friends and benefactors Phan Chu Trinh and Phan Boi Chau.

As a result of this break, Quoc lost his relatively comfortable place in the Villa Gobelins and, courtesy of his radical friend Vaillant-Couturier, took up residence in quite a vile little working-class hovel in the north of Paris—a single dingy room on the second floor of the Impasse Compoint. But his surroundings belied the power and influence he was accumulating, at least in certain circles. His performance at the Congress of Tours clearly had been a memorable one for the leading participants. Forty-eight years later, the great communist leader and writer Jacques Duclos recalled "a young Vietnamese who all the militants loved and who was an ardent defender of the October Revolution. His name was Nguyen Aï-quac [sic]. This young man has become the president Ho Chi-minh." It was Duclos who decades later, in the early nineteen-fifties, as secretary-general of the French Communist Party, led mass demonstrations into the streets of Paris against the war in Indochina that France was waging against the Viet Minh who were led, of course, by this very same Ho Chi Minh.

Back in the early 1920s, the secessionists, as the majority at Tours became known, constituted a powerful underground communist organization in France that was of great use to Quoc in what had by then become his revolutionary goals. The PCF [Parti Communiste Français] quickly formed a colonial wing called l'Union Intercoloniale, led by Lamine Senghor of Senegal, whose executive committee included, besides Quoc, representatives of La Réunion, Dahomey, Guadeloupe, the Antilles, Guyana, and Martinique. By this time, the police seemed to be regular visitors to Quoc's apartment, rifling through his papers in his absence and taking note of his every movement. By the fall of 1921, some of these documents suggested that Quoc and the so-called

Indochinese Study Committee, which he formed, decided to move to an action phase. They envisioned the birth of an indigenous communist party in Indochina marked by an escalating propaganda campaign. The campaign was launched in France by Quoc's by now regular contributions to *L'Humanité*, of which he had become virtually a permanent member, and by the founding of a new weekly, *Le Paria* (The Outcast).

Despite all of Quoc's efforts, by early 1922 the French government remained all but implacable in its refusal to entertain independence or any degree of self-determination for Indochina. Moreover, all the rhetoric being produced in France was having little impact back home in Indochina. As Phan Chu Trinh wrote to him in 1922 (they remained friends even after their ideological split and Trinh's return to Saigon), the vast mass of the Vietnamese people were either illiterate or unable to read the French language in which his anticolonial diatribes were written. At the same time, under the tutelage of Cachin and other leaders of the French Communist Party, Quoc was being gradually transformed. No longer was he merely a young Annamese agitator who wanted the delegates of the Peace Conference to free his country. His dream of the Allies granting self-determination and independence for Vietnam crushed, he had embraced a broader agenda. Suddenly he had become an international activist whose demands for emancipation extended to the world's entire underclass in the form of a communist revolution of global dimensions. And Lenin continued to hammer at his theme that the Treaty of Versailles represented "an unworthy, repressive peace [which] is winning us friends throughout the world every day and the imperialist victory reveals the true nature of English and French imperialism and is the beginning of the end for them."

It was probably for an amalgam of these reasons that Quoc finally decided to throw up his hands and leave France. But unlike his fellow Annamese intellectuals and activists who were returning to Saigon or Hanoi, Quoc decided to head for Moscow. Like much of his life before or since, his very departure was filled with intrigue, mystery, and a modicum of danger that baffled the Sûreté and many of his closest friends alike. Quoc's departure was preceded by ever closer attention from the Parisian authorities, especially the Sûreté and the Deuxième Bureau. Their surveillance of Quoc had intensified after reports arrived from Switzerland that an assassination was being planned of the Emperor Khai Dinh, a French puppet who was the nominal ruler of Vietnam.

The emperor was due to visit France to open the Colonial Exposition in Marseille. French exiles, led by Quoc, planned a series of protests, describing the emperor as "a marionette with the voice of the Minister of Colonies."

The visit actually went off in relative peace, but Quoc was increasingly uneasy. He had begun to fear now that he could be arrested and charged with treason. He was also anxious to get on with what he had begun to see as his broader mission of liberating the enslaved people of the entire Third World. Quoc knew that he risked a lot—imprisonment or worse—if he was caught leaving France, especially for Moscow, which had by 1923 become as bitter and feared an enemy of most of the Western European democracies as Germany had been a decade earlier. So in the spring, he let it be known that he needed a rest and had decided to go on vacation to the Savoie in southeastern France near the Swiss and Italian frontiers. It was some weeks before his absence began to be noticed. Even his closest friends thought that he had left on a simple vacation. In fact, he had already slipped out the rear entrance of a movie theater near the Gare du Nord in Paris. He had won the financial help of a few members of the Intercolonial Union. A twenty-six-year-old radical lawyer and activist, Gaston Monnerville, the black grandson of a Guyanese slave, and Elie Bloncourt, a young left-wing veteran blinded in the war, bundled Quoc aboard a train bound for Germany. Passing through Berlin, he adopted the pseudonym Chen Vang, and wound up in Moscow a few days later.

It took the French authorities until October to work all this out. It was not until October 17, 1923, that the Sûreté reported to the governor general of Indochina: "In Moscow our agents have uncovered a recent reorganization of Soviet propaganda for the Far East and it is probable that Nguyen Ai Quoc left for Russia to consult with the Soviets on what form their communist propaganda should take in Indochina." Nguyen the Patriot had been lost forever to the West. In Moscow, however, he was an important addition to the Comintern in its campaign for the hearts and minds of the Third World. Quoc was put immediately to work on the International Peasants' Committee at a critical moment for world communism—the transition from the rule of its founder Lenin, who died in January 1924, to the more autocratic rule of Joseph Stalin. Yet Quoc, too, had been hardening—from the timid young émigré who left his native land in 1911 fired only with a passion to win a measure of freedom for his people, to the tough international revolutionary and propagandist whom Stalin's Comintern later dispatched to China and ultimately back to Vietnam.

Still, one must wonder if deep in his heart Quoc, or Ho Chi Minh as he would soon become known, did not for some considerable time guard a sliver of hope for the enormous expectations raised by Wilson's Fourteen Points and the grand vision of the League of Nations he saw unfolding around him, which remained so inaccessible in the Paris of 1919. As late as 1926, with the U.S. Senate having rejected the Treaty of Versailles and U.S. membership in Wilson's beloved League of Nations, Nguyen Ai Quoc dispatched a final plea to this now all but toothless body. Certainly this could have been a Comintern-inspired propaganda ploy. The communist leadership shared Lenin's view that the League was simply a mechanism designed to serve as a guardian of the territorial acquisitions of the Great Powers—Indochina being only one of many. Still, Quoc, along with his compatriots Phan Boi Chau and Phan Chu Trinh, both now back in Vietnam, did petition the League, describing the deteriorating social, political, and economic situation of their countrymen, and pleading with this body to take up their cause:

In the name of the true friendship between the French and Annamite people, in the name of their common interests, of course, in the name of peace in the Far East and the world, in the name of the sacred right of peoples for self-determination which France and her powerful Allies proclaimed the morning after the Great War, we ask of the League of Nations the total and immediate independence of the Annamite people, with the conditions that we pledge:

1. Contract to pay in cash or goods, for a number of years to be determined, a portion to be determined of the war debts that France contracted with the US and Britain.

2. Conclude a political and commercial alliance with France.

3. Place in effect a political and social constitution inspired by the principles of self-determination with respect to the ethnic peoples, serving as the base of an Indochinese Federative Republic.

4. Create a national army based on our ancient system of militia, and charged with maintaining order at home and security abroad.

5. Send a delegation to the League of Nations of the same nature as Siam, and China.

None of the three signatories ever received a reply. Their final effort to invoke the great principles under which the Allied delegations first assembled in Paris seven years earlier had been totally ignored. The only recourse was revolution. There were, however, a number of future ironies as Nguyen Ai Quoc retreated to the jungles of Southeast Asia where in 1940 he assumed the nom de guerre Ho Chi Minh ("He Who Enlightens"). He was, for instance, the rare Asian face at sightings of leaders of the Communist Party and the Communist International through much of the Stalinist period. By 1930 he had returned to Vietnam, his revolutionary target, and presided over the founding of the Indochinese Communist Party. Its principal objectives were the overthrow of the French, establishment of an independent Vietnam ruled by a people's government, land reform, and universal education. These goals were little different from those Nguyen Ai Quoc had sought more than a decade earlier in his Eight Claims that everyone from Colonel House to Georges Clemenceau had dismissed so cavalierly or rejected so definitively.

By the time Germany invaded France in 1940, Ho Chi Minh's communist cadres had established a revolutionary administration in extreme northern Vietnam near the Chinese border. In 1945, though their country had been overrun by Japanese invaders, they prepared to seize a new opportunity. Japan's occupation forces had defeated the French and taken full control of the government, revoking the French protectorate established in 1883, while declaring Vietnam independent under Japanese oversight. In August 1945, however, the United States dropped its first atomic bomb on Hiroshima. Ho Chi Minh appealed for a national uprising. Within days, his Viet Minh forces seized control of Hanoi, followed quickly by Saigon. Ho announced the formation of the Democratic Republic of Vietnam. On September 2, the day the Japanese surrendered, from a hastily erected reviewing stand in a Hanoi park, Ho Chi Minh read to half a million cheering Vietnamese his nation's

Declaration of Independence, based on his Eight Claims of the Vietnamese People.

Ho was still trying to pick up where he left off in Paris during the
peace talks, where he had been so roundly rebuffed. In November he
sent a radiogram to President Truman praising "the declaration in twelve
points you made on the US foreign policy . . . enthusiastically welcomed
by our people as the opening of a new era for the oppressed nations
all over the world." But by 1946, the French wanted their lost Asian
colonies returned to them. They found that Ho Chi Minh was the
one politician in Vietnam with whom they could negotiate.

That summer, Nguyen Ai Quoc returned to Paris as Ho Chi Minh,
by then an important interlocutor of the president and the prime minister of the French republic. Quoc had come a long way from the young
communist upstart being tailed by agents of the Sûreté who had fled
the Republic nearly three decades before. His escort was a successor to
Sarraut—Jean Sainteny, a youthful-looking World War II resistance
hero (hence a revolutionary in his own right), veteran of the Banque de
l'Indochine in Hanoi and Haiphong, and commissioner of North
Tonkin. This time Ho was received with deference, not disdain. Photographs of the era show Prime Minister Georges Bidault smiling and
shaking hands deferentially with the Vietnamese leader on the steps of
his offices at the elegant Hôtel Matignon. But a series of meetings at
Fontainebleau turned out to be no less contentious than his youthful
sessions at the Rue Oudinot headquarters of the Minister of Colonies.

By December 1946, full-scale war broke out between the French and
the Viet Minh. It was the beginning of an all but uninterrupted period
of bloodshed, first with France, then with the United States, that ended
only in April 1975 with the final takeover of Vietnam by the communist
government that Ho Chi Minh had led for four decades. While he died
of heart failure on September 2, 1969, and never lived to see the results
of his long years of struggle, his legacy was the strong, unified, and independent nation that he had sought to claim nearly a half-century earlier
in Paris.

So what went so badly wrong? What sent Nguyen the Patriot into
the arms of the Communist International and ultimately the jungles of
Vietnam to create a workers' paradise? The proximate cause seems to
have been a senior Comintern operative from Moscow. Dmitri Manuilsky met Quoc in Paris at a communist conference and was impressed

with the fiery young Vietnamese agitator who had brought the throng to their feet by shouting, "It is every Communist's duty to further the liberation of the colonial peoples." It was Manuilsky who urged Quoc to come to Moscow to help lead the communist revolution in the Third World. But should he ever have gotten this far?

While Feisal and Lawrence had failed to win the unified Arab nation they sought, still they had their hearing before the international community. So had a host of other nationalists and revolutionaries. Nearly a half century later, Ho Chi Minh confided to two American editors, Harry Ashmore of the *Arkansas Gazette* and William Baggs of the *Miami News*: "We have been fighting for our independence for more than twenty-five years, and of course we cherish peace, but we will never surrender our independence to purchase a peace with the United States or any party."

Nguyen Ai Quoc never managed even a single hearing before the statesmen who came to Paris to establish the framework of a peace that would end all wars. Given the many other priorities, real or imagined, in Paris in 1919, an independent, even a self-governing Indochina under a French mandate was probably an unrealistic dream. Indeed, given the experience of citizens of the French mandates in the Middle East, this might even have proven counterproductive. Still, Nguyen Ai Quoc and his Eight Claims must be chalked up as yet another failure of the peacemakers of Paris. Each individually and all collectively failed to understand the enormous bloody consequences of their actions or their failure to act—in this one case, 58,000 American dead, 153,000 wounded, and as many as two million Vietnamese who lost their lives in a jungle war that was the longest the United States has ever waged.

6

A Pair of Princes

WHILE NGUYEN AI QUOC WAS BEATING IN FRUSTRATION against locked doors in Paris, two other national revolutionaries had already been inside for years. Each was a far more persuasive and effective advocate for freedom and self-determination for his nation. Each had blazed his own particular route to the pinnacles of political power. Tomáš Edvard Masaryk, leader and advocate of Czech nationhood since his earliest days as a member of the Austro-Hungarian parliament at the turn of the century, was an engaging, adept, and utterly sympathetic figure. A professor by training and temperament alike, he was prepared to forsake a promising academic career for the independence of his beloved homeland. By contrast, the route of Poland's Ignace Jan Paderewski was through the great concert halls of the Western world. From Royal Albert Hall in London to Carnegie Hall in New York to the Salle Erard in Paris, Padereweski was celebrated by everyone from Tchaikovsky to George Bernard Shaw as one of the foremost musical geniuses of his age. He, too, was prepared to relinquish a brilliant career, in this case, as a virtuoso of the piano, to win freedom for his homeland and lead it to independency and prosperity. That their contiguous aspirations should collide dramatically was one of the great tragedies of the Peace Conference, touching off turmoil and oppression for generations in Central and Eastern Europe.

Indeed, it is only in the past decade that the dual visions of Masaryk and Paderewski have finally been realized. Each turned out to be a supremely tragic figure—a victim of the strong spirits of nationalism that the world war had liberated in their countries after centuries of oppression by larger, outside forces. Yet each, too, had his own aspirations for the role his country could play in shaping the history of Europe. Had the diplomats and statesmen who converged on Paris been more farsighted and less self-absorbed, less starstruck, less inclined to rely on personal friendships, less receptive to political manipulation, they might have been able to bring together more effectively these two paths toward the same goal in Europe. Instead, what should have been cooperation between these two key figures, which many technocrats in the delegations of the Allied powers sought frantically, turned into petty political squabbles, bitter clashes of wills, and spreading battlefield skirmishes. All of this set the stage for the Nazi Holocaust and a half century of communist totalitarianism.

Tomáš Masaryk was born on March 7, 1850, in a small Moravian village in the Czech region near the Slovak frontier—part of the ancient kingdom of Hungary, which by that time had been absorbed into the Austro-Hungarian Empire. In his early years he was more fluent in Slovak than in Czech or German, which helped explain decades later his desire to incorporate rural Slovakia into the industrial regions of the Czech provinces, creating that most improbable nation, which until 1993 was called Czechoslovakia.

From a part of Europe where languages and ethnicities are as fluid as the shifting national boundaries, Masaryk early on acquired the skills to succeed in such a kaleidoscopic political environment. Fluency in German and Latin succeeded his early schooling in Slovak and Czech, followed by French and Polish at high school in the provincial capital of Brno. By the

The father of Czechoslovakia, the nation's first president, Tomáš Masaryk.

time he reached university in Vienna, he'd added Russian, followed by a smattering of Arabic picked up in Oriental school, where he flirted with the idea of a career in the foreign service. English he learned at the feet of the woman he loved and married, Charlotte Garrigue, the American daughter of a wealthy New York insurance executive of Danish origin. The two met and wed following a tumultuous courtship that took the young scholar from the Ringstrasse in Vienna to the Bronx in New York.

By 1882 he was back in his beloved homeland as one of the first lecturers at the new Czech University in Prague. Its establishment was one of several gestures by the Austro-Hungarian government to the strong nationalist feelings that were growing throughout the ethnically diverse kingdom. Masaryk was quickly embraced by his young students, who were swept up by the spirit of independence and freethinking that marked his lectures and the Friday salons he and his wife became known for in their home near the university. It was only a short leap to the founding of the magazine *Athenaeum*. This quickly became the center of a bitter political controversy over ancient manuscripts that showed Czechs were producing real governments while German tribes were still rooting for acorns.

In 1890 he hooked up with the newspaper *Cas* (Time). A year later, after joining the Young Czech Party, Masaryk returned to Vienna as a member of the Austro-Hungarian parliament, where he refused to take the oath of office in German. Not surprisingly, he didn't last long. He repeatedly demonstrated his strong nationalist sympathies in shouting matches on the floor of the Reichsrat, accusing his Austrian brethren of turning their backs on the Slavic portions of their nation while favoring the Teutonic. Masaryk began traveling widely in Slavic Europe, visiting Russia, Bosnia-Herzegovina, Montenegro, Croatia, and the Dalmatian coast. Other friends from his early university days, like Karel Kramář, were even more openly embracing Russia as the mother of all Slavs. Masaryk, however, was skeptical that the czar would ever care very much about preserving the sovereignty of the smaller Slavic nations of Central Europe. Masaryk was right. But by the outbreak of the world war in 1914, the Romanovs had little time left on the throne at St. Petersburg. Instead, Masaryk threw in his lot with the West.

By the fall of 1915, he managed to assemble enough resources— including contributions from Chicago industrialist Charles Crane, who would play such a critical role in efforts to bring stability to the Middle

East—to head to Rotterdam and Switzerland. There he sought support for an independent nation of Czechoslovakia. In Switzerland he was warned by friends at the Austrian legation that it would be dangerous to return to Prague. So he stayed on in the West, eventually finding his way to London and a teaching position at Kings College, where he spent nearly two years of the war. Together with an old Prague colleague, Edvard Beneš, and a thirty-six-year-old Slovak astronomer, Milan Rastislav Štefánik, they formed the Czech Committee Abroad, which in November 1915 declared war on Austria-Hungary.

Fearing a power vacuum in Central Europe from what they saw as the inevitable collapse of the empire, and backed by nearly 100,000 expatriate Czechs, by January 1916 the committee had formed a nucleus of the powerful Czech legions. Following the February revolution in 1917 and the abdication of Czar Nicholas II, Masaryk headed to Russia, traveling on a British passport under the name Thomas George Marsden. Already he was thinking about what he would tell the victorious Allies after the war. Though his vision of a postwar Czechoslovak nation was still only a distant dream, he described it vividly to the newspaper *Epocha*: "We want to be free and independent, we are asking for self-determination, like every other nation. The achievement of these aims is the basis of my activity. . . . But the concept of self-determination cannot be expressed under the constraining influence of Austria-Hungary. . . . Self-determination means the possibility of free organization of the nation and of its representatives."

By this time, Masaryk was effectively in command of a powerful armed force. The Czech legions had grown to some thirty-nine thousand men through recruitment and defections from the Austro-Hungarian armies. Masaryk stayed in Russia for ten months to observe the progress of the revolution, the growing civil war between the Reds and the Whites, and pitched battles in the streets of Petrograd, Moscow, and Kiev. Masaryk shared a deep bitterness with the Allies over the decision by Lenin and the Bolsheviks to pull Russian forces out of the war just at the moment when a strong eastern front was so important to draw resources from the Central Powers and ease pressure on the Allies in the West. So Masaryk drafted a memo for the United States secretary of state Robert Lansing that revealed this quiet, bearded university professor as a master of realpolitik. He warned that the small peoples of Eastern and Central Europe—the Czechs and Slovaks, as well as the Poles, Finns,

Latvians, and Lithuanians—needed a strong Russia. Otherwise, they risked finding themselves at the mercy of a Germany that might eventually be defeated but would remain a powerful military force. Realizing that he needed to reinforce this view in person, Masaryk headed to Washington, beginning with a brutal trek across Siberia to Vladivostok, then via Pusan in Korea to Tokyo and by ship to Vancouver.

On May 5, 1918, Masaryk arrived in Chicago, which had become the second-largest Czech town in the world after Prague. The census of 1910 showed a population of 500,000 Czechs and 280,000 Slovaks in the United States. Ten years later, their combined numbers had risen to 1,200,000, with the Slovaks concentrated in Pittsburgh outnumbering the Czechs, who gravitated to Chicago. As Masaryk's train pulled into Union Station, vast throngs spilled over the platforms to cheer his arrival. He set off on a cross-country swing through Czech and Slovak centers, winding up in Washington, where he was well introduced. Charles Crane's son, Richard, was serving as the private secretary of Robert Lansing, Woodrow Wilson's secretary of state. So on June 18, 1918, Masaryk met the president. It should have been a meeting of like minds. Each was a distinguished academic by training, each believed deeply in similar ideals of self-determination for minority peoples wherever they might be found. But tragically, Masaryk was unimpressed. "My relations with Wilson were always pretty matter of fact," the future president of Czechoslovakia recalled. "Perhaps the President was a greater pacifist than I was. . . . For an American, Wilson is more of a theorist than a practical person, a deductive rather than inductive thinker . . . a solitary, perhaps isolated person."

Masaryk was particularly put off by Wilson's priorities. The principal focus of their initial conversation was "the question of intervention in Russia, the question of whether the Japanese could intervene in Siberia and administer Siberia and whether our Czech units could be used for that purpose." Masaryk was quite aware of the military value of the thousands of Czech legionnaires he commanded. He was miffed that Wilson's paramount interest seemed more intensely focused on the Bolshevik menace than on the plight of his own people trapped between Germans, Austrians, and Hungarians. By this time the Central Powers were fighting a losing rear-guard battle, yet had failed to offer freedom to his homeland. During his audience with Wilson, Masaryk was reluctant to unleash his Czech legion, adding that "I expressed my view of the matter, that I am not an advocate of the so-called intervention, because I cannot see what the results would be." Clearly the Czechoslovak leader was miffed that the Wilson administration had been so slow in recognizing Czechoslovak independence. He was aware that the president had long been captivated by the other Central European leader—Poland's Paderewski. Freedom for Poland had already been expressed specifically six months before in Wilson's Fourteen Points, the basis on which the United States formally entered the war in Europe. But the friendship of Wilson and Paderewski and the political clout of more than three million Poles in the United States clearly outweighed the military muscle the Czech legions might exert during the conflict in Europe that was drawing to a close.

Masaryk stayed on in the United States while his colleagues in London and Paris were working feverishly on the other Allied leaders. And on June 29, 1918, France became the first Western power to recognize Czechoslovakia. Prime Minister Georges Clemenceau provided a foretaste of the bias the French would show for that nation and its views when the Peace Conference convened six months later. Clemenceau's diplomatic mouthpiece, the amiable though somewhat ineffective Foreign Minister Stéphen Pichon, broke the news to Edvard Beneš, who'd been working toward this moment for months:

> The Government of the [French] Republic, witnessing your efforts and your attachment to the cause of the Allies, considers it equitable and necessary to proclaim the rights of your nation to independence. . . . During long centuries, the Czechoslovak Nation enjoyed the incomparable benefits of independence; it was deprived of them by the violence of the Hapsbourgs allied to the German princes. The historic rights of a nation cannot be destroyed. It is in defense of those rights that France, who was attacked, fights today with her Allies. The cause of the Czechoslovaks is particularly dear to her. . . . True to the principle of nationality and of liberation of oppressed peoples, the Government of the [French] Republic considers as just and well-founded the claims of the Czech nation and at the proper time will endeavor with all its means to secure your aspirations to independence within the historic boundaries of your provinces finally liberated from the oppressive yoke of Austria and Hungary.

Six weeks later the British followed suit. Lord Arthur Balfour's pronouncement stopped sort of Pichon's unrestrained endorsement of
Czech aspirations and far short of his earlier declaration in favor of a
Jewish homeland in Palestine. Still, the British foreign secretary welcomed Czechoslovakia officially as an "Allied nation" and the exiled
National Council as the future Czechoslovak government. It took
another month for the United States belatedly to recognize that "a state
of war exists" between Czechoslovakia and Germany and Austria Hungary, and that the National Council was the nation's de facto government. The American statement contained none of the commitments to
guarantee the new nation's historic nineteenth-century boundaries that
were contained in the French note three months earlier.

It was left to Masaryk to issue the first public pronouncement of his
country's independence. The Czech leader was still in Washington on
October 18 when he summoned a group of journalists to read the declaration of independence of the Czechoslovak nation. It was a document
not unlike the Eight Claims that Nguyen Ai Quoc would struggle so
unsuccessfully to present to President Wilson during the Peace Conference. The young Vietnamese had none of Masaryk's introductions,
nor the Czech leader's deep understanding of how to manipulate the
levers of the Western press and politics. Ten days after Masaryk had
announced his nation's independence, and with the Austro-Hungarian
Empire collapsing, the proclamation was issued in Prague to the cheers
of tens of thousands. A few brave souls ripped from buildings the
double-eagle standard of the Hapsburg monarchy. The next day a cable
arrived in Washington from Beneš, newly chosen as foreign minister, who reported that Masaryk had been designated "President of the
Republic and should return at once . . . you have boundless authority,
and are being expected."

But there was still much for Masaryk to do in the United States
negotiating a $10 million loan for the new state, for instance, and a
farewell call on President Wilson. So it was not until November 20 that
the president of Czechoslovakia was able to sail for Europe aboard the
luxurious Cunard liner the SS *Carmania*. Forty years after his first ocean
crossing aboard a leaky tramp steamer, he was returning in style as the
designated head of state for a victorious Allied power. In Paris, Masaryk
and Clemenceau met for the first time. The Czech leader also discussed
the plight of the small nations of Europe with Greece's Eleftherios

Venizelos and Rumania's Take Ionescu. Each would play critical roles in the Paris Conference and ultimately in the formation of the Little Entente—the ill-fated Central European alliance that was so dear to the hearts of Masaryk and Clemenceau.

By December 20, a week after Wilson and the U.S. delegation arrived in Paris, a train carrying Masaryk crossed the Italian border into Czechoslovakia. The next morning, a cannon shot announced his arrival in Prague, as the presidential train pulled under the glass arch of the capital's central station. Cheering crowds surrounded the imperial coach pulled by four white horses decorated with white and blue lilac that were to carry the new president to his home. But Masaryk refused to enter the carriage, preferring to ride instead in a modest motorcar for the triumphal procession to Hradčany Castle high upon the hill above the old city.

Paderewski's route to Paris was a far different one from Masaryk's. Paderewski was born in the fall of 1860 in the village of Podolia in southeastern Poland. His mother, who died several months after her son's arrival, had been born in a remote penal colony in Siberia, where her parents were serving a sentence of exile by Czar Nicholas I after some intemperate remarks by her father over Russian rule. Paderewski's father, steward of the lands of a gentleman farmer, was a descendant of a long line of prosperous peasants who affected a crest and prided themselves on their lineage.

From his earliest years, the young Paderewski was fascinated by an old upright piano in his father's house. By the age of twelve, he was brought to Moscow to begin lessons at the Conservatoire, where his teachers failed to perceive much talent. Still, he persevered, and by the time he turned sixteen he had begun a series of traveling studies—from Berlin to Vienna to Strasbourg and back to Vienna. There, in 1887, Paderewski scored his first concert triumph on the piano. A year later, March 3, 1888, he made his debut on the international stage to a packed house at Paris's Salle Erard on the Rue de Mail. Parisian nobility eagerly awaited the appearance of the strikingly handsome young man with a mane of golden curls, clad in a long white waistcoat. "This is a genius who also plays the piano," exclaimed the great French composer Camille Saint-Saëns.

Then it was on to London, where doors from Grosvenor Square to Marlborough House opened amid more triumphs, including a concert at Windsor Castle for Queen Victoria and her daughter Princess Beatrice. Finally, on November 17, 1891, just as Masaryk was taking his parliamentary seat in Vienna, Paderewski debuted in New York's Carnegie Hall—the first virtuoso to give a recital in the newly built facility. He promptly boarded a private railway car complete with a Steinway piano for a six-month coast-to-coast tour of the United States, finally winding up back in New York to play both Carnegie Hall and the Metropolitan Opera House, the city's two largest venues, in the same day. Paderewski Soap and Padereweski Candies appeared, as well as Christmas toys of him seated at a piano in formal white tie, his hands running up and down the keyboard, his head with golden-red hair swiveling as the screw was turned. He began to live like a monarch, with shirts of the finest Japanese silk, silk top hats custom-made by Lock's of St. James Street, traveling the world with his private secretary, personal French piano tuner, and valet, his hair done fondly every evening by his new wife, Helena de Rosen, daughter of a Baltic nobleman and a Greek mother.

The world war broke out when he was on his estate, the Chateau de Riond Bosson, in the village of Morges, overlooking Lake Geneva. He had already thought long and hard about what he could do for his native Poland, still divided and enslaved under the boot heels of the czar of Russia, the emperor of Austria, and the chancellor of Germany. As a neutral resident of Switzerland, which took no part in the war, he could give free rein to what had been growing in his mind—a need to express overtly his passion for his native land. So Riond Bosson became a center for various currents of Polish politics that were already sweeping the nation. For while Paderewski had been busy building his personal image as a virtuoso, many back home had been busily searching for more direct ways to liberate their country—often at the point of a gun.

One of those working feverishly at home while Paderewski was building his reputation abroad was Józef Pilsudski. By contrast with the virtuoso concert pianist and political novice, Pilsudski was a full-blooded Polish revolutionary. Born into an impoverished family in Russian-occupied Poland, schooled in Vilnius, the capital of neighboring Lithuania, he was reared to believe deeply in a free nation that Poles of his own generation had never known, nor had his parents or grandparents. By the outbreak of the world war, Pilsudski had already been exiled to eastern Siberia for five years for conspiring to assassinate Czar Alexander III. He also had joined a group of radical Polish socialists; published in his tiny flat in Lódz an underground newspaper, *Robotnik* (The Worker); been imprisoned in, then escaped from a mental hospital in St. Petersburg; masterminded a series of armed uprisings against Russian rule in Poland; and finally founded a series of sporting gun clubs across Poland that were a thin cover for developing a national underground militia that had grown to twelve thousand men by the outbreak of hostilities in 1914. Pilsudski's early strategy for a free Poland was to use his Polish Legions first to help the Central Powers defeat Russia, then to turn and help the Allies defeat Germany and Austria-Hungary. But the Germans quickly caught on to his strategy of playing both ends against the middle and clapped him into prison in the fortress of Magdeburg for the rest of the war—rendering him instantly a national hero. Released three days before the armistice in November 1918, he headed straight for Warsaw, where he was welcomed as the nation's liberator and the first president of the new Polish republic.

While Pilsudski had been busy building his legions and an immensely popular following at home, Paderewski had begun busy building strong political and diplomatic ties in the West with the Allied powers that he believed would eventually determine the real course of Poland's future. He was confident the Allies would guarantee Polish independence by drawing defensible borders at the Peace Conference that would add the final coda to the years of war. He also came to believe that the idealism of the Americans could be the real driving force on which Poland could build its independence and its future. So Paderewski embarked for the United States to mobilize America's three million Poles and tens of millions of music lovers to his cause.

As with the Czechs and Slovaks, the United States at the outbreak of the World War had more Poles than anywhere else in the world outside of Poland. Moreover, Paderewski's years of crisscrossing the nation with his piano had created an instant name recognition and unparalleled magnetism that Masaryk could scarcely match. Many of America's leading figures in music, society, politics, and academia were close friends. He had been invited into their homes and dined at their tables. Now Paderewski embarked on the largest nationwide tour of his career—from men's and women's clubs to university lecture halls, theaters and concert spaces, before cheering throngs numbering in the tens of thousands and intimate soirees for a handful of carefully chosen opinion-makers. At more than three hundred performances on a whistle-stop tour

Poland's Ignace Jan Paderewski, internationally famed pianist turned statesman, campaigning with his wife in the United States for his nation's freedom just before the start of the Paris Peace Conference.

that would surpass the most vigorous efforts of presidential candidates, Paderewski offered an impassioned plea for Polish independence, and for his nation's fealty to the Allied cause against the Huns. Then he would launch into great works of Chopin and other Polish composers before boarding his train again, cheers still ringing in his ears.

But while Paderewski continued his campaign for the hearts and minds of the people, he scarcely lost track of the principal targets of his campaign—America's political leadership. And they were impressed with what they saw. Listen to Colonel Edward House, introduced to Paderewski by the industrialist Robert Wooley:

When Paderewski reached America, the entire situation under his direction was immediately changed. He gave to the American Poles a single purpose. . . . Having foreseen before others the part the United States was to play in the great tragedy, Paderewski never lost faith in the ultimate outcome. . . . In what measure the efforts and sagacity of Paderewski were crowned by success may be gauged by the fact that towards the end of 1916, his countrymen in America, without dissent chose him as their plenipotentiary, conferring upon him power of attorney to act for them and decide all political matters in their name and on their behalf. . . . Paderewski encouraged Polish youth to enter officers' training schools and presently he brought about the foundation of a Polish organization for the training of officers. Finally when the United States entered the war, he sounded an eloquent call to arms.

House and Paderewski quickly became close friends. The confidant and top aide to President Wilson was so impressed by his charm, brilliance, and enthusiasm for the Polish cause of freedom that he introduced him personally to the president and Mrs. Wilson. In the summer of 1916, when U.S. entry into the war in Europe on behalf of the Allies was still only a distant dream, Paderewski was summoned to the White House. There, in one of the drawing rooms, as guest of honor at a state dinner, Paderewski played for members of the government, foreign diplomats, and the Wilsons. Afterward, as Paderewski biographer Rom Landau wrote in 1934, "Wilson stepped forward and thanked him with the greatest cordiality with a smile showing he had not remained untouched by the music. . . . In the conversation after, Poland was the only subject, Wilson's keen sense of justice and the rights of man shocked by the historic crime committed on the Polish nation." Soon Paderewski and House were dining together tête-à-tête. After their lengthy dinners, the two would retire to House's study and pore over maps of Central and Eastern Europe, drawing and redrawing Poland's frontiers. "Together, we traced what we thought should be a homogeneous Poland," House recalled. "The Poland we outlined during those fervid days proved to be practically the Poland created by the Versailles Conference."

But Paderewski's biggest success came on Election Day. On November 5, 1916, almost single-handedly, he turned out the huge Polish vote that sent Wilson back to the White House for a second term by fewer than 600,000 votes out of more than 18 million cast. In January 1917, Wilson spoke, for the first time publicly promising "a united, independent and autonomous Poland," language that was reflected one year later in the thirteenth of his Fourteen Points, which guaranteed an independent Poland.

Paderewski spent the rest of the war in America, leaving for Paris a month after the armistice to meet with Roman Dmowski and the Polish Comité National, which would represent Polish interests at the Peace Conference. He returned finally to his beloved Warsaw on January 3, 1919, to the cheers of thousands, each man, woman, and child waving a tiny Polish flag. But he found a nation with decidedly divided loyalties. Only days before, the people had given a similarly effusive welcome to Pilsudski, and strong undercurrents of socialism and communism were bubbling among the workers. All were in desperate straits after the years of war and privation. The nation's two leaders—Pilsudski as president and Paderewski, who was proclaimed prime minister—had vastly different priorities. Pilsudski aimed to consolidate military and political power within his nation's borders. Paderewski's goal was a commitment from the peace delegates in Paris for borders that were both just and defensible.

The bitter divisions between the two leaders were apparent even within what should have been a united delegation assembled for the peace talks. With thirty Polish delegates, however, there were at least thirty different perspectives and thirty different factions. Indeed, the bickering began from the first days in Paris and reached a point when finally Colonel House himself was forced to intervene, ordering his deputy, Colonel Stephen Bonsal, to take matters in hand:

> This is a situation that must be handled sternly but with soft gloves, if you can. All the Poles must be summoned to come to my office tomorrow morning. I will not be there; you must take my place. This is the ultimatum that you must deliver to them: "Poland will be allotted two delegates—no more." They must fight it out among themselves as to the choice, but no one will be admitted unless all the delegates agree to his selection. There must be no more of the *liberum veto* which, as all historians agree, killed independent Poland in other days.

Bonsal ushered the whole delegation to Room 360 in the Crillon, though when the door flew open, "there stood before us a man who had just sprung from a disheveled bed . . . simply clothed in a union suit of flamingo red." Another room was quickly found and the delegation locked inside. After hours of shouting and quarrels that sounded as though they were approaching fisticuffs, Bonsal listened at the door. "A holy calm seemed to have settled over the place," he recalled. "At first I thought they were all dead. Timidly I opened the door and heard these words: 'We have reached complete agreement. St. Michael and all the angels have guided us. By common accord we have chosen Paderewski and Dmowski as our delegates.'" It was an inspired, and really inevitable choice—Paderewski, with the enormous reservoir of goodwill he had built for Poland in the West, and Dmowski, a brilliant biologist and true Polish patriot who had from his earliest days struggled against the occupation of his nation under the Russian czars and the German military machine. Unfortunately, he had also struggled for much of his life against Pilsudski and everything he stood for. The inevitable result was a disastrous split between the Poles of Paris, who would determine the nation's future character abroad, and the Poles of Pilsudski, who were actively steering the country toward his vision of the future at home.

But as the delegates of Central Europe joined their Western counterparts in Paris at the turn of the new year, one overwhelming reality overshadowed all their plans and their maneuverings. If oil and Islam were the motivating forces in the Middle East, it was coal and Bolshevism that overhung all the deliberations on the future of Central Europe. In the end, the peoples of Poland and Czechoslovakia, as well as Hungary and the Balkans, were forced effectively to place their bodies and their way of life in the breech as buffers between the forces of capitalism and communism—especially between Russia and Germany.

The leading delegates of both Poland and Czechoslovakia recognized these fears and did their best to capitalize on them, to the long-term detriment of both these nations and indeed the bulk of the civilized world. But few recognized this at the time. The immediate concerns were expressed in different fashions by each of the Allied powers, and in the final analysis it was their needs and desires that took precedence over any aspirations of the peoples of the small nations of Europe.

For France the primary fear, as it had been for a century or more, was neighboring Germany. Marshal Ferdinand Foch, commander of the Allied forces and a powerful political figure in setting France's agenda at the Peace Conference, still believed the Boche were capable of returning from the vanquished, and if French boots were removed from their neck, wreaking havoc once again on their bitter foe. Prime Minister Clemenceau, ever the realist, recognized that the real danger to France lay not in a thoroughly prostrate Germany—its economy, even its spirit drained to the dregs by five years of trench warfare. The real threat to his nation was represented by a German industrial machine revitalized by the vast resources of the Saar and the Sudetenland, animated by the Bolshevist ideology of the working class, and backed by millions of Russian communists knocking on Europe's eastern frontiers.

England's fears were not dissimilar from the French. Still, by virtue of their "special relationship" with the United States, British statesmen felt some primordial need to balance what Prime Minister David Lloyd George saw as the naive and foolhardy idealism of President Wilson with a recognition that England did need to prevent new hostilities from breaking out on the Continent. It was, after all, separated by barely twenty-six miles of water that was easily bridged by the new engines of war known as the aeroplane and the submarine. Both, with a single stroke, had all but neutralized the naval supremacy that had guaranteed Britain's safety for centuries from attacks originating in mainland Europe. Moreover, there was the other immediate vulnerability of its own working class succumbing to the blandishments of Bolshevism that was appealing to all workers of the world to unite and throw off their chains.

None of this was any dark secret. Europe's leaders had been crystal clear about their concerns for some time, though privately they expressed these worries to one another far more directly than they did to their citizens. The last thing they wanted, just as a Peace Conference to end all wars was opening, was to spread panic among their own people that risked sparking demands for a more draconian peace than could ever be enforced. Such a document might even prove counterproductive in the end by leading to a desperation among the vanquished.

The one large black hole was the intellectual baggage Woodrow Wilson was bringing with him to the conference table. The backbone of Wilson's decision to enter a distant war was the concept of self-determination for the world's oppressed peoples, and especially those for whom the war in Europe was being most directly fought. In the absence of his Fourteen Points, there was no real moral justification for the sacrifice of 126,000 American lives. But just what did Wilson's ideal of self-determination mean when it came to redrawing frontiers that for centuries had snaked their way in and around a kaleidoscope of different nationalities of Europe? Did Wilson even know what he meant when he first enunciated that seductive concept? At that moment, Europe's darkest hour, the humblest citizen and statesman alike across the continent prayed for the arrival, at any cost, of American doughboys and the vast weaponry they commanded.

As it turned out, from the moment he proclaimed what immediately became catnip to oppressed people, until he returned home from Paris and tried to sell his fellow citizens on the treaty that had been drafted with barely a gesture to these principles, neither Wilson himself, nor indeed any of those who acted in his name, had any real idea what he meant by self-determination. Still, he managed to conceal this dangerous lapse most adroitly even from many members of his own delegation who would be struggling gamely to navigate the thickets of national desires at the negotiating tables. By the time they began to arrive at the Peace Conference, some suspected, indeed feared, as much. Wilson barely touched on self-determination in his only real meeting with the delegation's professional staff—en route to Paris on the *George Washington*, leaving confusion and bewilderment in his wake.

On December 10, six days into their Atlantic voyage, members of the Inquiry were called into the president's stateroom for "an hour's conference," as Columbia history professor James T. Shotwell wrote in his diary, for a "whole talk [that was] frank, witty and full of charm." Many in the room, however, emerged with some deep concerns. William C. Bullitt, who in a few months would, at the age of twenty-eight, become the first U.S. official to meet Lenin, was "worried about vagueness of President's plan and wanted to get him to elaborate and stiffen it," Shotwell observed. Another of their colleagues, Charles Seymour, who was to be involved in trying to read the president's mind as he worked with fellow Allied specialists in drawing Central Europe's new frontiers, lamented the lack of any workable definition of self-determination. The entire staff, Seymour wrote, suffered from "a confusion of purpose . . . made worse, confounded by looseness of phraseology. . . . Phrases such as 'justice,' 'viability,' 'self-determination' were freely bandied about without clear definition of their meaning."

Into this vacuum poured the tough, single-minded members of the

Czech and Polish delegations—each determined to make use of this uncertainty for his own particular purpose. It was the Czechs who first and most shrewdly perceived which way the political winds were blowing in Europe—winds propelled by fear. Both Masaryk and Beneš recognized that Germany was the old fear. Bolshevism was the new one. So the Czech leaders prepared to capitalize on this fear and turn it to the benefit of their people and as much enlargement as possible of their fledgling nation. For they also recognized that the larger the Czechoslovak nation—both in territory and in population—the more difficult it would be to ignore or, for that matter, to intimidate or conquer. Masaryk had several key goals that would guarantee this security. First, he needed former German territories that contained vast resources of coal and the industries it fueled. At the same time he desperately needed access to the Danube, which meant a corridor across Hungary, to allow his landlocked nation an outlet to the sea. Second, this new greater Czechoslovak nation had to be closely tied to its neighbors—Poland on the north, Yugoslavia and Rumania on the south—for strategic purposes of protection against their larger and ultimately more powerful neighbors, Germany and Russia. He won on the first counts of territory and population. But it turned out to be a pyrrhic victory because he failed miserably on the second. Czechoslovakia was born and remained an isolated, vulnerable state whose demands in Paris would only leave it more desperately alone than ever.

Still, Masaryk had several key cards to play in his dealings with the Allies in Paris. Beyond the political power of more than a million Czechoslovak voters in the United States, there was the moral debt accumulated by the Czech legions. The French, at least, had recognized the strategic effectiveness of harnessing their loyalty as early as two years before the armistice. Their power went far beyond mere numbers to the moral authority they wielded. Slav soldiers in the Austro-Hungarian armies threw down their arms and refused to fight their Czech compatriots to whose side they deserted en masse. Finally, there was a negotiating tactic that Masaryk sought with considerable success to employ from the moment his nation's independence had been declared—what the French called a "fait accompli." In many cases, the Czech leader recognized, boots on the ground counted far more than words at a conference table when it came to redrawing the map of Europe.

To assemble the Czechoslovakia Masaryk envisioned meant effectively purloining territory from each of his once powerful neighbors who were now, at the end of a long and debilitating war, thoroughly crushed. Slovakia on the south and east was a long-standing part of Hungary—a central component of the Austro-Hungarian Empire. In 1919 the Slovaks were faced with a difficult choice. There had never been any real love lost between the Czechs and the Slovaks. But there was an even longer and more fraught history of total subjugation by the Hungarians, who had rendered the small, largely rural and agrarian nation incapable of sustaining any viable form of independence. So the realists decided to throw in their lot with the devil who at least spoke the same language. Vavro Šrobár, a young Slovak leader who'd admired Masaryk as a student in Prague and knew his professor as someone who spoke his language, led the movement to bring Czech troops into Slovak territory as quickly as possible. Certainly, Šrobár believed, this would have to happen "before the Hungarians could recuperate from their defeat [since] the one who first lays his hands on Slovakia would have it for keeps." By the time the Allies gathered in Paris, it was done. Slovakia would remain a part of Czechoslovakia for another eighty desperate years—until 1993, when real self-determination finally came to this tiny republic.

As for the coal and industrial regions along the German frontier, the Czechs already held large swaths under their control, and were well on their way to contesting areas along the Polish border. Beneš in Paris and Masaryk in Prague could sit back smugly as the Allied delegates began arriving in Paris. After all, how much could they really undo at the conference table? It turned out to be enough damage to make a hash out of Central Europe and the Balkans for generations to come. Masaryk brazenly described such a fait accompli to Bonsal in Paris on December 16, 1918, well before the Peace Conference convened:

These districts where the Germans are intermixed with our people is our territory, and ours it shall remain. We have recreated our state with assistance from the democratic world and most of all from my second country, America. We hope that these Germans may collaborate with us, but I for one understand the difficult position in which they find themselves. They were so ready to support the Pan-German attacks on the Czechs! They were intoxicated by the ephemeral military victories and failed to realize what was the true balance in the world situation. But because we understand these people who have remained strangers in our midst for so many generations is the strongest reason why we are not disposed to sacrifice our important and very precious Czech population who are their neighbors in what some propagandists call, mistakenly, German-Bohemia [Sudetenland.] It remains where it belongs, our bulwark against invasion where the danger is greatest.

Masaryk's forces were already making his remarks a reality on the ground. Moreover, this single statement contains within it the seeds of the colossal problems that the Allies failed to comprehend in Paris and that blossomed into the malignant plant of the Third Reich, World War II, and ultimately a half-century of communist domination in his nation and its neighbors.

Still, Clemenceau and the French were very much on the side of these faits accomplis. And Beneš, in salons and intimate tête-à-têtes in Paris, was doing his level best to press the Czech cause and win over the Allies. One of the earliest calls Beneš made was on Harold Nicolson. The two lunched together on January 16. The newly arrived British diplomat, who would be assigned to redraw Czechoslovakia's boundaries, found Beneš "altogether an intelligent, young, plausible, little man with broad views." Not a bad beginning, especially since he also "wants to reconstruct Mittel Europa on a new basis which is neither German nor Russian," but founded on a collaboration of small nations. This was entirely consonant with Nicolson's own personal views, not to mention Clemenceau's. Of course Nicolson's own leader, Lloyd George, remained to be convinced.

As the various parties plunged into the rounds of lunches and dinners where the real work of the conference was being done, some members of the delegations were outspoken in letting their most private thoughts be known. Beneš and Karel Kramář, leader of Masaryk's Young Czech Party, dined with Russian Grand Duke Alexander, who had narrowly escaped death at the hands of the Bolsheviks; some French officers; and a top aide and confidant to Colonel House—Frederick Hobbes Allen, a prominent New York attorney who had served as an early U.S. envoy to Hawaii. "The French can understand us," Kramář began. "They are faced by the same danger as ourselves, i.e. Germany. They and we stand in the front line trenches: therefore we must have security . . . a geographical boundary that affords some measure of protection."

The French believed it was necessary to form Central Europe into a shape that would work effectively within its framework of a cordon sanitaire before the fluid nature of war had hardened into an unbreakable mold of victory. Clemenceau told his principal aide, General Jean Mordacq, that his goal was a barricade of small states from the Baltic to the Mediterranean that would prevent German advances on the east or Bolshevik moves on the west. The concept was to have a sad echo less than thirty years later, when British Prime Minister Winston Churchill told an audience at Westminster College in Fulton, Missouri, on March 5, 1946, that "from Stettin in the Baltic to Trieste in the Adriatic an iron curtain has descended across the Continent. Behind that line lie all the capitals of the ancient states of Central and Eastern Europe—Warsaw, Berlin, Prague, Vienna, Budapest, Belgrade, Bucharest and Sofia, all these famous cities and the populations around them." The route this line would follow was largely laid during the Peace Conference of Paris in 1919, which was creating nations at the same time that a variety of armed forces were marching into towns and villages to plant their flags and their challenges.

One key problem was that Paderewski and Pilsudski in Warsaw and Dmowski in Paris had no interest in Poland becoming a part of a Clemenceau or Masaryk framework—a small state in a Franco-Czech dominated bloc. And the Poles were prepared to resist at all cost. One of the earliest and most bitter tests was over the small but economically critical enclave of Teschen, whose coal heated the foyers and powered the industry of Central Europe from Krakow to Vienna. With the Peace Conference barely under way, Polish and Czech troops faced off at gunpoint over Teschen. The Czech claim had never been recognized by the U.S. experts of the Inquiry. Indeed, Polish troops had already moved into the region in which the Inquiry had suggested the Czech claim had only "a weak basis of historic rights." Paderewski, however, while not on the scene in Paris, knew what he was doing. He had laid the groundwork most effectively for his request, which he cabled to Colonel House on January 12, for arms, munitions, and above all recognition of the justness of his cause. Wilson accepted House's recommendations on all counts, supporting Paderewski's demands, to the dismay of the British. They feared yet another fait accompli, while the French, equally dismayed, saw only the value of a powerful Czechoslovakia as the anchor of a cordon sanitaire.

The result was one of the early major debates before the Peace Conference. On January 29 Poland's Dmowski accused the Czechs of a violent breach of the peace by moving their forces into Polish territory. Kramář promptly exploded that Poland had violated a wartime agreement and invaded the historic Czech Kingdom. Secretary of State Lansing was one of the first to recognize what was going on, confiding to his diary: "Poles, Czecho-Slovaks, Ukrainians, Jugo-Slavs, Montenegriens [*sic*], Serbs, Albanians, all the races of Central Europe and the Balkans in fact are actually fighting or about to fight with one another. Just as the Russian, Austrian and German Empires have split into national groups, so the great war seems to have split up into a lot of little wars."

Even Clemenceau had begun to recognize the seriousness of the developments in this volatile region and the likelihood that the breakout of widespread, armed conflict could destroy all the grander aims of each of the major powers. "Everybody seems to be on the loose," he confided to Mordacq. So it began to appear that one of the earliest tasks of the Allied peacemakers would be to separate the various warring factions, wading in much as a referee throws himself between two boxers in a clinch, sending them to neutral corners for a moment of cooling down. The Allied delegates recognized that at least for a year or more they would have to be the referees, even the supreme governing body, of much of the Western world.

By late January most of the leading delegates were already fed up with the bickering that seemed likely to consume their energies. What remained of the goodwill between the major powers, the Allies had already come to believe, should more constructively be used to dictate peace terms to Germany and to establish a mechanism that could prevent future global conflicts. So instead of coming directly to grips with these complex issues, they happily dumped the whole matter in the hands of a fact-finding mission consisting of British and Italian colonels, a French consular officer, and the mission's improbable leader, Marcus A. Coolidge. His dubious credentials consisted of being a Democratic supporter of Woodrow Wilson and serving as the mayor of Fitchburg, Massachusetts, where he had worked in his father's rattan factory. Yet even as the mission was arriving in Central Europe, the peacemakers in Paris also decided—anticipating weeks of fruitless debate over a myriad of details of boundary lines and conflicting claims of displaced nationalities—to refer all these matters to individual national commissions for the respective countries. The top delegates still had little understanding of how interdependent most of these issues were in each of these territories where real people were living, often hating, and occasionally even fighting. Paderewski and Beneš were persuaded to halt all military engagements and to exchange cables agreeing to abide by the ruling of the Czech and Polish commissions. This accord brought at least a momentary end to the Masaryk-Beneš tactic of the fait accompli. Alas, for the future of Czechoslovakia, it also dealt an all but fatal blow to Masaryk's efforts to establish his nation as the anchor in a modern, peaceful alliance of Central European democracies.

By the end of March, with the commissions in Paris still mired in the details of how to dispose of millions of effectively dispossessed and disenfranchised populations throughout Europe—millions of Germans in the Czech republics of Bohemia and Moravia, Slovaks in Hungary, Czechs and Germans in Poland—Paderewski decided that it was high time that he weighed in personally before the Peace Conference. On April 6, the prime minister's train pulled into the Gare du Nord, where Roman Dmowski and the rest of the Polish delegation were assembled to greet their leader. On the ride to the delegation's headquarters at the Hotel Wagram just down from the Arc de Triomphe, Dmowski expressed his fears that all of Poland's most precious needs and desires were in jeopardy. Lloyd George, hence Britain, had lined up firmly behind Czechoslovakia. Dmowski failed to note that Lloyd George was especially put off by Dmowski's strident anti-Semitism. This shocked members of the British delegation, especially when, in private conversations, the Polish delegate used the Balfour Declaration to demonstrate the influence of Jews over the British government.

Undeterred, Paderewski plunged right in. Clearly he was aware that he needed to do little work with the Americans, having spent so many years during the war cementing his ties with Wilson and House. He also set aside for the moment the British (though Lloyd George remarked on learning of Paderewski's arrival, "what can you expect from a country that sends as her representative a pianist"). Instead, the Polish leader elected to begin by chipping away at the Czech advantage with the French. Arriving in the chambers of Foreign Minister Stéphen Pichon, Paderewski requested an interview with Prime Minister Clemenceau himself. Pichon excused himself and in the next room phoned Clemenceau, who arrived promptly to meet the maestro.

"You have just expressed the desire to see me? Well, here I am," Clemenceau announced, holding out his hand without removing his trademark thin gray glove. "Tell me, are you the cousin of the famous pianist Paderewski?"

"That is I, myself," replied Paderewski.

With mock surprise, Clemenceau cocked a practiced eye and shot back, "And you, the celebrated artist, you have become prime minister? What a disgrace." Both dissolved in laughter.

The ice broken with the French, the next stop was President Wilson who, learning that his old friend had arrived in Paris, summoned him to his home on the Place des États-Unis. Paderewski assured him that his name was worshiped by Poles from rural peasants to factory workers as the liberator of their nation and guarantor of its freedom. Moved by his words, Wilson confided to the great pianist that his people's faith was not misplaced. Paderewski could count on his support. Even Wilson's skeptical secretary of state was won over. Lansing conceded in his diary that while "my original impression was not of a complimentary nature, my second impression was that IJP was a greater statesman than he was a musician—wonderfully resourceful and apparently had an instinctive sense of the possible."

It was left only to bring Lloyd George under his spell—which proved to be a simple matter for Paderewski, the master showman, who by now had left the seedy Hotel Wagram for the more congenial surroundings of the Ritz. Watching him carefully in action, the British prime minister came to a grudging admiration of his political and diplomatic gifts to the point where Lloyd George invited the renowned pianist to a concert of the British Guards' band at the Trocadero. As the two sat in the British prime minister's box, Lloyd George leaned in close and warned him that the experts' commission on Poland was preparing to reject his nation's claim to Danzig. Even then, the Baltic seaport was deemed as critical to the commercial and political health of Poland as it would be more than six decades later. Then, under its Polish name of Gdansk, it would serve as the birthplace of Lech Wałęsa's Solidarity free trade union, the first step toward an independent and democratic Poland. Paderewski should do all he could, Lloyd George advised, to get the report altered, and he would do all he could to bring the commission into line.

The biggest problem faced by those specialists redrawing the maps of Poland, Czechoslovakia, and Hungary was the presence of vast numbers of minorities within the frontiers of each of these nations—but especially the numbers of Germans who inhabited the border areas. With Germany the defeated nation, and with the belief in much of Western Europe that Germans everywhere needed to be crushed, the rights of German minorities were scarcely a top priority for the peace delegates. But many of the Peace Conference's experts—especially Britain's Nicolson and America's Charles Seymour and Gordon Auchincloss—believed that German minorities were a present reality that needed to be dealt with if they were not to become major forces of instability in the future. At the same time, the U.S. experts were operating under the concept of "self-determination." This was becoming increasingly awkward, as it remained virtually undefined with respect to all minority peoples. And the body that might have served to define the concept and police its ongoing application, the League of Nations, was proving to be equally elusive at this point in the Peace Conference deliberations. Seymour confided his deep concerns to his friend Henry Pomeroy Davison, founder of Bankers Trust, partner of J. Pierpont Morgan, a participant in the meeting that led to the creation of the Federal Reserve, and chairman of the League of Red Cross Societies. Davison was himself very concerned since many of his Red Cross workers were dealing with displaced minorities under horrific conditions. The study of boundaries "has been very difficult," Seymour wrote, "inasmuch as we have been unable to estimate how strong a force the League of Nations is going to be."

Still, the Germans in the border territories seemed to be an all but intractable problem. "If all the territories inhabited by the Germans of Bohemia were separated from Czechoslovakia," the American members of the Czechoslovak commission reported, "this separation would cause a great danger for the Czechoslovak state, as well as serious difficulties for the Germans themselves; the only possible solution is, therefore, to attach them to Czechoslovakia." There ensued an endless round of horse-trading among the young technocrats of the great powers, closeted in fabulously ornate conference rooms, poring over hand-drawn maps with multicolored lines snaking across the page, at times on their hands and knees crawling around the edges of Europe. Nicolson, in one diary entry, captures the flavor of the frustrations and the pettiness of swapping back and forth thousands of lives they would never see:

March 13, Thursday

Czech sub-committee in the morning. We discuss Rumberg and Eger enclaves. The Yanks want to take both away from the Czechs. [By this time the Americans were solidly on the side of Paderewski and the Poles and opposed most desires of the Czechs.] The French and ourselves oppose this. In order to secure unanimity I agree to give the Yanks Rumberg, if they will give me Eger. This they refuse to do, so that we shall not have an unanimous report. This means further delay. Damn!

The questions of minorities, their rights, and the boundaries that would define who would rule them rapidly became the single most contentious issue of the early days of the Peace Conference. The principal problem was that the various experts, at the behest of their delegations' leaders, were seeking to draw boundaries in areas that had never before been separated in quite this manner by international frontiers—and drawing them on linguistic and ethnic grounds rather than on the grounds of any naturally occurring geographic criteria. Nicolson in particular was concerned more about the Czechs digesting too many enemy citizens. In other words, while most of his fellow Brits and other commission members, even his close pal Allen Dulles, worried about long-term threats to the Czechs and Poles from abroad—particularly from Germans or Hungarians—Nicolson was more concerned, and quite rightly, about the immediate threats at home: "I cannot persuade them out of it. I am sure they are wrong and it is heart breaking to have to support a claim with which I disagree. I am anxious about the future political complexion of the Czech state if they have to digest solid enemy electorates, plus an Irish Party in Slovakia, plus a Red Party in Ruthenia, to say nothing of their own extreme socialists."

From Prague, Masaryk battled desperately to influence the Peace Conference to let it retain territories with heavy German populations, delivering an impassioned speech to his own parliament:

The American Republic went to war rather than allow the secession of its south. We shall never allow the secession of our ethnically mixed north. . . . The Germans will have to be satisfied with self-determination of the second class. . . . We want to devote ourselves to peaceful work of administration. The basis of democracy lies in administration and autonomy. Democracy does not mean domination, but work for the securing of justice. And justice is the mathematics of humanism. . . . We, the Czechs and the Slovaks, could not stand aside in [the War] . . . the fate of our nation is quite logically linked with the West, and with its modern democracy."

But from the other side of Europe, it was too little, too late. Czechoslovakia failed to win the full control over Teschen that it believed it so desperately needed. As for other areas, the Czech commission decided to leave the final decision to the Big Four—Wilson, Clemenceau, Lloyd George, and Italy's Vittorio Emmanuele Orlando—to put together the whole puzzle of disassembling Austria-Hungary and creating stable, democratic new nations out of the myriad bits and pieces of the old empire. They never did.

Instead, the delegates sought something elusive that proved just beyond, perhaps way beyond, their grasp: a powerful, unified group of small nations in the heart of Europe that would be a guardian of future peace, or a trip wire against future war. As Lloyd George lamented in an extraordinarily prescient document he called "Some Considerations for the Peace Conference Before They Finally Draft Their Terms," later known simply as "The Fontainebleau Memorandum":

I cannot conceive any greater cause of future war than that the German people, who have certainly proved themselves one of the most vigorous and powerful races in the world, should be surrounded by a number of small states, many of them consisting of people who have never previously set up a stable government for themselves, but each of them containing large masses of Germans clamouring for reunion with their native land. The proposal of the Polish Commission that we should place 2,100,000 Germans under the control of a people . . . which has never proved its capacity for stable self-government throughout history must, in my judgment, lead sooner or later to a new war in the East of Europe.

. . . I would therefore take as a guiding principle of the peace that as far as is humanly possible the different races should be allocated to their motherlands, and that this human criterion should have precedence over considerations of strategy or economics or communications which can usually be adjusted by other means.

By mid-April, the various commissions of experts had put the final touches—as best they could—on the frontiers of Poland and Czechoslovakia, and the Paris Conference had moved on to even more intractable problems. But across Central Europe, out where the vast populations were just beginning to adjust to their new status as free people or their new enslavement under strange governments with different languages and customs, the troubles had only just begun. In Czechoslovakia, under the lines drawn by the Peace Conference, Czechs constituted barely 51 percent of the total population; Germans were more than 22 percent, a powerful and concentrated minority in the border areas with Germany, particularly the Sudetenland, which would become the flashpoint for the next world war; Slovaks accounted for 16 percent of the total, though three-quarters of a century later they would become an independent nation in their own right; Hungarians 5 percent; Ruthenians 2 percent; with the remaining 4 percent divided between Jews, Poles, and Gypsies. Effectively, the Peace Conference had turned Czechoslovakia into a polyglot highway from Germany to the Balkans and onward to the Middle East with a fifth column in its midst. The nation would prove to be simply the toll collector who'd swing wide the gates and speed the invaders on their way.

And despite all the valiant efforts of the experts' commissions Dulles, Nicolson, and other specialists in the fine points of minorities and boundaries of Central Europe in all their intricacy—the final determination was left to an offhanded chance meeting on a fine spring afternoon in April, as Colonel House described it to his diary:

At four o'clock I went to the Ministry of War where a meeting of the Council of Four was to be held. We had decided this morning to take up the question of the Czecho-Slovak boundaries. Our experts had drawn a line which ran in and out of the old territory, throwing some of the old Austria into Germany and placing many Germans in Austria [*actually the Bohemian region of*

Czechoslovakia]. The French and English agreed upon the entire line. I reached the Ministry of War five or six minutes in advance of [Lloyd] George and [Italian Prime Minister] Orlando, and by the time they arrived, Clemenceau and I had agreed to adopt the old historic boundary line and not attempt the new one. It was so much simpler and less full of possibilities for trouble. We had but little difficulty in persuading both George and Orlando to accept our conclusions. George seemed to know but little about it.

In fact, Colonel House, acting for the absent Woodrow Wilson, who had returned for a fence-mending operation back home in Washington, had merely compounded Czechoslovakia's problems. Its frontiers were expanded, but at the cost of adding to that nation more than 330,000 irredentist Germans as a vocal and rebellious minority. Many of the experts, like Nicolson, were appalled. Yet most of the well-intentioned drones of the Paris Conference had become powerless at this point to move the Great Powers with their geopolitical priorities that proved ultimately to be so misguided. Writing in his diary, Nicolson described from his perspective the cavalier manner in which the issue of Austria-Hungary was finally settled along the very lines House and Clemenceau had privately worked out in their brief moment together:

During the afternoon there is the final revision of the frontiers of Austria. Go round to the Rue Nitot at luncheon and coach A.J.B. [Lord Balfour]. Down with him to the Quai d'Orsay. There (in that heavy tapestried room, under the simper of Marie de Medicis, with the windows open upon the garden and the sound of water sprinkling from a fountain and from a lawn-hose)—the fate of the Austro-Hungarian Empire is finally settled. Hungary is partitioned by these five distinguished gentlemen—indolently, irresponsibly partitioned—while the water sprinkles on the lilac outside—while the experts watch anxiously—while A.J.B., in the intervals of dialectics on secondary points, relapses into somnolence—while [Secretary of State] Lansing draws hobgoblins upon his writing pad—while Pichon crouching in his large chair blinks owlishly as decision after decision is actually recorded—while [Italian Foreign Minister Baron Sidney] Sonnino . . . is ruggedly polite—while [Japan's Baron Nobuaki] Makino, inscrutable and inarticulate, observes, observes, observes . . . After some insults flung like tennis balls between Tardieu and Lansing, Hungary loses her South. Then Czecho-Slovakia, and while the flies drone in and out of the open windows, Hungary loses her North and East. . . . Then tea and macaroons. Bob Vansittart's play in the evening.

As a result, in terms of their borders and the territory that the government in Prague controlled, Czechoslovakia did wind up, largely, with the nation Masaryk had envisioned before the war and even during the darkest days of jockeying during the Paris Conference itself. Still, it was a pyrrhic victory.

The new Poland that emerged from the conference rooms of the Quai d'Orsay and the smoking rooms of a dozen hotels turned out to be an equally unstable and militarily indefensible hash, if somewhat more ethnically homogeneous than its neighbor to the south. Its 27 million inhabitants consisted of 70 percent Poles, 15 percent Ukrainians, 7 percent Jews, 4 percent Byelorussians, and 4 percent Germans. It did allow Polish access to the sea via Gdansk, complying with the letter of Wilson's Thirteenth Point, but the port itself would become a "free city," not part of Poland. It was a point on which Lloyd George would not budge, and Wilson, as he did on innumerable occasions, caved—hoping to win the British leader's support for his beloved but inevitably doomed League of Nations. The status of the "free city" would be guaranteed by a League that would wind up having little power to guarantee anything beyond a meal ticket for the hordes of international civil servants and diplomats who would attend to its modest needs and even more modest mandate. The Peace Conference did, however, also tack onto Poland the economically critical slab of Silesia, the coal and industrial region of Germany whose residents were more victims of the defeat of the Central Powers.

Neighboring Czechoslovakia stood in sharp contrast to the largely impoverished nation of Poland the Allies created. Even their most astute experts failed to appreciate just how prosperous was this country they were assembling out of the detritus of a prostrate Austro-Hungarian Empire. From the moment of its creation, it was already the world's tenth most industrialized nation. The Czechoslovakia that the Peace Conference assembled included 70 to 80 percent of all the industry in Austria-Hungary—from china and glass factories to sugar processors (the fabulous country homes of the old Czech sugar barons still line the hills around the spa of Karlovy Vary) to the breweries of Plzen and the Skoda works producing world-class armaments, locomotives, autos, and machinery. The wealth these companies generated would make Czechoslovakia coveted by Germany and envied by its other, less amply endowed neighbors.

The biggest failure of the Allies in Paris, however, was their inability or unwillingness to appreciate the personal dynamics of the leaders of these new nations they were creating. Masaryk and Paderewski emerged into the postwar world with a profound dislike for each other. This prevented them from leading their governments into the kind of joint efforts against common enemies that might have slowed, if not halted, the progress toward their enslavement by the two great nations on their western and eastern borders. Perhaps the only individual prescient enough to recognize this possibility was Clemenceau:

> The Conference has decided to call to life a certain number of new States. Can the Conference, without committing an injustice, sacrifice them, out of consideration for Germany, by imposing upon them inacceptable frontiers? If these peoples, especially Poland and Bohemia, have been able to resist Bolshevism up to now, it is because of a sense of nationality. If violence is done to this sentiment, Bolshevism would find the two peoples an easy prey, and the only barrier which at the present moment exists between Russian Bolshevism and the German Bolshevisms will be shattered. The result will be either a confederation of Eastern and Central Europe under the domination of a Bolshevist Germany, or the enslavement of the same countries by a reactionary Germany, thanks to general anarchy. In both cases the Allies will have lost the war. On the contrary, the policy of the French government is resolutely to aid these young peoples with the support of the liberal elements in Europe.

All the Allies, except the U.S. delegation led by Wilson with his fanciful ideals of a League of Nations that could pick up the detritus left by a failed Peace Conference, were operating from the same balance of power calculations that had propelled European diplomacy into a succession of failures since the Congress of Vienna a century before. The British believed that the Germans, as soon as they had adequately recovered from the last war and motivated this time by a Teutonic form of Bolshevism, would swallow the smaller nations of Central Europe if these were not provided with defensible frontiers. The French believed that the only chance for these nations to survive was to make them as hard to consume as an armadillo. Their only possible defense would have been a broad sense of common purpose—an entente of a military, diplomatic, economic, and political nature. Alas, the personal animosities generated in Paris rendered such a scenario unlikely, if not impossible. As for President Wilson, he appeared to be all but criminally unconcerned, reasoning that his beloved League of Nations would fix it all and guarantee the peace no matter what forces might attempt to dominate these regions. Imagine if the delegates had the foresight they so lacked in their dealings with the Middle East and carved Central Europe into a series of ethnically unified mini-states, united in a strong, multifaceted alliance. Europe would manage this more than a half century later, preserving the ethnic character of each of its components, while dropping trade and tariff barriers, unifying banking and commercial systems into a common European Union. By May 1, 2004, this encompassed all of the nations of Central Europe that had caused the delegates in Paris such angst eight-five years before.

When Paderewski and Beneš stepped to the front of the Hall of Mirrors at the Palace of Versailles on June 28 to add their signatures to the Treaty of Peace, little beyond the boundaries delineating their nations had been resolved. Their economies were in desperate straits. War continued to engulf much of Central and Eastern Europe. And the Allies, who had placed themselves in charge of the world for a year of suspended animation, had lost all control over the situation and, for the most part, seemed not to care a jot.

"Gloom is everywhere," Lansing lamented. "Paris is steeped in it. There is nothing to indicate that we are nearer peace than we were ten days ago. Meanwhile Central Europe is aflame with anarchy. The people see no hope." Wilson's grand construct of self-determination simply did not work in the real world, as even his own technocrats might have warned him. The president left Paris within hours of signing the treaty, but others, including some key witnesses to the impact of their deliberations in the field, remained behind. Barely a week later, Archibald Carey Coolidge, newly returned from Central Europe, provided a status report:

Along the boundaries of these little independent states there are sections inhabited by peoples whose blood is alien to their allegiance and who really desire union with a neighboring state which covets the territory occupied by them. Here is a ceaseless cause of trouble and unrest. For a time, open rupture may be avoided, but it will certainly come in the near future because each country with alien population within its borders will seek to impose its nationality upon these aliens. . . . We might as well look the truth squarely in the face. . . . Wars are by no means over. We must be prepared for a future of disputes and conflicts between these covetous nations. Possibly France and Italy have shown themselves wiser and more practical than the United States and Great Britain in their belief in strategic frontiers as a means of preserving peace in the world. I confess that my own opinion has been shaken.

But words from young and powerless academics were too little, too late.

With each of the great powers at Paris out for itself, these small nations had little hope of determining their own fate. Instead, most quietly devoted the bulk of their energies to raising the largest possible armed forces at the very moment their diplomats in Paris were busily negotiating the largest possible territories for them to defend. As early as February 26, General Tasker Bliss, the brilliant military tactician who had served on the Supreme War Council, expressed his personal fears. The French, he believed, and particularly the supreme commander Marshal Foch, were quietly encouraging armed conflict in Central Europe in a desperate effort to keep U.S. troops on the Continent and drag the United States into a continuing war in the East:

We see that the Poles, the Czecho-Slovaks, and a dozen newly revived or newly created states in Europe are bending every energy to the creation of as formidable an army as they can rate. All of the assistance in food supplies . . . that we are giving to them assists them in this detestable purpose. Every dollar's worth of food that we give them enables them to spend a dollar on military equipment. With the best intentions in the world, we are doing what we can to enable Europe to maintain another 30 years' war.

Indeed, many of these new governments found their people on the brink of starvation or frostbite as a cold winter dragged on in regions denuded of coal to heat homes and apartments. All of which reinforced the perception among the people of Central Europe that their leaders' inexperience in shaping the forces of society, politics, and history would ultimately doom them. Powerful forces of nationalism and anti-Semitism had begun to spread in efforts to assign blame everywhere but where it belonged. By December, aware that Pilsudski and his allies within the Polish military had emerged as the only real power in postwar Poland, particularly with new military threats from Bolshevik Russia, Paderewski threw up his hands and eventually returned to his beloved keyboard. While Masaryk was seen by his own people as the George Washington of the Czech nation, the father of his country, Paderewski was never seen as much more than a foreign celebrity, whose fame derived not from any deep sense of "la patrie" but from acclaim on far-off stages, before strange audiences. Pilsudski, whom the Western nations never came to understand or trust, was the true father of his country. Yet he played little role in the negotiations that established the boundaries of the nation he was to rule.

Throughout the long, hot summer of 1919, an eighteen-member Polish-Czechoslovak bilateral commission met in Krakow in an effort to find some way of bringing peace, even an alliance between these two nations that were critical to peace in Central Europe. On the side, however, Masaryk was making a stab at assembling his beloved Entente that he believed was the last hope for guaranteeing the security of the nation he and Beneš had struggled so diligently to assemble. He negotiated frantically with the Rumanians and the newly constituted Yugoslavia to the south. At the same time, Pilsudski was working independently to assemble a separate federation known as Międzymorze, or "Between the Seas," from the Baltic to the Black Sea and encompassing Poland, Lithuania, Belarus, and Ukraine. Such an alliance had protected its people in past centuries from a succession of barbarian invaders ranging from the Teutonic Order to Russians, Turks, Swedes, even Genghis Khan and his Mongol horde, whose advance had been halted at the gates of Europe.

The nations Pilsudski was now courting had once prevented the barbarians from sweeping across the European continent. But these were different times. The result of Pilsudski's efforts was a losing war for the

Ukraine in 1920. Victorious Russian Bolshevik forces pursued the fleeing Międzymorze armies to the very suburbs of Warsaw amid Lenin's brazenly announced plan to press on with an invasion of Western
Europe. As the Bolshevik's principal theorist Nikolai Bukharin trum-
peted in *Pravda*, "Immediately to the walls of Paris and London."
Pilsudski's army halted the Soviet advance at enormous cost. In the
subsequent Treaty of Riga, Russia brought an ignominious end to the
Polish leader's dream of federation. Poland was forced to surrender
large parts of Belarus and Ukraine to the Soviet Empire. Elsewhere
across the region, other violence was spreading. Polish and Czech forces
were doing battle over the rich mines of Teschen, since for much of the
world, coal was still in those years what oil is today.

Throughout all this, the Allies continued to operate the mechanism
of the Paris Conference. Though pledged to act as a global government,
however, they were behaving little like one. Beyond supplying food to
some of the most deprived regions of Europe through the Hoover Commission, they completely abrogated any responsibility for resolving the
intense personal, national, and ethnic feuds that continued to pit one
government and one nation against the other. They refused repeatedly
to insert their own military forces between the increasingly emboldened
armies that each of these countries was frantically raising. Instead they
chose to exercise their will through a succession of local plebiscites which,
under the international scrutiny accorded such votes today, would have
been called outright frauds. This was how the vast bulk of Teschen was
awarded to Czechoslovakia, despite the valiant efforts of a delegation of
Polish peasants. In desperation, they had walked fifty miles to the nearest
railroad station in their homeland, finally showing up at the Crillon in
their thick white felt coats decorated with red embroidery and high Cossack caps of black shaggy fur. They pleaded for the rights of 120,000 of
their countrymen who they feared would be forcibly amalgamated into
Czechoslovakia. Wilson himself was so touched that he pleaded with his
aides to do their maximum for this sliver of Poland. They won.

But others did not—especially the Slovaks. Once they realized they'd
been freed from Hungarian oppression, many Slovaks had no interest in
swapping one overlord for another in the form of the Czech leadership
in Prague. Father Andrej Hlinka, leader of the Slovak Peasant Party,
slipped into Paris and through an intermediary arranged a midnight
meeting on September 19 with House aide Stephen Bonsal. Leaving

the Crillon by the baggage entrance on the narrow rue Boissy d'Anglas, Bonsal "walked along in the pelting rain for several minutes before my mysterious escort would allow me to hail a cab." Then after wandering back and forth near the Luxembourg Gardens to make sure they weren't tailed, they wound up in a dead-end alley before an ironbound gate, guarded by a priest who summoned Father Hlinka from the shadows of a tiny monastery. Hlinka pleaded for his nation's independence, but he was too late. The Versailles treaty had been signed months before, and there was little that either Bonsal or House could do. Within days, the Slovak mission had been discovered by the French and expelled from France. Some months later, Czech soldiers broke into Father Hlinka's home and carried him away to prison, touching off a bloody uprising and yet another problem for the Masaryk regime.

The situation continued to deteriorate across the region. Through-out the summer that followed the signing of the peace treaty, the Allies maintained the fiction of governing a defeated Europe through an ad hoc commission that consisted of second-string Allied leaders. They were receiving regular and detailed reports from the agents that Dulles had set up in the field through Hoover's Relief Organization; a French military delegation to Poland that included a young French captain named Charles de Gaulle; and a British mission led by a war hero with one arm and one foot, General Adrian Carton de Wiart, who impressed the Poles even more than de Gaulle by his complete disregard for danger and his willingness to fight duels. When he arrived, much to his horror, he found the Poles "engaged in five wars: they were fighting the Germans, the Bolsheviks, the Ukrainians, the Lithuanians and the Czechs." De Wiart became very close to Pilsudski, a tough, like-minded warrior. Still, the veteran British officer quickly sized up his Polish counterpart for the one quality that indeed caused him and his nation the paramount difficulties with the Peace Conference and its outcome: "Unfortunately, Pilsudski had the *défauts de ses qualités*, for he was a very jealous man, brooked no opposition, and when anyone rose higher than it suited him he got rid of him. His ruthless dismissal of Paderewski [and] Sikorski were instances of his jealousy, and he lost these great patriots [who] stood high in the eyes of the world."

De Wiart, himself a passionate military professional, busied himself with visiting each of the major fronts, escaping at times by only the slimmest of margins and the blindest of luck. His specially constructed

wagon-lit was assaulted by Cossacks during the Bolshevik advance on
Warsaw, the mounted warriors circling the train much like Indian raid-
ers of the previous century. At one moment De Wiart debated whether
to waste one of his two final rounds dispatching a Cossack before turning his revolver on himself. But after the general abandoned his special
car and ordered it cut loose, the train managed to pick up speed and
outrun the invaders.

De Wiart spent considerable time on the Czech front and quickly
came to appreciate the problem. None of the expert negotiators holed
up in Paris ever fully understood that this was a conflict between two
peoples who shared a host of fundamental identities—historic, social,
cultural, linguistic. Each side would therefore bicker and toss a few gre-
nades halfheartedly. But it was difficult for them to put their hearts into
this war. They preferred to lob verbal sallies across conference tables,
preventing the conclusion of any true cooperation until the time for
both nations was simply too late. Or as de Wiart put it:

> The war against the Czechs proceeded equably, and more or less
> on a domestic basis. The Poles have a natural aversion to the
> Czechs, partly because they are neighbors and therefore prone to
> quarreling, and partly because the Poles look down on the Czechs
> for being, like the Brits, 'a nation of shopkeepers.' To the agrarian
> Pole, commerce is a despised occupation to be left to the Jew, and
> they had great contempt for the Czechs who thought otherwise.
> Their chief bone of contention were the coal mines at Teschen.

From the Czech side, Nicholas Roosevelt, a twenty-six-year-old
American observer, reported that the Czechs were encouraged in their
militant pursuit of territory by George Creel. This Wilson crony headed
the U.S. propaganda effort in Europe during the war, and after the
armistice found himself in Prague. That's when he told Masaryk that
the Czechs were America's "favorite sons," and they'd support Czech
actions "through thick and thin." Placards signed by a junior American
officer stating that the Czech seizure of Teschen had the approval of
the Allies, were a carte blanche for troops to move in, touching off the
armed confrontation with the Poles. This kind of confusion, a product
of inaction and inattention from the West's leaders in Paris, only compounded the problems of Central Europe's hottest flashpoints.

Still, amid these kinds of pressures of ongoing battles with powerful Hungarian forces on his southern frontier and the continued skirmishes in the north with Poland, Masaryk finally managed to conclude what came to be known as the Little Entente with Rumania and Yugoslavia. Both probably reaped more benefit from the recognition the treaties carried of their own viability as nation-states than Czechoslovakia ever gained as a means of self-defense. Meanwhile, at home matters were only deteriorating. By 1929 Klement Gottwald had been named general secretary of the Czechoslovak Communist Party and a senior member of the Moscow-based Comintern. Allied forces had withdrawn from Central Europe.

Still, for more than a decade, Czechoslovakia, under its First Republic, prospered as a liberal, democratic nation. But with the Treaty of Versailles defeated by the United States Senate, a toothless League of Nations opened its doors on the shores of Lake Geneva. It quickly demonstrated it was powerless to affect the economic situation that began deteriorating in much of Europe as America's Great Depression spread across the continent, leaving riots and chaos in its wake. By July 1932, the communist trade union had been banned in Czechoslovakia, its headquarters ransacked by Czech police and Gottwald arrested. But communism was not the most immediate menace to the continued independence of Czechoslovakia. On its western frontier, the economic catastrophe called the Weimar Republic had sprung from the reparations foisted on a defeated Germany by the Allies. Hyperinflation sent prices doubling every month, spawning a right-wing phenomenon known as National Socialism led by an Austrian housepainter named Adolf Hitler. The ill-drawn boundaries of Czechoslovakia and the German-incited agitation of the irredentist minority left in Bohemia and Moravia provided Hitler with his first excuse to embark on a campaign that would bring much of Europe under the boot heels of his panzer divisions. In September 1938, British, French, German, and Italian officials decided that their predecessors had indeed erred in Paris less than two decades earlier. Two and a half million Germans in the Sudetenland region of Czechoslovakia had been living in the wrong country for nearly a generation. Within ten days they and the lands they inhabited would be returned to their rightful overlords in the Third Reich.

"How horrible, fantastic, incredible it is that we should be digging trenches and trying on gas masks here because of a quarrel in a far away country between people of whom we know nothing," British Prime Minister Neville Chamberlain told an England broadcast two days before he signed over the lives of these people to Hitler. "However we may sympathize with a small nation confronted by a big and powerful neighbor, we cannot in all circumstances undertake to involve the whole British Empire in war simply on her account." Three days later, he returned to 10 Downing Street from Munich, announcing that, "for the second time in our history, a British Prime Minister has returned from Germany bringing peace with honor. I believe it is peace in our time."

The Czechs weren't quite so sanguine. Czech Foreign Minister Kamil Krofta observed starchily that the Munich Agreement was made "without us and against us." In the end, the Czechs could do little to resist Nazi forces that rolled first into the Sudetenland, then not long thereafter into Prague and across Slovakia. This small nation, which its defenders at the peace talks so rightly predicted could be little more than a highway to Russia and the Balkans, proved to be just that. Indeed, it turned into a two-way highway when just six years, and millions of deaths later, Soviet forces rolled across it heading west.

Throughout World War II, the Czechs sought to use the same playbook they had during World War I—playing one ally against the other. But Wilson and Clemenceau were not Franklin Delano Roosevelt and Joseph Stalin. These leaders of the 1940s had vastly different views of the world, and of the role of small powers in it. By July 1947 Czechoslovakia's fate was sealed for another half century. "I went to Moscow as the Foreign Minister of an independent sovereign state," moaned Foreign Minister Jan Masaryk, the son of Tomáš. "I returned as a lackey of the Soviet government." Six months later he was in Lake Success, New York, for the organizing session of the United Nations. It proved as powerless in halting the advance of communism in Europe as the League of Nations, in which his father had put equally limited stock, had been in halting the advance of the Nazis. During the younger Masaryk's visit, he managed to dislocate his shoulder. "You must have been leaning too hard on the iron curtain," a friend remarked. By March of the following year he was dead—his body found in the courtyard of the foreign ministry. Whether it was an accident, a suicide, or a successful operation by the KGB would never be determined. Czechoslovakia had disappeared firmly behind the iron curtain.

.   .   .

The route Poland followed after the signing at Versailles was even more direct and in many respects far bloodier. A March 1921 plebiscite, established by the Paris Conference to determine the fate of Silesia, led to a 60 percent vote by German residents operating under the protection— or intimidation—of German police. So the region was annexed to Germany. Silesian Poles staged an armed uprising, and the League of Nations stepped in, awarding Poland the eastern, wealthier, and more industrial region. The western portion, including Wroclaw and the agrarian lands of Opole, went to Germany. In the Teschen portion of Southern Silesia, Poles and Czechs battled over the spoils. The Czechs won the richer area south of the Olza River, where 55 percent of the population happened to be Polish. A plebiscite designed to resolve this dispute peacefully could not have come at a worse time for a struggling Poland. The Red Army was advancing on Warsaw and Czech troops had taken the opportunity to move into Teschen. With the autonomy of Poland hanging by the most slender thread, less than half the Polish population of the region turned out for the balloting. The Allied ambassadors in Paris agreed to award the western portion of Teschen to Czechoslovakia— shocking the Poles and putting a stake through the heart of any chance of Poland joining Masaryk's Little Entente.

All this unrest, of course, only stiffened Soviet determination to use Poland as a bridge to bring communism to Germany. Stalin, in one of many moments of pique, had told Lenin that the destruction of the Polish army was a necessary step in the Soviet revolutionary drive to the West. The Red Army's defeat on the doorsteps of Warsaw in 1920 was yet another consequence of the half measures taken by the Allied leaders in Paris. Backing away from every opportunity of dealing with the nascent Bolshevik menace, the Allies simply postponed Stalin's plans for a quarter century. Never a man to stomach defeat without vengeance, in 1940 he ordered the NKVD secret police to take to the Katyn Forest near Smolensk some four thousand Polish reserve officers his army had seized while supporting the Nazi invasion of Poland. There they were massacred to the last man.

World War II ended far differently than World War I. Slavery replaced self-determination. Stalin created the cordon sanitaire that Clemenceau so urgently and passionately desired, turning it 180 degrees to face west instead of east. He called it the Warsaw Pact and Comecon. These respectively military and economic alliances were formed with a

single purpose, to guarantee the security and prosperity of only one of
their "members"—Russia. And while Clemenceau and Stalin shared a
common goal of using the Central European nations—especially Poland
and Czechoslovakia—as a buffer between Soviet Russia and Germany,
the real aims of the two world leaders, a generation apart, were far different. Stalin's goal was not to guarantee the independence of the members
of this cordon sanitaire, but their enslavement.

In 1919, the French ostensibly sought a free and independent Poland
as a counterweight to German power, while the British saw it as a buffer
against Russian Bolshevism. But when it came down to putting words
on paper, all any of these Allies really demanded in Paris was to keep
Silesia and the Saar out of the hands of Germany. "Out of the ore fields
may be fashioned the weapons of the next world war," Clemenceau
confided prophetically. "There, unfortunately, is to be found everything
necessary to the rearmament of the Bavarians we have only just brought
to heel after four years of costly war." It is curious how prescient this
French leader, reared in nineteenth-century realpolitik, was in predicting how the twentieth century would turn out. It is curious, as well,
how contiguous the view of many of the minions of the other allied delegations turned out to be, though for far different motives. Recall Nicolson's words as he prepared to embark for Paris, filled with the optimism
and idealism of the young: "We were journeying to Paris, not merely to
liquidate the war, but to found a new order in Europe. We were preparing not Peace only, but Eternal Peace. There was about us the halo of
some divine mission. We must be alert, stern, righteous and ascetic. For
we were bent on doing great, permanent and noble things."

Along the way, there were many leaders who aspired to realize the
twin visions of Masaryk and Paderewski. Some, such as Czechoslovak
communist leader Alexander Dubček and his "Socialism with a Human
Face" nearly succeeded, but were quickly dragged back into line by
Soviet tanks rumbling through Prague in 1968. Others, including Polish dissidents Adam Michnik and Jacek Kuroń, tried again a decade
later with their underground KOR movement. It surfaced just as their
Czech counterparts playwright Václav Havel, novelist, poet, and playwright Pavel Kohout, and diplomat Jiři Hájek were roiling the waters in
Prague with Charter 77.

It was the better part of a century after Masaryk and Paderewski first
sought for their nations a place of their own among the community of

democratic nations before both states could become full-fledged members of the European community. On March 12, 1999, Poland and the Czech Republic joined the North Atlantic Treaty Organization, followed five years later by Slovakia. And on May 1, 2004, Poland, the Czech Republic, and Slovakia became full members of the European Union. All this was made possible only by an improbable series of events so ill-foreseen by the myopic peacemakers in Paris: the arrival of a Polish pope as leader of the Roman Catholic Church in October 1978; the founding in 1980 of the Polish trade union Solidarity by Lech Wałęsa, an obscure shipyard worker in Gdansk, that same city the Peace Conference delegates found so difficult to award outright to Poland; the arrival of a reformist Russian leader, Mikhail Gorbachev; and of course the fall of the Berlin Wall in November 1989, the final symbolic end to communism and Soviet rule in Eastern Europe.

How differently events might have turned out if the peacemakers of Paris had looked at the Europe they sought to raise from the dead in some less self-serving fashion. Europe might have looked very different had they not been paralyzed by the specter of Bolshevism exploding out of Russia, infecting Hungary, and which, they feared so desperately, could arrive on their own doorsteps before long.

7

ALL ABOARD THE
ORIENT EXPRESS

IN THE DAYS BEFORE AIR TRAVEL, PARIS'S ARCHING, ART DECO rail stations were the crossroads of the world. It was the heyday of the Train Bleu café in the Gare de Lyon—the starting point of the fabled Orient Express. On the morning of April 1, 1919, Ÿ Harold Nicolson— the same young British diplomat who just three months earlier had arrived in Paris filled with hope for the world he would be building— boarded a special train. He was joining a top-level delegation of Western military observers and diplomats bound for Budapest. By then the peace talks had become all but paralyzed with fear of the Bolsheviks—their apparently overwhelming success in Russia against a host of challengers and their ability to spread their gospel westward into the realms of the defeated Central Powers.

The goal of the delegation, headed by South African General Jan Smuts, a hero of the Boer Wars, was to explore the reality of Bolshevism—and to probe how real the menace might be to the New Europe that the Peace Conference was attempting to build. Then there was the issue of Béla Kun—Hungary's Red stalking horse. Would he accept a peace treaty that would wind up shredding the Ÿ former Austro-Hungarian Empire and his own nation as well? Or, even more critically, might he serve as a viable intermediary between the Peace Conference and the united powers of the West and the Bolshevik leadership of

Russia? A young Harvard professor—Archibald Carey Coolidge, a cousin of the future president—also came along, as did the Archbishop of Spalato (today's Dalmatian coast town of Split in Croatia). His stiff silk robes rustled through the corridors of the wagon-lit. ItŸwas a formidable collection of diplomats and specialists. Still, it was not the only probe launched by the Paris Peace Conference into the dead zone of communist Europe.

From their first days in Paris, the heads of state and their advisers had been grasping for a means of dealing with what was already clearly becoming a central challenge to the new world order. It was here, through the failures of the leaders of the West to appreciate the forces already at work in Russia, that the cold war began. Though it was not to acquire this name until George Orwell first used it in an article in the left-wing British weekly *Tribune* in October 1945, its reality was, perhaps, inevitable from the moment Lenin and his entourage were sealed into that rail car headed for Finland Station in 1917. By the time the delegates were assembling in Paris, the Bolsheviks had managed to field the single most potent, and most threatening, fighting force in Europe, whose immediate battle was with their White Russian opponents. Under intense political pressure from a war-weary West, the Allies had begun standing down their armies at the very moment Lenin was building his, sweeping across Russia and subduing vast reaches of the neighboring republics that were to become the Soviet Union. At the same time, though, the political philosophy of communism was gaining an even more menacing foothold. Far outside the immediate reach of Lenin's military machine, the tired and impoverished workers laboring in factories of the victors and vanquished alike in Europe were turning their faces and their hopes eastward toward Moscow.

Moreover, Lenin understood from the start the valuable propaganda the Peace Conference was promising to hand him from the moment the armistice was declared: "The Peace Conference is a device for dividing the territorial and financial spoils of the imperialist war under the hypocritical cloak ofŸWilsonian justice while the League of Nations is an international concern of reaction dedicated to suppressing the world revolution."

Still, the end of the war could not have come at a worse time for the Bolshevik leader, who was struggling with a host of internal problems.

Six separate offensives had been launched by military forces in various parts of his empire. At the same time, near economic collapse and a breakdown of fuel, transport, and distribution systems had brought vast stretches of Russia to the brink of famine. Even the sympathetic left-ist journalist Lincoln Steffens described the "deserted factories, factory buildings with machinery for thousands of workers struggling along with a few hundred, closed shops and houses, straggling crowds on dead streets—and always cold . . . and there was very little food."

From the beginning, Woodrow Wilson felt strongly that the Russians needed to be dealt with as though they had a place at the negotiating table in Paris. The Bolsheviks effectively left an empty seat at the Peace Conference. They had removed themselves from the conflict at a critical moment in the midst of hostilities after the czar and his family had been executed and Lenin was busying himself with seizing power. Moreover, as Gregory Zinoviev, son of a Jewish dairy farmer, who was sealed into the railway car with Lenin and later became the first editor of *Pravda*, observed, the Bolsheviks believed that proletarian revolutions could be expected to break out in Western Europe "momentarily."

Lenin was also persuaded that the Bolsheviks should do whatever they could to win breathing space to gather their strength at home so that they might be well placed to encourage revolutionary movements in the capitalist West. Accordingly, Lenin authorized at least seven overtures to the West between October 1918 and January 1919. Many of them were carefully framed to appeal to Wilson's idealism and liberal views of self-determination and human rights. In January the president even went so far as to dispatch to Stockholm a personal emissary, William H. Buck-ler, a Baltimore lawyer and part-time diplomat and archaeologist, whose brief was to listen to his Russian counterpart, the sly roving diplomat Maxim Litvinov, son of a wealthy Jewish banker. Litvinov offered a host of concessions, including hints of supporting Wilson's beloved League of Nations, none of which Lenin ever intended to honor. But Buckler's report that the Bolsheviks were prepared to accept some of the principles for which the Allies had fought the war in Europe had the impact at the Peace Conference that the Bolsheviks intended. It provided sup-port for those delegates who were casting desperately for some excuse to avoid sending in their own exhausted troops to neutralize the Bolshevik menace so that a diplomatic solution could carry the day. Or as David

Lloyd George put it: "If a military enterprise were started against the Bolsheviki, that would make England Bolshevist and there would be a Soviet in London."

Instead, the Allies agreed to invite the Russians to a conference of their own—a thinly disguised effort to draw the Bolsheviks into the global peace process and defuse an increasingly volatile situation in Central and Eastern Europe. Wilson sat down at an upright typewriter in his quarters on the Place des États-Unis and prepared the invitation to the Russians himself. The venue was Prinkipo—the largest of nine islands that make up the Princes' group in the Sea of Marmara a few miles off the Turkish port of Constantinople. The decision to extend the invitation to the various warring Russian parties in the ongoing civil war was taken late on the afternoon of January 22 at a private session in the French foreign minister's personal offices in the Quai d'Orsay. Wilson presented his fellow delegates with the typically understated remarks that he'd drafted:

> The associated Powers are now engaged in the solemn and responsible work of establishing the peace of Europe and of the world, and they are keenly alive to the fact that Europe and the world cannot be at peace if Russia is not. They recognize and accept it as their duty, therefore, to serve Russia in this matter as generously, as unselfishly, as thoughtfully, and as ungrudgingly as they would serve every other friend and ally.

Even before this session formally ratified the initiative, Wilson had already managed to win the agreement of his fellow Allies. Georges Clemenceau gave his reluctant approval to a meeting on Prinkipo after putting his foot down against inviting the Bolsheviks to Paris. There they would have had a propaganda field day among French communists, who were rapidly growing in power and reach. For the moment, Clemenceau relinquished his desire to intervene militarily on behalf of the anti-Bolshevik forces that were still challenging Lenin. With this concession, he hoped to sway the Americans toward his personal crusade of removing Germany once and for all as any sort of military or economic threat to his own nation. Of course, Clemenceau was still hoping desperately to win Allied approval for his "cordon sanitaire," which was evaporating by the moment.

The British also gave their reluctant approval to Wilson's Prinkipo initiative. "Bolshevik Russia has no corn, but within this territory there are 150,000,000 men, women and children," Lloyd George proclaimed. "There is now starvation in Petrograd and Moscow. This is not a health cordon, it is a death cordon. . . . Two-thirds of Bolshevik Russia is starving." Still, this marked the moment, as Clemenceau confided to his principal aide, General Jean Mordacq, when the aging French leader realized that, despite his earlier hopes, President Wilson "in reality understood very badly both Europe and its political reality."

The fundamental problem of Prinkipo was its aim—to assemble at one table all the various Russian forces that were systematically attempting to exterminate each other, all of which thought they could win on the battlefield. On February 15, 1919, the so called Whites, who were both prodemocracy and moderately proczarist, led by Generals Anton Denikin and Aleksandr Kolchak, would in theory be talking directly with the Reds, the hated Bolsheviks. The Whites promptly turned down Wilson's request, torpedoing the entire initiative and opting to continue their armed struggle against their foes. At that point, they were still hoping that Bolshevik propaganda—whose ideals were far removed from the Wilsonian ideals of freedom, justice, and self-determination—would persuade the Allies to come to their aid with military force.

The Bolsheviks, for their part, were delighted with the way the Prinkipo initiative turned out, recognizing they had momentum on their side. It had become crystal clear that the West failed to understand in even the most rudimentary sense just how desperate the scene in Russia had become. Each side in this civil war had developed positions so hardened by battle and ideology that it was truly a fight to the death of the last man on the losing side, bringing horrific suffering to the peasants trapped between the advancing armies. Moreover, Wilson by now had lost all faith in the White Russians and especially their leaders Denikin and Kolchak as holding the keys to a free and democratic Russia he so earnestly desired. At the same time, Lloyd George had come to believe it would take an Allied army of at least five hundred thousand men to stand even a chance of defeating the Bolsheviks on the battlefield. There was no democratic government in the West that could survive if it suggested a mobilization of that magnitude just as voters were beginning to welcome home the survivors of the last war. Instead, as Lloyd George suggested, perhaps the people of Russia were about to get what they deserved:

I see no reason why, if this represents their attitude toward Bolshevism, the Powers should impose on them a government they are
not particularly interested in or attempt to save them from a government they are not particularly opposed to. . . . We are bound to
give moral, political and, if necessary, material support to protect
Finland, Poland and other states carved out of Russia . . . against
Bolshevik invasion.

It was, of course, a typically shortsighted approach to the entire Russian question, but with the collapse of the Prinkipo initiative, it did lead
to a succession of other ill-conceived and ineptly executed measures in
an effort to cope with what was still viewed as a sideshow to the main
work of the Peace Conference. Characteristically, Wilson and Colonel
House were behind most of these efforts of direct personal diplomacy.

One of the members of the U.S. delegation to Paris was a twenty-
eight-year-old diplomat, William C. Bullitt. Although Bullitt came
from the patrician, well-educated background of most members of the
Inquiry, and indeed accompanied them and the president to Europe
on the *George Washington*, he was officially a member of the foreign
service. The product of a distinguished Philadelphia family, a 1912 Phi
Beta Kappa graduate of Yale, Bullitt had traveled widely in Europe and
Russia before the war. Turning briefly to journalism as Washington correspondent for the Philadelphia *Public Ledger*, he quickly attracted the
attention of Colonel Edward House. It was only a short step to the State
Department under Dulles's uncle Robert Lansing, where he first began
to agitate for U.S. recognition of Lenin and his Bolsheviks after the
overthrow of the czar. By the time he had arrived in Paris with the U.S.
delegation, Bullitt's views of the need to reach some accommodation
with Lenin had become a full-blown obsession.

In early February, Bullitt was detached from his role of preparing,
with Allen Dulles, the daily current intelligence report for the U.S.
peace delegates. Instead, he was sent on a quick side trip to Bern for
the Congress of the Second International, where socialists decided to
send their own mission to inquire into conditions in Russia. Immediately after his return, Bullitt prepared the latest of a series of memos to
Colonel House urging mediation with the Bolsheviks. On February 17
House called the young diplomat to his rooms at the Crillon and told

him to pack for Petrograd and Moscow. Bullitt was elated. It was, he fervently hoped, the world's first stab at peaceful coexistence.

The young journalist-turned-diplomat promptly began a whirlwind round of meetings of the other Allied powers, describing his mission. At the same time, the delegation's membership grew to include Lincoln Steffens; Captain Walter W. Pettit, a military intelligence officer who had done relief work in Russia before and during the revolution; and R. E. Lynch, a young naval stenographer. Steffens had been invited along as a face that was friendly and familiar to the Soviet leadership. The other two delegation members were young technicians who would have no input on matters of substance.

Bullitt's meetings included several sessions with Philip Kerr, private secretary to Lloyd George. The two cooked up an eight-point set of conditions the delegation would present to the Russians. This included an immediate end to all hostilities on every front, free entry for Allied citizens to all Russian territories, amnesty for all political prisoners, full restoration of trade between Russia and the outside world, hence an end to all blockades that proved so catastrophic for the Bolsheviks, and finally, a withdrawal of all Allied forces from Russian territories once a major demobilization of Russia's own troops had taken place and their arms destroyed. It was an enormous agenda, especially since Wilson never saw the Bullitt mission as any more than a fact-finding visit. Even House, who'd proposed it, never gave the whole program more than a passing glance. The mission was all the more daunting in that Bullitt himself was little more than a diplomatic dilettante who had spent most of his postcollege years as a newspaperman.

The British assured their safe passage from Paris via Norway, Sweden, and Finland and on into Russia. On February 22, the delegation pushed off from Paris. Steffens described the atmosphere on the trip as light-hearted and carefree: "On trains and boats they skylarked, wrestling and tumbling like . . . bear cubs all along the Arctic Circle. A pretty noisy secret mission we were, but Bullitt knew just what he was about; nobody could suspect us of secrecy or importance." By the time the group had reached Stockholm, the U.S. ambassador to Sweden, Ira Morris, put them in touch with Bolshevik agents to arrange for an official guide— a Swedish communist named Kil Baum. Bullitt blustered himself across frontiers, especially the Finnish-Russian border, until the ragtag

delegation finally arrived in Petrograd, where they found at night "a
deserted city . . . nobody at the station, nobody in the dark, cold, broken streets, and there was no fire in the vacant . . . palace assigned to us."

Steffens, who was known to the Russians from his writings and previous visits, was mistaken as the leader of the mission and promptly
taken in hand for a search "through dead hotels for officials at midnight
teas." Finally they stumbled on Zinoviev, who had been sent personally
by Lenin to determine just how serious the delegation was. When he
learned that Steffens was not the leader and that none of the delegation
was an official emissary, Zinoviev snorted in disgust, promptly disappeared, and was replaced by Georgi Vasilyevich Chicherin. A veteran
Russian diplomat of noble origins, Chicherin had entered the revolution as an aide to Trotsky and was at the moment the Soviet foreign
minister. Steffens explained that Bullitt's aim was to wring from the
Russians the best possible concessions so that Wilson and Lloyd George
could win over Clemenceau and the French. The goal would be for all
the Allies to recognize the Bolsheviks as the true Russian government,
thereby ending military assistance to their opponents and helping to
eradicate the famine that was sweeping the nation.

The Bullitt delegation had left Lynch in Finland and Captain Pettit in Petrograd, so it was reduced to only Steffens and Bullitt. They
boarded a train for Moscow with Chicherin and Litvinov, the same
individual who, just a month before in Stockholm, had attempted to
hoodwink Wilson's previous emissary to the Bolsheviks, William Buck-
ler. Moscow was at least sunny, dry, and warmer. The palace where they
were housed was heated and staffed with servants. The two Americans
also had had the foresight to bring supplies with them, so they were
never at a loss for dinner companions, who arrived unexpectedly and
promptly just in time for the tinned food that was served for dinner
every day. Bullitt opened his talks with Chicherin and Litvinov. Lenin
hovered nearby, monitoring each move.

By March 14 the Russians had agreed to virtually every point that
Bullitt and Kerr had prepared. Lenin promised that each conflicting
party would retain control of the portion of the Russian empire that it
held at that moment. This meant the Bolsheviks would relinquish their
claims to the Urals, Siberia, the Caucasus, Archangel and Murmansk,
the Baltic states, part of White Russia, and the bulk of Ukraine. Most
important for Lenin's future plans, Allied troops would be pulled out,

all their aid to anti-Soviet forces would be terminated, and the blockade of Russia would be lifted. The Bolsheviks also offered to recognize a share of the repudiated Russian foreign debt and requested a formal peace conference with the Allies. They were better terms than anyone had managed to wring from Bolsheviks until then and indeed ever since—until the fall of Soviet communism more than seven decades later. Clearly Lenin was hoping to buy time to marshal his own military forces and consolidate his gains, and that his economically prostrated territories would revive with the lifting of the blockade. With this agreement in hand, though, Steffens decided to see if there was any way he could improve on the terms. Banking on his personal relationship with Lenin, Steffens obtained an audience with the Bolshevik leader:

A quiet figure in old clothes, he rose, came around in front of his desk to greet me with a nod and a handshake. An open, inquiring face, with a slight droop in one eye that suggested irony or humor, looked into mine. I asked whether, in addition to the agreement with Bullitt, I could not take back some assurances: that, for example, if the borders were opened, Russian propagandists would be restrained from flocking over into Europe. "No," he said sharply, but he leaned aback against the desk and smiled. "A propagandist, you know is a propagandist. He must propagand. . . ."

"What assurance can you give that the red terror will not go on killing—"

"Who wants to ask us about our killings?" he demanded, coming to his feet in anger.

"Paris," I said.

"Do you mean to tell me that those men who have just generaled the slaughter of seventeen millions of men in a purposeless war are concerned over a few thousands who have been killed in a revolution with a conscious aim—to get out of the necessity of war—and armed peace. . . . If we have to have a revolution, we have to pay the price of revolution."

Steffens failed to come away from his efforts with anything much more concrete than an impression. "Wilson, the American liberal, having justified his tackings, forgot his course," Steffens observed before leaving Moscow. "Lenin was a navigator, the other a mere sailor."

Indeed, Lenin, Chicherin, and the rest of the communist leadership had offered what they viewed as some extraordinary concessions to the capitalist powers—trying, in their own way, to show that they took the Bullitt mission seriously. Alas, they were the only ones who did.

After a week in Moscow, and with the Bolshevik terms in hand, Bullitt decided to bolt for Paris—particularly since the Russians had set a deadline of April 10 for an acceptance of the agreement by the Allies. On March 16, the U.S. negotiator arrived in Helsingfors (now Helsinki), cabled the terms to Paris, then promptly continued onward to the French capital to push the terms of the agreement in person. But the agreement went far beyond his original assignment of gathering information and reporting. He was returning with a document more sweeping even than anything envisioned from the failed Prinkipo plan. It was, effectively, peace with Lenin and the Bolsheviks, a Western- guaranteed end to the civil war, and an Allied-Bolshevik conference with implied full recognition of the communists as the successors to the czar as the government of the Russian heartland. Not surprisingly, there were many problems in store for Bullitt in Paris.

On the evening of March 25, Bullitt arrived at the Crillon and rushed immediately to Colonel House's suite. House liked what he heard but recognized that he needed a quick buy-in from Wilson and from the other Allies. He got neither. While House told Wilson it was imperative that he hear this critical initiative from Bullitt, and the president scheduled a meeting the next night in House's suite at 6 P.M., he never kept the rendezvous. Wilson pleaded a headache, but it could well have been a ploy. Steffens tried on his own at the same time, counting on Wilson's "old promise to me . . . to receive me if I should send in my name with the words, 'It's an emergency.'" But Steffens's messenger reported that this time the president "sprang to his feet. 'No,' he said, and he walked across the road. 'No, I won't see that man.'" Even in the twenty-four hours after Bullitt met with House, as the young newspaperman-turned-diplomat began his campaign with the other Allied powers, it was clear the mission was in deep trouble.

Bullitt began with the British. They had, after all, drafted the terms with which the young American had left Paris a month earlier. In the interim, however, much had changed. Four days earlier, Hungary's Western-oriented president, Mihály Károlyi, had been ousted by a young communist named Béla Kun, and a "soviet" had been proclaimed in this nation in the heart of Central Europe. Communism was clearly on the march. In a dangerous fashion it was threatening the heart of the Entente Powers that the Allies were attempting to bring into the orbit of a peaceful and democratic Western Europe. Still, when Lloyd George invited Bullitt for breakfast at his Rue Nitot apartment on March 27, the young American expected a warm reception. He was shocked when, after a cordial greeting, the British prime minister unfolded a copy of the *Daily Mail,* Lord Northcliffe's powerful London paper, which during the Peace Conference was publishing a daily Paris edition. Henry Wickham Steed, the paper's veteran foreign editor, had penned a vicious diatribe against any proposal to recognize "the desperadoes whose avowed aim is to turn upside down the whole basis of Western civilization."

It seems that while Bullitt was in Moscow, other powerful forces had been frantically at work to undermine his mission. As Wickham Steed observed:

Potent international financial interests were at work in favour of the immediate recognition of the Bolshevists. These influences had been largely responsible for the Anglo-American proposal in January to call Bolshevist representatives to Paris at the beginning of the Peace Conference—a proposal which had failed after having been transformed into a suggestion for a conference with the Bolshevists at Prinkipo. The well-known American Jewish banker, Mr. Jacob Schiff, was known to be anxious to secure recognition for the Bolshevists, among whom Jewish influence was predominant; and Tchitcherin, the Bolshevist Commissary for Foreign Affairs, had revealed the meaning of the January proposal by offering extensive commercial and economic concessions in return for recognition. At a moment when the Bolshevists were doing their utmost to spread revolution throughout Europe, and when the Allies were supposed to be making peace in the name of high moral principles, a policy of recognizing them, as the price of commercial concessions, would have sufficed to wreck the whole Peace Conference and Europe with it.

By the morning after Bullitt returned to Paris and reported so eagerly to House, an unidentified source on the U.S. delegation—later identified as House's own son-in-law, Gordon Auchincloss—had already tipped off Wickham Steed to the proposal Bullitt had brought back with him. The British editor promptly fired off a fiery cable to Lord Northcliffe: "The Americans are again talking of recognizing the Russian Bolshevists. If they wanted to destroy the whole moral basis of the Peace and of the League of Nations they have only to do so." Then he sat down at his typewriter and wrote the incendiary editorial blasting the "evil thing known as Bolshevism," which the *Daily Mail* published the next morning. It was this paper that Lloyd George threw down in front of an entirely innocent and unsuspecting Bullitt, whose youthful enthusiasm was cut promptly and irrevocably short.

As Bullitt described his breakfast to a congressional hearing in Washington six months later, Lloyd George shouted, "As long as the British press is doing this kind of thing, how can you expect me to be sensible about Russia?" With that, the Bullitt mission and the entire initiative he had drafted so diligently with Lenin and Chicherin came to a crashing end. Indeed, two weeks after that fateful breakfast, Lloyd George himself dismissed the entire affair to the House of Commons with a wave of his hand: "Of course there are constantly men of all nationalities coming and going from Russia who are always coming back with their own tales. . . . There was some suggestion that there was some young American who had come back. All that I can say about that is that it is not for me to judge the value of these communications."

Bullitt was furious when he learned how his efforts had been dismissed so quickly and so offhandedly by the British prime minister. As he told Congress in his September testimony: "It was the most egregious case of misleading the public, perhaps the boldest that I have ever known in my life. . . . So flagrant was this that various members of the British mission called on me at the Crillon a day or so later and apologized for the Prime Minister's action in the case."

In view of the fact that it was actually Auchincloss who had leaked news of the Bullitt accord to Wickham Steed, one has to wonder just how committed House, and by extension Wilson, ever was to the theory or the reality of any comprehensive accord with the Bolsheviks. Indeed, there was more going on behind the scenes, especially among U.S. delegates and specialists, whose quiet lobbying played a substantial role in torpedoing the Bullitt initiative. Colonel Ralph Van Deman, the father of U.S. military intelligence, a distinguished éminence grise to whom House was deeply beholden for having set up the entire U.S. security apparatus in Paris, wrote on stationery of the "Office of Negative Intelligence Department":

> Wouldn't such a peace as [Bullitt] recommends merely give immense prestige and moral support to the existing Soviet Government without corresponding benefit to the rest of the world? If, as the Bolsheviks contend, their conception of society cannot exist side by side with the present social structure, why should existing society lend moral support to an organization which, by its very nature, must destroy it or cease to exist?

Was the first real prospect of détente in the end sacrificed in the interest of unanimous Allied approval of Wilson's larger agenda—the ill-fated League of Nations? Certainly, as was evident by the firestorm touched off in the Northcliffe-dominated British press, Wilson and House had to recognize that they would have a similar problem among right-wing journalists—or for that matter, right-wing, anti-communist senators who would be voting eventually on the Treaty of Versailles and the League. An agreement with Lenin would only sidetrack the Peace Conference from Wilson's primary goal of a world body, dominated by the democracies, that could guarantee the concepts of freedom and self-determination for which the United States had fought a world war.

In any event, Bullitt's mission and his agreement were all too little, too late. Bullitt had, as he recognized, developed a first, and unique, opportunity to open a direct channel to Lenin. Years later Dulles reflected that, like his own personal lapse in Switzerland when he chose tennis with a lady over a chat with Lenin, "here [in Paris] the first chance—if in fact it was a chance—to start talking with the Communist leaders was lost."

Bullitt, however, continued to lobby alone for his proposal, increasingly marginalizing himself and his cause. As Harold Nicolson observed after a chance meeting with Bullitt on April 11: "Bullitt there. A young man with beliefs. He was sent to Russia by the President and returned with a pro-Bolshevik report. He talks about them. I blink politely." On May 17, disgusted by the direction the Peace Conference was taking, Bullitt resigned from the State Department and headed for the Riviera for a rest. In September he was back in the United States, trout fishing in Maine, when he was summoned to testify before Senator

Henry Cabot Lodge's hearings on the Treaty of Versailles. He seized the moment to blast the document and the lost opportunities in Russia, which he described as "the acid test of good will."

For a time, Bullitt continued to romanticize the Russian revolution, eventually divorcing his wife and in the 1920s marrying Louise Bryant, widow of the American Leninist John Reed who had so glowingly portrayed the Bolshevik seizure of power in his book *Ten Days That Shook the World*. In 1933 Bullitt, who had become a close confidant of Franklin Delano Roosevelt and his secretary of state, Cordell Hull, lobbied hard for recognition of communist Russia and was rewarded by his designation as the first U.S. ambassador to the Soviet Union. By 1934, after Leningrad police had detained Bullitt and his daughter for "improperly crossing the street," the newly minted diplomat and veteran communist apologist was growing disenchanted. Within two years, he had come thoroughly to detest everything the Soviet Union represented—particularly the terror tactics of Joseph Stalin and the activities abroad of the Soviet secret police. "It is . . . perfectly clear that to speak of 'normal relations' between the Soviet Union and any other country is to speak of something which does not and will not exist," he cabled in 1935. The once avowed Bolshevik sympathizer had come to appreciate the nature of the beast he had earlier sought so ardently to embrace.

But the efforts to deal with communist Europe by no means came to an end in March 1919 with the collapse of the Bullitt initiatives. Not by a long shot. Bolshevism was a reality that continued to overshadow the Peace Conference during its formal deliberations and long afterward. The biggest problem faced by the delegates was how to deal with a regime that believed a global class war was inevitable and that it was only a matter of time before the masses of the West rose up against their oppressors, threw them over, and united with their Russian brethren in a global proletarian empire.

The peacemakers in Paris were finding it difficult, if not impossible, to deal directly with the Bolsheviks for their own peculiar domestic reasons, if nothing else. Still, they were faced with an immediate challenge in Central Europe that needed a resolution if all prospects for a comprehensive peace treaty with the Entente Powers were not to collapse. But the Peace Conference delegates really had no idea how to deal with any of these forces—Bolshevism, non-Russian communism, or a host of social-democratic political entities that were challenging the established order. Some of the Allied leaders, especially France's Marshal Ferdinand Foch, believed that force was the only way of expunging leftist tendencies from Europe—East or West. Others, including Bullitt and from time to time Wilson and House, believed that these forces needed to be drawn into a comprehensive European settlement based on principles of democracy and self determination. Ultimately, of course, the Peace Conference accepted neither course. And its reaction to the complex and kaleidoscopic situation in Hungary was a clear indication of its failure of will.

When we last saw Harold Nicolson, he was on the platform of the Gare de Lyon, preparing to board the Paris-Bucharest Express that would pass through Vienna, where a special five-car train was assembled to take them onward to Budapest. The goal of the Hungarian mission was twofold: first, to derail the French plan of sending a Rumanian force headed by General Charles "The Butcher" Mangin, victor of Charleroi, Verdun, and the Second Battle of the Marne, to pacify Hungary; second, to see if there was any way of using the new Bolshevik ruler of Hungary, Béla Kun, as a means of opening a permanent back-channel to Lenin.

Hungary had gone through a desperate period. A core component of the Austro-Hungarian Empire, one of the two defeated Entente Powers, it was in the process of being carved up—some might call it butchered. The goal of those doing the carving at the Peace Conference was to create new nations whose leadership and peoples had been at least nominally loyal to the victorious Allies during the war. Hungary was becoming the ultimate victim of every sort of prejudice, desire, and ultimate diplomatic and political error of the powers gathered in Paris. It had no real advocate there—no world-class virtuoso or wildly popular political figure who'd passed the war in America or Britain lobbying for his people. Its tiny population had sent few emigrants to the West to form a substantial voting bloc in any of the Allied nations. Few understood its people, its culture, even its language—a curious amalgam of Finnish and Mongolian, a remnant of the Mongols' invasion of Europe seven centuries earlier, which unlike any Latin, Germanic, or Slavic tongue was understood by few of the experts in Paris.

Hungary, which might have played a key role as an anchor in Clemenceau's cordon sanitaire, instead became a victim on every side. On one side there was the French desire to bolster the Czech Republic, which demanded all of Slovakia; on the other side there was the desire of Wilson to build a viable new nation of the South Slavs, or Yugoslavia, out of the remains of the Balkans and southern Hungary. Even the remote Rumanians, whose romantic culture won them at least a modicum of sympathy in Paris, had been awarded portions of southeastern Hungary while their armed forces were in the process of seizing even more territory. Back in January, Count Mihály Károlyi, the moderate president of what was left of Hungary, questioned Allen Dulles's friend Hugh Gibson, who reported the bitter remarks to the young coordinator of U.S. intelligence: "Why do you go on pretending you are fighting for the rights of small peoples? Why not say frankly, 'We have won and shall now do with you exactly as we please.' Hungary would then know definitely where we stand."

On March 19, 1919, the Allies effectively did just that. French Colonel Fernand Vyx, head of the Allied mission to Budapest, handed Károlyi the final delineation of the borders. It was the last straw. Károlyi resigned, and the communists under Béla Kun promptly seized power and announced the formation of the Hungarian Soviet Republic. Now the Smuts-Nicolson delegation heading to Budapest from Paris would effectively hammer the last nail into Hungary's coffin.

The new Hungarian leader whose measure they intended to take was a decidedly odd duck. Béla Kun, the thirty-three-year-old son of a Jewish father and a Protestant mother from Transylvania, looked as though he might have emerged from a Béla Lugosi film. Attracted to politics after schooling in a Calvinist grammar school in the Transylvanian town of Kolozsvar (now Cluj-Napoca in Rumania), at the age of twenty he changed his Jewish surname, Kohn, to the more politically acceptable Magyar equivalent, Kun. He developed into a fiery young man who fought several duels in his youth, became a muckraking journalist before the world war, but was forced to flee Kolozsvar after he was accused of embezzling funds from the local Social Insurance Board where he worked. Seized by the Russians during the war, he was sent to a POW camp in the Urals. There he was converted to communism and became caught up in the romance of the Russian Revolution. He fought for the Bolsheviks, became a protégé of the hard-line revolutionary Zinoviev, and organized the Hungarian Communist Party in Moscow, whose members Lenin began to call "kunerists."

After the armistice, backed by satchels of cash from the Comintern,

Kun returned to Hungary and began a vicious campaign against Károlyi, whose support from Paris was somewhat tenuous. Communist-led demonstrations against Károlyi's Social Democrats began to build in intensity until finally on February 22, 1919, a violent protest in front of a newspaper building left four policemen dead. Kun, arrested for high treason, was cursed as a Jew and beaten in public. As Kun was imprisoned, word spread of his bravery in the face of police brutality. With the fall of the Károlyi government on March 21, he was released from prison and promptly formed a "social democratic" government. Within days, he had purged the few socialists remaining in the cabinet. On March 21, Béla Kun proclaimed the Hungarian Soviet Republic. In Moscow, Lenin was delighted, but was as cautious in his own way as officials in Paris were in theirs. So two days later, he wired the new communist leader personally:

> Please inform us what real guarantees you have that the new Hungarian Government will actually be a communist, and not simply a socialist government, i.e., one [of] traitor-socialists. Have the Communists a majority in the government? Will the Congress of Soviets take place? What does the socialists' recognition of the dictatorship of the proletariat really amount to? It is altogether beyond doubt that it would be a mistake merely to imitate our Russian tactics in all details in the specific conditions of the Hungarian revolution. I must warn you against this mistake, but I should like to know where you see real guarantees.

While seeking the measure of his newest client state, Lenin was anything if not cautious. With no international telephone service available, he added, "So that I may be certain that the answer has come to me from you personally, I ask you to indicate in what sense I spoke to you about the National Assembly when you last visited me in the Kremlin."

The Peace Conference delegates in Paris clearly had similar aims—to take the temperature of the new Hungarian Soviet Republic that was promising a revolution in Central Europe. The Monday after the coup, a decidedly anti-Bolshevik Dulles handed Wilson a memo titled "The Present Situation in Hungary: Action Recommended by A.W. Dulles." The document included a three-point program to isolate Hungary while at the same time concluding that "France should no longer be allowed to make mischief to preserve her own power position in Eastern Europe."

So, two weeks later, the train bearing the Paris-based delegation pulled into Vienna en route to Budapest. For everyone on board, it was the first glimpse of life in the defeated half of Europe. "Town has an unkempt appearance," Nicolson wrote in his diary. "Paper laying about, grass plots round the statues strewn with litter, many windows broken and repaired by boards nailed up. People in streets dejected and ill-dressed. . . . I feel my plump pink face is an insult to these wretched people." He was embarrassed by the delegation's lavish lunch at the famed Sacher. "From now on we shall feed only upon our own army rations, and not take anything from these starving countries." At the "Bolshevik headquarters," where Nicolson went for a promise of safe passage for the delegation to Budapest, "the whole building reminds me of the refugee camps in the Balkan Wars." Still, the "commissar, a Galician Jew, educated in America, speaks English perfectly." After a series of hasty phone calls to Budapest, the consul, Elek Bolgár, produced the central question: Does the visit "mean that you recognize the government of Béla Kun?"

"That means nothing of the sort," Nicolson replied. "It means only that we are proceeding to Buda Pesth, and wish to discuss with the authorities at present in control of the capital the terms by which an armistice can be arranged between them and the Rumanians." The Allied mission was only, he added, seeking "safe conduct and civilized treatment." After a series of hastily exchanged telephone calls with Budapest, Bolgár conveyed the regime's agreement to receive the Allied delegation. That evening he joined Nicholson, Smuts, and their band aboard the special five-car train. Following an all-night trip across the Hungarian Puszta, they arrived at dawn the next day at Budapest's Ostbanhof rail station, where their sleeping cars were promptly surrounded by uniformed Red Guards with fixed bayonets. The delegation was on army field rations, and tempers were a bit short. Huge crowds pressed in to gawk at the long brown train parked at the platform.

Before long, Béla Kun arrived—described by Nicolson as "a little man of about 30, puffy white face and loose, wet lips, shaven head, impression of red hair, shifty suspicious eyes, he has the face of a sulky and uncertain criminal. He has with him a little oily Jew—fur coat rather moth-eaten, stringy green tie, dirty collar. He is their Foreign Secretary." They began by expanding at great length about the enormous benefits that Bolshevism could bring to Central Europe—as Nicolson put it, "work and happiness for all, free education, doctors, Bernard Shaw, garden suburbs, heaps of music, and the triumph of the machine. I ask him what machine. He makes a vague gesture embracing the whole world of mechanics." The discussion continued along similar lines. In the end, Béla Kun wanted to arrange a conference in Vienna or Prague of the states that were emerging from the Austro-Hungarian Empire. Smuts wanted him to come to Paris.

For the moment, the Paris folks got an eye-opening tour of Budapest. Most shops were shut, Nicolson reported, with everything shabby and bedraggled as the rain poured on pedestrians shuffling along the cracked sidewalks in little more than rags. Groups of fifteen to twenty Red Guards, armed with bayonets, swaggered through the streets carrying wooden hat-stands they had liberated from restaurants, each draped with "presents"—boots, sausages, red underwear that they had been "offered" from the few shops that were still open along their route. These were the overt signs of the Bolshevik Revolution in Hungary. At the Hungaria Hotel, a sad scene, a Potemkin village was assembled for the benefit of the visiting delegates. Lemonade and coffee were carefully placed on each table, and the revelers—all, it turned out, let out of a Red Army prison—were paralyzed with fear and totally silent. The delegation fled in horror back to their train for a final meeting with Béla Kun and his delegation, this time including the commander of the Red Guards.

Before the arrival of the Hungarians, however, the Paris delegation had another visitor. Ellis Ashmead-Bartlett, a patrician, Oxford-educated correspondent of the *Daily Telegraph*, boarded the train with a personal account of the revolution since, Nicolson observed, "he had the guts to remain when all the other people had bolted." His account of Béla Kun was somewhat different from the sketchy reports reaching Paris. The Bolshevik leader, Ashmead-Bartlett reported, "has little influence outside the capital, and the whole thing would collapse at the slightest push." That push, Béla Kun clearly feared, could be the very terms that Smuts presented. They seemed quite favorable—a standstill cease fire, with its implied recognition of the Bolshevik government of Hungary, followed by Allied occupation of a neutral zone between Hungarian and Rumanian forces that was fifteen miles more favorable to the Hungarians. And Smuts even accepted the notion of a major-power conference on Hungary that would have included its representatives.

After "consultations," most probably with Moscow, Kun returned to the train. He announced that he would accept Smuts's plan with a single condition—that the Rumanian army be ordered to withdraw behind the Maros River, which runs from southeastern Hungary (where the Rumanians had advanced) into northwestern Rumania. This condition was unacceptable to Smuts. He promptly ushered Kun and his delegation to the platform, where they watched with astonishment as the train began to roll out of the station, headed west to Prague and Paris—and with Ashmead-Bartlett at the last moment also on board. As Nicolson observed, "a plucky fellow. But his nerves were about to break."

Within days the Smuts-Nicolson mission was pronounced a "fiasco" in the press and the halls of the Peace Conference alike, and Hungary was fully at war with Czechoslovakia and the Kingdom of Rumania. At home, Kun's bloodthirsty mob descended into a Thermidor-like reign of terror, with revolutionary tribunals ordering as many as six hundred executions, including of clerics and landowners, and even seizing grain from defenseless peasants. Wilson, who believed that "to try and stop a revolutionary movement with field armies is like using a broom to stop a vast flood," succeeded in blocking Clemenceau's desire to send Allied forces into the country. Eventually a July military offensive by Kun's troops ended in disaster as the promised reinforcement by Russian Bolsheviks failed to materialize when they were pinned down in Ukraine. By late July Rumanian forces, advised by General Louis Franchet d'Espérey, nicknamed "desperate Frankie" by the British, had fought their way to Budapest. They seized and looted the capital and began their own reign of terror, which led to five thousand executions, quickly eclipsing the communists and especially targeting the Jewish minority as responsible for the nation's dire economic straits. As for Kun himself, he fled to Austria, made his way to Moscow, and in 1939 became a victim of Stalin's bloody purge of the Comintern.

The Allies had counted on the Smuts mission as a way to build a truly free and independent Hungary. It was equally clear, however, that Wilson's naive concept of self-determination would never work in Central and Eastern Europe, where every power simply wanted as much territory as its military forces could grab and a plague on whatever nationality or ethnic group happened to be living on those territories at the moment. In Hungary, instead of at least a nominally democratic government like those the Allies managed to encourage in Czechoslovakia and Poland, a right-wing government came to power that continued to drift even more sharply to the right as the depression of the 1930s deepened. Separated from its natural resource–heavy regions by the Peace Conference's imposed boundaries, Hungary saw its industries slowly strangle. The nation's right-wing ruler, Miklós Horthy, appointed a succession of increasingly reactionary prime ministers. Each moved Hungary closer to Germany, especially after the arrival in power of Hitler, who appeared to promise relief from its economic suffocation. The Nazis were followed by the Soviet communists, who came to power in 1944 to 1945 and who appeared to promise their own form of relief. This relief, however, came with its own high price—the nation's freedom, which it was unable to regain until early 1989, when Soviet leader Mikhail Gorbachev announced at the United Nations that he was withdrawing Warsaw Pact troops. Hungary was finally free to determine its own future.

Throughout the occupation of their territory during the nearly five decades of communist rule after World War II, it was clear that the Hungarians intended to find a truly Hungarian way of assuring their own intellectual and social survival as a race and as a nationality. What the misguided and self-serving national leaders failed to give the Hungarians in Paris was any clear road map toward legitimate self-government—the same way they failed most of the other nations they had either created or destroyed. Blinded to the reality of Hungary's situation, they also failed to provide the artificial nation they created out of the ruins of war with the wherewithal to become a viable country—in economic, political, diplomatic, or military terms. Stripped of its natural resources and of defensible natural frontiers based on geographical realities, it was forced to fend for itself and look to what was often the least palatable ally for its very survival.

Small, ethnically homogeneous states (when the dust settled, Hungary was 90 percent Magyar) can survive, even thrive—witness the nations that emerged from the breakup of Yugoslavia in the past decade—if their creators simply give them the wherewithal. None of the major powers in Paris had the vision or the gumption to do that. Ironically, however, in the end the strong-willed Hungarians proved theirs to be the Central European nation most capable of surviving over the rest of the century. While Clemenceau and his French military advisers were scheming with Czechs and Rumanians to divide up Hungary and make certain that the Austro-Hungarian Empire could never rise again in alliance with Germany, the Hungarian people were cultivating their own peculiar national identity. It was a self-image strong enough to carry them through an abortive and violent uprising against the Soviets in 1956 and into a long rule by a benevolent home-grown communist, János Kádár. In the late 1970s, Kádár's house in the hills of Buda was across the street from the modest home of one of the nation's leading intellectuals, the poet Gyula Illyés who, unlike such Czech counterparts as Václav Havel, never spent a day in a communist prison. Today Hungary, as a member of the European community, has one of the strongest economies and most active capital markets in Central Europe.

The most important reality in 1919 was the great power that was on the march on the eastern fringe of Europe and that remained both a threat and an enigma to the Allies. The failure of the Smuts mission to Budapest and its inability to open a back channel communication via Béla Kun to Lenin by no means discouraged the peacemakers in Paris from seeking some way of dealing with the Bolsheviks in Moscow. Throughout the period that the conference was proceeding, various forces—public and private—were doing their best to move the conferees toward some accommodation with the Russians. Two of these individuals were Vance McCormick and Oscar Straus. McCormick was one of the quiet giants of the U.S. delegation to Paris. A former newspaper publisher and gubernatorial candidate in Pennsylvania, he was chairman of the Democratic National Committee at the time Wilson sailed for Paris. Not surprisingly, Wilson and House paid very close attention to his views. He believed devoutly that the Allies needed to formulate a policy that could reach, and neutralize, the Bolshevik menace. He believed with equal fervor that the most direct route to the Bolsheviks' heart was through their stomachs. At the same time, McCormick rarely saw a party or gala dinner he could pass up, so by the end of January 1919, as the social whirl of Paris was moving into high gear, he often made his way to the most auspicious tables for pushing his points of view.

On the evening of January 30, McCormick found himself sitting at dinner with Lloyd George. The American seized the opportunity to broach the subject of a limited program of feeding the starving masses of Petrograd, the city where the Russian Revolution had begun. The British prime minister was unimpressed, but this hardly fazed a veteran politician who had managed to bring to heel a host of ward bosses from Chicago to Boston. He spent the ensuing weeks building alliances and renewing old acquaintances. One of these was with Oscar Straus.

Straus was one of three extraordinary brothers, the sons of a German Jewish immigrant peddler. Nathan and Isidor Straus owned two of New York's most prominent retail establishments: R. H. Macy's in Manhattan and Abraham & Straus in Brooklyn. When President Theodore Roosevelt tapped Straus as secretary of Commerce and Labor, he became the first Jew ever to hold a Cabinet seat in the United States. A lawyer by training, Straus spent much of his life in public service while his two brothers built the family business. Straus came to Paris with unofficial, but nevertheless powerful, portfolios. He represented the American Jewish community in support of Jewish minorities in Europe and served as chairman of the League to Enforce Peace, a grassroots group that Wilson was counting on to get his beloved League of Nations past a skeptical U.S. Senate. With Jews representing one of the largest minorities in Russia (many of Lenin's top deputies were themselves Jewish), and with his son Roger serving as a member of the eight-thousand-man American Expeditionary Force in Siberia, it wasn't a long stretch for Straus to expand his portfolio of interests to the plight of this beleaguered nation.

With the collapse of the Prinkipo initiative and while Bullitt was in the midst of his own mission to Moscow, Straus laid on a dinner on March 4, 1919, in the fabulous Paris apartment he'd been loaned by the wealthy Jewish philanthropist Edward Mamelsdorf on the fashionable Avenue Montaigne. The guests included both sides in the bitter

Oscar Straus, the former United States Commerce Secretary, the first Jew to hold a cabinet office. Representing the American Jewish community, he arrived in Paris without an official portfolio, but he became an important behind-the-scenes figure.

civil war in Russia. Boris Bakhmetev, the Russian ambassador to Washington, had arrived in Paris as a Bolshevik observer. Sergei Sazonov, once the czar's foreign minister and then ambassador to London, represented White Russian interests. Also breaking bread at this rare gathering of opposing forces was Herbert Hoover, Europe's food czar, and Vance McCormick. Straus recalled later that they simply "discussed the rehabilitation of commerce with Russia." But there was much more, and McCormick was ready. Before the group had even arrived at dessert, the wily negotiator was on his feet, as he later described it, presenting a "scheme for economic relief of Russia by joint Allied and neutral action, and distribution under proper military protection." Afterward, apparently pretty satisfied with the results, McCormick recalled that he "walked home [under a] beautiful moonlight night. First fine day." On arriving at his rooms in the Ritz Hotel on the Place Vendôme, he learned that the Queen of Rumania had taken the suite next door. "Things are certainly doing tonight," he concluded. (The next morning he learned, however, that the queen had asked that his sitting room be turned over to her, confining him to a single bedroom to live and work, observing "but we have to give way to Royalty, notwithstanding we hear so much of 'Bolshevism.'")

Over the next few weeks, pressure built for some action to be taken on behalf of the starving people in Russia as reports arrived in Paris. The most graphic came from Major Robert Whitney Imbrie, nominally vice consul in Viborg, Finland, but in fact a close friend and agent of Allen Dulles. Imbrie was a confirmed anti-Bolshevik and the last U.S. diplomat in Petrograd when the Bolsheviks took over in 1917–1918. A flamboyant and volatile personality, the young Yale Law School graduate made a name for himself by repeatedly pounding on the desk of Moissei Ouritsky, confronting the feared head of the Chekha secret police who terrorized thousands of Russians. Finally forced to flee Russia, he ended up in Finland where, during the Peace Conference, he operated a vast intelligence network in Bolshevik Russia. Imbrie was later murdered while serving as an agent for Dulles in Tehran in 1924.

Many of the dispatches he relayed to Dulles made a powerful case for food aid to the Russian people, especially in the Bolshevik-controlled zones. Imbrie reported widespread starvation in both Petrograd and Moscow that was leading to rapid depopulation of the cities, a flight to the countryside with potentially catastrophic results for a desperate and widening group. The scope of the problem was clearly beyond the means of the International Red Cross, whose resources in Central Europe were already stretched to the limits despite the most valiant efforts of its chairman, J. P. Morgan banker Henry Pomeroy Davison. Even before Bullitt returned from Moscow, Wilson had realized that his initiative would never fly. A food plan might be just the ticket—one led by Hoover who, himself a confirmed anticommunist, no doubt believed it was a way to extend U.S. influence into the interior of Russia. Perhaps this might even help tilt the mass of the people away from the Bolsheviks and toward the Western capitalists who were feeding them.

Whatever others' motives might be, Wilson was becoming increasingly desperate to reach out in some fashion to Lenin, the Bolshevik leadership, and particularly the people of Russia. Wilson continued to believe that they should be the ultimate targets of his efforts. Now, under the prodding of McCormick, Straus, and Colonel House, Wilson turned to Hoover. Ironically, Bullitt himself may have given Wilson the idea when the cable of his peace proposal included the information that "the economic conditions of Soviet Russia are tragic. . . . Everyone . . . is pitifully under-nourished. . . . There are no medicines; men, women and children die by hundreds who might otherwise be saved."

Since Wilson had designated Hoover as the man to be responsible for feeding the starving masses of Europe, especially the conquered territories, in the months following the armistice, his possible involvement in Russia was by no means a new idea. As early as June 13, 1918, with the war in Europe still raging and U.S. troops in the thick of it, Colonel House had written to Wilson from his vacation retreat in Magnolia, Massachusetts, just outside Gloucester. He suggested that Hoover head a "'Russian Relief Commission' [that] will typify in the Russian mind what was done in Belgium, and I doubt whether any government in Russia, friendly or unfriendly, would dare oppose his coming in. . . . Hoover has ability as an organizer, his name will carry weight in the direction desired, and his appointment will, for the moment, settle the Russian question as far as it can be settled by you at present." Hoover even journeyed personally to Magnolia to discuss this plan. But despite House's approval, it went nowhere.

At the time, there was mounting pressure from the Allies for the United States to expand its involvement in the war in western Europe by sending military forces into Russia, nominally to safeguard prepositioned military supplies from seizure by the Germans and eventually the Bolsheviks. Indeed, small American Expeditionary Forces were dispatched to Murmansk in northwestern Russia (five thousand men under British leadership) and Siberia (eight thousand men) mainly to guard supplies stockpiled in the west and the Trans-Siberian Railroad in the east, which was the evacuation route of fifty thousand members of the Czech legion. These forces were still in place when the Peace Conference convened, and while they had been nominally neutral in the civil war, they had fought some scattered skirmishes with Bolshevik forces. Still, throughout the last months of the war and into the Peace Conference, Wilson resisted any wide involvement in the civil war or, for that matter, feeding the Russian people.

With Hoover in charge of a broader food plan to feed postwar Western Europe, the army of food experts he assembled did provide the best regular snapshot of life in each of these nations, including Russia. According to his informants, large portions of these regions were imminently faced with widespread starvation. As many as 100,000 persons a month were dying in Petrograd alone. Then, of course, there was the political situation. "Russia was probably among the worst problems before the Peace Conference," Hoover reported. "It was the Banquo's ghost sitting at every Council table." Finally, on March 27, Wilson told House to talk with Hoover about a food mission to Russia. Hoover was ecstatic, immediately embracing as his own the scheme first cooked up by McCormick and Straus. Understanding what truly motivated Wilson, Hoover wrote the next day to the President:

> As the result of Bolshevik economic conceptions, the people of Russia are dying of hunger and disease at the rate of some hundreds of thousands monthly in a country that formerly supplied food to a large part of the world. . . . The Bolshevik ascendancy . . . represent the not unnatural violence of a mass of ignorant humanity, who themselves have learned in grief of tyranny and violence over generations. Our people, who enjoy so great liberty and general comfort, cannot fail to sympathize to some degree with these blind gropings for better social conditions. . . . [There is danger] the Bolshevik centers now stirred by great emotional hopes will undertake large military crusades in

an attempt to impose their doctrines on other defenseless people. We have also to contemplate what would actually happen if we undertook military intervention. We would probably be involved in years of police duty.

From the outset, Hoover saw this mission from a humanitarian perspective but very much as an anti-Bolshevik measure as well. As Gordon Auchincloss described Hoover's views for House, "He feels that as soon as the fighting stops the Bolshevik army will disintegrate and the distribution of food to the people of Russia will make them less eager to continue their policy of agitation." Still, ÿHoover also recognized that any initiative involving the direct hand of a major capitalist power would be viewed with deep suspicion by Lenin and his crowd. So he proposed a neutral intermediary "of international reputation for probity" as a front for this effort. The person he settled on was Fridtjof Nansen. The renowned fifty-eight-year-old Norwegian explorer, product of a wealthy, even titled family, had distinguished himself in 1895 by departing Siberia and becoming the closest man to approach the North Pole at the time. He had come to the attention of Hoover and McCormick during the war when, by then a neutral statesman and opposed to conflict, Nansen had come to Washington seeking food for his isolated homeland.

By the start of the Peace Conference, Nansen had little to occupy himself. His days of exploration were long finished and he was living on a fading reputation. He had brought to Paris a letter of introduction to Colonel House from Lady Kathleen Scott, widow of Antarctic explorer Ronald Scott. Her beauty and charms had won over both House and, particularly, Nansen, seventeen years her senior. Nansen's unpopularity with Norwegian politicians at home coupled with his irrepressible womanizing had excluded him from his nation's tiny delegation to the Paris conference. Still, he had the introduction to House and he had maintained ties to the Russia he had loved since his early days in Siberia. As Nansen sat around Paris seeking a mission, Sazonov, representing the White Russians at the Peace Conference, asked the Norwegian to help raise $100 million to arm White Russian forces in the fight against the Bolsheviks. While there's no evidence Nansen actually embarked on this fund-raising effort, such companions were unlikely to win him many friends among Lenin's crowd. It's not clear that

Hoover, McCormick, or even House was aware of all his extracurricular activities at the time. What they sought was a "neutral" with an impeccable image back home in the United States. And that's what Nansen seemed to bring to the table. By April 3, 1919, Nansen had drafted a proposal for Wilson:

> to organize a purely humanitarian commission for the provisioning of Russia, the foodstuffs and medical supplies to be paid for perhaps to some considerable degree by Russia itself, the justice of distribution to be guaranteed by such a commission, the membership of the commission to be comprised of Norwegian, Swedish and possibly Dutch, Danish and Swiss nationalities. It does not appear that the existing authorities in Russia would refuse the intervention of such a commission of wholly non-political order, devoted solely to the humanitarian purpose of saving life.

On April 9, the day the Smuts-Nicolson mission returned to Paris and was branded a "fiasco," the Big Four—Wilson, Lloyd George, Clemenceau, and Italy's Vittorio Orlando—gave Nansen their approval to put together a plan. The devil, however, was in the details—or at least the caveats. The plan, while enormous and expensive, would carry with it several key provisions: "neutral" (that is, Western, capitalist) observers would be responsible for distributing food in Bolshevik-controlled regions; the Bolsheviks would have to halt all military action at home and cease all foreign military adventures in support of disturbances (Hungary was top of mind, of course). But at the same time, as Hoover wrote, "This plan does not involve any recognition . . . of the Bolshevik murderers now in control." In short, the plan involved substantial intervention by the Allied powers in Russian territory controlled by Lenin's forces. What appeared at the outset to be a reasonable concept, involving a tentative extension of a hand of friendship, had turned into yet another capitalist method of co-opting and slowing the communist advance in Eastern Europe. Even this, however, was too much for the White Russians in Paris, who also turned thumbs down on a proposal that seemed calculated to extend the life and power of the Bolsheviks in the regions they controlled. In short, the proposal appeared to be fraught with problems across the political spectrum in Russia.

Eight days later, however, an undaunted (or oblivious) Nansen was ready to dispatch his plan to Lenin—though it was couched in less inflammatory language than had been circulated among the Allied leaders in Paris. Alas, the dispatch was to have been sent by the French government–controlled Eiffel Tower Radio Station; but while Clemenceau had consented to the plan, he had concluded privately that White Russian forces were on the verge of defeating the Bolsheviks on the battlefield, and he wanted to give no aid and comfort to the enemy. So Nansen's message never went out. Another colossal error in judgment. Even that brief delay may have made all the difference. Ten days later, with no response, Hoover recalled, "I became suspicious and sent Nansen's dispatch to Lenin to our [food committee] representative in Holland with instructions to send it again from the Dutch radio station." Nansen also had it dispatched via the Norwegian foreign ministry in Christiania. Then he sat back to wait, indulging in a round of parties that included, as Nansen biographer Roland Huntford described, one marathon evening beginning in the Bois de Boulogne and winding up in the Paris studio of a Norwegian artist, where one guest injured his knee trying to lift a fat Pole, and a young woman fell and broke her leg.

In Moscow, the Nansen cable was met with mixed reactions from the Bolshevik leadership. The Russians acknowledged they'd received it on May 3 from the Dutch. Lenin quickly decided it could be turned to the Bolsheviks' advantage. He told Foreign Minister Chicherin and his deputy Maxim Litvinov to draft a reply: "My advice is to use it for propaganda, for clearly it can serve no other useful purpose. . . . Be extremely polite to Nansen, extremely insolent to Wilson, Lloyd George and Clemenceau. This is . . . the only way to speak to them." Lenin instantly recognized the plan for what it was—at least after the Big Four had finished with it. So he told Chicherin and Litvinov how to reply to Nansen: "This is politics! You are an educated man, Mr. Nansen, you know perfectly well that every war and every truce is politics. This means YOU have linked the 'humanitarian' with the 'political.' You have lumped them together. Explain to him, as you would to a 16-year-old schoolgirl, why a truce is politics."

And that was, effectively, the end of it. The final draft of the Bolshevik response included a lengthy diatribe against the Allies' inhuman blockade of Russia, asserting it to be the root cause of the widespread starvation. The note suggested that with the blockade ended, the Bolsheviks could do very nicely on their own feeding their people, thank you very much. If it was a cessation of hostilities in the civil war that the Allies really wanted, this end should not be thinly camouflaged by a humanitarian gesture. "It is of course impossible for us to make any concessions referring to these fundamental problems of our existence under the disguise of a presumably humanitarian work," Chicherin concluded his message.

The reply went out by wireless on May 7, though it took eight days to reach Paris. It was the last substantive communication between East and West through the Peace Conference mechanism. By this time, it appeared as though Clemenceau was right—the White Russian forces were having some substantial victories on the battlefield against the Bolsheviks. The very narrow window of opportunity of some accommodation, or at least dialogue, between the West and the Bolsheviks that a prompt and reasonable exchange of messages might have opened had slammed shut.

The peacemakers in Paris never fully understood the Russian people, nor did they make much of an effort in that direction. The Allies paid scant attention to the handful of their specialists who did appreciate the peculiar pride and the xenophobia that had motivated that nation for centuries under the despotism of the czars and the Bolsheviks alike. Instead of accommodation, relations descended into a long freeze of isolation and bitterness that was to mark the rest of the twentieth century. Might the tentative overtures to communist Russia have been framed differently—less confrontational, less clearly a challenge than a genuine openhanded offer? Perhaps. But not in the context of all the other fears and hopes that were washing through the corridors of power in Paris in 1919.

Motivated by their prejudices and fears, each of these arrogant leaders was intent on his own particular agenda. Containing Russia, communism, and Bolshevism took precedence over a real possibility of détente in an age before the word ever acquired the fraught meanings it would conjure up later in the century. Instead, all was lost for generations of men and women east and west. To the end, Wilson held out for his principle of self-determination—at all costs, and the cost for the Russian people for eight decades was a very high one indeed. Five days before he signed the final Treaty of Versailles and left Paris for Washington, Wilson told McCormick: "The Russian people must solve their own problems without outside interference. . . . Europe had made a great mistake when they attempted to interfere in the French Revolution. It seems hard on the present Russian generation, but in the long run it means less distress for Russia."

Another grotesque miscalculation, of course, by a confirmed ideologue whose efforts to adhere unswervingly to a concept that was proven again and again inapplicable to rapidly evolving conditions on the ground was simply a foretaste of similar failures by successive Western dealings with Russia. The final months of the Peace Conference, after the collapse of the Hoover-Nansen and Bullitt initiatives, were devoted largely to inventive methods of helping the White Russian military activities on the ground. For a brief period, these succeeded in slowing Bolshevik advances into some of the non-Russian territories that eventually became part of the Soviet Union and Lenin's efforts to extend communism into Central and Western Europe. But by the late fall of 1919, after the world leaders had departed from Paris, though not before the Peace Conference finally disbanded, and on into the early weeks of 1920, the White Russian movement collapsed. The Bolsheviks began moving into and annexing Azerbaijan and Armenia. In 1921 the Bolsheviks were solidly in control, and as a famine swept across the nation, they finally accepted Hoover's assistance. Ironically, by 1922 Hoover's food administration was feeding at least ten million Russians—all in Bolshevik-controlled regions. None of this, however, did much to remove the bitter taste left by the attitudes of the peacemakers of Paris.

As the treaty was about to be signed, British Foreign Secretary Lord George Curzon lamented that he had serious doubts that "this moribund conference is capable in its death throes of producing a Russian policy." And on June 6, Lloyd George warned his fellow heads of state that "there is one Power which was constantly overlooked in this Conference, namely, Russia. At the moment it has gone to pieces but in five years who could tell what it would be." An even more shortsighted Wilson dismissed the British prime minister's fears with a flip remark that "the Slavs have nowhere shown the organization that made the Teuton [German] so dangerous." Of broader importance, none of these world leaders was able to see further than his own self-interest.

Three days before Christmas in 1919, with Bolshevik military fortunes on the ascendancy, Soviet leaders proposed to British representatives in Copenhagen that they would be prepared to exchange Russian flax and raw materials for manufactured goods. Two weeks later, E. F.

Wise, a leading British socialist and the nation's representative on the Allies' Supreme Economic Council, stressed that Russian raw materials could bring down world industrial prices substantially. By January 16, 1920, the West agreed to end its support of all anti-Bolshevik activities in return for opening trade and banking to Western, particularly British, interests. In short, many of Wilfred Sheed's worst fears came to pass—that British bankers would drive a procommunist agenda and cement the forces of Bolshevism in Europe for pecuniary interests.

Still, all of this was too late to resolve the fundamental problem the Allies faced at the Peace Conference—the intellectual and moral construct of believing Wilson's "democratic" solutions were in the best interests of all peoples. Much the same dilemma has bedeviled successor administrations dealing with such disparate societies as Vietnam and Iraq. What, after all, was the real difference between supporting the White Russians of 1919 and supporting Ngo Dinh Diem in Vietnam or anti-Saddam forces in Iraq? For the peacemakers in Paris, the religion of Bolshevism and Lenin's political shock troops of the Comintern were today's Islam and terrorism. The West reacted similarly to these parallel threats. In January 1920, a British War Office communiqué, riffing on a speech by War Minister Winston Churchill, detailed how if Bolshevism were allowed to continue its expansion, ultimately joining forces with the rising nationalism of Islam and a desperate, defeated Germany, the world would know no mercy. These Western opponents of communism were, perhaps, listening to the words of Leon Trotsky (né Lev Bronstein), Marxist theorist, founder/commander of the Red Army, and the People's Commissar of War, when he described the world war just ended as: "destined to do away ruthlessly with existing frontiers between the states, establishing upon their ruins the United States of Europe. . . . This would be the next task of the triumphant revolutionary proletariat. . . . Salvation of the Russian Revolution lies in its propagation all over Europe [while] India, Morocco and Egypt were to be liberated, along with all the colonies in general."

As seen from this perspective, to those dealing with these apparently deadly issues of that era, the stakes appeared even higher in Russia and Hungary of 1919 than today. Then, the entire capitalist economic and political system seemed under attack. Yet today, the West has still failed to learn from its errors, which played out on an even broader stage than during our own time. While the peacemakers of Paris considered themselves at once the world's government and supreme court, they failed to behave as such on numerous fronts, but none more catastrophically than in their dealings with communist Europe. Leaving the communist nations out of the European peace accord and barring them from the League of Nations baked major instability into the system, particularly as economic dislocations developed globally in the 1930s. Even Lloyd George recognized this, warning Clemenceau and Wilson prophetically in a private meeting at Wilson's house on the Place des États-Unis that since "Russia is not in the League of Nations, there is no control over her." Wilson made no reply.

So when Lenin gave way to Stalin, unchecked by any foreign forces, the Soviet despot had a free hand to embark on an all but unprecedented reign of terror against his enemies, real or imagined. With Russia absent from the League of Nations, no international mechanism was in a position to challenge Stalin's actions at home or the vast propaganda and espionage machine the Comintern assembled abroad. At the same time, the Allied actions in Paris in 1919 set the stage for a Russian tilt toward the Allies' enemy, Germany, and the Soviet-German Non-Aggression Pact of 1939—the scenario most feared by Clemenceau, who never lived to see that day. The Molotov-Ribbentrop agreement gave Hitler the free hand he needed to embark on his catastrophic adventures across Europe.

Lenin was actually delighted by the entire outcome in Paris—even the League of Nations that had failed to include him. "Every day of the existence of the Covenant [of the League] is the best agitation for Bolshevism,"ŸLenin told the Comintern in 1920. Still, the delay by the West in lifting the blockade of Russia, which even on June 17, 1919, Wilson admitted, had no real legal justification, contributed substantially to the great famine that swept Russia in the bitter winter of 1919 to 1920. And despite the late arrival of Hoover's food brigade, that famine helped persuade a vast part of the Russian people that perhaps Lenin was right in his portrayal of the capitalist West. As late as the 1980s, Russian citizens would still on occasion bring up their abandonment by the West to American visitors probing the origins of the great gulf between capitalism and communism.

As there descended across Europe first what the Peace Conference managed to assemble of Clemenceau's cordon sanitaire, then Churchill's iron curtain, the Bolshevik half of the continent was severed socially and economically as well as politically from the democratic half. The vast mass of the Russian, then the Central European, population was effectively cut off from any contact with the West, with no criteria to measure the performance of their own leaders—or their way of life. The Bolsheviks did manage to assemble a Teutonic-style bureaucracy of remarkable brutality, if not the efficiency that a shortsighted Wilson had so little credited them with the ability to evolve. It sufficed for seventy years to keep half of Europe enslaved. Moreover, the lack of economic engagement and the resource-drain of the cold war kept their standard of living virtually unchanged for decades.

From the 1950s through the 1980s, the Soviet Union managed to maintain a nuclear parity with the United States, but Moscow remained a city dominated by the same seven huge, grim, wedding-cake-style buildings Stalin built in the 1950s that served as the characteristic feature of the skyline until capitalism returned. While Moscow sought to extend the power of communism far beyond its frontiers—fomenting "independence movements" from Asia across the Middle East to Africa and into the Caribbean and Central America—it never once achieved, or even aspired to, the kind of self-governing democracy that Wilson had sought to establish so many years before. This should, of course, have come as no surprise. The peacemakers in Paris gave no incentive to any such accommodation, made no effort to understand the needs and wants of the Russian people. The monolithic structure that was the result of the Bolshevik success did help the Soviet Union get through desperate times during the Nazi invasion of World War II and survive a debilitating postwar reconstruction. But it also kept the nation mired in a primitive isolation that left the bulk of its people living at little above subsistence level and under the thumb of a vicious internal security apparatus.

The various paths not taken have only now come full circle, with the West welcoming these nations into the world economic and political community—from NATO and the European Community for much of Central Europe to the G8 group of developed nations that now includes Russia, serving in 2006 as its chair. It was an outcome promised by the West in Paris nearly a century earlier, and never delivered.

8

INTO THE
BALKAN SOUP

A HAIL OF CABLEGRAMS URGING JAN SMUTS AND HAROLD
Nicolson to continue eastward, past Budapest to Bucharest and Belgrade, failed to reach the delegates on board their special train. For in
their absence, the focus of the Peace Conference had shifted suddenly
to what had been Europe's tinderbox for centuries—the Balkans. There
were many sparks for this tinderbox. The principal fireworks were the
land grabs in this remote corner of southeastern Europe. Yugoslavia
(known then as the Kingdom of Serbs, Croats, and Slovenes) and neighboring Rumania both sought to improve the size and shape of their own
lands. At the same time Italy, one of the four Allied Powers, had its own
designs on many of these same territories.

If the anchors of Central Europe, Poland and Czechoslovakia, had
Józef Pilsudski and Ignace Paderewski, Tomáš Masaryk and Edvard
Beneš, then the bulwarks of the Balkans—Yugoslavia and Rumania—
had Nikola Pašić and Ante Trumbić, Ion Brătianu and Queen Marie.
But these Balkan leaders had far different attributes; their nations, far
different agendas. The hatreds and emotions that motivated them were
different from anything the West had ever needed to deal with or might
imagine. But now, at the peace talks, they all found themselves again
right in the middle of bitter and complex intrigues as a host of contesting

parties jockeyed for position and the Allies debated the creation of a new European power—Yugoslavia, nation of the South Slavs.

It was, from its birth, a nation in name only—a curious hodgepodge of nationalities, languages, alphabets, and religions from Latin to Slav, Orthodox Christianity to Catholicism to Islam. Yugoslavia's creation, not to mention its long-term viability, was far more a tribute to potent external forces than to any natural or internal cohesion. There was, first and foremost, Serbia. The region's dominant kingdom jealously guarded its Orthodox religion, its Slavic language and alphabet, and the independence it had won centuries before from invading Ottoman Turks. Then there were Croatia and Slovenia—Catholic states with a Latin alphabet, which for centuries had been the oppressed backwaters of the Austro-Hungarian Empire. Serb and Croat, Orthodox and Catholic, Balkan and European—a volatile and explosive mixture, all forced to become one nation.

And each of the principal players was a product of its own unique background. The guardian of Serbian preeminence was seventy-three-year-old Nikola Pašić, born in 1846 in Zajecar, barely five miles from the hotly contested border between Serbia and Bulgaria. The region could trace its history to the Emperor Gaius Galerius Valerius Maximianus who, in the late third and early fourth centuries, used it as his base for conquests of Persian territory and the eastern Roman Empire. By the time the delegates began arriving in Paris, Pašić himself had seen a host of Balkan wars, conflicts, and assassinations that marked the nineteenth and early twentieth centuries, long before any Western power became very interested in what had become a remote backwater of Europe. By the age of thirty-seven Pašić had already become deeply involved in radical politics, narrowly escaping a death sentence for plotting against King Milan I of Serbia, and finally, in 1904, rising to the post of prime minister that he was to occupy for another twenty years. Pašić was every inch a Balkan politician—from his piercing blue eyes that were as lethal as a Serbian scimitar, to the dense white beard that cascaded to his belt. While his knowledge of French and German was rudimentary, he had a working knowledge of Bulgarian and Russian, but more often used a sloppy Serbian argot, expressed in a powerful voice, to cut opponents down with a single phrase. And among his opponents he numbered anyone who failed to recognize the supremacy of Serbia in the Balkan arena.

Not surprisingly, one of these opponents was Ante Trumbić—a brilliant Croatian diplomat, a sharp-faced, owl-eyed little man who was the antithesis of everything Pašić represented. Pašić was eighteen years old when Trumbić was born in the Dalmatian town of Split, a bastion of Roman Catholic Croatia, which overlooks the crystal blue waters of the Adriatic. Trumbić studied law in the provincial capital of Zagreb before moving on to graduate studies in Vienna, capital of the Austro-Hungarian Empire of which Croatia was a remote outpost. At the age of thirty-three, Trumbić joined the lower house of the Austrian Parliament in 1897. In Parliament, he was a reformer in name only, arguing for constitutional changes that would have provided greater autonomy for Croatia and his beloved Dalmatia, but firmly within the imperial system. It was an evolutionary attitude and state of mind that was to prove enormously frustrating in his later years at the negotiating table as he crossed swords repeatedly with Pašić. For this aging Balkan politician, reform meant revolutionary change and Serbian supremacy. Trumbić, as it turned out, had little interest in swapping one imperial overlord (Austria-Hungary) for another (Serbia). But it was the war that truly separated the one from the other.

With the outbreak of hostilities, Trumbić fled his beloved Split for Italy, then to Paris, where he set up the Yugoslav Committee. Along the way, he managed to win the friendship and admiration of some Western experts who would prove crucial to the Yugoslav cause—the powerful London journalist H. Wickham Steed and the brilliant British historian and propagandist R. W. Seton-Watson, among many others. Still, Trumbić's Yugoslav Committee was, from its earliest days, but a poor imitation of the powerful exile committees of Masaryk and Beneš's Czechoslovakia and Paderewski's Poland. The committee's leadership was heavily Croatian, as well as Slovenian, and from the start, was particularly active abroad. The neighboring Kingdom of Serbia was preoccupied at home—under direct attack from the armed forces of Germany and Austria-Hungary.

By October 9, 1915, Belgrade had fallen to Austro-Hungarian and German forces, and within a month the Serbian army, accompanied by Pašić and his nation's government, were in full flight across Montenegro to the Adriatic, where they crossed to the island of Corfu and set up a government in exile. And they began looking for friends and allies. These were hard to find. Despite its alliance with Britain and France and its battles with the Central Powers, Serbia was a defeated nation with no territory, a battered army, and a remote government with few ties to the West. Croatia was not much better off—officially, in fact, a unit of the very empire whose forces had sent the Serbs on their long retreat to Corfu. But the Yugoslav Committee, representing the rebellious provinces of Croatia and Slovenia, was very much a reality. Indeed, as early as May 12, 1915, Trumbić's organization had proclaimed a federation of the South Slavs, including Serbia—all Balkan nationalities united in their hatred of Austria-Hungary. At that point in time, though, Serbia seemed to have little need for such an alliance. Russia was still Serbia's principal guarantor, an alliance cemented by family and blood ties. Grand Prince Nikolai Nikolaevich, the czar's cousin, was the great-uncle of Prince Alexander, the ruler of Serbia. And Russia was fighting on the side of the Allies.

But Pašić began picking up some disturbing rumblings. On April 26, 1915, France, Britain, and Russia had concluded a secret Treaty of London with Italy in an effort to bring that nation into a conflict that had proven not to be the simple six-month romp in the park that was envisioned at the outset. To bring its forces into the war on the Allied side, Italy had set some stringent demands, including a takeover of the entire Dalmatian coast of Croatia, much of its Istrian peninsula, and— the most difficult for Serbia to swallow—the territory of Albania as well.

At the same time, the Allies were in the midst of serious negotiations in efforts to bring into their camp the other principal Balkan states, Rumania and Bulgaria. Each was making its own demands. The Bulgarians wanted to recover Macedonia, which the Serbs had won in the Second Balkan War. Rumania had its eyes on all of the Banat, much of it occupied predominantly by Serbs. With Serbia overrun by enemy forces, it had little negotiating power while these secret treaties were being discussed behind their backs. Serbia and Croatia would need some powerful political and diplomatic muscle—and were better off together rather than separate. In this atmosphere, Yugoslavia—the Kingdom of Serbs, Croats, and Slovenes—was born.

From the start, Pašić and Trumbić each guarded very different concepts of what any union of the South Slavs might resemble. For Pašić, Yugoslavia was simply a Greater Serbia—an expansion of the historic core Balkan kingdom with the western provinces of Croatia and Slovenia tacked on. In short, it would be a reconstituted Austro-Hungarian

Empire but ruled this time from Belgrade. Trumbić, by contrast, saw
the Kingdom of Serbs, Croats, and Slovenes as a union of equal partners, a group of united states that voluntarily joined together for their
common good. The one problem with this concept was the unlikely
ethnic, political, and religious diversity of this would-be nation. A table
of the population tells only part of the story:

Serbs	43%
Croats	23%
Slovenes	8.5%
Bosnian Moslems	6%
Macedonians	5%
Albanians	3.6%
Germans, Hungarians, Vlachs, Jews, and Gypsies	14%

Among these various nationalities were three religions, two alphabets,
and a multiplicity of dialects. Trumbić believed a federalist system
was the only type that could truly bridge the vast ethnic divides. This
concept was particularly congruent with Woodrow Wilson's doctrine
of self-determination. Pašić, on the other hand, intended that Serbia
should emerge from the war as the single dominant nation in the Balkans. There were other contenders as well for Balkan supremacy: Italy,
Rumania, even Bulgaria, though it had the misfortune to guess wrong,
linking up with the Central Powers, who looked like winners in the winter of 1915. So Bulgaria wound up on the short end of everyone's stick
after the Allied victory.

These early days, in the depths of the war in Europe, were when each
side began choosing partners—just as the Poles and Czechs were in the
process of lining up their supporters on both sides of the Atlantic. By
November 1916, with the Serbian government-in-exile firmly established on Corfu, and the Yugoslav Committee solidly implanted in London and Paris and already gathering strategic friends and allies, Pašić
and Trumbić papered over their differences and began what would turn
out to be a long and painful partnership. The partnership was formal-
ized by the Declaration of Corfu, signed July 20, 1917, at the Serbian
government-in-exile headquarters. The document pledged to work for
a union of all southern Slavs in a single independent, democratic

state. It would be a constitutional monarchy under the House of Karadjordjević, with a guarantee of freedom of religion, though the gulf between Orthodox, Catholic, and Moslem has never been bridged to the present day. More immediately, there was no agreement on a single political system. Pašić continued to hold out for a Serb-oriented centralized government, while Trumbić continued to press for a federalist organization. For the moment, they agreed to disagree.

Still, there was now a unity of sorts. And throughout the war, the Yugoslav Committee did its best to work both sides of the Atlantic, just like their brethren from Poland and Czechoslovakia. In Washington, the Yugoslavs enlisted the services of Ljuba Mihajlović, Serbia's chief diplomat in the United States. Representing the Yugoslav Committee was the veteran Serbian diplomat Milenko Vesnić, who later would become prime minister and who had the good fortune to have married an American heiress—a close friend of Mrs. Woodrow Wilson. Vesnić was indeed the only Balkan national consulted by the president before he delivered his Fourteen Points address. The fifty-five-year-old emissary embarked on a whistle-stop tour of the United States designed to mirror those undertaken by the likes of Masaryk and Paderewski. On January 8, 1918, Vesnić became the only Central European, indeed the only minor-power figure, to address the House and Senate during the war. The only others so favored were leaders of France, Italy, Britain, Japan, and Russia. Neither Paderewski nor Masaryk was accorded that honor. Still, Vesnić's impact was substantially less than either of his Central European competitors. In part this was due to a simple failure in his negotiating skills.

Wilson had been in the final process of preparing his Fourteen Points message when Vesnić arrived in Washington from Paris in December 1917. The president was anxious to perfect the complex point dealing with the Balkans. This was a part of the world that he little understood beyond the fact that it was potentially of enormous strategic significance to the Western world—indeed, it was the tinderbox where the world war had begun. So he asked Colonel Edward House to meet with Vesnić and show him the text of the message, as the colonel noted in his diary:

> I sent for Vesnitch [sic] to meet me at Gordon's [Auchincloss]
> house as I did not think it advisable to have him come to the
> White House. . . . He [Vesnić] totally disagreed with what had

been written and said it would not satisfy Serbia. He also said that peace should not be made at this time and that the discussion of peace should be frowned upon. . . . I asked him to set forth concretely what he would suggest in preference to what I submitted to him. He wrote with some difficulty, underneath the paragraph which the President . . . had framed."

Vesnić's cramped scrawl beneath Wilson's typ script noted that "there will [not] and there cannot be in Europe any lasting peace with the conservation of actual Austria-Hungary. . . . Bulgarian treachery can and shall not be rewarded. I sincerely believe that serious negotiations for the peace at this moment of the war would mean the complete failure of the policy of allies and a grave collapse of the civilization of mankind."

House was upset. The United States was not yet prepared to carve up the Hapsburg Empire unequivocally, but Vesnić was not to be deterred. It was an extraordinary opportunity—to indicate flexibility and an understanding of the U.S. goals and principles, to plead for prompt recognition of an independent Yugoslav nation or at a minimum, the Yugoslav Committee as the government of an eventual free and independent people. Vesnić had the undivided attention of the figure who, at the moment, was the second most powerful man in America— perhaps the most persuasive counselor among all the Allies. But instead of reasoning with House, Vesnić launched into an interminable history of the Balkans—a foretaste, the colonel feared, of what was in store as the Allies attempted to frame a fair and equitable peace. House, short on patience with the clearly inflexible Serb, cut him short. Observing that he had an engagement with the president, he left Vesnić and went directly to the White House carrying the page with the diplomat's scrawl. "The President was depressed at this first and only attempt to obtain outside opinion regarding the message," House reported. "I advised him not to change the paragraph in the slightest."

And it was not. Point X, dealing with the Croatian and Slovenian regions of Austria-Hungary, and Point XI, dealing with Serbia, Montenegro, and Rumania, needed to be of a piece with the rest of the document in terms of guaranteeing the fundamental principles for which the United States went to war—independence and self-determination of all peoples. Indeed, the text reflected with considerable precision these views and, for that matter, those of the Yugoslav Committee—particularly after the insertion on the draft, with a small caret, the key words "and economic":

X. The peoples of Austria-Hungary, whose place among the nations we wish to see safeguarded and assured, should be accorded the freest opportunity of autonomous development.

XI. Rumania, Serbia, and Montenegro should be evacuated [by the Central Powers]; occupied territories restored; Serbia accorded free and secure access to the sea; and the relations of the several Balkan states to one another determined by friendly counsel along historically established lines of allegiance and nationality; and international guarantees of the political *and economic* independence and territorial integrity of the several Balkan states should be entered into.

Though Vesnić was a Serbian diplomat—far more concerned with Point XI than Point X—in Wilson's final draft, both items turned out to be pitch-perfect with respect to the fundamental needs and desires of all the Balkan nations. Meanwhile, Vesnić and Serbia's Washington representative, Ljuba Mihajlović, embarked on an extensive campaign to rouse American public opinion to the side of a South Slav nation—public meetings, advertisements, and petitions, culminating in Vesnić's appearance before the House and Senate the same day Wilson presented his Fourteen Points. The United States and indeed, all the Western powers had their own motives for treating the Yugoslavs so well at this particular juncture of the war. The hope, expressed most vividly by the Italians, whose forces were directly facing those of Austria-Hungary, was that Western support for Croatian and Slovene independence would persuade troops of those nationalities to desert. This would have the effect of further neutralizing the military muscle of the Central Powers.

The problem was that sympathy for the Balkan cause among the Allied leaders fell apart even more quickly than for the Czechs or the Poles. In part this was due to a host of negotiating issues that developed from the earliest days of the peace process. In part, however, it was due to the reality of electoral politics and political pressure in the United States. The Balkan nations simply were never a very potent voting block. While in the 1920 U.S. census Poles numbered 1,268,583 and

Czechoslovaks totaled 491,638, Yugoslavs weighed in with just 211,416 and Rumanians numbered 146,393. For that matter, there were just 8,814 Albanians scattered across the United States.

At the same time, there were other, more powerful, forces at work seeking to torpedo Yugoslav aspirations. The Italians, who had finally entered the war a year after signing the secret Treaty of London, were doing their best to make sure their allies would not recognize the existence of a Yugoslav state. Italy was hoping to dismember the entire region, ruling key areas and dominating the rest. Italy's fondest hope was to re-create the Adriatic as a mare nostrum. Istria, Dalmatia, and Albania at a minimum would serve as component parts of a resurgent Mediterranean Italian empire that would mirror the lost glory of ancient Rome. So while Poland and Czechoslovakia had the Allies unanimously working to create vibrant bulwarks against Germany and Bolshevism, with France, Britain, and the United States recognizing these nations even before the armistice in November 1918, Italy was lobbying strenuously, and effectively, against any such action on behalf of a Kingdom of Serbs, Croats, and Slovenes. Indeed, at the time of the armistice, Italian troops were landing in Dalmatia and, facing no Austro-Hungarian resistance, were moving resolutely into Slovenia, causing panic, followed by political and economic paralysis. The final armistice lines set in November 1918 were virtually identical to lines set forth in the secret Treaty of London that brought Italy into the war. At the same time, Italy sought to seize the entire Austro-Hungarian fleet, most of which was based in Yugoslav ports.

The Yugoslavs were not silent, but were virtually impotent. Their protests over Italy's actions fell on all but deaf ears. Wilson, whose Fourteen Points declaimed against secret treaties, retreated in the face of potential Allied disunity that could jeopardize creation of his beloved League of Nations. Privately the president observed to House that "without U.S. support, Italy could never secure what she went into the war, on cold-blooded calculation, to get." Still, the price might prove too high for the United States to pay. At the same time, Britain and France shrank from repudiating the Treaty of London, a formal, if secret, diplomatic document.

As delegates from the various nations began to converge on Paris, louder voices were heard urging the Americans to intervene to prevent

Italian forces already in place from having their own way with vast swaths of territory. "The attitude of the population is in no way hostile to a joint landing of the Entente [Allied] forces but only to the Italians being allowed to act alone," H. Percival Dodge, the U.S. diplomat at Serbian government headquarters at Corfu, wrote to Secretary of State Lansing. "The landing of American forces would be especially agreeable and quieting to the population. In this connection I may mention that the feeling between Italians and French at Corfu has become very bitter." But U.S. forces would not arrive in any significant numbers.

At the same time, Italy was embarking on a secret plan to destabilize Yugoslavia and create an image of chaos in the Balkans—disorder that only a strong Italian presence could neutralize. Italian Prime Minister Vittorio Emmanuele Orlando personally authorized a three-pronged attack designed to undermine the very foundations of the fledgling nation. The Italian military had already landed on Dalmatian territory. An economic blockade was designed to starve the Yugoslavs into submission. And Italy enlisted a frustrated King Nicholas of Montenegro, who had been sitting in penurious exile in Paris while at least one of his daughters, married to a Russian prince dethroned by the Bolsheviks, took in sewing. He was easily persuaded to back a separatist movement and independence for what Serbia saw as an integral part of its territory. Some two hundred Italian agents were launched into the heart of Serbia, Croatia, and Slovenia with the mission of fomenting internal disorder. The price was a steep one. Every officer was given 10,000 lire in cash for payoffs and political subversion. Three newspapers would each be bought off for 150,000 lire. Clergymen would be enlisted at a cost of 300,000 to 500,000 lire, while top government officials would be subverted for 200,000 to 500,000 lire, or $17,000 to $57,000 (worth $200,000 to $600,000 today). A not inconsiderable sum. Such Italian efforts did not go unnoticed even by U.S. representatives in the region who, by the end of December, were already complaining, as General Tasker Bliss warned Wilson:

American troops are being used to further a policy of occupation and penetration [by Italian forces] which, if not contrary to the terms of the armistice with Austria-Hungary is at least unnecessary under that armistice. In one case, an attempt was made to use a small American force to effect, without any apparent justifiable reason, a penetration into Montenegro. . . . The result seems to be that the regiment is being employed not for legitimate military purposes but to further political aims.

The French realized precisely what the Italians had in mind. A population bomb was ticking in France's own backyard, which the shrewd and calculating Georges Clemenceau was desperate to defuse. The accelerating Italian birthrate and the catastrophic loss of a large chunk of France's productive male population in the war was threatening to turn Italy into the dominant nation of southern Europe. At the same time, Clemenceau was committed to the secret treaties he had negotiated when the Central Powers had his back to the wall three years earlier.

Wilson, for his part, had two priorities—an early and lasting peace that would bring American boys home quickly and a League of Nations that would assure they would never again have to be dispatched abroad to fight someone else's war. The result was that Wilson kept his head firmly buried in the sand. He wanted no part of these internecine conflicts in Europe. Moreover, even among the various Balkan peoples there was no real sense of nationhood, no true pan-Yugoslavian nationalism, no real, viable nation to recognize and support as the various ethnic groups continued to feud among themselves. Wilson's self-determination, if strictly construed, would have meant a kaleidoscope of mini-states, not dissimilar to the map that has finally emerged in this region since the turn of the twenty-first century. Unlike any internal, homegrown product of self-determination, the Balkan nations that emerged from the foundry that was Paris were products of external forces and external priorities. The disparate, feuding, grasping delegations that arrived in Paris should have provided the Western powers some sense of what was in store—had the Allied leaders looked closely and thoughtfully enough.

By early January 1919, the Yugoslav delegation—ninety three strong—was installed in the Hotel de Beau-Site on the Rue de Presbourg just steps from the Arc de Triomphe and, strategically, just steps from the British delegation in the Hotel Majestic. While outnumbered by the Allied missions, particularly the Americans and the vast personnel of the Inquiry, the Serbs, Croats, and Slovenes were by no means outgunned intellectually. There were law professors from the universities of Belgrade and Ljubljana, brilliant geographers and demographers such as Jovan Cvijić, whose academic studies of Balkan ethnography were globally renowned. Eventually other experts were called to Paris to lend their support. Michael Pupin, the Serbian physicist and father of the long-distance telephone call, who by 1919 was a distinguished Columbia professor, was a colleague of many members of the Inquiry and arrived to lend a hand. But the internal feuding continued. Serb versus Montenegrin versus Croat versus Macedonian versus Slovene versus Albanian is not a pretty sight in the best of times. Yet the Yugoslavs were not alone in this noxious political arena. Delegates from the already independent nations of Rumania and Bulgaria arrived to claim their own slices of Russian or Austrian, Serbian or Macedonian territory, and were not in the least reluctant to stir the ethnic pot. For Paris in 1919, it was a cattle call.

Rumania began the sessions with Take Ionescu, a dapper, well-fed ambassador who'd studied law at the Sorbonne and whose principal claim to a seat at the table was his cheerful English wife, Bessie. Take was quickly supplanted by the nation's prime minister, Ion Brătianu, who persuaded Queen Marie to write to her uncle, King George in London, warning him that Ionescu represented neither Rumania nor herself. Most Rumanians saw Brătianu as an individual of undeniable genius, mixed with guile, though he managed to alienate virtually every foreign official with whom he came in contact. Harold Nicolson described him in a deft turn of phrase as "a bearded woman, a forceful humbug, a Bucharest intellectual, a most unpleasing man. Handsome and exuberant, he flings his fine head sideways, catching his own profile in the glass. He makes elaborate verbal jokes imagining them to be Parisian." This view was widely held, with even House's even-tempered aide Stephen Bonsal observing that "Brătianu is undoubtedly the most unpopular of the prime ministers who are assembled here." Still, women swooned over him and his "eyes of a gazelle and jaw of a tiger."

Brătianu was determined to turn the force of his personality to the profit of his native country. He had already managed a clever diplomatic maneuver during the depths of the war. At the time, Rumania was just one of the neutral powers that the Allies were determined to bring on board. The goal was to open a Balkan front that would suck military reserves of the Central Powers away from the western front where their own armies were taking a pummeling. But Brătianu drove a hard bargain, demanding expanded territory and population in return for military action. He wanted large swaths of territory inhabited by Hungarians and Serbs. At the time, Brătianu was untroubled by the addition of substantial minorities to Rumania's population mix. His nation was ethnically more homogeneous than Yugoslavia, as its population grid demonstrates:

Rumanians	71.9%
Hungarians	7.9%
Germans	4.1%
Jews	4.0%
Ukrainians	3.2%
Russians	2.3%
Bulgarians	2.0%

While ethnic Rumanians constituted nearly three-quarters of the population, the nation had learned to accommodate its diversity. Rumania was an ancient and long-standing amalgam of disparate regions and origins—from Transylvania, Bukovina, and the Banat on the north and west to Moldavia and Bessarabia on the east, Walachia on the south, and the rich oil-producing regions of Dobruja on the Black Sea. At the same time, Rumania was surrounded by other countries whose territories it coveted and which coveted Rumanian soil—Hungary and Yugoslavia on the north and west, Russia on the east, and Bulgaria on the south. In one small corner of this Balkan region, it is still possible in the course of an hour to travel through three different nations (Yugoslavia, Hungary, and Rumania), each with a separate currency, language, police, and government.

At the outbreak of hostilities in 1914, an ostensibly neutral Rumania was sandwiched between the Central Powers in the form of Hungary, and the Allies in the form of still czarist-era Russia and Serbia. The sympathy of many Rumanians was with the Allies. While King Ferdinand was nominally a Hohenzollern of Germany, his wife, Queen Marie, was the first cousin of both England's King George V and Czar Nicholas II of Russia. The czar had pledged to send large forces to Rumania's defense if it was attacked by the Central Powers. Which it was, of course, as soon as it ended its neutrality in August 1916, after Brătianu finally accepted the lavish offers of territory he had wrung from the Allies. This secret treaty (which followed the one the Allies had signed in London with Italy) awarded Rumania huge swaths of Hungary's

Transylvania and the entire Banat region, at least half of which was claimed by Serbia. Both were far beyond the boundaries of ethnic Rumania. The promised Russian troops, however, never materialized. By the end of 1916, on the heels of a powerful advance by Austro-Hungarian and German forces, the capital of Bucharest was overrun. King Ferdinand, Queen Marie, and the Rumanian government fled into internal exile in Iasi, a remote area of Bessarabia near the Russian frontier. Rumania was occupied by enemy forces until the final weeks of the war, when it finally managed to enter the conflict on the side of the Allies.

None of this prevented Brătianu from arriving in Paris determined to take his place as a full-fledged Allied delegate. After all, Article VI of the secret treaty he had negotiated more than two years earlier stated that Rumania would be entitled to "the same rights as her allies" at the peace conference. He conveniently ignored Article V, of course, which specified that none of the parties would conclude a "separate peace" with the Central Powers. Rumania had done just that when the nation was overrun. Moreover, Brătianu promptly brushed aside Take Ionescu, who had spent a good part of the war in London meeting with British officials and a host of Balkan émigrés, especially Serbia's Ante Trumbić. The two exile leaders sought to assemble a coalition of Balkan forces that they hoped might lend the entire region some joint negotiating power as a major bloc in Paris. Brătianu dismissed all of this, since he fully anticipated being able simply to walk in and claim Rumania's full rights under his secret treaty. But Take had many friends at the Peace Conference, if not back home in Bucharest. Indeed, two days after Nicolson arrived in Paris, he went round to see the Rumanian at his rooms at the Hotel Meurice:

> On to see Také Jonescu [sic] at the Meurice. A hot stuffy bedroom and in the passage outside the dim fustanellas of King Nikita's Montenegrin bodyguard. Lounging exotic on the Turkey [sic] carpet of the corridor.
>
> Také is rubicund, dapper, continental. Tries to speak English and then relapses into French. He is extremely bitter about his treatment by Brătianu. . . . Také says that the Brătianu Cabinet is very unpopular in the country. . . . Také had come to some arrangement with Trumbić under which the Banat would be amicably divided between Rumania and the S.C.S. [Serbs, Croats,

and Slovenes], and the Succession States would present a united bloc in Paris as against the Great Powers. Brătianu had used his knowledge of this arrangement to discredit Také in patriotic circles in Bucharest. . . .

Také [is] evidently embittered and revengeful. This rather affects his moderation and judgment. . . . This is a pity since he is the only man who realizes that it is a mistake for the Rumanians to insist upon the 1916 Treaty.

There would be nothing amicable or moderate at all about relations between any of the Balkan states in Paris. The hands of the major powers had been tied with respect to the Balkans more firmly than with any other region by the time they reached the negotiating table. Certainly the intentions of the Allies, and especially the Americans, were the right ones—particularly as stated in the First of Wilson's Fourteen Points: "Open covenants of peace, openly arrived at, after which there shall be no private international understandings of any kind but diplomacy shall proceed always frankly and in the public view."

Already, a month earlier, the Inquiry had submitted its definitive report on how peace should be concluded in the Balkans—a position the Americans held firmly to the end:

No just or lasting settlement of the tangled problems confronting the deeply wronged peoples of the Balkans can be based upon the arbitrary treaty of Bucharest. That treaty was a product of the evil diplomacy which the peoples of the world are now determined to end. That treaty wronged every nation in the Balkans, even those which it appeared to favor, by imposing upon them all the permanent menace of war. . . . The ultimate relationship of the different Balkan nations must be based upon a fair balance of nationalistic and economic considerations, applied in a generous and investive spirit after impartial and scientific inquiry. The meddling and intriguing of great powers must be stopped and the efforts to attain national unity by massacre must be abandoned. . . .

We are strongly of the opinion that in the last analysis economic considerations will outweigh nationalistic affiliations in the Balkans, and that a settlement, which insures economic prosperity is most likely to be a lasting one.

It would take at least eight decades for economic considerations to trump ethnic and nationalistic prejudices, but in the near term all of these rational, albeit somewhat academic, aims fell victim, yet again, to Wilson's overwhelming desire to win a League of Nations and lay the basis for an eternal peace. The economic prosperity of the Balkans was very far down on most of the Allies' lists. From the first days of the Peace Conference, every move by the major powers turned into a slap in the face for all these nations.

The week preceding the formal opening of the Peace Conference on January 18, 1919, was filled with frenetic political maneuvering—particularly with respect to who would receive a coveted seat at the conference table, indeed, how many seats would be awarded in the first place. At a minimum, the Yugoslavs had hoped for four, but counted on three—one each for a Serb, a Croat, and a Slovene. When House and the other Allied negotiators had prepared for the conference, they'd allotted three each to Serbia, Rumania, Belgium, and Greece. Poland and Czechoslovakia (both unable to enter the war until the final days) received two apiece—which, as we've seen, caused no end of consternation in those quarters.

So imagine the horror when on January 12, six days before the opening, David Lloyd George announced to his fellow Allied leaders that he feared an "unwieldy assembly," and proposed holding all of the small states to two seats apiece. Moreover, under heavy pressure from the Italians, the Allies postponed any formal recognition of the Kingdom of Serbs, Croats, and Slovenes. Only the Kingdom of Serbia would officially be seated. When Wilson succeeded in raising Brazil's quota to three (as the largest representative of South America), all hell broke loose among the other small nations—particularly the Belgians, on whose territory much of the war in the West had been fought, and the Greeks. Belgium threatened an outright boycott, while Vesnić relayed a formal protest on the part of the Yugoslavs. Under strong pressure from Clemenceau and Lansing, Yugoslavia's quota was raised to three—but they would be seated at the opening session under the banner of the Kingdom of Serbia.

Pašić, Trumbić, and Vesnić attended the opening session on January 18, then later that evening, around 9 P.M., the Yugoslav delegation caucused for an assessment meeting. It was only the first of a long string of such sessions, embittered by endless wrangling over the shape of the new nation, its territory and boundaries, and the tactics needed to win a semblance of respect from the Western world. Josip Smodlaka, a leading Croat politician who would later become foreign minister of a communist Yugoslav government during World War II, urged that the delegation's demands must "adhere strictly to the ethnographic boundaries of our nations." He warned prophetically that exceeding these boundaries would "facilitate and lend justification to Italian claims in Dalmatia and will, moreover, incur retribution in the future." Pašić shot back that "a political frontier cannot be drawn strictly along an ethnographic line, because the nationalities are mixed, and as much as we might receive of a foreign element so much of ours will have to go to others."

The debate might equally have dealt with the Kosovo conflict of 1998–1999. Unfortunately, at the Hotel de Beau-Site in January 1919 there was little outside pressure that could be brought to bear to paper over these internal disagreements. As Vesnić pointed out: "If we do not agree on details, neither will the experts. Men charged with such a lofty and delicate mission must be prepared to bear responsibility for their work." Indeed, the principal external pressure, from Italy, only served to intensify these internal disagreements. Moreover, while Nicolson and many senior members of the Inquiry backed the concept of a united Yugoslavia with defensible frontiers, some, including Columbia historian George Louis Beer, were definitively in the Italian camp. As Beer wrote in his diary on March 16: "The Poles and Jugo-Slavs may become a nationality but as yet they are merely a potential one. It is far preferable to have Poles under Germans and Jugo-Slavs under Italians."

At least for the early days of the conference, the Balkans were scarcely on the front burner as the Allies juggled a host of priorities, particularly dealing with Germany and its western frontiers, not to mention the likes of Poland, Czechoslovakia, even the Hejaz. Eventually, though, it was the Balkans' turn. At noon on January 31, Pašić announced to the Yugoslav delegation that they had been summoned to appear at the Supreme Council—at three o'clock. They had high hopes. Much spadework had been done in the intervening days by the likes of R. W. Seton-Watson and Wickham Steed in an effort to get the Brits on their side. Senior members of the Inquiry tried to make certain Wilson was on board. These maneuverings sought several key results in terms of territory for the new Yugoslav state: sovereignty over the Dalmatian Coast and Fiume (later to be called Rijeka) as well as the Istrian Peninsula adjacent to Italy, a chunk of the Banat claimed by Rumania, plus the bulk of Macedonia claimed by Bulgaria and Montenegro, where King Nicholas and his princesses were still holding out hopes of returning to power.

When Pašić and Trumbić arrived in the anteroom of the Quai d'Orsay for the afternoon session, they found Wilson's personal body-guard sprawled on a settee reading "A Bed of Roses." The session proved to be nothing of the kind. For there was a surprise awaiting the Yugo-slavs. Milling around in the anteroom were Brătianu and his deputy, Nicolas Misu, Rumanian ambassador to London. French Foreign Minister Stéphen Pichon arrived momentarily to escort all four into the hall. Nicolson, who'd accompanied Foreign Minister Arthur Balfour, set the stage in his diary:

> A high room, domed ceiling, heavy chandelier, dado of modern oak, Doric paneling, electric light, Catherine de Medici tapestries all around the room, fine Aubusson carpet with a magnificent swan border, régence table at which Clemenceau sits, two chairs opposite for the Rumanians, secretaries and experts on little gilt chairs, about twenty-two people in all. The lights are turned on one by one as the day fades behind the green silk curtains. The Big Ten sit in an irregular row to Clemenceau's right. Pichon crouches just beside him. [French Ambassador Paul] Dutasta behind. Silence— very warm—people walking about with muffled feet—secretaries handing maps gingerly.
>
> Bratianu, with histrionic detachment, opens his case. He is evidently convinced that he is a greater statesman than any present. A smile of irony and self-consciousness recurs from time to time. He flings his fine head in profile. He makes a dreadful impression.
>
> A.J.B. [Balfour] rises, yawns slightly, and steps past his own armchair to ask me for our line of partition in the Banat. [Allen] Leeper, whose subject it is, produces it at once. A.J.B. shows it, with marked indifference, to Sonnino. Vesnic replies to the Rumanian case. He does it well and modestly. He attacks the Secret Treaty. Then Bratianu again. Then Trumbic and old Pasic. President Wilson gets pins and needles and paces up and down the soft carpet kicking black and tidy boots. He then goes and sits down for a moment among the Jugo-Slavs. Then we all disappear again

through the double doors. General feeling that Bratianu has done badly.

Nicolson's account of this session suggests that the issues in the Balkans had come to revolve almost entirely around the two key secret treaties, though stunningly Clemenceau tossed off the remark that he "was not aware that the Treaty of 1916 had been secret." Pichon trumped his boss by reading the last article of the treaty that "required the maintenance of its secrecy to the end of the war." Vesnić, as he had done with House months earlier, then launched into a lengthy history of the region. The official record of the session shows that Clemenceau asked offhandedly whether Brătianu "would agree to the general principle of a referendum" to set the borders of the Banat. Brătianu maintained that he "considered the question already settled" by the treaty, which France had signed. Brătianu in turn played the demographic card—which should have been close to the heart of Wilson and his concept of self-determination—pointing out that "on ethnical grounds it would be impossible to justify the placing of 580,000 Germans and Magyars under 272,000 Serbs. Therefore, the Banat could not be divided into two for ethnical reasons." Trumbić responded that the part of the Banat Yugoslavia desired contained 272,000 Serbs and just 266,000 Rumanians.

This opening confrontation set the tone and established the issues that were to trouble much of the rest of the Peace Conference and beyond. The European powers were unprepared or unwilling to destabilize Europe's ancient systems of realpolitik that revolved around treaties, secret or otherwise; while the Americans had their own issues. Indeed, the background to this first seminal Balkan encounter on January 31 turned out to be the fact that Wilson and Italian Foreign Minister Sidney Sonnino had nearly come to blows four days earlier. As Wickham Steed wrote in a memo to his boss Lord Northcliffe: "[Wilson] had just had a stormy interview with Sonnino, who seems to have lost his temper and to have gone to the length of telling Wilson not to meddle in European affairs but to stick to his American last [sic]. When referring to Sonnino, Wilson had clenched his fist and used un-parliamentary language."

Steed believed that Sonnino and Brătianu had even concluded their own private deal "to stand or fall together over the maintenance of the

Secret Treaties." Each stood to gain substantially at the expense of the Yugoslavs, while at the same time dramatically altering, no doubt for the worse, the balance of power in the Balkans. Only Wilson really barred the way—but he was a thin reed. France certainly was opposed to Italy gaining power in that region, but at the same time it was particularly close to Rumania for a host of ethnic and cultural reasons. Rumania, with the only Latin-based language in southeastern Europe, has long considered itself a "Latin island in a sea of Slavs." Britain was somewhat interested in the shape of power on the continent, provided its economic interests were looked after. While it did seriously covet Rumanian petroleum reserves, Britain was mainly interested in its continued pretensions to a global empire. It would be unlikely to welcome Italy turning the Mediterranean, or even the Adriatic, into its own mare nostrum—particularly as these seas represented principal shipping routes to the Suez Canal and on to India.

The Yugoslavs seemed only vaguely aware of, or were determined to ignore, most of these powerful realities that underlay the early weeks of negotiations in which their aspirations were given short shrift. Still, they and their friends among the Allies did manage to forestall any definitive action on Italy's claims. The Italian demands had placed the Yugoslavs in an untenable position: being judged by a plaintiff in what was becoming, much to their chagrin, increasingly a juridical rather than a negotiating process. As Steed recalled:

> Dissatisfaction grew rapidly with the tendency of the 'big men' to decide important matters without consultation of the smaller Allies. It was increased when . . . Clemenceau attempted to bully the small Powers and told them, in effect, to mind their own business. He declared that the Conference was mainly a concern of the Great Powers to which the Little Powers had graciously been invited; and that had it not been for the desire of the Great Powers to form a league of nations, it was not certain whether the small Powers would have been invited at all. Too many cooks might not only spoil the broth but dangerously protract the cooking.

Italy was of course one of the Great Powers. But all the Balkan nations did their utmost in the ensuing weeks to make certain they were not ignored. They sought to ensure that the value of their demands for the future peace and well-being of their remote region and for the balance of Europe was appreciated by those who were in a position to establish their boundaries and assure their future prosperity, or even survival.

So Trumbić opened an extended series of back-channel communications with the Americans. This included Robert Lansing and Allen Dulles, but also Inquiry member Douglas W. Johnson, a thirty-nine-year-old Columbia University cartographer and physiography instructor whose critical task was to draw the maps of the Balkans; and Arthur Hugh Frazier, a diplomat who with Gordon Auchincloss, Stephen Bonsal, and Dulles was a member of House's personal staff. Trumbić's immediate goal was a formal recognition of Yugoslavia by the United States, which he managed to win on February 7. The formal letter, released by Lansing, also put a stake through the heart of Montenegro's aspirations for independence and sent King Nicholas into an even deeper funk. After the American statement, Brătianu took some comfort from the door that Lansing had left open a crack in the document, which pointed out that Yugoslavia's "final frontiers will be determined by the Peace Conference in accordance with the wishes of the peoples concerned." In the end the "peoples concerned" turned out to be the same inner circle of European political leaders.

Meanwhile, in an effort to accelerate the process, and frustrated that he had managed to acquire precious few supporters in key quarters to win the kinds of territorial gains he'd expected from his secret treaty during the war, Brătianu decided it was time to wheel in his heavy guns. Rumania's Queen Marie left Bucharest on the morning of March 1, seen off at the railway station by a cheering throng that included Rumanian aristocracy, generals, and top government officials. In her diary she recorded her reservations: "My Roumanians have an almost mystic belief in my powers which flatters and upholds me but which makes me a bit anxious." She need not have been.

Paris threw itself at her feet, and particularly the diplomats and politicians whom this forty-three-year-old granddaughter of Queen Victoria was to hold in her thrall. Among the Americans, Frazier, Bonsal, and Auchincloss even fought over who should be allowed to greet her at the Gare de l'Est and "to see that the red carpet is worthy of royal feet and properly spread." As Bonsal continued, the result was "quite an uproar in the 'family,'" until House himself stepped in and declared that the delegation would "await her appearance at the Crillon. He was confident she would not fail to put in an appearance." House was right, of course, but her arrival at the U.S. headquarters would have to wait until she had made an overwhelming impression on the rest of Paris.

Descending on the Ritz Hotel, she displaced, as we have seen, such notables as Vance McCormick, so that the twenty rooms she required for her entourage, including her three daughters, might be available. Gardens were emptied to provide the cascade of flowers that swamped her from the moment she stepped off the train, garlanded with strings of her famous pearls. Paris became bathed in red, yellow, and blue, the national colors of Rumania, whose flag flew above the entrance to the Ritz throughout her stay. The queen was mobbed on each of her repeated ventures into Paris's smartest shops and evenings at the opera where, on one occasion, a throng of overwrought Parisians actually lifted her car into the air.

But while all of Paris society threw themselves at Queen Marie, she was quite aware that her real value would be in the private conversations with the Western leaders who were debating the future of her nation. So, after a press conference with forty reporters from the various

Queen Marie of Rumania in 1919 at age forty-three.

Allied nations, she began to make the political rounds. Her first call was on Clemenceau. Leaving Brătianu behind, she decamped to the Quai d'Orsay accompanied by her maid of honor, Princess Marthe Bibesco, a Rumanian beauty and former mistress of King Ferdinand, whose salon had made her a doyenne of Parisian literary and political society; and Rumania's extremely francophile ambassador to Paris, Victor Antonescu. Clemenceau, the gruff, unflappable Frenchman known as "the Tiger," who was frank in how much he detested Brătianu, turned on all the charm for the arrival of a queen, ordering the playing of the Rumanian national anthem as he ran down the stairs to greet her.

Antonescu waited outside the meeting room, regaling Clemenceau's top aide, General Jean Mordacq, with stories of the queen's extraordinary reception in Paris. Mordacq was clearly smitten: "Before the Queen had even arrived in our country, she was already effectively a legend. It is said—and it is not far from the truth—that she was 'truly the man of the Romanian royal family' . . . the one person who declared that honor as well as the national interest commanded that [her nation] fight to the end and that she had made superhuman efforts to prevent a surrender to the Central Powers."

Still, while Mordacq's views of the glamorous royal were personally shared by Clemenceau, the prime minister bridled when the subject came to Rumania's frontiers. Marie urged that her nation's boundaries be extended to the Tisza River, as provided by the secret treaty. Clemenceau shot back that she had requested "the lion's share" of the Banat region. "This is just why I came to see his first cousin, the Tiger," Queen Marie replied, as the two dissolved in laughter.

Having charmed Clemenceau, as he admitted on several occasions to close aides, Marie next set her sights on the Brits—particularly Lloyd George and his foreign secretary, Lord Arthur Balfour. To make this dual conquest, the wily queen made use of two of her principal attributes— her direct descent from Queen Victoria and her slightly scandalous reputation. On March 10, Balfour invited Lloyd George and Queen Marie to lunch at his rooms in Paris. While she immediately won over Balfour, the prime minister was not so quickly taken in. As Lloyd George's secretary (and mistress) Frances Stevenson recorded in her diary:

D. [Lloyd George] says she is very naughty, but a very clever woman, though on the whole he does not like her. She gave a

lengthy description of her purchases in Paris, which included a
pink silk chemise. She spoke of meeting President Wilson on his
arrival [back from a quick trip to Washington]. "What shall I talk
to him about?' she asked. "The League of Nations or my pink chemise?" "Begin with the League of Nations," said Mr. Balfour, "and
finish up with the pink chemise. If you were talking to Mr. Lloyd
George, you could begin with the pink chemise."

Before meeting Wilson, Queen Marie traveled briefly to London,
taking her public relations campaign to her first cousin, King George
V, and the British establishment—from the Prince of Wales to acting
foreign secretary Lord Curzon. By April 10 she was back in Paris and
prepared to meet Wilson, whom she rather grandly summoned to her
apartment at the Ritz at the ungodly hour of eight-thirty in the morning. Ghibbering away gaily, she jumped from Rumania's territorial
demands to the Russian menace, her desperate fear of the Bolsheviks
and their espousal of free love and emancipation of women. She hoped
some of this might touch a chord with the Calvinist Wilson and his
wife, Edith, who had accompanied her husband. But here the queen
succeeded only in shocking the one man who might have held a key to
Rumania's future prosperity. As Edith Wilson observed:

> She reviewed the new Russian laws concerning sexual relations,
> saying the proximity of Russia to her country made the menace
> very real. . . . When my husband did not yield the Queen tried
> another tack. Lifting from the mantelpiece a photograph of a
> dark-haired girl of ten or twelve years, she held it up to him, say-
> ing: "This, Mr. President, is a picture of my youngest daughter,
> Ileana. My love child I call her. Is she not lovely? My other girls
> are blonde, like me; but she—oh, she is dark and passionate. . . . "
> When we got in the car, Admiral Grayson, who as naval aide to
> the President, had accompanied us, said: "Well, in all my experi-
> ence I have never heard a lady talk about such things. I honestly
> did not know where to look, I was so embarrassed." . . . My hus-
> band said nothing. So I looked around and seeing his jaw set, knew
> this very beautiful woman had met one man whom she had failed
> to charm.

The queen tried once again the next day at lunch. Sweeping in with her entourage to the Wilson residence thirty-five minutes late, the president observing privately, "This is extremely rude," she again made little further headway in impressing either Wilson or the first lady. At the end of April, she was back in Bucharest. Wilson exhibited so little sympathy for the Rumanian cause largely because it appeared, even with the royal veneer of Queen Marie's elegant intervention and lighthearted spin, that it was little more than a territorial grab with barely a nod to his deeply held belief in self-determination of the people involved.

As the Balkan minuet continued among the leaders of Yugoslavia, Rumania, Italy, and the rest of the Allied powers in Paris, back home the situation was rapidly taking on a momentum of its own. As the Poles and Czechs had also recognized, boots on the ground—the brutal realpolitik concept of "faits accomplis"—was applicable in the Balkans as well as the rest of Central Europe. By March 1, Italian forces were preparing to occupy the Dalmatian port of Split, and within two weeks were firing on crowds of unarmed civilians protesting the hard-line Italian rule. On the island of Krk, the Glagolitic liturgy, based on the oldest known Slavic alphabet of the ninth century, was banned by Italian occupiers. Clergy who resisted, including sixty-eight-year-old Bishop Antun Mahnić, were exiled to Rome. There he was confined for a year until his release after becoming critically ill, only to die back in the Croatian capital of Zagreb. Ironically, most Croats and Slovenes shared with their Italian neighbors a deep belief in Roman Catholicism. The faith of these Slavs brought the region into repeated clashes with the Orthodox religion of Serbia over the next century, and finally led to the definitive breakup of Yugoslavia nearly eight decades later. None of this really mattered to Italian military forces, of course. Their intention was to control territory—religion be damned.

For the peace delegates in Paris it was all deeply disturbing. So they took the same route they took in most of the other regions—and with a comparable lack of impact. They sent a mission. The one positive product of the Miles-King mission—headed by two U.S. army officers, Lieutenant Colonel Sherman Miles and Lieutenant Leroy King, both part of Archibald Carey Coolidge's mission to Vienna—was the series of reports sent back. These so horrified and infuriated most of the Allies in Paris that they provided substantial propaganda for the Yugoslav position. At the end of March, for instance, Lieutenant Colonel Miles described the situation in Croatia:

> The Italians are running things with a high hand and are clashing with the French and to a lesser degree with the British. . . . The Italian determination to antagonize the Jugo-Slavs is a most amazing piece of stupidity, when one thinks of the opportunity Italy might have seized in the Balkans. . . .
>
> The issue of Dalmatia is very plain. The province is Jugoslav by blood and sentiment. . . . The Italian claims on Fiume and upper Dalmatia are pitiably weak when compared with those of Jugo-slavia. It is a case of a bargain made under the morals of the old diplomacy as against national rights.

Lieutenant King's reporting was even more depressing:

> The Bulgars are making preparations on the Macedonian front by organizing bands of from 100 to 200 men, whom they are expected to send across the provisional frontier in the spring, for the purpose of sowing discord among the Macedonian people and turning it against the Serbs. . . .
>
> The Italians are choking Croatia by their occupation of Fiume and are doing everything to cause discontent and trouble, both there and in Slovenia. They are determined to break up Jugo-Slavia if they can.

By May 10 matters were only getting worse, as Lieutenant King observed that "the Italians have occupied Fiume and are fortifying their lines. They are digging trenches and putting up barbed wire." A mere lieutenant colonel and a lieutenant managed a pitch-perfect summary of the situation now confronting the finest political and diplomatic minds of the Western world, as the Peace Conference moved through the heart of its deliberations, confounding many who watched them at work. "I can't understand the Italian attitude," observed Nicolson. "They are behaving like children, and sulky children at that. They obstruct and delay everything—and evidently think that by making themselves disagreeable on every single point they will force the Conference to give them fat plums to keep them quiet."

As winter gave way to spring in Paris, the Allied leaders dumped the entire Balkan mess into a committee comprising the multinational staffs of the various delegations. American Charles Seymour was among the members, and of course Nicolson, whose interest in the Balkans went back at least to the day the armistice was declared, when he was already deeply immersed in maps of his beloved "Strumnitza enclave." Seymour and Nicolson were both prepared to defend manfully Wilson's principle of ethnic justice and self-determination, which led to some brutal confrontations with the Italians. As Nicolson wrote to his father, Lord Carnock, until recently the permanent undersecretary, or highest-ranking civil servant, in the Foreign Office: "On the whole I find that the Americans are a great help, since they are well-informed, broad-minded and extremely honest. The French are behaving far better than I imagined . . . the great difficulty comes on the side of the Italians. . . . The unanimity of action is frustrated at every point by perfectly willful obstruction on the part of the Italians. It is all working up to a real row."

The row was to lead to a complete pullout of the Italians from negotiations, with Vittorio Emmanuele Orlando, Sidney Sonnino, and the entire delegation stomping off to Rome in a huff after seeing the full committee report, which was completed and passed to the delegations' leaders on April 6. This Solomonic document divided the Banat down the middle. Yugoslavia received the western portion, Rumania the east. The carefully drawn frontier lines threaded the needle, leaving just 75,000 Rumanians in Serbia and 65,000 Serbs in Rumania. But the key element was the effective end to Brătianu's beloved secret treaty. The toughest issues were left unresolved due to Italian obstruction—the fate of Dalmatia, Albania, and the entire Istrian Peninsula, including Fiume.

For the next four weeks, before the Italian pullout, a variety of diplomatic stratagems and maneuvers were tried to break this bitter, and back in the Balkans themselves increasingly violent, logjam. Wickham Steed resurfaced. A journalist of the old school who believed in wielding his power and relishing his influence, he was persuaded to act as intermediary. He never succeeded in accomplishing much. At the same time, two fabulously wealthy Yugoslav shipping magnates—Bozon Banac and Melko Cingrija, whose stunning Dubrovnik villa was ironically furnished with masterpieces of Venetian cabinetry—met with their Italian counterparts. It was a final (and as it turned out, successful) private effort to divide up the Austro-Hungarian fleet and keep it out of French and British hands.

The momentary absence of the Italian delegation from Paris gave the rest of the Allies an opportunity to grant formal recognition at long last to the Kingdom of Serbs, Croats, and Slovenes—or, as Nicolson put it, "to twist the Italian tail." Whatever the excuse, it was welcomed by the Yugoslav delegation. Meanwhile, the Americans were warming to the idea of putting much of the disputed territory into the hands of the League of Nations. At least in part, perhaps, they hoped to provide some real mission to this body that by this time was close only to the heart of Wilson, and by extension, Colonel House.

The Italian absence lasted just ten days. By May 6, they were back in their seats. And ready for what was easily among the more bizarre mise-en-scènes of the entire Peace Conference—a bout of shuttle diplomacy between Italians and Yugoslavs, all taking place in three adjoining rooms at the Crillon. The idea was House's. Put Trumbić in one room with two Americans he had come to trust (Frazier and Johnson). In another room, put Orlando and Italy's ambassador to Washington, Vincenzo Macchi di Cellere, with two other Americans they believed were in their corner (Beer and David Hunter Miller, an Inquiry member who'd been a New York law partner of Gordon Auchincloss). In the middle was a "control room" manned by House, who was to shuttle between both parties, neither of whom was to see the other. On May 16, at four o'clock in the afternoon, both parties presented themselves at the Crillon. Beer, who had quite a little downtime while the shuttling was occurring, described in his diary what happened in his room:

> I remained with the Italians from 4:15 to 8:15. Yugo-Slavs immovable. Italians are satisfied if Fiume is a free city. Chief difficulty is eastern boundary in Istria. Orlando said such a settlement such as he was proposing would ruin him politically and that he was preparing to go back to his University to teach. He comes from Palermo and is a charming little chap. Told me all about himself. Feels that Italy has been badly treated by her Allies and said there was a great resentment against France in Italy. Personally he favored an alliance between Italy and France, a Latin bloc against the German one, but France was jealous of Italy and distrustful. Already Italy surpassed France in numbers.

Plan now is to get President Wilson to agree to Italian plan and to have it put into effect no matter what the Jugo-Slavs think. Attitude of Trumbitch [*sic*] showed that they will make no concessions. In fact as de Cellere said they cannot because if a concession hurts a Croat, he will complain against Serb or Slovene making it. As a result any concession tends to disrupt this artificial unity of the Slovenes, Croats and Serbs.

As it turned out later, Beer's Italians had come to the meeting with the single-minded hope that he and House would apply sufficient pressure on the Yugoslavs to have them cave to their demands. In the ensuing weeks, as the clock ticked down to the official windup of the Peace Conference, a host of other ideas were broached and shot down by both sides. British aides Nicolson and Allen Leeper came up with an idea of turning over central Albania to the Italians, giving southern Albania to the Greeks, and creating a Union of North Albanians in the form of an "autonomous zone" to be overseen by the Yugoslavs. As it developed eighty years later, such a scenario would have been like putting the fox in charge of the henhouse.

As June rolled around, the Allies had come to recognize that there was unlikely to be any shape to the Balkans by the time the Versailles Treaty was signed with Germany and the leaders, particularly Wilson, would head home. The treaty with Austria-Hungary would have to be delayed in hopes that some definitive resolution of the Balkan boundaries might somehow be found. Two seminal events in this respect changed the entire dynamics of the peace process, however. On June 19, Orlando suddenly made good on the threat he had tossed out to George Beer a month earlier and resigned as prime minister of Italy, thereby removing as well his foreign minister, the obstructionist Baron Sonnino. Though their successors signed the Treaty of Versailles with Germany on June 28, it was to be some time before any sort of meaningful talks could be resumed on the Balkans. By then Wilson was back in Washington and facing his own problems—trying to ram through a distinctly skeptical, isolationist, often downright hostile Senate the Treaty of Versailles and the League of Nations.

The power realities of Europe did not really change very much at all with the signing of the treaty. France believed it had removed Germany as a serious menace in the near term. But now there was Bolshevism to deal with as well. More than ever, Clemenceau wanted a system of balances to neutralize any future revival of the military and diplomatic aggressiveness of both of these potentially hostile powers—Germany and Russia. The French statesman was still committed to the concept of a strong cordon sanitaire from Central Europe down through the Balkans. The Central European component was largely in place, as we have seen. Only the Balkans remained in doubt. Italy's priorities were quite different. It wanted to replace Austria-Hungary as the principal force in all of southern and southeastern Europe. And the Americans were happy to retreat into a period of postwar isolation across the Atlantic. In other words, a whole new set of realpolitikal structures needed to emerge as the newly configured kaleidoscope of European nations came into focus. But across the region, forces of all sides were seeking to establish faits accomplis—bringing further misery, death, and destruction to millions of people.

Suddenly, on September 12, a new complication arrived in the form of a self-styled poet-condottiere, a mercenary in the style of the warrior-adventurers of the old Italian city-states of Venice, Florence, and Genoa of the late Middle Ages. Gabriele D'Annunzio, an admirer of Mussolini and the Italian fascists, led a band of heavily armed followers into Fiume. This colorful freelancer, whose favored pose was with a large flower in his boutonnière, became a wild card in the complex game that was still playing out in the ministries of a half dozen European capitals. Son of a wealthy Dalmatian landowner, he produced volumes of poetry, even a uniquely daring tragedy for the celebrated French actress Sarah Bernhardt, before winning renown during World War I as an Italian fighter pilot. Horrified by what he feared was an impending Italian surrender of Fiume to the Yugoslavs, he organized a group of two thousand Italian irregulars. He seized the port and the surrounding countryside, proclaiming himself Il Duce and managing to hold on to the city for eighteen months. It was a frightening prequel to the arrival to power in Rome two years later of Benito Mussolini, so strongly influenced by D'Annunzio that he would adopt the same title before leading his nation into World War II.

Through the summer and into the fall of 1919, negotiators and military forces continued their efforts to establish a series of new nations in the region. Serbian troops maintained their occupation of northern

Albania while Italian forces controlled the rest of that nation. The Rumanian army pushed into Hungary, seizing Budapest. This followed a summons to the French Foreign Ministry on July 11, to the Yugoslav, Rumanian, and Czech delegates in Paris. Pichon "suggested" their nations should mount an offensive to dislodge Béla Kun from Hungary. He asked the Rumanians to contribute eight divisions, the Czechs two divisions, and the Yugoslavs eight thousand men. In the end, the Rumanians went it largely alone. Eventually Beneš warned the Yugoslavs that the Rumanians were thinking seriously of driving all Serbian forces out of the still-contested Banat, since military action seemed to be working so well in Hungary. For diplomats, these maneuvers, real or imagined, were only more reasons to conclude some definitive agreement quickly.

By September 10, 1919, an Austro-Hungarian treaty was ready for signature. But Yugoslavia still refused to sign. This time the sticking point was the issue of minorities whose rights were too closely defined in the treaty for the taste of Yugoslav politicians. "One people with three names," was the way the Belgrade government described the new union of Serbs, Croats, and Slovenes. But what about the others? What rights for the Macedonians, for instance, or the Moslem Albanians? Guaranteed by the Serbian-Turkish Treaty of March 14, 1914, the Serbs observed. For the moment, this had to satisfy the Allies, though their fears were eventually corroborated eighty years later when Serbs and Albanians faced off at gunpoint in Kosovo. Ultimately, the Yugoslavs believed, these guarantees spelled out in the Austro-Hungarian treaty represented outside influence on their internal affairs. This was especially ironic since from the start of the negotiations, the Yugoslavs had relied heavily on Wilson's Fourteen Points, a core element of which guaranteed the rights of national minorities. In fact, the Yugoslavs were less concerned about such rights than the methods of policing how these minorities might be treated. Plainly, it did not want the League of Nations calling them to task, much as the Organizaton for Security and Cooperation in Europe or the European Union would do decades later.

The border issues also continued to drag on—far beyond the point of interest of most voters in the nations concerned, especially the Italians. Indeed, as Wilson pointed out on November 13, 1919, in a note to Italy's new prime minister, Francesco Nitti, three days before critical Italian elections: "The Italian people are not seriously interested in the question of Fiume, but rather in a solution of their major social and economic problems." Then, in an effort to bring the still recalcitrant Italian around, Wilson held out the carrot and the stick in the form of America's food-for-Europe program, which was then in full swing: "The Government of my country [would] assist in the task of economic reconstruction [and food relief] only in those countries which adhere to its program" for settling the Fiume issue. Wilson turned out to be right. Italian voters were most concerned with filling their bellies. Socialists tripled their seats in the Italian Parliament.

Setting aside Yugoslavia's western borders, on November 27, the Treaty of Neuilly was signed with Bulgaria. The Yugoslavs won their beloved Strumica Valley, straddling the Bulgarian frontier, which Nicolson was so anxious to see them awarded. The border with Bulgaria was fixed, with the Yugoslavs adding some 960 square miles (and 100,000 Bulgars) to their territory. Of even greater immediate importance, Bulgaria's army was limited to 33,000 men. A week later, on December 5, 1919, the Yugoslavs finally signed the Treaty of St. Germain with Austria in what they hoped would be a gesture of goodwill toward the Italians and the other Western Allies.

There followed another flurry of negotiations in a host of venues—from the salon of the Baroness Grazioli, one of Paris's great dowager socialites, at 1 Rue Buenos Aires in the shadow of the Eiffel Tower, to the Quai d'Orsay to Claridge's Hotel in London. By June 4, 1920, the Italian frontier was still not settled, but the Allies did sign the Hungarian treaty at the Trianon guaranteeing Yugoslav frontiers with that nation. They have remained little changed until today. By then there was yet another Italian government.

This one seemed prepared to do business. Its first step was a unilateral decision on August 2 to withdraw all Italian forces from Albania, evacuating the strategic port of Vlorë and recognizing the independence of the nation, thus renouncing all claims on Albania. The Italian government had finally come to recognize that it simply did not have the means to continue its occupation of Albania or, for that matter, to sustain a mare nostrum in the Mediterranean or the Adriatic—at least not for the moment. This freed the Yugoslavs from the pressure of Italians on their southern frontier. Wilson and his Democratic Party were also on their way to utter defeat in his efforts to ratify the Versailles Treaty, create a powerful League of Nations, or even win election for Democratic canddate James M. Cox in the 1920 presidential contest. It was finally time for Yugoslavia to throw in the towel. On November 12, 1920, ten days after Republican Warren Harding swept to an overwhelming 60 percent victory as Wilson's successor, Yugoslavia and Italy signed the Treaty of Rapallo. The war officially came to an end for both feuding allies two years and one day after the armistice had called a halt to the armed conflict.

So what did the Yugoslavs get after all? First, full recognition by Italy of the Kingdom of Serbs, Croats, and Slovenes. Italy did manage to retain its beloved secret Treaty of London line along the northern part of the Italian-Yugoslav frontier. But it relinquished the entire Dalmatian coast to Yugoslavia, apart from a small enclave reserved to Italy around the ancient stone-walled port of Zadar, a Roman colony from the earliest days of the empire in the first century B.C. Italians in Dalmatia were allowed to become Italian citizens without leaving Yugoslav territory. Under the agreement, Fiume became "independent in perpetuity," though linked to Italy and formally absorbed by Mussolini in 1924 as he began his own efforts to turn the Mediterranean into a Roman lake. Italian military forces had already managed to oust D'Annunzio and his dwindling band of supporters after he impulsively declared war in Italy on December 1, 1920. He retired to his estate on Lake Garda. On his death in 1938, Mussolini gave him a state funeral with full military honors. In 1947, after World War II, Fiume, by then known as Rijeka, finally assumed its rightful position as part of Yugoslavia, though Tito's communist partisans oversaw the execution of hundreds of suspected Italian fascists who remained in the city. In 1978, an old woman living in a stone hut there since the late nineteenth century told me that she had lived under seven different flags in her lifetime and never moved from her cottage.

By the end of 1920, Yugoslavia was finally whole. Still, some 720,000 Yugoslavs were left beyond the nation's various frontiers, including 480,000 in Italy. Within Yugoslavia's frontiers were 231,000 Rumanians, 467,000 Hungarians, and 505,000 Germans among a total of some two million non-Slavic peoples, the largest group of whom were Moslem Albanians concentrated in Kosovo and never assimilated into Serbia. Indeed, for decades after the war, minority citizens of Yugoslavia were called "foreigners." The Treaty of Rapallo and the various peace treaties that the Allies had assembled brought little real stability to the perpetual caldron known as the Balkans. Had Wilson managed to establish the frontiers drawn by the Inquiry, much future conflict could have been avoided.

After the dust settled, the clear winner from all the peace talks in the Balkans turned out to be Rumania. With three strikes against it—disgust with Brătianu that spread throughout the major delegations, its late reentry into the war only at the very last minute, and its piggish demands for territory—Rumania still wound up the winner. In the Treaty of Trianon with what was left of Austria-Hungary in June 1920, Rumania managed to scoop up Transylvania, Bessarabia, Bukovina, and a large chunk of the Banat. Rumania nearly doubled from its prewar size. Some 1.7 million Hungarians found themselves in the new Rumania, which numbered five million minorities among its eighteen million population. Much of this was a tribute to the Western powers' fear of a resurgent and expansive communism. The Allies were determined to make certain that a Bolshevik-dominated Hungary would be as small and weak as possible, and that Bessarabia was kept out of the hands of the Russian Bolsheviks, while the nations of the Little Entente (finally created by Yugoslavia, Rumania, and Czechoslovakia in June 1921) would pack some real heft in territory and manpower. Brătianu had deftly played to these fears in a session of the four Great Powers plus Poland, Czechoslovakia, Serbia, and Rumania that Wilson convened in his quarters on the Place des États-Unis on June 4, 1919. As Brătianu pleaded: "Rumania is actually in a state of war, formally declared on her by the Bolshevists [*sic*] both of Russia and Hungary. It [may be] a good thing to disarm the police, but the thieves must be disarmed first."

Just a week later, Brătianu agreed to Pichon's request to provide Rumanian forces for this very purpose—to crush Béla Kun and his communist forces in Hungary. It was clear that the Comintern, led first by Lenin, then by Stalin, intended to seize the opportunity posed by the large, disaffected, often disenfranchised, and frequently abused minority populations the Allies created in Paris. And the Balkans were an especially fertile breeding ground for violent insurrection by these very minorities. In 1924 the Comintern called for self-determination for the "oppressed people" of Macedonia, Thrace, Carpathia, Slovenia, Transylvania, Dobrudja, Bessarabia, and Bukovina. Its plan was a devious one—to pull Bessarabia and Bukovina into an expanded Soviet Union, while turning the rest into a series of small communist nations that would band together as a Soviet-dominated federation. It was a fiendishly clever plan that never seemed to occur to the Allied peacemakers of 1919, most of whom wanted a unified Balkans with which they could deal easily and that would stabilize this critical region. The Comintern's concept failed to bear fruit until the final decade of the twentieth century, when ethnic fragmentation finally came to the Balkans after communism had been relegated to the history books.

By the middle 1920s, across the Balkans and southern Europe, the seeds sown by the peacemakers in Paris quickly began to bear some very bitter fruit. In Rumania the disparate peoples herded into the nation's new national borders led to increased instability and enormous problems of political management. Brătianu returned home only to resign in dismay after what he saw as a personal failure of losing a slice of the Banat to Yugoslavia. Unable to stomach his archfoe Take Ionescu, who took over in his place, Brătianu resurfaced in a succession of unstable governments that failed to win sustainable electoral majorities. Finally he succumbed, in perhaps the ultimate irony, to a terminal case of laryngitis, dying of complications in November 1927, and was succeeded by his brother. Queen Marie's only son, Charles, turned out to be a rake, running off to France with a string of flamboyant commoners, including Magda Lupescu. In 1930 Charles returned to Bucharest and was crowned Charles II. Eight years later, with the nation unable to sustain an elected government for more than a few months, and with the help of a powerful homegrown fascist organization known as the Iron Guard, King Charles seized power, proclaiming, effectively, a dictatorship. Another nation was lost to Wilsonian-style democratic self-government.

A similar path was being followed in neighboring Yugoslavia, also choking on the rich stew of minorities and multiplicity of languages, religions, and ethnic origins all thrown together during the peace process. A succession of cabinets and a parade of elections followed the war, through the Treaty of Rapallo and on into the 1930s. Milenko Vesnić, who'd scrawled his "corrections" on House's copy of the Fourteen Points during the war, returned home from Paris to become prime minister of the newly formed Yugoslavia. By 1921 he was succeeded by Pašić, who like Brătianu couldn't stay away from power. Pašić wound up presiding over ten cabinets in the five years before his death in 1926, eight days before his eightieth birthday. In 1920, after completing negotiations for the Treaty of Rapallo, Trumbić resigned as foreign minister. He was unable to stomach the rising tide of Serb domination of a kingdom that had all the appearances of a Greater Serbian version of its prewar predecessor. All seven prime ministers of the twenty-four cabinets between December 1918 and January 1929 were Serbs, as was every minister of the army and navy, and all but four of the one hundred sixty-five generals who served until the outbreak World War II. Most Croatian and Slovenian parties eventually refused even to take their seats in the Serb-dominated parliament. There was bitter opposition as well from Macedonians, Bosnian Moslems, and most of the other ethnic minorities. Serbia's King Alexander, by then crowned the ruling monarch of Yugoslavia, threw up his hands and in January 1929 dissolved parliament and proclaimed a royal dictatorship. Five years later, on a state visit to France, he was assassinated in Marseille by a Macedonian fascist with links to Mussolini. The Serbian monarch had never managed to return any unity to his disparate nation of Yugoslavia and its fractious nationalities.

The rest of the Balkans fared little better. Bulgaria, the only regional power on the losing side in the war, was forced by the Paris peacemakers to give up four border areas to Yugoslavia and was socked with a staggering bill for reparations, equal to the entire national wealth of the country. By the end of 1919, Boris III had been crowned king, a powerful communist party had been formed, and a right-wing Orange Guard of peasants armed with clubs was organized to break up communist-led strikes. Still, amid this chaos, the nation managed to organize a democratically elected government dominated by the Agrarian Union Party, which won double the number of seats the communists collected in the first postwar election. In 1920 Bulgaria became the first of the defeated Central Powers to join the League of Nations. But there was considerable internal instability, due in part to the persistent economic problems that only deepened as the global depression of the 1930s swept across the Balkans. A succession of military coups, revolts, and communist disturbances marked most of the interwar years until finally, as in both of its neighbors, a royal dictatorship was declared in 1935 by King Boris.

The smallest Balkan nation, Albania, which managed to escape Italian domination while losing a slice of its territory in the north to Yugoslavia, was also rent by political strife. The major landowners, led by Ahmet Zogu, sought to preserve their system of feudal tenure and opposed all social reforms that were pressed by Bishop Fan S. Noli. A Harvard graduate who had founded the Albanian Orthodox Church in Boston in 1908, Noli returned to Albania in 1920 determined, with Wilson's blessing, to establish a Western-style democracy. He succeeded in doing this in July 1924 at the head of a peasant-backed insurgency—though with no help from the United States. By 1925 Zogu, at the head of an army he'd raised with the support of Yugoslavia, where he'd fled after Noli seized power, recaptured Tirana and three years later proclaimed himself Zog I, king of the Albanians. His reign lasted until 1939, when Mussolini decided to consummate what his predecessors had sought for twenty years. With Albania in desperate need of foreign economic assistance and after a huge loan in 1931 of a hundred million gold francs that the nation was unable to repay, Italian fascist forces invaded Albania and turned it into yet another outpost of Italy's neo-Roman Empire.

By the outbreak of World War II, in sharp contrast to the desires of the best-intentioned peacemakers at Paris, all of the Balkans had become royal dictatorships of one form or another. Most of them were carefully designed to do away with self-determination and a host of national and minority rights. Desperate political, social, and economic consequences grew out of these efforts to impose Western systems on nations that had no previous experience with such concepts. These basic realities, together with overwhelming problems of survival following the end of a catastrophic war, combined to push them all into various extremes on either the right or the left. During World War II all of the Balkans were overrun by the Nazis, producing a polarization of homegrown political forces—from the barbaric Iron Guard in Rumania to the fascist Ustaše of Ante Pavelić and the communism of Josip Broz Tito's partisan freedom fighters in Yugoslavia.

The end of World War II mirrored very closely the end of World War I. In Rumania, the communist dictatorship of Nicolae Ceaușescu replaced the royal dictatorship of Charles II, while in Yugoslavia Tito's rule replaced King Alexander's. Tito, however, sought a different route to unity. Abolishing all preexisting religions in favor of communism as the one true religion at least papered over some of the deeper faultlines that had caused such irreparable divisions among Yugoslavia's nationalities in the past. Communism appeared as a welcome respite from the continuous instabilities, chaos, and repression that marked the post-Versailles years.

Each Balkan leader succeeded in bringing into his central government representatives of all the major nationalities. Ceaușescu welcomed

Rumania's chief rabbi as a member of parliament, with all the perks—including a chauffered black Mercedes. Tito's partisans were a truly multiethnic band. During the war, they were united in what the population saw as a heroic struggle against the Nazi invaders. At the end of the fighting and on into the postwar era, they joined in their efforts to present a common front against hard-line Soviet communism and to preserve their nation's position as a leader of the world's nonaligned nations. Tito was careful to bring into his early inner circle Slovenes such as his foreign minister Edvard Kardelj, Croatians like Dr. Vladimir Bakarić, and the Montenegrin intellectual Milovan Djilas. Tito himself was born in Croatia, son of a Croatian father and Slovenian mother, and he married a Serbian woman who was born in Croatia. Such a personal and political family was designed to create a single, polyglot nation with considerable internal and external strengths. It was precisely the type sought by the peacemakers of Paris, though absent any suggestion of Wilsonian democracy. Tito's Yugoslavia, however, proved to be little more than a transitory creation of a single individual that barely survived his own lifetime.

At its heart, Yugoslavia remained an artificial union, held together only by the force of Tito's charismatic personality. For a decade after his death on May 4, 1980, the "collective leadership" system he had established, including one member from each of the six Yugoslav republics plus Kosovo and Vojvodina, managed to hold the various parts of the nation together. Finally by 1990, with Slobodan Milošević, a fervent Serbian nationalist, in power, and communist regimes collapsing across Eastern Europe, Yugoslavia began to break apart—violently. A decade of bloody warfare erupted, tearing apart the nation into component territories and forcing the intervention by armed forces of NATO and the United Nations to enforce a peace brokered by the United States. It was only after the deft diplomatic negotiations by Ambassador Richard Holbrooke and his carefully engineered Dayton Accord of November 1995—which separated so adeptly those nationalities joined at the hip in 1919, finally righting the wrongs of Versailles—that the bloodshed was ended. The Balkans returned to the path they exited so long before. "We were, in effect, burying another part of Versailles," Holbrooke wrote seven years later. "At Dayton we were working on only one small part of the puzzle; in Paris they worked on the world."

The end was perhaps inevitable from the outset. The centrifugal forces of the individual nationalities, the deep power of religious beliefs, languages, and alphabets eventually split Yugoslavia apart into individual nation-states far more violently than the peacemakers in Paris might ever have feared.

What finally brought a degree of self-determination and stability to the Balkans was prosperity and the prospect of becoming full-fledged members of the European community of nations. Slovenia, always the most prosperous of the Balkan nation-states, joined the European Union on May 1, 2004, eight years after it applied and the same day as the Czech Republic, Hungary, Poland, and Slovakia. Bulgaria and Rumania were set to follow suit in 2007 or 2008, while Croatia and Macedonia applied and became candidates. Still considered potential candidates, though they have not yet applied for membership, are the independent nations of Albania, Bosnia and Herzegovina, and Montenegro and Serbia (though the Kosovo Albanians are still demanding independence and their own nation). Montenegro declared its independence from Serbia on June 3, 2006, and was admitted as the 192nd member state of the United Nations twenty-five days later.

Finally, it would seem, nearly nine decades after the peacemakers of Paris gave these nations life, they were finally obtaining the type of self-determination that some had envisioned as their future from the beginning. Many of the boundaries drawn so painstakingly by the expert committees of diplomats and cartographers did manage to last for the rest of the century. Still, true self-determination would have meant independent nations of Serbia, Croatia, Slovenia, Bosnia and Herzegovina, Montenegro, Macedonia, and more. This would have left far too complex a map of Europe for the peacemakers in Paris to create, much less dominate and control. The new nations born at the Allied conference table were victims of great power paranoia—the fear that any smaller units could wind up spinning off in different, and uncontrollable, directions. With Bolshevism on the rise, such micro-states could become fertile ground for Lenin's Russia and its deep pan-Slavic ties. Instead, the road not taken was joined nearly a century later after decades of untold suffering, bloodshed, chaos, and poverty.

9

GREATER ASIAN
INSECURITY

ON DECEMBER 13, 1918, THE *GEORGE WASHINGTON* STEAMED into the harbor of Brest, and to the clash of cymbals and the cheers of hundreds of thousands of French, discharged President Woodrow Wilson—set to begin his conquest of Europe and the world, wrapped in the self-righteous glow of his beloved Fourteen Points. At the same time, another passenger, a slender young Chinese gentleman, slipped all but unnoticed to the dock. He, too, carried a powerful hope. It sprang from the selfsame document—that the promises it contained might transform the future of his own nation, restoring it to its one-time glory, or at a minimum guarantee the rights of its people to determine their own destiny. It was to prove a futile and empty dream—as empty as those of any of the other disappointed peoples across Europe, the Middle East, and on into Asia who also found their aspirations crushed beneath the realities of geopolitics and the armed forces that still overwhelmed diplomats and statesmen.

V. K. Wellington Koo, the thirty-two-year-old ambassador plenipotentiary of China, the youngest full delegate who would appear at the Paris Peace Conference, had been invited to accompany the president of the United States to Europe. It was a unique honor and, he believed, a signal that the United States was prepared to place particular effort in readjusting the balance of power in Asia that had tilted so dramatically, indeed tragically, against his nation. In terms of population, China was then, as it is now, the world's largest country. In the course of his lifetime, however, Wellington Koo had seen the fortunes of the once great Qing Dynasty plummet to the point where it collapsed in 1912. Riven internally by battles between rival warlords and political factions, China now found itself under the boot heels of its powerful and covetous neighbor, the Empire of Japan.

China's delegate to the Peace Conference, Vi Kyuin Wellington Koo.

Wellington Koo was born into a prosperous merchant family in Shanghai. Their forebears had begun their journey from Hunan Province on the Middle Yangtze River in the late sixteenth century at about the time the Qing Dynasty was launched, brushing aside the last Ming emperor. By the 1860s Koo's grandmother was well established in Shanghai. His father, first apprenticed in a customs brokerage by day, studying the Confucian classics by night, was on his way to becoming the leading hardware merchant in Shanghai. His shop on Foochow Road provided a center for the gentry merchant to spread his influence. Vi Kyuin Wellington Koo was born on January 29, 1887, and like his two brothers was reared in the classic Chinese style, studying at the feet of Master Chu, a scholar based in an ancestral temple. Beginning with the *Trimetrical Classic*, a Song Dynasty primer on Confucianism, he progressed rapidly through the *Book of Family Names*, expanding his education in the traditional Chinese spirit and principles of loyalty, piety, and diligence, and above all the concept of duty toward his family and his country. At the age of twelve, Koo continued his schooling at the Anglo-Chinese Junior College of Ts'angshan Road, winning first prize and developing a remarkable fluency in English—his second language. But it was here, in 1899, that Koo came hard up against the reality of contemporary China.

One day the young Koo, riding his new bicycle near the Shanghai racecourse, came upon a British boy about his age who was riding his own bike ahead of him. When the British youngster moved to the sidewalk, Koo followed. Suddenly an Indian policeman appeared, let the British youth pass, then turned on Koo and handed him over to a nearby Chinese police officer. Koo was taken to a police station, where he protested indignantly about the unfair and inequitable treatment. "I didn't know the rule, I only followed that English boy," Koo recalled telling the police—a version he recounted to his biographer, Pao-chin Chu, more than a half century later. Koo's protests fell on deaf ears. He was fined five yuan, which he ran home to borrow from his sister so that he could ransom his bike. It was a story he never forgot. There would be little that the peacemakers two decades later could do that might fix this attitude. Or even, as it developed, its underlying causes.

China, already powerless and divided, had been carved up and partitioned by the major military powers of the outside world beginning with the end of the First Opium War in 1843. The Qing emperors, it seems, had gone so far as to ban gunpowder, though it had been in wide use as early as the Song Dynasty and on into the Ming period. China had become vulnerable to a succession of foreign invaders, beginning with the British in the eighteenth century, who sought to expand the opium trade as payment for silk and spices so sought after in the West. As the Qing emperors never maintained a national army, relying instead on a network of regional warlords to maintain order, China was ripe for the plucking by powerful, disciplined national invaders. By the time Koo was confronted by the Indian officer in Shanghai, China had already been divided into spheres of influence by the British, the Germans, the French, the Russians, the Italians, the Austrians, and especially the Japanese.

For while China was being carved up by these foreign traders, its military weak and fragmented among a host of feuding warlords, Japan was growing in unity, power, reach, and above all ambition. This, too, was a response to foreign encroachments. Japan and China approached the arrival of foreign military and economic might on their shores in sharply different manners. In 1853 U.S. Navy Commodore Matthew C. Perry led a flotilla of black ships into Japan's waters in an effort to pierce that nation's determined isolation. This shock to the system, the likes of which would later all but paralyze the Chinese, energized the Japanese. In 1868 the empire embarked on the Meiji Restoration, designed to transform Japan within a generation into a modern state and a major world power, while fending off foreign domination and colonization.

The Japanese, especially the leadership surrounding the court of the emperor, had long believed in their cultural superiority over other Asian peoples. This profoundly racist concept proved ironic in view of Japan's later demands for racial equality with the Western world, particularly the United States. What quickly mutated into an especially pernicious form of manifest destiny was reinforced by a renowned Japanese educator, Fukuzawa Yukichi, who in 1882 published a landmark work— *Japan's Mission in Asia*. By the last decade of the nineteenth century, the nation's leadership recognized that it was faced with some hard realities. Japan, confined to a narrow group of islands off the Asian mainland, would eventually run out of space for its rapidly expanding population. The natural resources needed to fuel its industry, especially its military-industrial establishment, would be exhausted as well.

The Japanese recognized that if they did not expand, they would die. So the empire took a leaf from the playbook of the Western nations. Europe's troops and traders had spread across Asia—the Dutch in the Indonesian archipelago; England, France, and Germany in China; and Russia in Manchuria and Korea. China had been forced to "lease" Liaotung to Russia, Guangzhou to France, Weihaiwei to Britain, and Kiao chau to Germany. Now, like a shark, which must move through the waters to feed, Japan embarked on its own rapid, often vicious, expansion to mainland Asia.

In 1895, four years before Wellington Koo wound up in the police station with his bicycle, Japanese forces had poured into Korea, prepared to face down troops of the Qing Dynasty, which had long considered Korea's Choson monarchy a tribute state. For its invasion, Japan fielded a fleet of ships including twelve modern battle cruisers built in Britain, France, and Germany, as well as 120,000 men divided into two powerful armies. China, which Western experts picked as an easy victor over the much smaller nation of Japan, was pummeled into submission. The Chinese military was plagued with corruption that in the middle of Battle of the Yalu River left its naval units actually running out of gunpowder. Its armies were weakened by divisions among Manchu, Mongol, Moslem, and Han Chinese units and further divided among feuding regional warlords.

The result was a series of quick, bloody, hammerlike confrontations with Japanese invaders that finally led to the Chinese caving in to the Treaty of Shimonoseki. On April 17, 1895, this humiliating document effectively turned over Korea and Taiwan to Japan. But the empire's expansion had only just begun. Barely a decade later, Japan went to war again—this time against a major Western power. Russia had long had its hooks out for Manchuria and Korea, its forces pushing across the forbidding frontier down from Siberia. In 1904 war broke out with Japan. The empire's disciplined forces made short work of the armies of the czar, sparking an abortive revolt by naval forces, weakening his rule. This helped lay the groundwork for his eventual overthrow in 1917 and the takeover by Lenin and his Bolsheviks.

These two confrontations had a profound impact on the societies of all these nations. The Russo-Japanese War marked the first real victory of any Asian state over a major Western country. It effectively catapulted Japan into the ranks of a global power—indeed, the single great power in Asia. Within Japan, it touched off a debate as to whether it would be better to conquer and establish a colonial relationship with China or strengthen purely economic ties that would make both countries more interdependent. For the Japanese leadership, it wasn't even a choice. Japan wanted China more fragmented, more isolated, hence more submissive. Within China, however, there was a sense that it needed to open more resolutely to the outside world, to seek understanding and partnerships, much as the Meiji Restoration had accomplished in Japan.

In this atmosphere, with war breaking out between Japan and Russia, Wellington Koo set forth for the United States. In 1905 the young scholar enrolled as a liberal arts student at Columbia University, where he distinguished himself in nearly every endeavor. He was elected to Phi Beta Kappa, edited the *Columbia Spectator*, won the Literary Prize of the Philolexian Society, whose aim was to "improve its members in Oratory, Composition and Forensic Discussion," and was elected a member of the Senior Society of Nacoms—a unique secret society not unlike Yale's renowned Skull and Bones. Most important for his future career, he was selected for the varsity debate team, where he won the Columbia-Cornell Debating Medal as an outstanding orator. At the same time, Koo accumulated a reservoir of admiration from key faculty members who, seven years after he completed his PhD with the dissertation, "The Status of Aliens in China," would wind up in Paris on the U.S. delegation to the Peace Conference.

In 1912 Koo received a cable to return home to Beijing to serve his country, and was promptly named English secretary to the Cabinet. It was a time of accelerating turmoil. Barely two years after his return, war had broken out in Europe, and Foreign Minister Lou Tseng-tsiang was rushing to Koo's bedside in Beijing's German hospital, where he was recuperating from surgery. The young diplomat stayed up all night to draft the English response to Japan's Twenty-One Demands.

This document was one of the most demeaning in the history of diplomacy. It was presented as an ultimatum to the Beijing government shortly after the start of World War I, and its provisions would effectively have turned over control of China to Japan. It was the most sweeping of a host of secret agreements in Asia that would tie the hands of the peacemakers in Paris as effectively as any of the pacts carving up the Middle East, Eastern Europe, and the Balkans would paralyze deliberations on each of these regions. The Twenty-One Demands were handed to the Chinese government by Japan's ambassador to Beijing. The document was designed as a natural extension of Tokyo's activities in the early months of World War I.

Less than three weeks after Germany declared war on France, Japan declared war on Germany. On August 23, 1914, Tokyo ordered its "Army and Navy to carry on hostilities against that Empire with all their strength." This was a carte blanche for Japanese forces to land on the north coast of Shantung Province with the ostensible purpose of seizing the German concession, or sphere of influence, centering on Kiao-chau. This province, about the size of the state of Iowa, jutting into the Yellow Sea, was in a commanding position along the densely populated coastline of China. For the Japanese forces, who respected few boundaries, Shantung was perfectly positioned as a foothold for the empire's ultimate goal—to convert China into the type of Japanese colony it had so successfully managed to implant in Korea over the previous decade. The Twenty-One Demands were simply a reflection of the military reality that by January 1915, four months into Tokyo's rapid strike into Shantung Province, Japan had become an occupying power. Curiously, the Twenty-One Demands constituted the kind of document a victor would normally offer to a defeated foe. Yet China at that point was more a victim than an ally of Japan's enemy, Germany. The Demands were divided into five groups, the first four largely detailing the turnover of the German concessions to Japan and promising the empire exclusive rights along the Chinese coast. Tokyo ordered the Chinese not to disclose the fifth group. They effectively ceded control of the most vital functions of China's government to Japan—"engaging influential Japanese as political, financial and military advisers . . . [placing] police under joint Japanese and Chinese administration." They also gave Japan control of vital rail lines running into the heart of China. With massive military forces of the empire already occupying large swaths of Shantung Province and threatening to push into the interior, China had little choice. After four months of largely futile attempts at negotiating, with a knife to its throat, the government capitulated and signed.

Two months later, Lou Tseng-tsiang dispatched Wellington Koo as ambassador to Mexico, but en route a cable arrived. It ordered the twenty-seven-year-old diplomat to change course. He was the new Chinese ambassador to the United States and Cuba.

The Washington where Koo arrived in late July 1915 was in the throes of a desperate tightrope walk. The two-year-old administration of Woodrow Wilson had managed to keep the United States out of the war in Europe, where its sympathies were deeply embedded with the Allied side. But Wilson was equally concerned by developments in Asia. There his sympathies lay with China, while he recognized that the Western European nations, with whom the United States would eventually ally itself, had just been joined by Japan. From its earliest days, the Wilson administration had gone to bat for China, while battling Japan on a host of diplomatic fronts. Asia, though still separated from the United States by weeks of travel in those years before intercontinental airline flights, was becoming an ever more important element of U.S. policy.

Barely two weeks after his inauguration on March 4, 1913 (in those pre-Twentieth Amendment days), Wilson found himself deeply embroiled in a complex six-nation consortium loan to China—a vital economic component of the Open Door Policy. Wilson's predecessor, William Howard Taft, had proposed this concept as a means of wedging a toehold of U.S. interests into a China whose territory had already been divided among Western powers in their concession zones. Wilson, seeing it as a means of defending self-determination for the beleaguered Chinese people, embraced the Open Door as well.

Wilson also moved quickly to put his own man in Beijing. His final choice, after several false starts, was a distinguished academic—Paul Samuel Reinsch, a professor of political science at the University of Wisconsin, trained as an attorney, whom Wilson had come to admire when the two helped to organize the American Political Science Association.

Reinsch arrived in Beijing on November 13, 1913, as another critical issue in Asia was coming to a full boil.

The morning after the inauguration, Sutemi Chinda, Japan's ambassador to Washington, appeared at the White House to call the new president's attention to the problem of land legislation in California. It was an issue that Wilson knew well—a holdover from the bitter political campaign when his own Democratic Party platform had proclaimed itself in favor of exclusion laws. These laws were aimed largely at Asian immigrants, most of them in the Western states and particularly California, where some one hundred thousand Japanese had settled in coastal cities and the rich inland valleys. These frugal and hardworking settlers very quickly sought to buy up fertile agricultural land—contesting with resident whites, first for employment, then for property ownership. By the beginning of 1913, some forty measures restricting land ownership and settlement by Asians were on the docket in the California legislature. During the 1912 presidential campaign, Wilson had already written to San Francisco Mayor James Phelan: "In the matter of Chinese and Japanese coolie immigration, I stand for the national policy of exclusion. The whole question is one of assimilation of diverse races. We cannot make a homogeneous population out of a people who do not blend with the Caucasian race. . . . Oriental coolieism will give us another race problem to solve, and surely we have learned our lesson."

Whether such an extraordinarily racist statement reflected Wilson's real, deep-seated views of Asians or merely the exigencies of a bitter three-party political campaign and California's thirteen electoral votes (which finally went to his Progressive opponent, Teddy Roosevelt), now, as president, Wilson had a far broader problem. It was standing in front of him in the person of Ambassador Chinda. This legislation, the ambassador observed frankly, branded the Japanese as inferior people. Wilson tried, with little success, to help the ambassador, and by extension his government, to understand that there was little he, even as president, could do to thwart the wishes of the California legislature, whose independence in dealing with its Japanese residents was to haunt most of his presidency.

A host of other frictions between the United States and Japan had also been building in as rapid, if less directly confrontational, a fashion as the California land issue. Paramount was America's extension of its reach into the Pacific. In 1898 the United States had acquired the

Hawaiian islands, where many Japanese already made their homes. Following the Spanish-American war, the United States acquired the Philippines as well, establishing a military base there. This was yet another stepping-stone across the Pacific and another perceived threat to Japan and its interest in dominating Asia.

There were more frictions as well. An especially sensitive issue was the hordes of American missionaries plying their trade in China. Most of them were bitterly opposed to Japanese activities on the Asian mainland. The missionaries' interests and well-being were also very close to the heart of Wilson. The new president also espoused the Open Door Po icy, calculated to frustrate Japanese intentions of unique domination of the Asian mainland. Finally, the Panama Canal was a little more than a year from opening. Indeed, as tensions with Japan rose, Colonel George W. Goethals added an extra shift to accelerate its completion, giving U.S. warships more rapid passage between the Atlantic and the Pacific. This sent new fears through Japan's powerful naval establishment that Japan's domination of the waters of the Pacific might be nearing an end.

It didn't take much for Ambassador Chinda to accumulate a wel spring of ill feeling in the White House—his government had already seen to that. The Twenty-One Demands, whose existence had been leaked in parts to Ambassador Reinsch in Beijing beginning three days after they were handed to the Chinese, had made Japan suspect in all the Allied capitals. Britain and France had already concluded that their alliance with Japan was acceptable only because of fears that the empire's military leadership—which already had openly expressed its admiration of the German war machine—might otherwise tip Japan into the arms of Germany and the Central Powers. So instead of Germany being ousted from China, it would have been Britain, France, and eventually the United States.

Washington was torn by what to do about the Twenty-One Demands, which Reinsch exhorted his bosses at the State Department and his friend Woodrow Wilson to keep secret (until they were finally leaked to the press in Beijing a month later). Wilson's then secretary of State, William Jennings Bryan (replaced by Robert Lansing in 1915), suggested that it might be "worthwhile for China to agree to the cession of Manchuria if, by so doing, she could secure the freedom as to the rest of the country." This, of course, did not even approach Japan's ultimate desires on the Asian continent. Wilson went even further, cautioning Reinsch in Beijing that "any direct advice to China or direct intervention on her behalf in the present negotiations would really do her more harm than good, inasmuch as it would very likely provoke the jealousy and excite the hostility of Japan, which would first be manifested against China herself." To his counterparts in Britain, France, and the Netherlands, he suggested "in strictest confidence" that "the United States frankly recognizes that territorial contiguity creates special relations between Japan and these [Chinese] districts." The State Department, surprisingly, agreed with this view—that some arrangement had to be made for Japan to expand on the Asian continent. In part, no doubt, this was a tribute to the fear by many, including Secretary Bryan, who had personally been dispatched by Wilson to California to deal with the land question, that if Japan didn't have lebensraum in Asia, its people would find their way very quickly across the Pacific to California. Some powerful voices in Congress and across the nation expressed very Homeland Security–style views. In the words of Hudson Maxim, inventor of the machine gun, Japan could land 250,000 troops on the California coast faster than the United States could dispatch 30,000 to fend them off.

When Ambassador Koo took up his post in Washington in July 1915, it was too late. Two months earlier, China had capitulated and signed the Twenty-One Demands. While Wilson had become "convinced that we shall have to try in every way practicable to defend China . . . [and] be very chary hereafter about seeming to concede the reasonableness of any of Japan's demands or requests," the die was cast. The best Wilson could muster was a declaration that the United States would not "recognize any agreement or understanding which has been entered into or which may be entered into between the governments of Japan and China, impairing the treaty rights of the United States and its citizens in China, the political or territorial integrity of the Republic of China, or the international policy relative to China commonly known as the open door policy."

Meanwhile, frictions were multiplying between the United States and Japan. Since 1913 the government in Tokyo had been shipping arms to General Victoriano Huerto in Mexico for use against the United States. On January 16, 1917, German Foreign Secretary Alfred Zimmerman dispatched a note promising the Mexicans that if they allied themselves with Germany, they would "regain the formerly held territory in Texas, New Mexico and Arizona," and urged Mexico's president to "use his good offices between us and Japan." Needless to say, the Zimmerman note provoked paroxysms of rage across America. But it was not the only point of friction between Japan and the United States. The leadership in Tokyo also unilaterally decided to occupy German-controlled islands of the northern Pacific, including the Caroline and Marshall islands, for the duration of the war. This action horrified U.S. Navy brass, who promptly sent fuel and ammunition to U.S. naval facilities in Hawaii and the Philippines. The British privately advised their American colleagues that there was an "understanding" that the Japanese would keep German islands north of the equator after the war. This was yet another secret pact that would return to haunt the peacemakers in Paris. On a trip to London, Colonel Edward House complained to British Foreign Secretary Sir Edward Grey that Japan was using the war and the Allies to further its own ends. Tokyo knew full well that the Europeans were in no position to object or enforce any objections as they fought a life-and-death conflict half a world away.

There were more than "understandings" afoot. Unbeknownst at the time to Colonel House or any U.S. official, Japan was moving to secure a broad series of secret agreements cementing its military and political position across Asia. On July 3, 1916, Russia and Japan signed an alliance pledging to prevent any third power from acquiring political influence in China hostile to either party. Ostensibly directed at Germany, the agreement was in fact intended to exclude the United States from the northern Chinese spheres of influence of the two signatories. Japan figured, correctly as it turned out, that it could deal with Russia after it was exhausted of men and supplies, with one million Russians lost in the war against the Central Powers in Europe.

There were more secret agreements to come. In February 1917, two months before the United States formally entered the war, Britain, Russia, and Japan signed a pact giving Britain all German islands in the Pacific south of the equator, and Japan all islands north of the equator. This went far beyond the informal "understanding" that Sir Edward Grey had tossed off to Colonel House. At the same time, Britain assured Japan it would support all Japanese rights to Shantung at the eventual peace conference, while Japan pledged its navy's help in escorting convoys in the Mediterranean (which was how Chaim Weizmann and his Zionist contingent came to be escorted to Palestine by a Japanese warship). In separate agreements, France and Italy also privately agreed to support Japanese claims after the war.

As Japanese military and diplomatic victories in Asia multiplied, her cockiness did as well. On September 1, 1917, a major Japanese mission arrived in the United States headed by Viscount Kikujiro Ishii, the wily former foreign minister. It was accorded the pomp and ceremony of a state visit—at formal receptions in San Francisco, New York, and Boston, at the White House, and the ultimate irony, even at Admiral (formerly Commodore) Perry's grave in Newport, Rhode Island. Ishii was carrying an important message. He took this message to Wilson, of course, but directly to the American people as well—effectively a whistle-stop tour of the power centers of the nation. There was no mention of any of the secret treaties that Japan believed had cemented its legal position in Asia. Instead Ishii proclaimed a Japanese Monroe Doctrine. He was confident the Americans could accept such a concept for the Eastern hemisphere since they had embraced such a doctrine to secure U.S. supremacy in the Western hemisphere.

From September 6 to November 2, 1917, Robert Lansing, by then secretary of state, met with Ishii thirteen times—far more often than with Wellington Koo, notwithstanding all the goodwill China seemed to possess in Washington and the diplomat's schooling in America. Lansing and Ishii were working toward an eventual exchange of notes—dealing largely with China, and especially with the Open Door Policy that Wilson and Lansing hoped to cement as dogma. The note was finally concluded on November 5. Both parties recognized that "territorial propinquity creates special relations between countries, and consequently the Government of the United States recognizes that Japan has special interests in China, particularly in the part to which her possessions are contiguous. The territorial sovereignty of China . . . remains unimpaired." The Open Door Policy was reaffirmed in a secret protocol of the agreement. The United States itself had now entered into a secret pact that would go a long way toward tying the hands of its negotiators in Paris.

China, not surprisingly, was horrified when word of the exchange of notes was leaked by the Japanese, who hoped to prove to the world, and certainly to Beijing, that Wilson had abandoned China. Reinsch promptly cabled Washington with China's reservation—which he had suggested—declaring the Beijing government was bound by nothing in the Japanese-American pact. The day Reinsch's dispatch was received at the State Department, Lansing summoned Koo for a chat. The secretary of state assured Koo that he had an enormous personal affection and respect for the young diplomat. Indeed, his counselor at the State Department was the very John Basset Moore who had served as Koo's professor of international law at Columbia. Then Lansing told Koo that he had no intention of putting China in a bind and that China's interests were paramount in his thinking throughout the negotiations. While never confiding this to Koo, in fact both Wilson and Lansing saw this pact as nothing more than a finger in the dike—a stopgap measure to rein in Japanese expansion in China while the Western powers got on with their priority: winning the war in Europe. Colonel House summarized this view for Wilson. The president agreed:

> We cannot meet Japan in her desires as to land and immigration, and unless we make some concession in regard to her sphere of influence in the East, trouble is sure, sooner or later to come. Japan is barred from all the undeveloped places of the earth, and if her influence in the East is not recognized as in some degree superior to that of the Western powers, there will be a reckoning. A policy can be formulated which will leave the door open, rehabilitate China, and satisfy Japan.

Still, the Asian Monroe Doctrine, first raised by Ishii on this visit and during these negotiations, would return—as the Amau Doctrine—to haunt the United States in Paris and, in an even more pernicious form, in the months leading up to Japan's first incursions into Manchuria that were a prelude to World War II.

Before World War I could end, however, there developed one final point of friction between the United States and Japan that was to overhang the entire Peace Conference. This time, it involved the Bolsheviks. By the end of 1917, the United States, China, and Japan were in the war and Russia was out of it following the overthrow of the czar. Now, with Russia embroiled in its own civil war, Siberia became a backdoor focus of those seeking to contain the Bolshevik advance. The fragmented forces of Russia in Siberia also seemed to pose an irresistible opportunity for Japan to seize large swaths of valuable territory. Japan's opportunity came with the realization that some 648,00 tons of Allied munitions were stockpiled in Vladivostok, while Bolshevik forces appeared to be ramping up an operation to seize stretches of the Trans-Siberian, Chinese Eastern, and Amur railroads.

By December 1917, Japan pressed the United States to engage in a joint military exercise to take strategic points in Siberia, allegedly to prevent any German army units from moving in. The United States demurred, particularly when word reached Washington that Chinese forces controlled by Japanese overseers had already occupied the Chinese Eastern Railway zone—intensifying suspicion of Japanese intentions in Siberia. Still, David Lloyd George liked the idea of an eastern front against the Bolsheviks, though at the same time House was telling Wilson that "it would be a great political mistake to send Japanese troops into Siberia." Wilson largely shared this view, though for different reasons. He feared pushing Russian moderates, whom he still hoped might carry the day in Russia, into the arms of Germany. On March 1, 1918, the United States finally agreed not to stand in the way of sending in an Allied force, as Wilson told the Japanese:

The United States has no objection . . . and it wishes to assure the Japanese government that it has entire confidence that in putting an armed force into Siberia, it is doing so as an ally of Russia, with no purpose but to save Siberia from the invasion of the armies and intrigues of Germany and with entire willingness to leave the determination of all questions that may affect the permanent fortunes of Siberia to the Council of Peace.

Wishful thinking. And there were realists in the administration who recognized what a colossal mistake this could be. William Bullitt sent a personal memo to Wilson via Colonel House charging that the United States had "tacitly agreed to Japan's invasion of Siberia. . . . Japan will take this step because of her desire to annex eastern Siberia which she covets so intensely. . . . We cannot wash our hands of this matter. Unless we oppose, we assent. Pontius Pilate washed his hands. The world has never forgiven him."

These were the kinds of emotions that Asia was raising in the United States. Still, the die was not cast. U.S. forces were not committed to the action, and House continued to warn Wilson that "we are treading on exceedingly delicate and dangerous ground, and are likely to lose [our] fine moral position." It was an argument calculated to appeal to Wilson's most deeply held beliefs. By late April, however, the war was going badly in Europe. Lord Arthur Balfour alerted the United States that the Germans were about to transfer some forty divisions from the Eastern to the Western fronts, where American boys were already deeply committed. By early August, an agreement was reached. Japan would send in 10,000 troops and Major General William Graves would lead a group of 8,000 Americans.

When General Graves arrived in Siberia on September 1, 1918, Japanese forces had already landed and were fanning out across Siberia. As he quickly reported, they were operating as a full-scale army of occupation. Moreover, the Japanese expeditionary force consisted of two full divisions—each with some 28,000 men, far more than the agreement called for. It was to take two international conferences and four years to dislodge them, although the timely arrival of General Graves and his U.S. troops did appear to have prevented full Japanese seizure of the Siberian maritime provinces. Fortunately, armistice in Europe also intervened. War came to an end. Now it was time, with lots of faits accomplis in Asia, as well as Europe and the Middle East, for the Allied powers to divide up the spoils.

On all fronts, the nations with the most at stake lined up the most potent diplomatic forces they possessed and sent them on to Paris.

For China, it was inevitable that Wellington Koo would emerge as its leader, its most vocal and articulate spokesman. But this was only after bitter political battles within the delegation that reflected the increasingly tangled political situation back home. China had become bitterly divided, north and south, in the immediate prewar years. This was a troubling, potentially lethal scenario as it faced down Japan—an increasingly powerful and unified enemy. A virtual civil war had broken out between Sun Yat-sen, the revolutionary republican leader based in Nanking in the south, and the Beijing-based government that had replaced the deposed Qing monarchy. Since the Beijing government was the one that most foreign governments recognized, it chose a majority of the delegation to Paris. The mission was led by Lou Tseng-tsiang, the foreign minister who had first recognized Koo's extraordinary talents and dispatched the young diplomat as ambassador to Washington. Alfred

Sze, a Cornell graduate, ambassador to London, and the man who had first escorted the young Koo to the United States as a student a decade earlier, was the second-ranking member of the delegation in seniority. He would become embittered and hostile as his young one-time protégé emerged as China's principal spokesman to the world. C. T. Wang, a Yale graduate, and S. T. Wei, another Columbia College alum, were the two representatives grudgingly granted to the south. And then there was Koo.

Aware even before the armistice that he'd been designated a member of the delegation, Koo had been carefully laying the basis for China's position in Paris. On November 15, 1918, four days after hostilities ended, Koo visited Secretary of State Lansing with details of the Chinese proposals for the Peace Conference. As an ally, if largely a noncombatant, China believed its wishes were fair and attainable, certainly in total conformity with Wilson's Fourteen Points. First Koo said that China wanted an end to all foreign "concessions" or settlements, which had functioned with their own governments, taxing powers, and as Koo had experienced firsthand as a youngster in Shanghai, police. China also wanted a return of all sovereign rights throughout its territory, evacuation of all foreign troops stationed in the country, as well as economic and fiscal independence, particularly freedom to set and administer tariffs. Ten days later, Koo visited Wilson at the White House to press these points, describing his nation's desire as "merely to restore to her some of the things which, in the view of the Chinese people, had been wrongly taken from her." Wilson replied that "there would be nothing for China to fear from the discussions at this conference." However, he then struck an ominous note. "There are many secret agreements between the subjects of China and other powers," the president observed.

In one respect Wilson was right China would have nothing to fear from decisions at the Peace Conference. That's because her worst nightmares had already been engraved in the secret treaties that largely preordained the outcome. Moreover, none of the Allied delegates saw enough reward to their own countries in circumventing or overturning these Asian treaties to expend valuable political capital. Nor was any Allied delegate—even Wilson—sufficiently farsighted to recognize the harm inaction would cause in this remote corner of the world. The delegates from Japan—which had itself engineered most of these treaties—effectively held all the cards, and were wise enough to play them at just the right points.

The Japanese sent some of their wisest and most adept politicians to the Peace Conference, an event for which they had been preparing since the outbreak of the war in Europe more than four years earlier. Heading the delegation was one of Japan's most distinguished leaders: Prince Saionji Kimmochi, last of the genros, the elders who for generations had quietly pulled the political strings of the nation and who were revered as the closest confidants of the emperor himself. Prince Saionji was born into an ancient noble family in the imperial city of Kyoto in 1849, so by the time of the Peace Conference he was nearly seventy years old. Growing up near the imperial palace, he was an early playmate of the young prince who would become the Emperor Meiji. The two remained lifelong friends. As a young man, Prince Saionji spent several years in France, researching European culture—part of the Meiji Restoration—and came to know a rising French politician, Georges Clemenceau. Throughout the late nineteenth and into the twentieth centuries, Saionji played an important role in bringing Japan out of its isolation, while as a liberal politician, and twice prime minister, he sought to restrain some of the more unbridled adventures of his nation's military elite. By the time of his arrival in Paris, he was a figure of reverence and wisdom, whose exalted position kept him largely secluded. Like his venerable Chinese counterpart, Lou Tseng-tsiang, Saionji was rarely seen in public. He pulled all the wires, however, behind the curtains.

It was, for instance, Saionji who suggested in a carefully choreographed audience he granted to his old friend Stephen Bonsal that "the Conference will have failed of one of its high purposes unless the Russians are placed in control of Constantinople and the Dardanelles." Bewildered that this Japanese diplomat would be so concerned with the entrance to the Black Sea, Bonsal reported back to Colonel House, who said, smiling:

> What a wise old boy he is. Certainly the outlet on the Mediterranean would keep Russia busy in Europe for decades to come and give Japan for the same period a free hand in Manchuria and Siberia, and indeed in the whole of Asia. What a boon that would be for Japan—and what a disaster for China. . . . He and those who think with him are contemplating a general advance on the continent of Asia. . . . And how easy that will be if Russia is

engaged elsewhere. I think the fair inference from what the Prince said is very important. . . . Japan is going continental.

These were the ploys of the master manipulators that the empire had sent to Paris. Accompanying Saionji on their diplomatic endeavors to cement Japanese hegemony were the delegation's two front men—a crafty pair of diplomats who were already well known in the West. The U.S. delegation quickly dubbed them "The Two Mikados."

Viscount Sutemi Chinda, ambassador to England and former ambassador to the United States and Germany, had dealt during the early years of the Wilson administration with most of the major players who now had come to Paris. A small man with a large drooping gray mustache, Chinda might have passed for an elderly professor of political science at a small Midwestern college. His American roots ran as deep as Koo's. Though he had none of the Ivy League credentials of some of his Chinese counterparts, still the young Chinda did pledge the powerful Deke fraternity at Indiana University when he arrived as a student in 1877. After graduation, he married the sister of a Deke fraternity brother from Japan. Thirty-five years later, she planted the second of three thousand cherry trees along the banks of the Potomac River that her husband, by then ambassador to the United States, had brought to Washington as a gift to the American people. (First Lady Helen Taft planted the first of the trees.)

Chinda's principal colleague in Paris was Baron Nobuaki Makino. His background and education were largely European, having served as Japanese ambassador both to France and Italy as well as foreign minister in Tokyo. Between the two, they had all four Allied powers covered. In contrast to Chinda, Makino was a large, dominating presence with a stern, military bearing. He more often took the floor in the debates with the Allied leaders to reinforce Japan's positions and its demands. Ironically, his young son-in-law, who served in a junior position on the Japanese delegation, came to detest Makino. As a result, he was one of the few Japanese officials spared by U.S. occupation forces in Japan after World War II, and he became the nation's first postwar foreign minister. The contrast with his father-in-law was striking. Makino was the iron fist of the Japanese delegation in Paris in 1919.

This rounded out the Japanese delegation. Other Asian nations failed even to win a formal hearing at the Peace Conference, which recognized only clearly independent and sovereign states. So while Siam (Thailand, as it's known today) was allowed to field a tiny delegation, Korea was not. It was not for lack of trying, however. From the United States, forty-three-year-old Syngman Rhee, who a decade before had studied for his PhD at Princeton under Woodrow Wilson, sought to lead a delegation from his home in Hawaii. He was refused a passport for his mission by a State Department that wanted no more complications in Paris than it already envisioned—especially with the prickly Japanese. Another Korean delegation was marginally more successful, at least managing to find its way to the French capital. Kim Gyu-sik, a graduate of Virginia's Roanoke College, made his way across Siberia to represent the New Korea Youth Party, which consisted of more than one million Koreans who'd fled into exile to China and Siberia ahead of Japanese forces. Setting up an elaborate propaganda system in Paris, he was the envy of Nguyen Ai Quoc, at least in terms of his access to U.S. officials, particularly Stephen Bonsal. Kim pleaded with House's aide, explaining, as Bonsal recalled, that "the people of Korea . . . regard the assembly of this Parliament of Man, and the convening of this High Court of world justice as a heaven-sent opportunity . . . to make known their wrongs to the world and to seek redress." Bonsal managed to raise the issue with Colonel House, but returned with some sad news. "The Korean problem [does] not come within the purview of the Conference," he told Kim. "If we attempt too much we may fail to accomplish anything."

"What a strange world this is," Kim replied, adding that the Japanese, "these scamps and scalawags, these pirates and land grabbers, are here and they are accepted as representing a great power while we are excluded from the World Congress." When news of Kim's failure reached Korea, the first of the violent demonstrations that were to mark the outcome of the Peace Conference in Asia erupted across the nation. An anti-Japanese march was held in Seoul, and in the smallest villages a "Declaration of Independence" was read. It was for many a death dirge, as Japanese troops moved in to crush the marchers, firing into groups of Korean Christians singing protest hymns, nailing leaders to crosses as mounted police decapitated young schoolchildren and burned churches. This Japanese colony was as central to the empire's economic and geopolitical interests as Annam was to the French or the Philippines, Hawaii, and Cuba to the Americans. In short, it was inviolate. Wilson's Four-teen Points clearly did not extend to the colonies.

Still, China trusted deeply in the sympathy it believed it had built up in all Allied capitals. As the U.S. ambassador to Beijing, Paul Reinsch, reminded Wilson in an urgent cable while he was on board the *George Washington*:

> You have become to the people of China the embodiment of their best hopes and aspirations. . . . Never before have the words of a foreign statesman entered so deeply and directly into the hearts of the Chinese people. . . . I have been forced through the experi-ence of five years to the conclusions that the methods applied by the Japanese military masters can lead only to evil and destruction and they will not be stopped by any consideration of fairness and justice but only by the definite knowledge that such action will not be tolerated. . . . China must be freed from all foreign political influences exercised within her border.

The realists on the U.S. delegation recognized, however, that a long, difficult road lay ahead. Lansing promptly dispatched a reply to Ambas-sador Reinsch that he should "make occasion to say orally to the Chi-nese Foreign Office that the American Commissioners will be unable to help China at Peace Conference if Japan comes here with China's grant of special rights in Shantung as a fait accompli." Which is precisely what the Japanese intended from the opening session. Japan would under no circumstances give up the special rights it had been granted by the Chinese government in Shantung, the empire's foothold on the Asian mainland, and return the territory to its Chinese owners.

China's problems were apparent from the outset. Japan, the earliest Asian member of the Allied powers, which had contributed land and naval forces to the effort from the Mediterranean across Siberia to the Pacific, was treated as a full-fledged member of the Council of Ten. China, while admitted to the proceedings (unlike Korea and Indochina), was present only when matters directly affecting its interests were on the agenda. In short, Japan was on the inside, while China's nose remained for the most part pressed against the window. Japan did have several issues of its own to deal with that had little to do with China, but that would certainly gum up the works in Paris.

While retaining the territory it had already seized in Shantung and the Kiao-chau German concession area was of paramount importance, Japan was also profoundly concerned with the issue of racial equality that still festered—particularly in the United States. Anti-Asian legislation continued to trouble the position of its settlers in California and a host of other states. Landowners in Louisiana were even proposing to bring Japanese to work their plantations, a move all too reminiscent of the slavery that had been abolished little more than a half century earlier. So the day after the ceremonial opening of the Peace Conference, Makino and Chinda appeared on the doorstep of Colonel House in the Crillon to solicit his help in inserting a racial equality clause in the treaty or the covenant of the League of Nations. Quite simply, this was not going to happen. Australian Prime Minister William H. Hughes, faced with the potential of thousands of Japanese overrunning his nation, which was even closer to Japan than California, dug in his heels. Hughes forced the British, as leaders of the Commonwealth bloc, to do likewise. Lord Robert Cecil told House, "the British would not agree to it at all, probably not in any form."

A month later, with the finishing touches being placed on the covenant of the League of Nations, the Japanese resurfaced with an amendment to the freedom of religion clause, seeking to add "racial freedom." The campaign continued at a low level throughout the deliberations in Paris with telegrams from Japanese residents of Hawaii and petitions from thirty-seven Japanese associations in Tokyo arriving at the Crillon. Ambassador Ishii even made a quick trip to New York from Washington to assure Americans at a dinner of the Japan Society that a race provision would in no sense interfere with U.S. immigration policy. Back in Tokyo, some leading Japanese political figures took a harder line, suggesting publicly that if the race issue was not addressed in writing, Japan should withdraw from the League of Nations. Neither frontal assaults nor these backdoor efforts went anywhere. In late April, Wilson sought to skirt the issue by observing that, though unstated, racial equality was a fundamental principle of the League of Nations where Japan would be seated as a charter member. Its delegation still demanded a formal vote of the Allies. The measure failed to acquire the unanimous approval required by the rules. The race issue was dead. But on other matters, the Japanese were having considerably more success.

Effectively, it relinquished the concept of racial equality in favor of the reality of Shantung and the North Pacific islands.

Before the Peace Conference opened, the State Department had suggested that the United States press for a return to Germany of its northern Pacific territories—especially the Mariana, Caroline, and Marshall islands that had been occupied by Japan. As for Germany's Shantung concession, also seized by Japan, that region had to be returned to China, whose people constituted the bulk of the population. All these issues came to a head when the conference turned to the issue of mandates. On January 27, Japan presented its two claims: Kiao-chau, a principal port of Shantung province, plus all German possessions in the Pacific north of the equator. Makino said that "the Japanese Government feels justified in claiming from the German Government the unconditional cession" of these territories. Australia's Hughes piped up and demanded that all German islands south of the equator be given to his nation; he was backed by New Zealand, France, and Japan. Wilson suggested that all these territories might prove perfect vehicles for his concept of mandates where "the fundamental idea would be that the world was acting as a trustee through a mandatory, and would be in charge of the whole administration until the day when the true wishes of the inhabitants could be ascertained." Moreover, it was pretty clear to the Chinese what the full wishes of the residents of Kiao-chau would be. C. T. Wang asked for a delay to respond. Wilson had already indicated that with respect to territories Japan coveted, he "did not trust the Japanese . . . in fact they had broken their agreement about Siberia and [he] would not trust them again." Still, the delay did not help the Chinese very much.

Wilson had largely made up his mind to accept the recommendations of the Inquiry over those of other elements in his administration. The Inquiry's view was that the North Pacific islands demanded by Japan be awarded it under a mandate with strict limits on their fortification. Denying this, the Inquiry wrote, would "not only be considered a gratuitous affront by Japan, but would undermine the moral influence of the United States in the settlement of other questions." The U.S. Navy, by contrast, wanted the islands returned to Germany and subject to negotiations with the United States as possible payment for reparations. In other words, eventually, the United States could wind up with the strategic northern Pacific islands. As for Shantung and Kiao-chau, the Inquiry wanted all preexisting treaties or secret agreements, especially the Twenty-One Demands, nullified, and the territories in Shantung returned to China. But the Inquiry seemed to leave a loophole. No time frame was suggested for this return. An interim mandate might just fill the bill.

The Inquiry's suggestions overall seemed to mesh neatly with Wilson's broader moral agenda. The United States had no substantial claim to any part of Asia. Any such claim would undermine the moral high ground that Wilson believed he had seized heading into the conference with his Fourteen Points. Self-determination again reared its ugly head. This was not, of course, to suggest that China would in any sense wind up with what it desired, no matter what the Inquiry might have recommended. Japan still had many cards to play. A formal debate loomed over all of these fraught issues. China put up its ace debater—Wellington Koo.

The evening of January 27, following Japan's assertive presentation earlier that day, Koo and Lou Tseng-tsiang met with Wilson at his home near the Trocadero. It would be Koo's turn the next morning and the two Chinese begged Wilson to understand the horrors the Japanese had perpetrated in Korea and parts of Manchuria. They feared being left at Japan's mercy and begged the president to understand that they had no confidence in Japanese promises. China was even prepared to restore to Germany all of its previous possessions in China—for the Chinese, a far preferable alternative to awarding them to Japan. Wilson advised Koo to speak as frankly and as powerfully as he was speaking to him—and as strongly as Makino had presented Japan's case. Wilson added that he "felt deeply sympathetic for China and would do [his] best to help her."

The next morning, Clemenceau called the meeting to order in Foreign Minister Stéphen Pichon's chambers in the Quai d'Orsay. Koo rose to begin the Chinese argument. He opened with an eloquent description of Shantung and Kiao-chau: "An integral part of China . . . Chinese in race, language and religion . . . the cradle of Chinese civilization, the birthplace of Confucius and Mencius and a Holy Land for the Chinese . . . with thirty-six million people in an area only thirty-five thousand square miles. The density of the population . . . renders the country quite unsuitable for colonization."

Turning to Makino and the Japanese delegation, Koo expressed his gratitude to "the heroic army and navy of Japan in rooting out German power from Shantung," then concluded: "But, grateful as they are, the Chinese delegation feels that they would be false to their duty to China and the world if they did not object to paying their debts of gratitude by selling the birthright of their countrymen, and thereby sowing the seeds of discord for the future."

Makino's rebuttal was brief. He recalled his remarks from the day before and observed that Japan had received these territories as a result of international agreements. Then Koo rose again. He knew that Makino was referring to the infamous Twenty-One Demands. China, he said, had agreed to them only after a Japanese ultimatum. Then, recalling his days in the Columbia classroom of John Basset Moore, he added the coup de grace: "Even if the treaties and notes had been entirely valid, the fact of China's declaration of war on Germany had altered the situation in such a way that on the principle of *rebus sic stantibus* they could not be enforced today." Koo had fallen back on a fundamental principle of international law that any treaty or agreement may become inapplicable due to a fundamental change of circumstances.

The brilliant Columbia University varsity debater had, as Secretary Lansing wrote in his diary, "simply overwhelmed the Japanese with his argument. In fact it made such an impression on the Japanese themselves, that one of the delegates [Viscount Chinda, who'd brought the cherry trees to Washington] called upon me the following day and attempted to offset the effect by declaring that the United States would be blamed if Kiaochow was returned to China."

No decision was taken on January 28. Wilson asked if notes detailing the various "understandings" might be laid before the Peace Conference. Japan, not to mention Britain and France, had no interest in opening that Pandora's box of secret treaties. Moreover, the Allies had way too many other priorities to deal with—not the least being the establishment of the entire mandate system that might govern vast stretches of the world from southeastern Europe, across Asia Minor through the Middle East, even Africa (where Germany had several valuable colonies), and on to Asia.

As weeks passed with no resolution, all sides continued their lobbying and horse-trading. Meanwhile, the whole tone of the Peace Conference began to shift. In the end, Lansing's darkest fears proved largely right. Seized and occupied territory, military and political muscle, threats and bluster would once again carry the day. But not for lack of effort on the part of Wellington Koo and his Chinese colleagues, who continued to press their cause wherever they could find a listener. One of Koo's Columbia history professors, James T. Shotwell, an early member of the Inquiry, lunched with his protégé and another of his students, fellow Chinese delegate S. T. Wei, at "a magnificent apartment in the aristocratic section of the city." They wound up the afternoon singing old Columbia songs around the piano.

No matter how much the matter might be postponed, eventually the Allies would have to come to terms with the nettlesome issue of Kiao-chau and Shantung Province. By April 21, Wilson had decided to propose that German rights in China be ceded to the five Allied powers—Britain, France, Italy, the United States, and Japan—as trustees. His aim was eventually to return these areas to China. At the same time, all spheres of influence in China would be terminated immediately. Japan, naturally, agreed with alacrity to the second half of the proposal. It would give Japan, the geographically closest power, all but free rein in China once the dust had settled and the peacemakers had gone home. On April 22, in a morning session before the Council of Four, Makino and Chinda continued to insist that the wartime secret treaties provided ample legal underpinnings for Japan's takeover of Germany's Asian territories. If this was the carrot, the pair then added the stick. Without these demands being met, Japan would refuse to sign the Peace Treaty with Germany. Wilson panicked. On the one hand, with Italy waffling at that point over the Adriatic and threatening its own pullout, Japan's withdrawal could destabilize the entire architecture of the peace, as well as his carefully crafted League of Nations. On the other hand, as he put it, in China, with its 400 million people, "if flames were put to it, the fire could not be quenched."

In the afternoon session of the Group of Four at Wilson's residence on April 22, the Chinese were summoned for what would turn out to be the last time. Koo turned on all his oratorical skills:

China stands at the crossroads. A great part of the nation wishes to cooperate with the western powers, and that is equally the desire of the present government. But if we fail to obtain justice at the conference, that can throw us into the arms of Japan. There is a party in China which favors Asia for the Asians. If we fail in our mission,

I fear that the effect of the reaction that will follow might be very strong. . . . I cannot insist too strongly on the serious consequences that can result. It is a question of whether we can guarantee a peace of half a century to the Far East, or if a situation will be created which can lead to war within ten years.

Wilson advanced his proposal for a five-power trusteeship. Makino rejected this out of hand. A report from two experts—Britain's Ronald Macleay and the State Department's Edward T. Williams—concluded with a warning contiguous with Koo's. "Japan in Shantung is much more dangerous to China and the peace of the Far East than Germany ever was," the experts wrote. Clemenceau, scarcely one to mince words, observed that Shantung was "China's Alsace-Lorraine and Japan is the Yellow Prussia."

Two days later, Makino and Chinda came for a seminal meeting with Lansing and Williams at the Crillon. Japan, the two diplomats pledged, would not modify any of its "understandings" with China, but would agree orally to return Shantung to China after the Treaty of Versailles officially turned over this territory to Japan, "retaining only the [same] economic privileges granted to Germany." It was an agreement shot through with loopholes. In Japan's hands these economic privileges could be used to turn Shantung into the very colony that the empire desired as a foothold in the world's most populous nation. At this point, however, Wilson had decided he must do whatever was necessary to win a Japanese signature on the peace treaty with Germany.

On April 27 it was done. Japan got its way as the Big Four ratified the proposal Makino and Chinda had presented at the Crillon. Lansing believed to the end it was an enormous mistake. It would have been better to leave Japan out of the League of Nations entirely than to abandon China, with the resulting damage to America's image across Asia. The next morning Wilson confided to his press aide, Ray Stannard Baker, that he "had been unable to sleep":

If Japan went home there was the danger of a Japanese-Russian-German alliance, and a return to the old 'balance of power' system in the world, on a greater scale than ever before. He knew that his decision would be unpopular in America, that the Chinese would be bitterly disappointed, that the Japanese would feel triumphant, that he would be accused of violating his own principles, but nevertheless he must work for world order and organization against anarchy and a return to the old militarism.

Wilson was right on nearly every score—beginning with the moment that Baker walked into the Chinese delegation to break the news to Wellington Koo and his colleagues. The news was not well received. "You can rely on me," one delegate shouted in despair, quoting Wilson as he flung himself on the floor in a fury of frustration. Lou Tseng-tsiang entered a formal protest. The delegation asked to sign the treaty "with reservations," a request that was denied at the last moment by Clemenceau, who feared that such a precedent would allow all signatories—including Germany—to do likewise, thereby eviscerating the entire document. In the end the Chinese delegates refused to sign or attend the signing ceremony at Versailles.

"If I sign the treaty—even under orders from Beijing—I shall not have what you in New York call a Chinaman's chance," Koo moaned to Bonsal, who feared for the young delegate's life. Not unreasonably, as it turned out. The Sunday after the Shantung sellout in Paris became known in Beijing, students from thirteen universities met in the capital and drafted a series of protest resolutions. As tempers rose, one student leader, Hsieh Shao-min, slashed open his finger and wrote on the wall in his blood, "Return our Tsingtao," the principal port of Shantung Province. That afternoon they took to the streets. Gathering in Tiananmen Square, where their counterparts seventy years and one month later would face down the tanks of another tyrannical regime, more than three thousand students launched the May Fourth Movement.

Chanting their opposition to everything from the Twenty-One Demands to what would become the Treaty of Versailles, as well as those Chinese leaders they saw kowtowing to the Japanese, the students were cheered by throngs that wept as they passed. The mob surged to the East City District. There, at 3 Front Zhaojialou Lane, they paused in front of the home of Tsao Ju-lin, the pro-Japanese vice foreign minister of China, who had become infamous for having signed the Twenty-One Demands. The students burned his house to the ground, though the minister escaped, taking refuge, ironically, in the U.S. legation. The flames lit up the sky, setting the stage for the New Cultural Movement.

Picking up momentum, merchants, dockworkers, laborers, even peasants were caught up in the wave that swept across China from Beijing to Shanghai, even into the interior in what became a nationwide boycott of Japan and Japanese products. It was the first mass-based political movement in China.

One of its young members was a fifteen-year-old student at the Chongqing Preparatory School, a middle school preparing its students to go to France on work-study programs. The young man had already embraced wholeheartedly the May Fourth Movement's slogan, "save the country by industrialization." He hoped to travel to France to learn the kinds of industrial skills that would help rescue his nation from the Japanese whose rule the Versailles peacemakers had effectively ratified. Teng Hsiao-ping had some simple patriotic ideas. Already he had joined his classmates in boycotting anything that smacked of Japan. In the summer of 1920, Teng Hsiao-ping graduated from Chongqing and, traveling steerage, boarded a ship for France, arriving, like Nguyen Tat Thanh a decade earlier, in Marseille. His reception in France, the menial jobs he found at Le Creuset ironworks in central France, at the Renault factory in suburban Billancourt outside Paris, and finally as a kitchen helper in restaurants were similar to those followed by the man who would become Ho Chi Minh. They were barely enough to allow the young Chinese man to survive.

A month after Teng Hsiao-ping arrived in Marseille, an older Chinese student embarked from Shanghai, also headed for France. Like Teng, Chou En-lai had embraced the May Fourth Movement, but his hatred of Japan had more tangible roots. He had studied in Tokyo, though his studies were cut short by his outspokenness against Japan's military and political stranglehold over China. Chou returned to Tianjin in 1919, arriving on May 9, just in time to assume an active role in the rebellion, quickly rising to national prominence as an organizer of the Tianjin Students' Union and editor of its newspaper, proclaiming the aim of "struggle against the warlords and against imperialism, and to save China from extinction." Chou was selected to carry the fight to Europe, to form and lead a Communist Party of Chinese Youth in Europe, that was eventually to embrace Teng Hsiao-ping and take both to Moscow and leadership in the Chinese Communist Party.

With Teng and Chou in Europe, back home, another young revolutionary also found himself inspired to take to the streets, deep in the province of Hunan, ruled by the brutal warlord Chang Ching-yao, who was known to be in the pay of the Japanese leadership. Two years later, this young provincial May Fourth Movement agitator joined with other student leaders of the revolt to found the Communist Party of China. His name was Mao Tse-tung. As the party's Central Committee observed later: "The May Fourth Movement's . . . great contribution lay in arousing the people's consciousness, and preparing for the unity of the revolutionary forces. The May Fourth Movement promoted the spreading of Marxism in China, and prepared the ideological founda-tion for the establishment of the Communist Party of China."

But there was more to it than that. Although the movement initially was directed at Japan, very quickly its student organizers turned their attention to the United States and what was viewed as its betrayal of solemn pledges to China, the ideology professed by President Wilson, and what turned out to be the empty promises of his Fourteen Points. While Colonel House and others in Paris were privately suggesting to Chinese, Koreans, and a host of others whose aspirations had been throttled in Paris that they might look eventually to the League of Nations to redress their grievances, the United States failed to join the League or ratify the Treaty of Versailles. A swath of Western liberal political philosophy had effectively been discredited with a single stroke. China, and especially its young, vibrant intellectuals, would have to look elsewhere for their inspiration. They would find it with Mao.

Back in Washington in the summer of 1919, Shantung and the China debacle were becoming just another nail in the coffin Wilson had been building for the Treaty of Versailles in the Senate. Senator Philander C. Knox pointed out that Japan had acquired hegemony over Korea, Inner and Outer Mongolia, and Manchuria largely through the economic rights the Allies had surrendered on China's behalf in Shantung. Wilson agreed that if the Senate failed to ratify the treaty—which by then was largely assured—then Japan indeed would be free to do with Shantung as it saw fit. On August 23, the Senate Foreign Relations Committee, under the leadership of Senator Henry Cabot Lodge, who led Senate opposition to the treaty, voted an amendment that would return all German territo-ries and rights in China directly to the Chinese government and people. Wilson refused to authorize his Senate Democratic supporters to agree to any of the treaty amendments and embarked on his futile whistle-stop tour of the country in a last-ditch effort to win its acceptance. In Salt Lake City, Wilson described the deep feelings he still held for China and explained just why everything had gone so wrong: "My heart goes out to that great people, that learned people, that accomplished people, hundreds of millions strong, but never adequately organized for the exercise of force, therefore always at the mercy of anyone who has effective armies and navies, always subject to be commanded, and never in a position unassisted by the world to insist upon its own rights."

Japan, meanwhile, emerged from the Peace Conference stronger than ever. Though its delegates returned to Tokyo to face demonstrations against their failure to win a racial equality clause in the Treaty of Versailles, its victory on virtually every other front gave new strength to the militant factions within the Japanese government and society. Japan's hegemony was virtually unchallenged across much of Asia—particularly Korea and vast areas of China. The empire embarked on an explosive military buildup, especially of its naval fleet. Capital ships (battleships and battle cruisers) were the nuclear weapons of the early twentieth century. They served as the principal means of projecting a nation's armed might across oceans to countries far out of range of the still limited power of propeller-driven biplanes that were the backbone of World War I air forces.

All the major powers embarked on a panicked arms race—to build flotillas of new capital ships. In 1920 the United States proclaimed its intention of producing a navy "second to none," laying down keels for five battleships and four cruisers. Japan embarked on an "eight and eight" program, building eight ships of each class. All this activity touched off two overlapping fears: first, that the world had embarked on a new naval arms race similar to the Dreadnought race between Britain and Germany that was a proximate cause of World War I; second, that Japan—with only one ocean it needed to control—was on the cusp of developing an all but unstoppable naval dominance of the entire Asia-Pacific region.

All these pressures came together in November 1921 at the Washington Naval Conference. Held outside the already feeble framework of the League of Nations, the conference was summoned by Warren G. Harding. The Republican had trounced his Democratic opponent, hobbled by Wilson's legacy, in the 1920 presidential election. Included in the Washington Conference were all nations with an interest in the Pacific:

the Big Five naval powers (the United States, Britain, France, Italy, and Japan); as well as Belgium, the Netherlands, Portugal, and China, which did not engage in the naval discussions that were the heart of the gathering. It was a brutal three months of negotiations that proved to be a perfect coda to the failures in Paris more than two years earlier.

On February 6, 1922, the Five Power Naval Limitation Treaty was signed. The treaty provided for a ceiling on capital ships allowed each of the powers that translated roughly to a ratio of 5:5:3:1:1. Japan wound up with 315,000 tons of ships versus 525,000 tons each for Britain and the United States and 175,000 tons each for France and Italy. The big winners were Italy—which needed only a navy capable of assuring dominance in the Mediterranean—and Japan. Japan's tonnage was the minimum it would have accepted without walking out of the conference—a fact that U.S. negotiators had ascertained by intercepting and decrypting Japanese cable traffic between Tokyo and Washington. While a crafty move, it did little to improve global security. To circumvent the treaty, Japan simply converted a battleship and a cruiser into aircraft carriers, both of which wound up launching the planes that struck Pearl Harbor on December 7, 1941. By that time, the treaty had been all but thrown out the window as Japan entered World War II with nearly 2 million tons of naval firepower. The Five Power Naval Limitation Treaty, in short, was about as effective as today's nuclear nonproliferation treaty.

The Washington Conference, however, did have some other short-term results. Wellington Koo, together with his wife, their English maid, a valet, and a sable-colored Pekinese dog, was on hand as China's representative to make sure that Japan and the United States did right by his country. Together with Alfred Sze, the Chinese ambassador to Washington, the delegation was determined to hold Japan to what was left of its pledges to China. After eighteen contentious sessions, China did manage to win the return of a modicum of autonomy over its tariff structure. Japan finally did make good on its oral pledge in Paris that it would return the territory of Kaio-chau to China. In the end it proved to be an empty pledge. Japanese troops and police were, for the moment, withdrawn. But Japan retained so many economic rights over railroads, mines, and cable communications that it surrendered neither its economic nor its political influence in China.

At the same time, Japan had a virtually free hand to bolster its military forces that would dominate Asia. Japan quickly set to work bringing some five million men under arms. Charles D. Tenney, United States chargé d'affaires in Beijing, cabled Secretary of State Bainbridge Colby, who succeeded Lansing during Wilson's last year as president: "The Japanese government and nation are drunk with ambition. They aspire to control the western share of the Pacific Ocean and the resources of the hinterland . . . [and seeking to control the trade of Asia, they dream] of the day when they can humble the United States and are systematically preparing for it."

A short time later Reinsch, in his farewell message from Beijing as he headed home, had his own warning of: "a sinister situation dominated by the unscrupulous methods of the reactionary military regime centered on Tokyo, absolute in tendency, cynical of the principles of free government and human progress. . . . If this force, with all the methods it is accustomed to apply, remains unopposed there will be created in the Far East the greatest engine of military oppression and dominance that the world has yet seen."

Both were ominous portrayals of the world that was coming into focus in the years following the Paris Peace Conference.

Most of Japan's political and military leadership failed to understand why China and the rest of Asia, which they would ultimately sweep across beginning barely a decade later, were unable to appreciate Japan's benevolent motives. The nation's leaders believed their mission was simply to protect Asian populations from the Western forces that throughout modern history had done nothing but attempt to turn them into colonial vassals for their own profit. Japan perfected the Amau Doctrine, its own Asian perversion of the Monroe Doctrine, which Viscount Ishii first had rolled out on his trip to Washington and Makino had invoked in Paris as justification for Japan's control of Shantung. Effectively this doctrine was designed to turn Asia into Japan's own sphere of influence, which became known as the Greater East Asia Co-Prosperity Sphere during World War II. Throughout the period between the two world wars, from Beijing to Seoul, Japan blamed the paroxysms of anti-Japanese feeling on British, and particularly American, interests— namely, businessmen, missionaries, and diplomats. Ultranationalist groups such as the Black Dragon Society had long believed that Japan needed to take a leadership role in Asia to expel foreign powers by means of a righteous war—effectively a jihad—if necessary.

It happened that Japan remained throughout the 1920s and 1930s one of Asia's only truly unified nations that was also domestically at peace. China was swept by internal discord that finally erupted into civil war. Chiang Kai-shek, succeeding Sun Yat-sen as head of the nationalist Kuomintang, battled forces loyal to the Beijing government. Meanwhile a tiny Chinese Communist Party flirted with joining forces with Chiang Kai-shek while seeking to gain its own footing.

Less than a decade after the Washington Conference, and barely twelve years after the Paris Peace Conference, Japan finally felt strong enough to return in force to the Asian mainland. In September 1931, after a small stretch of the Japanese-owned South Manchurian Railway was blown up near Mukden in southern Manchuria in what may have been a deliberately manufactured provocation, Japan invaded the strategic region. In overt defiance of protests from the all but powerless League of Nations, Tokyo installed a puppet government under the deposed Qing Dynasty emperor Puyi. Over the next seven years, Japanese forces pushed into the interior, heading for Beijing, and after a three-month battle, seized Shanghai.

By now the Chinese Communist Party was growing in strength as it united with the forces of Chiang Kai-shek in an effort to expel Japan once and for all from China. With the end of World War II and the departure of Japan from mainland Asia, an enormous power vacuum developed. Civil war erupted again in China, this time between nationalist and Communist forces. It took four years for Mao to drive Chiang Kai-shek's forces off the mainland to Taiwan. Finally, for the first time in a century, China was united and in control of its own territory under a single government of its own people. It was a government whose principles dated back to the early postwar days of the May Fourth Movement, but whose methods were akin more to the gulag than to the Fourteen Points.

Korea did not fare much better after World War II. Cleared of Japanese forces by Soviet troops pushing down from Siberia and U.S. troops landing in the south, it became a nation divided at the artificial demarcation line of the thirty-eighth parallel. Half of the country eventually did achieve the aspirations of self-determination promised by Wilson but never delivered to a delegation that was marginalized and abandoned in Paris in 1919. Still, this deliverance did not come before it was forced to suffer for decades under a home-grown dictator, the same

Sygman Rhee who was unable to find his way to the Paris Peace Conference. It took one more conflict—the Korean War from 1950 to 1953, which left 600,000 Korean soldiers, more than a million civilians, as well as 54,000 Americans soldiers dead—for a tenuous peace and democratic rule to return to the southern portion of the peninsula. The other half remains a blight on the planet and a menace to civilization.

For much of this period, Wellington Koo played a seminal role. By refusing to place his signature on the reviled Versailles Treaty, he escaped the vitriol ladled on other Chinese leaders. In 1926 and 1927 Koo served as acting president of the Republic of China. Later, in 1931, he crossed swords again with Japan, presenting China's protest over the invasion of Manchuria to the League of Nations—with little more impact than he'd had in Paris. In 1945 he was a founding delegate to the United Nations. As Chiang Kai-shek's forces retreated ahead of the Communists, Koo retired from the diplomatic service. In 1985 he died in New York City at the age of ninety-eight.

The problem from the start was that Wilson, unlike Koo, never truly appreciated the dark Japanese nationalist streak—one that truly believed its race, with its militarist religion, was stronger and more righteous than any forces in the West. Wilson, whose Presbyterian upbringing was so inclined to see the good in everyone or any situation, was destined to perpetuate an Asia dominated by a nation bent on a militarist jihad—long before that term entered the contemporary political vernacular. In the end in Asia, as in large swaths of Europe and the Middle East, military might and seized territory prevailed—especially where backed by a determination and set of values calculated to keep the invaders in place. While World War I opened with Britain, Germany, and Russia as the principal rivals for world hegemony, the Peace Conference ratified Britain, the United States, and Japan as the new global powers, at least for the moment.

As historian Roy Watson Curry observed in 1957, "Wilsonian idealism assumed all the symptoms of a fatal political blindness." By then, however, we were only halfway to the present.

10

SETTING UP A
GLOBAL ECONOMY

ON FEBRUARY 17, 1871, A TWENTY-NINE-YEAR-OLD NEWLY
elected Radical member of the Assemblée Nationale watched in horror as Prussian troops staged a victory parade through the streets of
his beloved Paris. He voted against the peace treaty with the newly
formed German Empire whose ruler, Wilhelm I, had just been crowned
emperor in a ceremony in the Hall of Mirrors of the Palais de Versailles.
He was horrified by the terms of the peace, appalled that five billion
francs' worth of French money would be paid as tribute—"reparations"
to the German government whose forces would remain on French soil
for five years or until the tribute was paid—two and a half years early, as
it would turn out. France also lost its provinces of Alsace and Lorraine.
Now it was a half-century later and the young parliamentarian, Georges
Clemenceau, was prime minister of the same nation that this time had
wound up victorious over its German foes. Bismarck, the Iron Chancellor who had sent his Prussian forces into battle then, was long dead.

Clemenceau was determined that this time the Germans would pay to
rebuild his nation—the one its troops had destroyed. And he needed to
make certain that France would never again be vulnerable across its eastern borders. This quest for security would motivate his policy in Central
Europe and the Balkans, the cordon sanitaire quaranteening Bolshevism
within Russia. And it would motivate his attitude toward the Reich—its

boundaries, its military and especially its economic muscle. An old man by now, he sought recompense, in all its forms. He was one of the few who would sit down at the conference tables of Paris in January 1919 with an active and vivid memory of the previous war and the last peace. David Lloyd George, prime minister of Britain, was barely eight years old when the Prussians had marched into Paris. Woodrow Wilson had just turned fourteen, son of a Presbyterian minister in Columbia, South Carolina, an ocean away from those violent, remote events. Other men and a few women, younger still, were converging on Paris, this time with a determination that the mistakes of their elders would not be repeated. Vengeance would not be exacted at this peace table, they vowed. And money—tribute—would not be exacted for the sake of retribution. How wrong they turned out to be.

There were many errors committed at the Peace Conference in Paris—many of them geographic, ethnic, and political. But redrawing of national boundaries and disenfranchisement of vast populations were not the only crimes. The nature of the economy of the Western world was shaped as well—the foundations laid for considerable suffering among the very people who had already paid most dearly during the conflict itself. This was done by the old men at the table and some of the young as well.

John Maynard Keynes was one of the young men. He took the same boat train from London via Calais to Paris that carried Harold Nicolson, but ten days later. Keynes, the thirty-five-year-old aide to Britain's chancellor of the exchequer, was cut from the same bolt of cloth as Nicolson, the assistant to the Foreign Secretary. Each was a product of late Victorian English intelligentsia—Keynes a towering (at six feet six inches) Cambridge don, son of a Cambridge economist; Nicolson an Oxonian born three years later. Both were members of the Bloomsbury group, a gaggle of patrician Edwardian aesthetes—Keynes by the brilliance of his intellectual accomplishments, Nicolson by his marriage to the writer Vita Sackville-West, the model whom Virginia Woolf took for her Orlando. Keynes was the first to join Bloomsbury; indeed, he was present at the creation after being inducted into Cambridge's most elite and secretive society, the Apostles, by two of its young denizens. Lytton Strachey and Leonard Woolf were attracted by his brilliant reputation at Eton and his parentage.

When war broke out in Europe, Keynes was pressed into service at the British Treasury, drafted in July 1914 from his rooms in King's College where he had taken up a lectureship in economics. His immediate mission was to help deal with a crisis in the remittance system that was threatening a run on the stock exchange. Keynes was a firm believer in using the nation's money and resources, rather than hoarding them—especially the gold reserves that backed the currency in those far-off days when the precious metal was still the world's monetary standard. Still, Keynes was troubled by the dangers of inflation, and he worried for much of the war about how to finance this colossally expensive effort without bankrupting the nation or, of lesser concern, ruining Britain's allies. He vaguely (somewhat more vaguely than much of the rest of Bloomsbury) disliked the war, but nevertheless believed if it was going to be fought, it might as well be efficiently managed. With his surfeit of self-confidence, he had no doubt that he was the man to make certain it was run in this fashion.

By January 1915 Keynes was comfortably installed in Whitehall at an adequate government salary of £600. A month later, he headed to France for the first inter-Allied conference on financing the conflict. It was here that the foundations for the entire edifice that was to become such a problem for the Peace Conference were laid. It was, effectively, the fiscal equivalent of the secret treaties that bound the Allies in dealing with so many troublesome issues in other parts of the world. Only in this case, it was not a secret, nor was there a treaty involved. But it was certainly binding—a system to finance much of the war effort by credits, not grants. France and Belgium were on the front lines. Vast swaths of their territories were being chewed up by the armies of both sides as they dug in for a long and bloody war of attrition in the trenches and barbed wire strung across hundreds of miles of once fertile farmland. Both countries were in desperate need of funds to buy and make arms, clothe their armies, and feed their people. The solution the British decided upon was credits to the continental powers rather than outright grants—credits to Allied accounts at the Bank of England that could be used to buy whatever was needed to keep the war machine ticking.

Dining with the likes of Bertrand Russell and D. H. Lawrence, partying with the Bloomsbury crowd, relieving his tension by weeding gardens with a small pocket knife for six hours at a stretch, kneeling on a small piece of carpet at Bloomsbury's summer place in Charleston outside London, Keynes found that the war passed quickly. A congenial and polished guest at their stately homes, he became a close confidante of many of the top British officials who were running the war—Sir Reginald McKenna, chancellor of the exchequer, and the Asquiths, especially the prime minister's wife Margot Asquith and their beautiful daughter Elizabeth, later Princess Bibesco. But Keynes was not a big fan of Lloyd George, and mutual antipathy led to his name being struck from the King's honors list the first time around. It was an unprecedented slight that the young economist never forgot. This was scarcely surprising. He was becoming even more insufferable than he had been at Cambridge—the kind of young man who believes he is the smartest person in any room and if you are unconvinced, won't let you leave the room until he has persuaded you. In his case, alas, he probably was.

Keynes's view of the war was a simple one. As his official biographer Roy Howard reports, he believed that "we must go through with [it, to] establish world affairs on a better basis so that this shall not happen again." This view was shared, if unconsciously, by many at the Paris peace tables—from Harold Nicolson to Woodrow Wilson. It fairly reeks of George Edward Moore, the Cambridge philosopher whose *Principia Ethica* appeared just as Keynes was coming up to university for the first time in 1902. "We accepted Moore's religion, so to speak, and discarded his morals," Keynes would recall later. "How did one compare the value of a good state of mind which had bad consequences with a bad state of mind which had good consequences?" A difficult path of reasoning for a young economist who was seeing to the financing of a war of which he barely approved, and which nearly cost him his own life though he never approached the field of battle. On June 6, 1916, British war minister Lord Horatio Herbert Kitchener, dispatched to Russia for negotiations with the then-Allied monarchy of the czar, was drowned off the Orkney Islands when his ship went down—a fate Keynes was spared only by his exclusion from the party at the very last minute.

Meanwhile, the continental Allies had become totally dependent on Britain for financing the war, while Britain, her own meager resources all but exhausted, had become totally dependent on the United States. Though it had not even entered the conflict officially yet, America was already shoveling into British accounts more than $200 million a month—or 40 percent of all war spending. Whitehall in turn was underwriting all of Italy's foreign war spending, most of Russia's, two-thirds of France's, and half of Belgium's and Serbia's. As Keynes observed acerbically, "We have one ally, France. The rest are mercenaries."

Keynes spent September and October of 1917 in the United States in an attempt to shore up the financial relationship with the newest Allied nation, America having recently entered the war officially. What he found was a collection of New York bankers, including one patrician J. P. Morgan partner whose goal was to make Wall Street the banker to the world. Thomas William Lamont (great-grandfather of the man who defeated Senator Joseph Lieberman for the Democratic nomination for a U. S. Senate seat in Connecticut in 2006) was raised in a parsonage and graduated from Phillips Exeter Academy and Harvard. Keynes would cross swords repeatedly with him in Paris. When Keynes first encountered him in New York, Lamont had spent fourteen years working his way to the pinnacle of the American financial establishment. What Keynes and the British Exchequer needed desperately from the Lamonts and, by extension, from the U. S. Treasury, was cash. Keynes recognized that the United States had Britain over a barrel. In July 1917 he had already warned: "Our resources available for payments in America are exhausted. Unless the United States can meet in full our expenses in America, including [foreign] exchange, the whole financial fabric of the alliance will collapse. This conclusion will be a matter not of months, but of days.

He'd been exaggerating, for effect, of course. But not by much. Keynes's goal was to have the United States take over all the financing of the war effort, rather than operate an elaborate Ponzi scheme that could ultimately result in Britain holding the bag. The Americans, it seemed, would rather loan huge sums to the Brits, who might eventually be expected to honor the debt and let London loan the money onward to the Allies. The unpleasant alternative was for the United States to accumulate a mountain of ultimately worthless French and Italian obligations. Keynes's American forays met with mixed success from the British perspective. On the one hand, the United States did continue to underwrite the war effort. But it did so for the rest of the war through the Bank of England. Britain would wind up holding the worthless Allied paper.

Ten days after the armistice, Keynes was attached to the British delegation to the peace talks. In the next two months his principal mission was to prepare the Treasury's position on German indemnities—reparations the victors would extract from the vanquished. The model he was given, not surprisingly, was the same that the German Empire had used with France in 1871.

By the end of the war in 1918, Europe was crushed in every sense of the word. Nearly an entire generation of young manhood had been wiped out in much of Western Europe. Vast territories had been rendered all but uninhabitable. Mines and other sources of vital natural resources had been blown up, spiked, or rendered unusable. Vast populations were on the verge of starvation as farms were neglected, farmers were killed in the war, and the transport systems that brought food to market were damaged or obliterated. Financial resources, too, had all but evaporated. Even the powerful Bank of England was living paycheck to paycheck and the paymaster was three thousand miles away across the Atlantic.

It was becoming increasingly clear that while many of the politicians were focused on redrafting the political and ethnographic map of Europe, the Middle East, and as much as possible of the rest of the world, money would be the real determinant of power and politics in the post war years. Keynes was profoundly aware of these realities as he set out to prepare his first reparations memorandum for the chancellor of the exchequer, Bonar Law. From the get-go, Keynes outlined the two realities that were to consume all discussions over reparations, money, and power for the next decade and beyond. First there was the damage done to France, Belgium, and the other Allies by Germany. (Austria-Hungary, being totally crushed and in the process of being broken up to form the new nation-states of Central Europe, never figured very deeply in any of these computations.) Second, and as it turned out far more importantly, there was the capacity of Germany to pay. Keynes's first pass at both efforts showed, in outline, direct damages to civilian populations, excluding the costs of pensions to the widows of dead soldiers, totaling £4 billion, with Britain claiming 15 percent. The maximum Germany might be expected to pay was £3 billion. So a satisfactory outcome, Keynes projected, would be £2 billion—payable over the course of decades in a form of annual tribute. "If Germany is to be 'milked,'" his Treasury report observed presciently, "she must not first of all be ruined." None of this would even come close to the conclusions reached by the peace delegates. Self-determination be hanged. This was money they were talking about.

Much of this Allied apparent rapacity was due to three potent forces at work—a powerful British lobby of conservative critics who wanted Germany to foot the entire bill for the war and nothing less; the U. S. political and financial network of Woodrow Wilson and his Wall Street boys; and finally Clemenceau and a small band of French financiers and bureaucrats who had their own very definite ideas of what the victors needed and wanted.

The French brought to the table a tag team of experts, each persuaded in his own way that the only real path to recovery for their nation was Allied (that is, American) assistance. First in the ring was Etienne Clementel, product of a modest family of flour millers in the Auvergne region, who became a *notaire* (a cross between an attorney and a notary public, but a powerful and well-remunerated position in France), before entering public life. His first ministerial appointment was minister of colonies from 1905 to 1906, five years before Nguyen Tat Thanh set out from Saigon to seek his destiny. Schooled at the Ecole des Beaux-Arts in his hometown of Clermont, one of France's oldest cities deep in the heart of the mountainous region, Clermont-Ferrand, Clementel retained an artistic sensibility for much of his life. He played a leading role in the creation of Paris's Musée Rodin. None of this, however, prepared him for the radical restructuring of the European economy he advanced as France's post war position at the Peace Conference. It was a daring, even visionary concept that was all but stillborn. And this despite the assistance he won from a thirty-year-old bureaucrat named Jean Monnet who, four decades later, would become the father of the European Economic Community.

Clementel's ideal was a vast trans-Atlantic pooling of resources to rebuild Europe, but particularly the most devastated areas of France—creating an Allied economic bloc. If Germany played along, eventually it, too, would even get its share. The goal was a steady source of raw materials at moderate prices, plus low tariffs to build strong export markets for all concerned. Clementel was decades—and another world war—ahead of his time. His plan was deliberately crafted to win over the Americans by appealing to Wilson's desire for a strong League of Nations. Clementel's "economic union of free peoples" would provide the strongest foundations for such a world body. Moreover, without such a system, it would be "a material impossibility for Germany [alone] to rebuild so many ruins . . . and would completely crush her and reduce her to a state of economic bondage."

Raw materials—particularly coal—were the core of the Clementel plan in lieu of huge cash payments, which the former *notaire* recognized would be a recipe for "an enormous monetary inflation [in France], a disorderly rise in prices and by virtue of their size would transform France into a country rich in mere cash, a buyer of products and incapable of working. . . ." But by the time the Peace Conference got under way, it was clear to Clemenceau that the Allies, particularly the Americans, weren't buying this effort to redraw the economic map of the world in France's image. So out went Clementel and in came the next member of the tag team, Louis Loucheur.

Loucheur's designation was a masterful stroke. A graduate of the prestigious École Polytechnique, Loucheur was an engineer and a technocrat to his core—none of Clementel's artistic yearnings. Loucheur had spent the war wielding virtually dictatorial powers as minister of munitions, building a French arms industry that was one of the greatest state-run enterprises his nation had ever known. When Clemenceau recognized that Clementel was on a wild goose chase with his pan-Allied economic union, Loucheur was the natural choice as a successor. His wartime Ministry of Munitions was transformed with a stroke of a pen into the Ministry of Industrial Reconstruction. Loucheur's goal was to rebuild France using American money, but without the Americans recognizing it.

The idea was apparently simple, but as it turned out, fiendishly complex: get Germany to commit to paying, over a number of years, a moderate, fixed sum. This could immediately be securitized—turned into an upfront cash horde by issuance of bonds, effectively backed by Germany's signature on the Treaty of Versailles. These bonds could then be sold on the one financial market of the world that had not yet been crushed by the war—Wall Street. Effectively, Americans would be paying for the rebuilding of France, but without ever touching the congressionally held purse strings of the U. S. Treasury. Loucheur, unlike Clementel, was able to win some powerful political support within France for this scheme. André Lebon, head of the Fédération des Industriels et Commerçants Français, was already backing the idea of moderate payments. His fear was that huge reparations demands on Germany would force the defeated nation to wage a trade war for foreign export markets to earn funds for these payments, crippling France's own foreign commerce.

The problem in all this was that the views of Clemenceau and Loucheur were not shared by either the Brits or the Americans. While it was clear even before the ink was dry on the armistice that Keynes had a largely sensible view of how the peace should be structured from an economic perspective, this view was by no means shared by that political shark Lloyd George. As early as August 1918, and possibly long before, the prime minister was campaigning for what would become known as a Carthaginian Peace. This concept harkened back to the Punic Wars. In A.D. 146, the Romans laid siege to Carthage, killed most of the inhabitants, sold the rest into slavery, burned the city to the ground, and then spread salt through the ruins so that nothing would grow there again. The British prime minister was in no position to spread salt across the landscape of Germany, particularly since Allied troops had halted their advance well short of the capital, Berlin. "Germany had committed a great crime, and it was necessary to make it impossible that anyone should be tempted to repeat that offence," Lloyd George told the War Cabinet three months before the armistice. "The Terms of Peace must be tantamount to some penalty for that offence."

The basis for such a peace was a finding on December 10, 1918, by a British government committee that the total cost of the war was in excess of £24 billion—or $100 billion, the equivalent today of some $1.2 trillion, nearly half the federal government's spending for the year 2006 in the United States. Such a staggering sum was far beyond the capacity of any nation—indeed, the entire Western world—to have even contemplated, let alone paid in the year 1919. The British War Cabinet rejected it as a "wild and phantastic chimera," but not before this illusory figure was seized upon by Lloyd George in a parliamentary campaign just weeks before the opening of the Peace Conference. The national election had been carefully designed to send Lloyd George to Paris as a newly reelected prime minister with just such an unassailable mandate. Rather than adopting a statesmanlike attitude of leading his people to a just and lasting foundation for an enduring peace, Lloyd George played to his electorate's basest passions. On December 11, a day after the incendiary war costs report was released, the prime minister delivered a stem-winding campaign speech. The location was Bristol, from whose port ships had ventured into the Atlantic only to be set upon by German submarines. Lloyd George laid down the principles of his "Indemnity policy." Its core was a demand that the Central Powers pay the whole cost of the war, not merely reparations. This was an important distinction. Reparations alone would have netted little for Britain, whose territory suffered minimal damage during the hostilities that ravaged France and Belgium. But the costs of war went far beyond the immediate physical destruction to include the huge pension burden that Britain was forced to bear for the millions of war widows and other surviving members of families whose men had been cut down on the battlefields of Europe. These were Lloyd George's voters who would send him and his party back to Parliament with an unquestioned majority and in a position to exact a Shakespearean tribute in Paris—a pound of flesh, and then some.

The electoral strategy worked. Especially when the prime minister told voters, archly, that a Cabinet committee had assured him that Germany could afford all indemnities. This included an assumption of the entire British national debt, which had risen to some $120 billion, including interest payments of $6 billion a year (respectively $1.44 trillion and $72 billion today). Then there was the final stroke. As Keynes put it baldly, "a vote for Lloyd George means the Crucifixion of the Anti-Christ." How could any responsible citizen have voted against that? Keynes continued, "The campaign for securing out of Germany the general costs of the war was one of the most serious acts of political unwisdom for which our statesmen have ever been responsible." He wasn't far off.

It was not surprising that Lloyd George brought along to Paris the two principal authors of the cabinet's indemnity report. The pair was quickly dubbed the Heavenly Twins: not Castor and Pollux, but Lord Walter Cunliffe, wartime governor of the Bank of England, a sixty-three-year-old merchant banker, product of Harrow and Trinity College Cambridge, who had repeatedly crossed swords with Keynes during the war; and William Morris Hughes, prime minister of the British dominion of Australia, who, as Bernard Baruch later put it, "insisted that every Australian who had placed a mortgage on his house to buy a war bond was as definitely entitled to reparation as was every Frenchman whose house had been burned by the Germans." On the British economic delegation the only realist was Keynes. The young Bloomsbury economist had been brought along because Lloyd George recognized he might need some accurate figures.

On the U. S. side, in moral terms, Woodrow Wilson seemed to hold many of the same views as Lloyd George. He viewed the war as a fairly straightforward struggle between good and evil. Good had won out, and now evil must be prevented from ever rising again. "This intolerable Thing of which the masters of Germany have shown us the ugly face, this menace of combined intrigue and force which we now see so clearly as the German power, a Thing without conscience or honor or capacity for convenanted peace, must be crushed. . . ." But despite the elevated nature of Wilson's rhetoric, the individuals who accompanied him were a far more pragmatic bunch. Their roots were as deeply planted in Wall Street as Wilson's was in the Presbyterian rhetoric of a preacher's family. Moreover, unlike their colleagues whose mission was to redraft the world's political landscape, their hands were little tied by any earlier pledges.

The Fourteen Points, which elaborated in great detail Wilson's desires to restore democracy to a host of different nationalities, dealt only in passing with a single economic issue: free trade. The Third Point demanded "the removal, so far as possible, of all economic barriers and the establishment of equality of trade conditions among all the nations consenting to the peace and associating themselves for its maintenance." The issue was of central importance to a resurgent American capitalist system on the cusp of assuming a commanding position as the world's preeminent trading nation, but of peripheral relevance to the post war economic troubles of Europe.

The U. S. delegation was carefully calibrated to represent these sensibilities. Thomas Lamont looked after the interests of Wall Street and the Morgan Bank, not always in that order. Norman Davis was a Tennessee gentleman who'd made a fortune as a trader in Cuba after the Spanish-American War, and now served as assistant secretary of the Treasury. Finally, there was John Foster Dulles, the thirty-year-old elder brother of Allen Dulles, who had spent the war as an associate at the white shoe New York law firm of Sullivan & Cromwell, which had represented German commercial and banking interests for years. Dulles was a late addition, having appeared on his own initiative in Paris late in 1918, pestering Allen and their uncle, Secretary of State Robert Lansing, for some role in the peace talks. He'd calculated that such an item on his resume wouldn't hurt in his efforts to reach partner status when he returned to Sullivan & Cromwell. He was right, of course. Meanwhile, this American trio was to carry the water for Wall Street. And what that meant was a repeated and persistent refusal to cancel Europe's war debts to America. As Calvin Coolidge was later to put it bluntly, "The [Europeans] hired the money, didn't they?"

So the battle lines on the economic front were already clearly drawn by the first week in January 1919 when all the players assembled in Paris. As Norman Davis warned Wilson in the early days of the conference, a "concerted movement [was] afoot to obtain an interlocking of the United States with the continental governments in the whole financial situation." To which Wilson replied, he was "on my guard against it."

By the time the conference had opened, it was clear that several immediate economic realities would take precedence over all others—Germany needed desperately to be fed, France needed desperately to find supplies of coal. The first order of business was the fact that Germany was starving. Bolshevik-sympathetic rioting was already breaking out all over the country. The leftist Spartacist League, led by Rosa Luxemburg and Karl Liebknecht, was opposed to the new post war government and attracted tens of thousands of war-weary soldiers, many wounded physically or psychologically. All were pouring back into the country and needed to be fed and cared for. Armed workers had taken to the streets of Germany. Pitched battles broke out with paramilitary Freikorps units, who wound up beating to death Luxemburg and Liebknecht. These same units managed to overturn a Soviet republic that sprang up in Munich. Elsewhere in Bavaria other small right-wing organizations had sprung up including one that called itself National Socialists—the Nazis.

Four days after Keynes arrived in Paris, he was told by Norman Davis that the Americans had stumbled on the fact that the French were opening secret financial negotiations with Germany. As Keynes put it, he and Davis "decided it would be extremely amusing and perhaps useful if we stepped aboard the Marshal [Foch]'s train on his journey a day or two later to Trèves" on the German border with Luxembourg, known to them as Trier, the oldest city in Germany. En route, Keynes and Davis played bridge with an American representative of Hoover's food agency and Sir John Beale, lawyer for Britain's Midland Railway. When the train reached Trèves, the Germans boarded. They were, Keynes observed:

> a sad lot . . . with drawn, dejected faces and tired starting eyes, like men who had been hammered on the Stock Exchange. But from amongst them stepped forward . . . a very small man, exquisitely clean, very well and neatly dressed, with a high stiff collar which seemed cleaner and whiter than an ordinary collar, his round head covered with grizzled hair shaved so close as to be like in substance to the pile of a close-made carpet . . . his eyes gleaming straight at us, with extraordinary sorrow in them, yet like an honest animal at bay. This was he with whom in the ensuing months I was to have one of the most curious intimacies in the world, and some very strange passages of experience—Dr. [Carl] Melchior.

Melchior was indeed an extraordinary individual who, from the sidelines, was to play a critical role in the financial aspects of the Treaty of Versailles and the entire question of reparations, the economic survival of Germany and the financial structure of the West. He was a Jew, though Keynes was to stumble on that fact only much later; he was trained as a lawyer; and he served as a partner in the venerable Hamburg-based bank M.M. Warburg. The bank, whose roots date to 1798, was later to do much business with John Foster Dulles's Sullivan & Cromwell and Lamont's J. P. Morgan. Dulles himself would, fortuitously and profitably, become Warburg's American counsel. But all this was in the future. In January 1919 the immediate, desperate need was for Germany to find food. And the Allies had it. Over the next weeks, through the most adroit back door diplomacy, Keynes and Melchior managed to hammer together one of the few economic successes produced by the Peace Conference.

Germany was in particularly desperate straits for two principal reasons: a catastrophic Allied naval blockade that had continued even after the armistice, and the desire of the Allies to seize the bulk of the German merchant fleet as part and parcel of the broader reparations package that would take years to negotiate. Germany didn't have years. It perhaps did not even have weeks. It needed food—now. Hoover recognized that fact; so did Keynes and Melchior. Even the armistice negotiators had recognized that reality, declaring that while the blockade should continue until a peace agreement was concluded, "the Allies contemplate the provisioning of Germany to the extent that shall be deemed necessary." The problem was that so few of the Allied negotiators at Trèves were prepared to accept this fact.

Hoover's solution was to sell Germany cheap U. S. pork that was rotting on the docks in Rotterdam. Since Germany's merchant marine was tied up in ports by the Allies who intended to seize the ships, the nation had no way of transporting even these pathetic stores to its shores. Nor would the Germans be allowed to pay for this food with gold currency that was still in their reserves since this, too, was to be used to pay reparations to the victors. After several fruitless visits to Trèves, however, Keynes and Melchior hit on a compromise that each managed to persuade his respective government to accept. Germany would turn over its merchant fleet, and the Allies would accept £4 million of gold in return for 200,000 tons of bread and 70,000 tons of pork, which these ships would be allowed to transport. Lloyd George recognized the urgent necessity for this compromise to go through. So, in a dramatic session in French Foreign Minister Stéphen Pichon's private offices in the Quai d'Orsay, the British prime minister with a flourish read out a cable he had just received from Field Marshal Herbert Plumer, commander of the British Army of Occupation on the Rhine: "In my opinion food must be sent into this area by the Allies without delay. The mortality amongst women, children and sick is most grave, and sickness due to hunger is spreading. The attitude of the population is becoming one of despair, and the people feel that an end by bullets is preferable to death by starvation."

Lloyd George observed that he would rather order British occupation troops back home than "continue to occupy a territory in order to maintain the population in a state of starvation." The objections of the other Allied representatives were overcome—even those of France's obdurate Minister of Finance Louis-Lucien Klotz. Though Clemenceau called him "the one Jew I know with no capacity whatsoever for finance," he was still holding out for Germany not relinquishing an ounce of the precious gold he believed he could ultimately claim for France. Klotz was eventually forced to give way before the onslaught, but not before Lloyd George pronounced his memorable prediction that "if a Bolshevist state is formed in Germany, three statutes will be erected—one to Lenin, one to Trotsky and the third to Klotz." To which Klotz, quite sensibly, made no reply.

In the end, it was this fear of Bolshevism poised to sweep across Germany that carried the day, coupled with a need for the conference to turn to the other critical economic imperative. France was nearly out of coal. In those pre-OPEC days, this was the fuel that heated peoples' homes. It powered industry and lit the conference rooms, hotels, and apartments of the delegates, who were fed by food cooked on coal-fired stoves. Retreating German troops had wreaked heavy damage on France's principal coal mines, adding to the sense that the defeated nation needed to pay for the suffering it had caused. As a result, the battle of reparations that was quickly joined became at once political and economic.

The issue of coal was almost from the start intimately wound up with the central question with which the Peace Conference was having to deal—how much would Germany have to pay and what would these payments, such as they were, comprise? By the end of the war, Germany didn't have much. In his later efforts to make the case for lightening the burden on Germany, Keynes toted up the balance, which turned out to be quite accurate. With respect to coal, in 1913, the last year before the start of hostilities, Germany produced 191.5 million tons, while consuming 139 million tons for its own railroads, electrical production, manufacturing, and household use. Some 60.8 million tons of this output came from mines in territories that the peacemakers were in the process of turning over to other countries—Poland and Czechoslovakia in particular. France, Belgium, and the other Allies were demanding at least 45 million tons, leaving Germany with barely half as much as it used before the war to satisfy its post war needs. Somehow, that didn't seem to bother the French very much at all.

But the question for the Allies was a broader one. Not only how much should the total reparations bill be, but how much of that should come in the form of natural resources, how much in labor and reconstruction, and how much in the form of cash? The failure of the peace delegates ever to arrive at an answer acceptable or tolerable to all sides or that was even realistic, turned out to be at the heart of Europe's post war economic and political problems.

The French wanted, particularly, a fixed sum of total reparations including delivery of "in kind" payments. Loucheur and Klotz, his counterpart at the finance ministry, were quite right in believing that such a structure was the only way of securitizing the debt, creating German bonds that would give France the immediate cash it needed to rebuild the country. The purchasers of these bonds—backed only by Germany's signature on the Treaty of Versailles, or the Allies' willingness to enforce it, if necessary at the point of a gun—would be providing the cash. These bondholders would be paid interest over the next thirty years and a final lump-sum principal when the bonds matured. In other words, if the French couldn't get relief from the U. S. government, they'd get it from U. S. investors—the only group with any hard currency left over after the war. The Americans, particularly the Morgan banker Lamont, liked this idea a lot. It was likely that J. P. Morgan would profit handsomely as a prime issuer of these securities.

There was one final wrinkle. Whatever lump sum was fixed had to be sufficiently modest that the Germans would not be either ruined by the periodic payments or so demoralized as to simply throw up their hands and say, do with us what you will. For a settlement of that nature would mean no investor in his or her right mind would ever buy these German reparations bonds when they came on the market, as they would likely be repudiated long before they were ever redeemed.

This, then, was where months of bickering and dealing were concentrated. On March 15, three of the top Allied experts—Loucheur, Norman Davis and Britain's Sir Edwin Montagu—observed that even before the war, Germany had been running a balance of payments deficit, importing more than it was exporting. So in the aftermath of a draining conflict, there would be no surplus for the foreseeable future that could be used to pay reparations. This trio, the ultimate pragmatists, set forth their fears for the post war era:

> Germany might within a few years repudiate the entire obligation as having been an imposition, and the moral opinion of the world might support her in this. . . . As to the estimates which have been given by some eminent bankers [especially Britain's Lord Cunliffe], to the effect that Germany would be able, over a period of 30 years to pay 3 or 4 billion dollars per annum, we can say only that we are satisfied that such a performance on the part of Germany is utterly impossible, because in the first place she would never agree to such an undertaking, and in the second place, even if she were able to do so, which is improbable, it could only be done by absolutely destroying the trade of England and France and other countries of

the world, and in order to do so Germany would have to develop a state of efficiency such as has never been known in the history of the world, and if she can do this, there is nothing we can do which would prevent Germany from overrunning the world thereafter.

In short, a prescient foretaste of what was indeed in store for the world from the Third Reich and Adolf Hitler, at that point a junior member of a Bavarian Freikorps devoted to suppressing communist uprisings. Keynes, too, saw numbers even approaching this magnitude as preposterous. He pointed out that less than 10 percent of all French territory had even been occupied by Germany, less than 4 percent had substantial devastation. Yet French damage claims amounted to one-third of the entire value of all of France's household property.

There was also the question of how this money was to be collected. Loucheur, the consummate pragmatist, had no interest in France taking over German mines, equipment or workers. "I confess that I would not want them at any price," he explained, "because the mines without the miners and the miners without political control is impossible." At the same time, Loucheur wanted no part of German equipment or matériel for the devastated regions. As he told John Foster Dulles at one point, such actions would "give Germany a stranglehold on the economic life of northern France as, once German machinery was installed, all replacements and spare parts would have to be supplied by Germany and orders, enlargements and new installations would similarly go to Germany." Britain's Lord Cunliffe, the Heavenly Twin, arguing to the end for crushing, purely cash payments, observed: "Do France and Belgium really want to take in a great number of men who are, at the very least, undesirable and who might even be spies? . . . I believe I know something of the psychology of our enemies, and I would not be astonished if they released their criminals from prison in order to send them."

Underlying all these very real and immediate fears was an even broader French paranoia—the same emotions that motivated Clemenceau in his dealings with Italy in southern Europe and the Balkans—the demographic imperative. In 1919, barely 40 million French faced down 60 million Germans, and that gap was only widening. For the moment the Germans were defeated, dispirited, and hungry, but eventually they would recover both their morale and their enormous talent for organization and military genius.

Meanwhile, the issue was just how much Germany could be made to pay under the contract that was gradually taking shape around the conference tables and halls of the Quai d'Orsay and in the parlors of the Big Three. Britain, France, and the United States were driving the reparations talks—and had the most at stake. In a series of meetings in early April, the economic issues were beginning to come into focus. First there was the fundamental issue of defining just what was meant by reparations. Second, there was the thornier issue of what levels to set—what could Germany and other Central Powers pay—collecting the maximum number of golden eggs without killing the goose. Lamont offered a summary of one session called by Wilson with his U. S. experts on April 1:

> Some of us were gathered in his library in the Place des Etats-Unis, having been summoned to him to discuss this particular question of pensions [for war widows and veterans]. We explained to him that we couldn't find a single lawyer in the American delegation that would give an opinion in favor of including pensions. All the logic was against it. 'Logic! Logic! I don't give a damn for logic. I am going to include pensions!' [Wilson shouted] Now Mr. Wilson was, least of all men, lacking in logic. For logicians who may stand aghast at his offhand utterance, I hasten to explain that it was not a contempt for logic, but simply an impatience of technicality: a determination to brush aside verbiage and get at the root of things. There was not one of us in the room whose heart did not beat with a like feeling.

The group had touched on an especially sore subject. John Foster Dulles had just pointed out to the assembled experts that adding pensions to the reparations bill being presented to Germany—an item very dear to the heart of Lloyd George, as we have seen, because otherwise Britain would realize little of the swag that was being divided—would be in direct violation of the armistice agreement all had just signed five months earlier. Indeed, the armistice agreement was overhanging the entire reparations battle as firmly as the secret treaties were overhanging the drafting of boundaries in much of the rest of the world. This could help explain at least a part of Wilson's frustrations. His Fourteen Points, on which the armistice was based, were yet again being torn to shreds.

Four days after this meeting with his own delegation, Wilson called together another session in his parlor at eleven o'clock in the morning. This time, the president played host to the Council of Four—Wilson, Clemenceau, Lloyd George and Italy's Vittorio Emanuele Orlando. The agenda was the same. The agreement they reached was diabolically clever. Germany, they finally decided, would pay enumerated damages until the point that the Allies became convinced that it could pay no more, at which point the debt would be reduced. For all other issues, they punted. Just as they dumped into the lap of the still unborn League of Nations the most noxious problems they'd left unresolved with respect to border issues, minorities, and self-government, rather than deal with yet another rat's nest of problems, they shoveled the entire question onto a Reparations Commission. This body, composed of representatives of the victorious Allies, was given nearly unlimited powers to inquire into the affairs of the German government and its people, becoming effectively a second, international government grafted onto the nation's own elected representatives. Germany would have until May 1921 to come up with a down payment of 20 billion gold marks, which would include the costs of the Allied occupation of German territory plus the value of food and raw materials it had turned over.

At this point the Treaty of Versailles turned into an almost comic-opera document. Germany, it seems, also was required to provide France with "500 stallions (3 to 7 years); 30,000 fillies and mares (18 months to 7 years), type: Ardennais, Boulonnais or Belgian; 2,000 bulls (18 months to 3 years); 90,000 milch cows (2 to 6 years); 1,000 rams; 100,000 sheep; 10,000 goats. And eventually it had to surrender 5,000 locomotives and 150,000 rail cars. The Belgians also got 40,000 heifers, 200 rams and 15,000 sows. Keynes objected strongly to these provisions, referring to "the desperate starvation conditions prevailing" in Germany. But there was more. It also had to provide 7 million tons of coal per year for ten years, plus the amount of coal that would have been produced in destroyed French mines until they were repaired. Finally, the treaty also required Germany to issue 60 billion gold marks' worth of bonds immediately, with more to follow when the Reparations Commission had determined Germany could pay. This would satisfy French needs for an immediate cash infusion. It would also mean, indirectly, help from the United States, since most of these bonds would be sold to Americans by Wall Street investment banks. Eventually a similar structure would be mirrored in the other treaties signed with the defeated Central Powers. For Bulgaria, the Allies fixed on a reparations bill of $450 million, or a quarter of the entire national wealth of this pathetically poor nation, which had the misfortune of joining the wrong side in the war, plus in-kind payments of 13,500 cows, 12,500 horses, 2,500 mules and 125 bulls. And this as the production of grain, the principal component of Bulgaria's national output, had fallen to 47 percent of its prewar average.

The entire reparations compromise, alas, turned out to be too clever by half. Germany, as Loucheur, Montagu, and Davis had already warned, was to be transformed into an indemnity machine whose levers would be manipulated by the hated Reparations Commission. The Germans recognized this reality from the first moment they laid eyes on the treaty, which was presented to them on May 7 at Versailles, where their delegation had been confined to the barricaded Hotel des Réservoirs. Leading the mission was Ulrich Graf von Brockdorff-Rantzau, Germany's foreign minister, who two years earlier had facilitated the passage of Lenin across Germany in a sealed train en route to St. Petersburg's Finland Station. Brockdorff-Rantzau was horrified by the reparations section, warning the Allies on May 13 that "those who will sign this Treaty will sign the death sentence of many millions of German men, women, and children" from famine. At the same time, Lloyd George was also beginning to panic that perhaps the Germans might not sign, plunging Europe back into war. He was most concerned with the harsh reparations clause and began to suggest a pullback. But Clemenceau and Wilson, by then all but fed up with the British prime minister's manipulations, refused to budge. Finally, two weeks later, Brockdorff-Rantzau fired one last desperate shot across the bow:

Although the exaction of the cost of the war has been expressly renounced, yet Germany, thus cut in pieces and weakened, must declare herself ready in principle to bear all the war expenses of her enemies, which would exceed many times over the total amount of German State and private assets. . . . No limit is fixed save the capacity of the German people for payment, determine not only by their standard of life but solely by their capacity to meet the demands of their enemies by their labour. The German people would thus be condemned to perpetual slave labour. . . . The

International Reparation Commission receives dictatorial powers over the whole life of our people in economic and cultural matters. Its authority extends far beyond that which the Emperor, the German Federal Council and the Reichstag combined ever possessed within the territory of the Empire. This Commission has unlimited control over the economic life of the State, of communities and individuals. Further the entire educational and sanitary system depends on it. It can keep the whole German people in mental thralldom.

Brockdorff-Rantzau wasn't far off base. Indeed, one might ask the very pertinent question as to whether under such conditions, wouldn't even an Adolf Hitler appear as a savior, determined to renounce the entire treaty document and show the Reparations Commission the door? Before we get there, however, there were other more immediate effects of this misguided treaty.

None of the Allies really wanted to crush the Central Powers. Each had separately come to the realization that a living, vibrant Germany was the only viable bulwark against the spread of Bolshevism across Europe to the English Channel and beyond. In the end, though, Wilson's unflinching morality (except where it suited him to compromise in the interest of promoting his beloved League of Nations) still led him to declare to Lloyd George that the treaty should "be a historic lesson, so that people might know that they could not do anything of the sort the Germans attempted without suffering the severest kind of punishment." This was in sharp contrast to members of Wilson's own delegation who were horrified at many aspects of the treaty, particularly the reparations clauses.

On June 3, with the treaty already in the Germans' hands, some forty members of the U. S. delegation held an extraordinary session at the Hotel Crillon. The discussion was often heated, and at the end, many walked out of the room frustrated and disgusted by both the process and its outcome. As George Beer described in his diary: "Obviously the treaty is in many points at variance with sound principles and it cannot be carried out. It is not executable and must be provided as a provisional, transitory agreement. Some things demand immediate changes, especially the absurd Reparations Clauses, but others must be adjusted from time to time."

Beer suggested that the most critical element was for "a definite and reasonable amount as indemnity, all payable in ten years." In the end, no changes were made. Germany was asked to trust the Allies, but there was no basis for any such trust, nor would any such basis be established in the ensuing months and years. Germany should, however, have examined the real motives of each of the Allies, but especially its closest neighbor—France. Loucheur, even Clemenceau, had no interest in crushing Germany. Or at least, the two had a much greater fear of crushing France in the process—especially French industry that was dependent on Germany for both markets and raw materials. At the same time, they feared the influx of cheap German products into France's own markets at home and abroad. Indeed, the entire character of the West's relations with Germany was determined for decades by the manner in which the reparations question played out.

Few of the experts, let alone the heads of state, who sat down to write the structure of the world's post war economic system had any formal training in economic theory. They were consumed by a host of phantom problems that suggested they had no real grasp of international economies, which they apparently believed were a zero-sum game. In fact, the international economic system is far more flexible and expandable than most experts thought at the time, though certainly the persistence of the archaic gold standard until the 1930s contributed to any embedded rigidities. Until then, equivalent amounts of gold were supposed to back every paper bill that was issued. Keynes called the gold standard "a barbarous relic." Germany was the first to cave in. With most of its gold marks earmarked for reparations, Germany abolished the gold standard and moved quickly to paper currency. It became virtually crack-cocaine for its economic system. Without the need to back every Reichsmark with gold, more could be—and were—printed at will. The result was a rampant hyperinflation that all but destroyed the German economy in the 1920s. In his diary, the British diplomat Sir Edgar Vincent, the Viscount D'Abernon, who participated in most of the twelve international conferences on reparations that took place from 1920 to 1924, described the problem:

In the autumn of 1920, when the first Brussels Conference of Experts came together, exchange stood at 254 marks to the £ sterling. In January, 1923 at the time of the Conference in Paris, which preceded the Ruhr occupation, the mark had fallen to 83,000 to the £ sterling. Nine months afterwards, when the Ruhr occupation had resulted in the complete discomfiture of German finance, the paper mark had fallen to the almost incredible level of 18 billion to the £ sterling. In other words, the mark in October, 1923, was worth in gold one-forty-millionth part of its value in 1914 at the outbreak of the war.

These numbers don't begin to describe the misery and suffering on the streets of Weimar Germany when 50 million mark banknotes, worth $1 when they were issued (and would have been worth $12 million nine years earlier), were all but worthless within a matter of days . Still, on May 31, 1921, Germany had managed to hand over to the Reparations Commission one billion gold marks in cash. By November of that same year, it was already begging for relief. France had a new finance minister, Frédéric François-Marsal, replacing Klotz, who was sent to a much-deserved retirement. The new minister believed that economic restoration of Germany just might be a good thing. Still, hostility to France was only intensifying across the Rhine. Though the German steel industry depended on French iron ore, known as "minette," nearly as much as France's steel producers were dependent on German coke, one German steel executive shouted in 1922, "They can choke on their minette." Very quickly Germany learned to make do with scrap steel and ore from other sources.

Meanwhile, Keynes had been doing his best to see if there was anything that could be salvaged from what he rightly predicted would be a truly devastating blow that the treaty's reparation provisions would deal to the Western world's economic system. Even before the treaty was signed on June 28, 1919, Keynes had left Paris, with one final shot to Lloyd George:

Dear Prime Minister:

I ought to let you know that on Saturday I am slipping away from the scene of nightmare. I can do no more good here. I've gone on hoping even through these last dreadful weeks that you'd find some way to make of the Treaty a just and expedient document. But now it's apparently too late. The battle is lost. I leave the

[Heavenly] twins to gloat over the devastation of Europe, and to assess to taste [sic] what remains for the British taxpayer.

Sincerely yours,

J. M. Keynes.

In fact, of course, the Heavenly Twins had not really had their way at all, but by now Keynes was determined to take his campaign against the reparations to the people. Friends urged him to put his concerns on paper—among them, Virginia Woolf, who on seeing him on July 18 was worried, as she confided to her diary: "He is disillusioned, he says. No more does he believe, that is, in the stability of the things he likes. Eton is doomed; the governing classes, perhaps Cambridge too. These conclusions were forced on him by the dismal and degrading spectacle of the Peace Conference, where men played shamelessly, not for Europe, or even England, but for their own return to Parliament at the next election."

The work Keynes finally produced—what some believe was truly his masterpiece, was certainly heavily influenced by Bloomsbury, especially Lytton Strachey's magisterial 1918 work, *Eminent Victorians*. Keynes's *The Economic Consequences of the Peace* ranged from caricatures of those in Paris whom he detested to a brilliantly reasoned formula for revising the entire reparations structure, which he was confident could lead to a new era of peace and prosperity across the Western world.

First, Keynes set up the context—chaos, madness, and confusion threatening to overwhelm the Western world's economy and undermine its political foundations, leaving the way clear for the arrival of Bolshevism, even anarchy. The war, and the abortive attempts at a stable peace that followed, had all but destroyed the delicate balance that existed in those halcyon days before the outbreak of hostilities. Then he picked apart the economic planks of the treaty—particularly the capacity of Germany to pay and the needs claimed by each of the European powers. In each case they were vastly overrated; indeed, by many orders of magnitude. Certainly there was some considerable hyperbole at work here, but not enough to enable even Keynes's sharpest critics on both sides of the Atlantic to discredit the work. Especially since Keynes offered a solution—an eminently reasonable one, in fact, that seemed on the surface to cut through all the rhetoric and various national self-interests. The formula that Keynes proposed was a simple one. First, cancel with one stroke all war debts. Second, cap German reparations at $10 billion, then deduct the value of various seized property like the German fleet, bringing the lump-sum total to $7.5 billion, to be repaid in thirty annual installments of $250 million beginning in 1923. This would allow the German economy to return to some semblance of stability. Finally, Britain must renounce all claims to this sum, turning her proceeds over to the "new states" of Central Europe, particularly Poland, Czechoslovakia, and Yugoslavia, that were in far greater need. Some portions of the bonds issued by the "former enemy powers" to help satisfy the reparations must carry some financial guarantees from the Allies. "All this implies some generosity by the United States," Keynes concluded.

The problem with this entire structure was simple. It would never work. It ignored the immediate political realities, as well as the deeply embedded passions, not only of rival political leaders, but of the peoples of most of these countries. With Wilson in the midst of a losing battle to win approval of the treaty and the League of Nations from a hostile Senate, he had no interest in forgiving U. S. debts to Britain. Recall the wartime financial loan scheme that Keynes hated at the time, but was forced to accept. Now as a result of this system, Britain had neither the interest nor the wherewithal to forgive the Continental Allies' debts without receiving comparable concessions from Washington. Particularly galling was Europe's new position with respect to the United States. Suddenly Europe, but especially Britain, was becoming a debtor region. For the political and financial leadership especially, it was demeaning to contemplate that for the first time, the colonies—the children, effectively—were holding the parents hostage.

Still, broad swaths of American and European readers embraced Keynes's work. To make certain that each word appeared as he wrote it, Keynes himself financed its publication on both sides of the Atlantic. Felix Frankfurter—the young lawyer, Harvard Law professor, and a cofounder of *The New Republic*, who'd actually come to Paris to lobby for the Zionist cause—got the book published in America and serialized in his new magazine. Keynes, it appeared, had pointed out every flaw— of personality and structure—that bedeviled the entire peace process:

The campaign for securing out of Germany the general costs of the war was one of the most serious acts of political unwisdom for which our statesmen have ever been responsible. To what a different future Europe might have looked forward if either Mr. Lloyd George or Mr. Wilson had apprehended that the most serious of the problems which claimed their attention were not political or territorial but financial and economic and that the perils of the future lay not in frontiers or sovereignty but in food, coal and transport. Neither of them paid adequate attention to these problems at any stage of the Conference. . . . The financial problems which were about to exercise Europe could not be solved by greed. The possibility of their cure lay in magnanimity. Europe, if she is to survive her troubles, will need so much magnanimity from America that she must herself practice it.

And this process, with the mechanisms it had created, was grinding inexorably onward. Keynes's monumental work, despite the widespread praise it attracted, never had much concrete impact on the peace process. Germany managed to make its first payment on the war reparations before the burden of what amounted to Mafia-style vigorish came crashing down on it. Keynes had pointed out that even at 5 percent interest, the reparations burden would double every fifteen years so that by 1936, with $750 million in annual payments (triple the sum he had called for), the overall reparations debt would have exploded to $65 billion, an almost unimaginable sum to a nation that by then had suffered through more than a decade of hyperinflation, depression, and mass unemployment. There were projections that Germany would still be paying reparations until 1961 or beyond.

It was at about this point that France trotted out the third, and in some respects most potent, member of its tag team. Jacques Seydoux was born to the breed—son of a French diplomat, first in his class at the prestigious École Libre des Sciences Politiques, trained in the great French embassies abroad—London, Berlin, Athens. He finally returned to Paris in time to assume his greatest mission of all. He was, effectively, father of the blockade. Throughout the war, Seydoux was in charge of making sure that nothing the Allies, or indeed any neutral nation, produced got through to the Central Powers. Debilitated by a degenerative disease that struck him at the age of thirty-six, all but paralyzing him for twenty-two years, he hobbled at first on two canes, eventually navigating in a wheel chair. Throughout, he remained cheerful despite constant though rarely expressed pain. And he was tireless in his mission that was devoted to strangling Germany into submission. So it was scarcely surprising that, the peace concluded and the necessity of wringing desperately needed reparations funds from the loser, France turned to this quiet, intensely focused bureaucrat. As François Charles-Roux, a distinguished French diplomat and later principal aide-de-camp of General Charles de Gaulle in World War II, observed in 1932: "Jacques Seydoux found in his hands all the elements of one of the largest and most complex problems ever posed to human intelligence, every part of a work as broad as it was arduous, and which include among its parts dealing with ex- Allies, ex-enemies and ex-neutrals. . . . What one might call the economic reconstruction of Europe was what occupied him totally."

For five years Seydoux raced from conference to conference—London, San Remo, Boulogne, Spa, Cannes, Brussels, Genoa, and back to London. He brought, as Charles-Roux put it, "his moral force" to the efforts to find funds to rebuild France while at the same time keeping Germany from descending into its own inferno that approached, on several occasions, civil war. The succession of conferences was yet another, miserable, legacy of the Peace Conference's abdication of its responsibilities. A viable agreement on the level and schedule of reparations might have set Europe on a workable path toward rebuilding strong, sustainable foundations and a lasting peace. As Wickham Steed described the situation:

> Even Clemenceau understood [the treaty's] defects but trusted that time would help to remedy them. President Wilson, and to a still greater degree, Colonel House, felt that the best features of the Treaty were those which would permit of its gradual modification, through the instrumentality of the Reparation Commission and the League of Nations, when the passions and appetites that prevailed in Paris should have cooled down.

A nice rationalization, and certainly part and parcel of Wilson's dual desperation. First, there was his overwhelming desire to give some raison d'être for his beloved League of Nations. Second, there was his fear of the spread of Bolshevism westward. Certainly with the arrival of Rosa

Luxemburg and Karl Liebknecht as early as December 1918, it was not unreasonable for Wilson to search for some mechanism that would monitor and calibrate the red menace with the means of extinguishing it. But both of these goals, at the time commendable, exhibited little or no understanding of the rapidly deteriorating realities in Europe, especially in Germany. Containing Bolshevism in Germany was as complex an undertaking—probably beyond the capacities even of the peacemakers in Paris—as was their effort to contain communist expansion everywhere else they turned.

In the end, this task was performed outside the entire Paris peace process, but led to accelerating chaos in Germany. By the early 1920s, a series of attempted putsches unsettled the Weimar government and led to a widespread feeling of near-anarchy in many portions of the nation. This in turn encouraged the rise of Bolshevist sympathizers and so-called workers or socialist parties. Some of these evolved into just the opposite. Violent right-wing organizations such as the National Socialist party, whose military wing, the vicious SA, or Sturmabteilung, the feared brown shirts or storm troopers, attracted many of the same Freikorps thugs who had suppressed the early Bolshevist revolts in the days after the armistice.

By the end of 1922, about the only incentive the Germans had to make the reparations clauses of the Versailles Treaty work was the threat of the Allied occupation of its territory to enforce the terms. That threat turned into a reality in January 1923, when Germany, its fiscal back to the wall and with the economy in hyperinflation, defaulted on reparations payments. French and Belgian troops promptly moved into the Ruhr Valley, seizing the heartland of German industrial production. The occupation lasted two and a half years and led to widespread strikes and civil disobedience, including the infamous Beer Hall Putsch, Hitler's first, abortive attempt to seize power in Germany.

The arrival of French and Belgian forces led also to the inauguration of Gustav Stresemann as Reichskanzler on August 13, 1923, and an end to Germany's most pressing fiscal crisis. With economic recovery spreading to Europe from the United States, already into the flapper era of the Roaring Twenties, Stresemann brought a measure of stability. Issuing a new currency, the Rentenmark, on November 15, he managed to halt the crippling hyperinflation by refusing to print more of the new paper money, reigning in the spiraling economy. Meanwhile, he,

Seydoux and a host of other Allied diplomats were shuffling back and forth to the string of economic conferences that finally culminated in the Dawes Plan which was signed in August 1924.

Charles Gates Dawes was America's answer to Jacques Seydoux. He was a brilliant Midwestern lawyer, banker, and utilities entrepreneur, whose great-great- grandfather, William Dawes, had ridden with Paul Revere to warn Massachusetts that the British were coming. Charles Dawes ran the entire Allied procurement system during the war. Afterwards, though a Republican, and flying in the face of his party, he urged the Republican-dominated Senate to approve the Treaty of Versailles, a losing proposition. In 1920 he was named the nation's first budget director, saving the government some $2 billion in his first year of office. This quickly drew the attention of European leaders to his masterful command of the niceties of financial manipulations. By late 1923 the Allies were desperate, since Germany had all but reneged on its reparation payments, leaving France to stagger under the burden of reconstruction. Vast swaths of the Ruhr Valley were still under French and Belgian occupation, depriving the Germans of income from its rich resources that could be used to pay reparations. The Reparations Committee asked Dawes to find a way out. And he did.

In a compromise that won him the Nobel Peace Prize in 1925, Dawes proposed a system that provided an immediate quick fix. His plan, issued in April 1924, included evacuation of the Ruhr region, reparation payments beginning at one billion marks in the first year, rising to two and a half billion per year after four years, and foreign loans, primarily from the United States, to help Germany through its immediate fiscal crises. The document contained a dash of Keynes, a dollop of Seydoux, and whiff of Lloyd George and Clemenceau. And for a time, it worked. But not for long. Like most of the structures established by the Allies, the Dawes Plan, while clever, even elegant in its outlines, failed to take into account the realities of the time. As Keynes had warned so eloquently, Germany simply couldn't make multi-billion dollar payments indefinitely.

So five years after the Dawes Plan, on June 7, 1929, twelve days after the death of Jacques Seydoux, a new Allied commission was assembled. Thomas Lamont and Owen D. Young on the U. S. side, with Carl Melchior on the German side—who for a decade had been pressing quietly the need for reduced reparations—came up with another, and as it turned out, final stab at bringing order out of chaos in post-war European finance and reconstruction. The Young Plan was actually the brainchild of this lawyer and industrialist who'd founded the Radio Corporation of America (RCA) while the Peace Conference was under way a decade earlier. By the time he was tapped to head the newest reparations effort, he had moved over to the chairmanship of the General Electric Corporation. Young was another financial genius, out of the same mold as Dawes and Lamont, but this time he took the long view. Reparations would be fixed at $26.35 billion—a sum that approximated, when adjusting for inflation, the figure that Lamont had been pressing on the Peace Conference ten years before (though more than twice the figure that Keynes had thought even remotely realistic). But this time, payment would be made over the course of an all but inconceivable period of fifty-eight and a half years. In other words, somewhere around 1988, Germany would finally have satisfied its war debt. Well, not exactly.

Even before the plan was officially signed into being, Black Thursday intervened. The Wall Street Crash of 1929 rippled rapidly across Europe, as failing U. S. banks were forced to call in credits that had just barely been issued. Ironically, it was Thomas Lamont who, as acting head of J.P. Morgan & Company, sent Richard Whitney onto the floor of the New York Stock Exchange on Black Thursday to "buy [U. S.] Steel at 205 . . . 25,000 shares," in a vain effort to inject a jolt of confidence into the plummeting market and halt the collapse.

By 1931 more than a third of all Germans were unemployed. A year later, that figure reached 40 percent. In July 1932 the Allies agreed at yet another conference in Lausanne, to reduce the entire German obligation to a mere $714 million. But six months later, on January 30, 1933, Adolf Hitler was sworn in as chancellor of Germany. The new Reichkanzler promptly repudiated the Versailles Treaty and all the war debts as well. Eleven months later, the Gestapo closing in on him, Melchior died of a stroke within weeks of marrying his long time French mistress, the aristocratic author Marie de Molènes. Europe was about to be plunged into a second world war having barely recovered from the first. And the grim prophesy of 1919 that a powerful, resurgent Germany could again prove a scourge to its neighbors and much of the civilized world, was about to come true.

On June 28, 1940, his panzer divisions having overrun France in a blitzkrieg attack, Hitler appeared on the Trocadéro to gaze at his Eiffel Tower. It was a sad, jarring parallel to Wilhelm I's coronation at Versailles three-quarters of a century earlier. Hitler's visit followed France's surrender and the signing of an armistice in the same railroad car in the Compiègne Forest where the armistice of 1918 had ratified the German defeat in the last world war. This time there would be no reparations. Germany simply seized half of France. By the time the Reich had been defeated yet again, there was little left to reclaim. The Allies occupied the western sector, the Russians the east. The goal, this time, was to rebuild a new nation with as little of the baggage of the past as possible.

That was not the end of the issue raised so long ago in Paris, however. The ghosts of Versailles, Dawes, and Young lived on in Europe. In 1953 a final international conference determined that Germany would pay off what remained of its debt only after the nation was reunified. Still, by 1980, a by now prosperous West German government had paid off the principal. In 1995, following reunification of the two halves of the nation, the new united German government said it would resume payments of the interest on that debt of so long ago.

Earlier, in 1938, on the eve of World War II, John Foster Dulles perhaps seeking to rewrite his own role in history, reflected back to those days of his youth and all the mistakes made in Paris—the roads not taken:

> If through inadvertence the draughtsmen [Dulles among them] of the reparation clauses contributed largely toward a German psychology which has changed the political complexion of much of the world, so through lack of prescience they set up a force which has contributed to a profound change in the commercial and financial structure of the world. . . . It was assumed that reparation could be permanently absorbed into an expanded world credit structure and there could be an indefinite postponement of the problem of actually transferring goods or services in payment of this portion of reparation. This conception might have been realizable if it had been held to modest limits."

It was not, of course. So in some respects, Keynes was even more prescient:

If we aim deliberately at the impoverishment of Central Europe, vengeance, I dare predict, will not limp. Nothing can then delay for very long that final civil war between the forces of Reaction and the despairing convulsions of Revolution, before which the horrors of the late German war will fade into nothing, and which will destroy, whoever is the victor, the civilization and the progress of our generation.

Keynes had never wanted Germany to become the whipping boy of Europe—pillaged, for the sake of domestic political profit, by the victorious Allies bent at the same time on destroying Germany's ability to restore any degree of prosperity for its people. Undeterred, the leaders of the major powers hammered out terms of payment that could only be described as confiscatory, effectively bleeding Germany white.

Did any good come of all these efforts through so many years, then? Certainly nothing the creators of the reparations system of the Versailles Treaty ever envisioned. Still, Jean Monnet, a young deputy on the French delegation, had come to understand deeply the role coal and steel played in the intersecting political and economic life of Europe. After World War II he was named planning commissioner by de Gaulle, effectively the role exercised by Louis Loucheur after World War I. Monnet recognized that the same friction between Germany and France for control of the Ruhr Valley that so devastated relations between the two nations post-Versailles was threatening the fragile peace yet again. This time Monnet succeeded where Loucheur, Seydoux, and a host of others had failed.

Without the overwhelming burden of a system of crushing reparations hanging over their heads, the principal European nations, supported this time by the United States, agreed to Monnet's proposal—a European Coal and Steel Community. By 1958 it had given birth to the European Economic Community (known as the Common Market), and finally on February 7, 1992, the Maastricht Treaty created the European Union. By then, oil had long superseded coal as the global economic weapon of choice, while OPEC vastly outstripped the European Coal and Steel Community as the leading geopolitical power.

All the leaders gathered at Versailles had their own political motives that drove their economic priorities, just as they drove the borders they drew on the map of the world and the methods they used to juggle

religious and ethnic groups. In each case, the consequences of their selfish actions proved equally catastrophic for the peace and stability of all
the regions they touched. As Keynes wrote after the treaty was signed and
the delegations and military forces headed home: "No political structure
for keeping the peace would stand up if the economic foundations were
rotten." But as the twentieth century morphed into the twenty-first,
motives turned out to be far less important than consequences.

11

WHERE DID
THEY ALL GO?

IN THE END, VERSAILLES PROVED A COLOSSAL FAILURE FOR
Woodrow Wilson, for the United States, and for the future of a world
that had hoped it might be governed by principles of freedom and self-
determination—even today. As a devastated Harold Nicolson observed,
covenants of peace were not openly arrived at. Freedom of the seas was
not secured. Free trade was not established in Europe; indeed, tariff
walls wound up being erected, higher and more numerous than any yet
known. National armaments were not reduced. German colonies and
the lands of its allies, Austria-Hungary and the Ottoman Empire, were
distributed among the victors as spoils—from the Saar to Shantung,
from Serbia to Syria—the wishes, to say nothing of the interests, of their
populations flagrantly disregarded. Russia was not welcomed into the
society of nations. Arab portions of the Ottoman Empire were assured
neither secure boundaries nor secure sovereignty. Vast territories in
Central Europe and the Balkans included millions of inhabitants who
were indisputably not native Polish or Czech, Serb or Rumanian, Slovak
or Slovene. The League of Nations, emasculated first by the peacemakers in Paris, then by America's failure to join up, was never able to fulfill
its vision of political independence for great and small nations alike.
Provinces and peoples were treated as pawns and chattels. Territorial
settlements in almost every case were mere adjustments and compro-

mises between the claims of rival states. Even the old system of secret treaties remained barely touched.

Above all, the Fourteen Points—under whose banner American boys had gone to war, and often their deaths, on the battlefields of France and Belgium—were eviscerated by America's own allies, all of whom had come to Paris with their own particular priorities. None of these involved self-determination, territorial integrity, or the various freedoms on which the Points were based.

There has been some debate among historians on whether Wilson, as a president, was a hit or a miss. Certainly, the document he took home with him from Paris was profoundly flawed in almost every respect. It failed to embrace any of the elevating moral vision that he had brought over with him. In his efforts to win acceptance by the Allies of his beloved League of Nations, he compromised at virtually every turn with respect to the world he and his fellow peacemakers were creating. Then, after returning to Washington with this perverted vision, he compounded the felony with a categorical refusal to entertain a single amendment or reservation to the treaty from the Republican-controlled Senate. Many of these amendments, ironically, would have restored some of the goals that Wilson had surrendered in Paris.

These revisions were proposed by men equal to Wilson in talent and imagination—in particular by the leader of the opposition, the brilliant and powerful chairman of the Senate Foreign Relations Committee. Massachusetts Republican Henry Cabot Lodge was the first student ever to graduate from Harvard University with a PhD in political science. Lodge was an attentive student of the U.S. body politic with a close, if at times adversarial, relationship to the media that were shaping the views of the American electorate on the deliberations in Paris. For months he and his fellow senators were closeted in Washington—far from the gilded conference rooms in France where they might have contributed substantially and constructively to the debate, had Wilson seen fit to include any of them on the U.S. delegation. A growing number from both sides of the aisle viewed with mounting concern what the president was giving away. They worried over the ties he was forging with an international community that, they believed, had dragged the United States into a war not of its choosing.

The amendments, or "reservations," to the treaty that Wilson presented to the Senate were seen by Lodge and many of his colleagues as simply preserving America's freedom of action —that could prevent the nation from being sucked into future conflicts in which it had little or no interest. Their goal, not so distinct from Wilson's, was to enable, though not require, America's participation in the work and funding of the League of Nations. Wilson categorically refused any compromise, ordering Senate Democrats to vote against the forty-five amendments and four reservations reported by the Senate Foreign Relations Committee on September 10, 1919. Two weeks later, in the midst of his whistle-stop campaign seeking in vain to drum up popular support from a nation worn out by the recent conflict and still licking its wounds, the president collapsed from exhaustion in Pueblo, Colorado, and returned to Washington. On October 2, 1919, he suffered a debilitating stroke that left him paralyzed and ineffectual for the last seventeen months of his presidency, as the Senate overwhelmingly defeated his beloved treaty.

Most of the young experts who populated the Allied delegations went home defeated and disillusioned. The dreams they had borne so confidently to Paris just a few short months earlier they saw ground between the rocks of large-power diplomacy and selfish priorities. At the outset, Harold Nicolson had been particularly anxious that the errors of the Congress of Vienna a century earlier, where the map of Europe was redrawn after the defeat of Napoleon, not be repeated. His most profound fears had come to pass. The errors were indeed repeated, even compounded. The great diplomats of the nineteenth century—Austria's Metternich, France's Talleyrand, Russia's Corsican-born Pozzo di Borgo—talked often of humanitarian principles while practicing palace intrigue, moving armies and frontiers around on the map of Europe as though they were tin soldiers on a chalkboard. But such old habits die hard. And an innocent such as Wilson, insulated from the realities of European politics, came like a lamb to the slaughter. As he moaned when he recognized how resoundingly his dreams had been rejected, he sought excuses, but found little comfort: "European diplomacy works always in the dense thicket of ancient feuds, rooted, entangled and entwined. It is difficult to see the path; it is not always possible to see the light of day. I did not realize it all until the peace conference; I did not realize how deep the roots are."

Lansing had seen it for months, but was never able to make Wilson understand what desperate trouble his Fourteen Points were encountering. On February 3, 1919, he wrote in his diary: "As I see it, the dominant spirit in the Peace Conference is selfish materialism tinctured with a cynical disregard of manifest rights. What will be the outcome? Will American idealism have to succumb to this evil spirit of a past era? Will principle or expediency control the work of the Conference?"

The answer, of course, was expediency. The diplomats the Americans encountered were playing by different rules from those preached by the upright Presbyterian from Princeton who carried the hopes and dreams of the world to Paris on his shoulders. At the Congress of Vienna, according to the British statesman Horace Walpole, "it was the mode of the times to pay by one favor for receiving another."

The fact is that Wilson, until the very end, had little notion that his European fellow statesmen had taken him to the cleaners, picking his pockets neatly of the last shred of hope for the principles he had brought with him. When it dawned on him, he was stricken to the core. On May 30, the Treaty of Versailles already printed in its final form and in the hands of the Germans, Beer had a passing conversation with Whitney Shepardson. An aide to Colonel Edward House, Shepardson later became a top member of the Office of Strategic Services (OSS), the precursor to the Central Intelligence Agency, and he served as a founding member of the Council on Foreign Relations. "House had told him [Shepardson] that until a few days ago, W.W. had no idea but that the proposed treaty was on all fours with [in all points similar to] the Fourteen Points, but that now he realized its defects," Beer recorded in his diary with what appeared to be both relish and horror, since, as the young Inquiry member continued, "it is just the mess that I foresaw months ago when I washed my hands of all responsibility and decided to adopt a purely detached attitude. But what a situation."

A situation indeed. But one that the experts who expressed horror and concern were powerless to correct. To the end there remained some considerable question as to whether Woodrow Wilson ever really understood what the grand principles he so eloquently enunciated really stood for—especially the central concept of self-determination around which revolved the most intractable issues that the Paris peacemakers confronted. The vast gap between rhetoric and reality was never fully breached. There had been, fundamentally, two different forces working at sharp counterpurposes throughout the conference. On the one hand, there were those who continued to espouse the powerful moral priorities of Wilson and his Fourteen Points. These forces foresaw a better world eventually. The forces of nationalism and self-determination, whatever this might mean, would enable the populations of each of the regions the peacemakers were restructuring to take control of their own destiny, their future, and their governments. On the other hand, eventually, for most European statesmen, was too long to wait. Eventually was now. Georges Clemenceau still recalled the methods Bismarck had used following the Franco-Prussian War four decades earlier. The Prussian leader had believed he was fully empowered by Providence to accelerate the grindingly slow process of historical evolution that operated over the course of decades. Moreover, the world that Europe's leaders wanted to bring forth from this Peace Conference was one they could understand and continue to manipulate in the same way they or their forebears had been pulling the levers for centuries. For the first time, however, they had embraced a larger task—remaking the entire world in their image. And quickly. For this they were hopelessly ill-equipped.

And there were many immediate concerns that further complicated matters. Clemenceau and David Lloyd George shared a very tangible fear of the Bolsheviks—poised on Europe's frontiers, but threatening to carry the revolution to their doors. For Lloyd George, there was a need to face an impatient electorate and an even more impatient Parliament to which he had made some importunate but apparently binding promises; for the Italians, there were similar imperatives of basic political survival. For Clemenceau, there was paranoia over the continued menace of the Germans and the destruction they'd wrought on his now stricken nation that needed to be rebuilt. For the French leader there was fear, as well, of the imperial ambitions of Britain, combined with France's need to hang on desperately to its fragments of a global empire. This he saw being challenged by Britain on every side and, increasingly, by an insurgent America. All Europeans recognized the United States as the only nation to emerge largely unscathed—economically and politically—from the war.

World War I and the Treaty of Versailles were meant to mark the debut of America on the world stage—as a global power in every sense of the word. Wilson came to Paris with the world at his feet. U.S. forces and its military-industrial complex had broken the deadly battlefield stalemate and effectively won the war for the Allies, whether or not they were prepared at that moment to acknowledge it. But it was Wilson who lost the peace. Through an adroit mixture of diplomacy, political maneuvering, and canny horse sense, Britain's Lloyd George and France's Clemenceau managed to retain their grip on their colonial empires and their global hegemony for at least another generation. Their clever manipulations skewed the world back to the nineteenth-century realpolitik with which they were most comfortable and away from the concepts of self-determination and democracy that Wilson espoused.

Even as the war was beginning, a British backbench member of Parliament had expressed a view that would fit the reality of those assembling to sign the peace treaty at Versailles five years later. T. Edmund Harvey rose on August 13, 1914, to respond to a speech by Foreign Secretary Sir Edward Grey just as Britain was plunging headfirst into the abyss: "I am convinced that this war for the great masses of the countries of Europe is no peoples' war. It is a war that has been made by men in high places, by diplomatists working in secret, by bureaucrats out of touch with the people, by men who are a remnant of an older evil civilization."

The conclusion to the ensuing conflict was written, as one observer of the process, E. J. Dillon, observed, by "a gang of benevolent conspirators, ignoring history and expertship, shutting themselves up in a room and talking disconnectedly." And each of them striving desperately to come out on top over the other—but particularly over that paragon of virtue, and naiveté, Woodrow Wilson.

Lord Riddell, a top British aide to Lloyd George, recalled a picnic on May 4, 1919, when most of the major decisions already had been taken, the die cast: "Went with L.G. and party to the woods near Fontainebleau, where we had lunch at the Hotel du Foret. I drove with [Chancellor of the Exchequer] Bonar Law. He said he thought L.G. had got the better of Wilson, who had had to give up most of his Fourteen Points."

It was difficult to find barely a gesture to the Fourteen Points in the Treaty of Versailles that Germany was forced to sign on June 28, 1919. Certainly it was a grand ceremony—in the great chateau of Louis XIV, fifteen miles west of Paris, as Walter Duranty described it in the *New York Times*:

There could have been found no nobler setting for the signing of peace than the palace of the greatest French kings, on the hillcrest of Versailles. To reach it the plenipotentiaries and distinguished guests from all parts of the world, who motored to their places in the Hall of Mirrors, drove down the magnificent, tree-lined Avenue du Château, then across the huge square—the famous Place d'Armes of Versailles—and up through the gates and over the cobblestones of the Court of Honor to the entrance, where officers of the Garde Républicaine, in picturesque uniform were drawn up to receive them.

But inside, amid the pomp and ceremony, there was the grim reality of the treaty and the peace it defined. "The stillest three minutes ever lived through were those in which the German delegates signed the Peace Treaty today," *New York Times* correspondent Charles A. Selden wrote the next morning. At that moment, many saw the document as something less than the triumphal conclusion to a victorious war and the opening of a new era of peace and concord that they had hoped for. "A huge crowd and two German delegates led like felons into the room to sign their doom," wrote the Inquiry's Beer. "It was like the execution of a sentence." For more than just the diplomats from both sides, to be sure.

If this pact had meant simply some short-term changes in a time long past, it would have made little difference to us today. But the statesmen went to Paris to transform the world as it was then known, and in that, alas, they succeeded only too well. Their goals, effectively met by the treaty as it was presented to the hapless German delegates, were fundamentally simple. Each of the European Allies was determined to take care of the needs and the security of his own nation, as he perceived it—and everyone else be damned. Bismarck, in an earlier era, had tossed off the perfect description of all their feelings: "The whole of the Balkans is not worth the bones of a single Pomeranian grenadier."

It is we, today, who are still paying the price—far steeper than Bismarck's lone Pomeranian. In each part of the world on which we have turned our spotlight in these pages, the failures of the peacemakers at Versailles—errors of judgment, or simply a surfeit of hubris—are only too apparent now. The goal Wilson so correctly envisioned, even articulated, but on which he failed in the end to follow through, is a fundamental lesson that is critical for our leaders to understand today: "What we seek is the reign of law, based upon the consent of the governed and sustained by the organized opinion of mankind." We must learn from the long-ago failures even to approach these lofty ends.

Wilson was also prescient enough to appreciate, but alas not sufficiently determined or adroit to have insisted upon, a fundamental
reality—that all nations ultimately return to a stasis, an equilibrium
that works for each of them and their people. It might take decades, at a
cost of untold bloodshed, millions of people lost or displaced. But from
my personal experience, each nation ultimately winds up where it really
belongs. Certainly this has been the case in each of the countries that the
peacemakers at Versailles created, redrew, or somehow tinkered with.

The states of Indochina—ignored completely by the peacemakers of
Paris, to their decades-long damnation and a bitter battle with colonial
powers, Western democracies, and communist manipulators at a cost
of millions of lives—wound up with the governments that suited them
perfectly. In Vietnam there is what might be called an entrepreneurial
communism. This is not dissimilar to the road taken by its neighbor
to the north, China, which for centuries had largely called the tune in
that part of the world, long before Western exploiters arrived in their
ships. Neighboring Laos has settled into a quiet, Laotian-style isolation
that appears to suit its people. In Cambodia, in the spring of 1975,
at the end of the war that had spilled over from Vietnam, the mantra
I heard from all sides was, "As long as the war is finished, we are all
Cambodians, and we can live together in peace." The price, of course,
turned out to be more than a million dead in a historic genocide that
cost the nation more than 20 percent of its population. But today it has
returned to an equilibrium that promises prosperity and freedom. Had
the peacemakers of Paris recognized the aspirations of Nguyen Ai Quoc,
they would have cut loose these nations to set them on a course they
themselves would determine. Quoc might never have become Ho Chi
Minh, and the history of the past century in Southeast Asia would have
been far different indeed.

Much the same has been the case in Central Europe and, especially,
the Balkans. Yugoslavia, a completely artificial nation assembled out of
the ruins of Austria-Hungary and remnants of the Ottoman Empire,
was predestined for a bitter and bloody future. This nation, created to
form a strong southern anchor for Clemenceau's cordon sanitaire, was a
collection of powerful centrifugal forces held together by a succession of
strong men with political muscle. In 1980, after spending nearly three
years in Belgrade, I wrote for *Foreign Affairs*:

Despite the 35-year effort by Marshal Tito to promote unity behind a single Yugoslav identity, the ancestral enmities between the various component nationalities of Yugoslavia, particularly the Serbs and the Croats, have barely cooled. These are deeply felt, highly emotional, even irrational animosities—the Catholic Slovenes and Croatians with their heritage of the Austro-Hungarian Empire, the Orthodox Serbs, Montenegrins and Macedonians, the Muslim Bosnians with their heritage of rule by the Ottoman Turks. The differences are as fundamental as alphabets and cultures—the Cyrillic used in the eastern republics and the Latin alphabet in the western provinces.

At the time, the editors raised a skeptical eyebrow to my thesis, finally publishing it only after receiving a supporting companion piece by the distinguished dissident author-politician, Milovan Djilas. Alas, Djilas lived only to see the chaos of the post-Tito era, not the denouement that he and I predicted—a return to the small, ethnically and religiously homogeneous microstates of the Balkans that, today, hold the promise of a peaceful and prosperous future. The cost was some ten thousand dead and a quarter million or more homeless or displaced.

Elsewhere it took eighty years, but ultimately the Czech Republic and Slovakia emerged from the artificial Czechoslovak nation that Tomáš Masaryk and Clemenceau cobbled together as another anchor of the cordon sanitaire. None of these Central European people, however, could withstand the eventual armed power of the Soviet Union. The Bolsheviks managed to accomplish what Clemenceau feared the most, seizing half of Europe—though in their westward march they did stop considerably short of the Atlantic. For the various peoples of the Soviet Union, it took nearly eight decades, but eventually they, too, returned to the individual governments that suited them best. Today Russia has a strong ruler, a latter-day czar, but one at least of their own choosing, while the various other components of the former Soviet empire have returned to their homogeneous ethnic and religious origins. Ukraine, Georgia, Kazakhstan, and all the rest of the Soviet republics are governed not by a distant regime with divergent priorities, but by their own leaders. Millions died in Stalin's gulags in the process, but while the final miles have been rocky, they have been far less bloody. Would the path have been easier had the paranoid negotiators in Paris reached out a hand to seek accommodation, to welcome Russia into the community of sovereign nations, allowed to find its own identity as a partner rather than an adversary, whose destiny we might have sought to influence rather than stymie? Again, we will never know.

Finally, we come to the single most intractable problem today Iraq and terrorism. Are there lessons to be learned here, too? Most assuredly. The nations whose boundaries the peacemakers drew for the remains of the Ottoman Empire were every bit as artificial in their own way as the boundaries drawn in Central Europe, the Balkans, or even the Pacific island territories of Germany. The peacemakers of Paris clearly had as little understanding of the differences between Shiite and Sunni, Bedouin Arabs and Palestinians, as do many of our statesmen today. These are not small distinctions. They are blood feuds, cemented by centuries of frequently violent hatred and religious beliefs that date to the founding of these faiths. These feuds pit Moslem against Moslem, Jew against Arab, at times Arab against Christian. To create the current nations out of these profound antagonisms is to lay the foundations of the civil wars we see today.

Yet there is no reason that all of these nations and peoples ca not exist, side by side in their own territories with their own forms of government. Palestinians in the Gaza and West Bank territories should be entitled to govern themselves in their own nation, as the Jews should be entitled to govern their people in the State of Israel. Shiites and Sunnis, each in their own territory should be allowed their own right to a peaceful existence, all worshiping in their own way, governing themselves as their history and religion have dictated for a millennium.

Early in 2006, on a trip through the Arabian peninsula, I heard a host of intelligent and thoughtful Arabs speculate that perhaps the best that could be expected from the terrible and escalating bloodshed was for the deals of the Paris Peace Conference to be undone—for Sunnis and Shiites each to find their roots in their own nation. Certainly, it would remain a complex reality. Millions could die in the process. If the same formula that was operative in Cambodia in the 1970s were applied to Iraq three decades later—20 percent of the population wiped out in unimaginable violence—then five million Iraqis could perish. It is a horrific prospect. At the end, the Middle East would be a very different place. Iraq could wind up as three nations—a peaceful and prosperous Kurdistan in the north, a wealthy oil-rich Shiite Iraq in the south, and a much shrunken Mesopotamia surrounding a Baghdad whose river, the Tigris, divides Sunnis from whatever Shiites might remain there.

The Greater Mesopotamia that the Paris peacemakers turned into today's Iraq would still be a dangerous region—dangerous to the West, that is. The Shiite crescent from Iran across Iraq and down through eastern Saudi Arabia would contain a frightening percentage of the world's oil. It would provide an enormous diplomatic and economic challenge, but one whose resolution is feasible—by statesmen who are sensitive to the national aspirations involved, to the power of religions different from our own, even if we cannot accept or understand them—and above all, who are aware that the currents of history move slowly.

> Men and women today feel an intense apprehension, when they think of the fate of their children in a world in which the unreasoning prejudices and unenlightened practices that have recently again come to the fore in international life should prevail, leaving mankind in a dazed confusion, and pushing the people from time to time into wholesale slaughter with ever more horrible instruments of destruction.

Those words were written not today, but in 1922—by Paul S. Reinsch, Wilson's ambassador to China. He concluded his thought with the following hope: "We cannot believe that the peoples of the world will be so foolish as to allow themselves to remain in this condition and not to find their way to a reorganization of public affairs which will make such a haphazard and perilous situation impossible."

Reinsch believed, quite rightly in hindsight, that the peacemakers in Paris never "got beyond the old methods of bartering the destinies of small and weak peoples, which had been used by the Congress of Vienna with disastrous results."

The question, of course, is whether our leaders today are falling into the same catastrophic traps. Only, those small people today are by no means weak anymore. New tactics of terrorism and new weapons of mass destruction have equalized the balance between small and large. Today, even large nations must beware. But other elements have not changed. In the first weeks of 1919, much of the world looked to the United States and President Wilson as a beacon to guide them. Wilson surrendered that beacon, in the process losing that sense of leadership.

We have regained it from time to time, only to lose it again for similar reasons of realpolitik or a failure to understand just how important we are—important in our ability to help others be what they want to be, not what we want for them. This was the failure of the other Allies in Paris—they sought to force their own vision of the world on nations and people far away who had no interest in accepting it and for which this vision was anathema at best, heretical at worst. Self-determination was Wilson's watchword then. It should be ours again today.

In the fall of 1974, as I was preparing to head for Asia as a correspondent for the *New York Times*, the paper's executive editor, A. M. Rosenthal, called me in for a talk. "There is one immutable reality that you must keep in mind over there," Rosenthal began. "It is the one constant that determines everything—politics, society, the economy, the culture. That is the heat. It is inescapable, inexorable. You must never ignore it." He was right, of course. It was also just one of many realities that neither a Frenchman from the Vendée, nor a prime minister from Wales, nor a university president from Princeton, could truly appreciate.

If there is a single lesson to be learned, it is that we cannot remake the world in our own image or the image we would like to have of it—politically, economically, socially, or in any other fashion. Moreover, if we don't try, there is a far greater chance that those parts of the world for which we wish the best will ultimately return to a certain stasis—the equilibrium that was intended. The best of intentions simply don't work with a bad plan. And if there is any question about that, we have only to look to the past to prove this point—provided we look far enough back to see where our troubles began.

MAPS

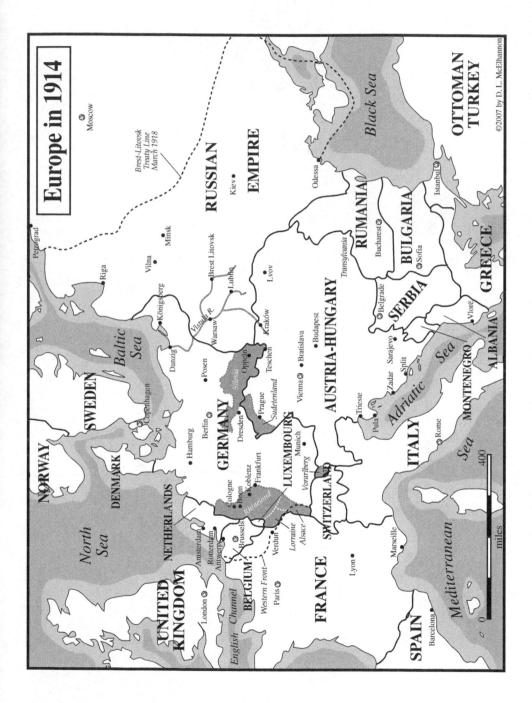

Europe in 1914

©2007 by D. L. McElhannon

OTTOMAN TURKEY

RUSSIAN EMPIRE

Brest-Litovsk Treaty Line March 1918

Moscow

Black Sea

Istanbul

Odessa

Kiev

RUMANIA

Bucharest

BULGARIA

Sofia

SERBIA

GREECE

Belgrade

Vlorë

ALBANIA

MONTENEGRO

Petrograd

Minsk

Vilna

Riga

Brest Litovsk

Lubin

Lvov

Königsberg

Warsaw

Kraków

Teschen

Budapest

Bratislava

AUSTRIA-HUNGARY

Transylvania

Sarajevo

Zadar

Split

Adriatic Sea

Baltic Sea

Vistula R.

Danzig

Posen

Silesia

Oppeln

Prague

Sudetenland

Vienna

Trieste

Pula

SWEDEN

Copenhagen

Hamburg

Berlin

Dresden

GERMANY

Munich

Vorarlberg

Frankfurt

Koblenz

LUXEMBOURG

SWITZERLAND

ITALY

Rome

Adriatic Sea

NORWAY

DENMARK

NETHERLANDS

Amsterdam

Rotterdam

Antwerp

Brussels

BELGIUM

Cologne

Bonn

Rhineland

Verdun

Lorraine

Alsace

North Sea

UNITED KINGDOM

London

English Channel

Western Front

Paris

FRANCE

Lyon

Marseille

SPAIN

Barcelona

Mediterranean Sea

400

miles

0

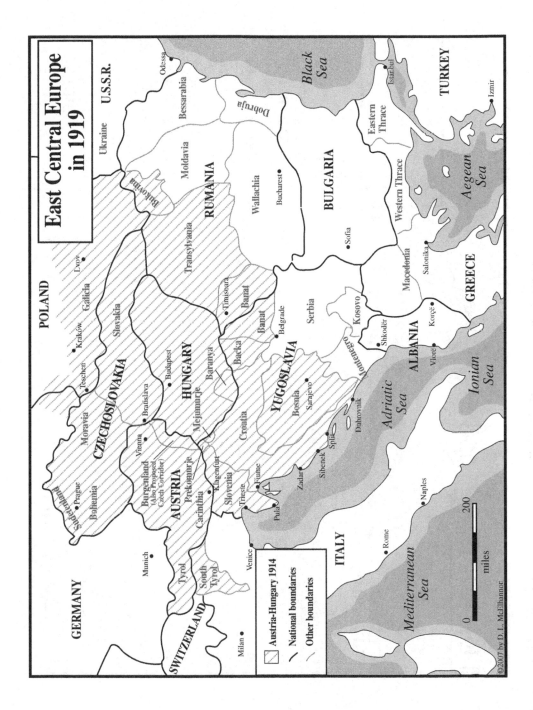

East Central Europe in 1919

Legend:
- Austria-Hungary 1914
- National boundaries
- Other boundaries

©2007 by D. L. McElhannon

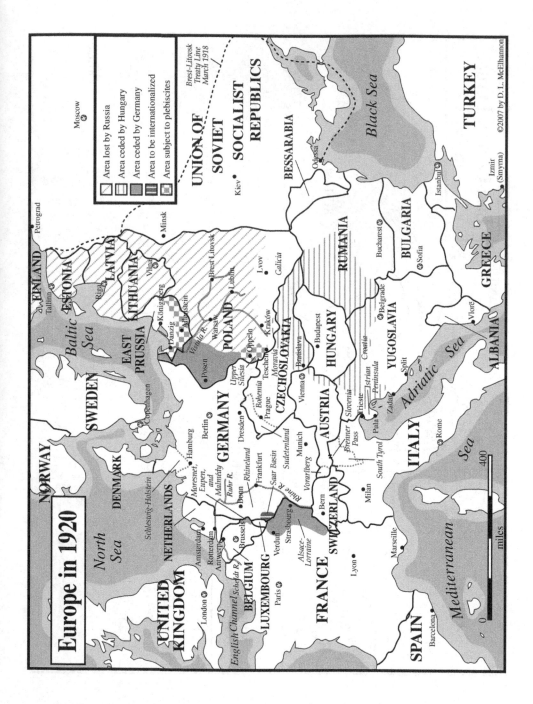

Europe in 1920

Legend:
- Area lost by Russia
- Area ceded by Hungary
- Area ceded by Germany
- Area to be internationalized
- Area subject to plebiscites

©2007 by D. L. McElhannon

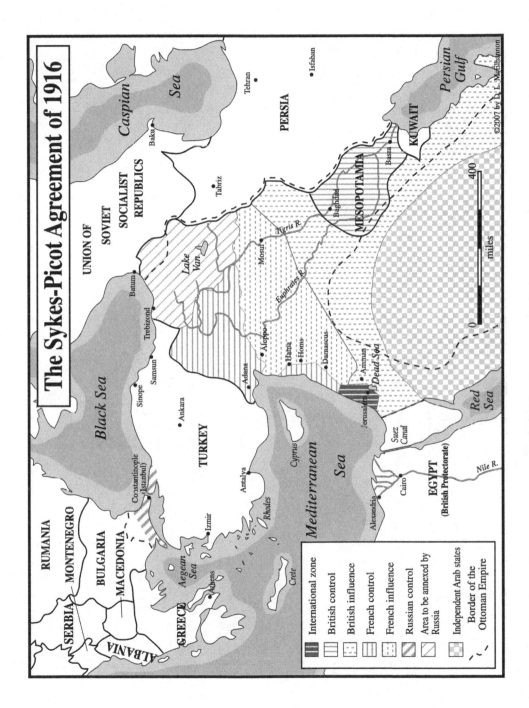

The Sykes-Picot Agreement of 1916

International zone
British control
British influence
French control
French influence
Russian control
Area to be annexed by Russia
Independent Arab states
Border of the Ottoman Empire

©2007 by D. L. McElhannon

333

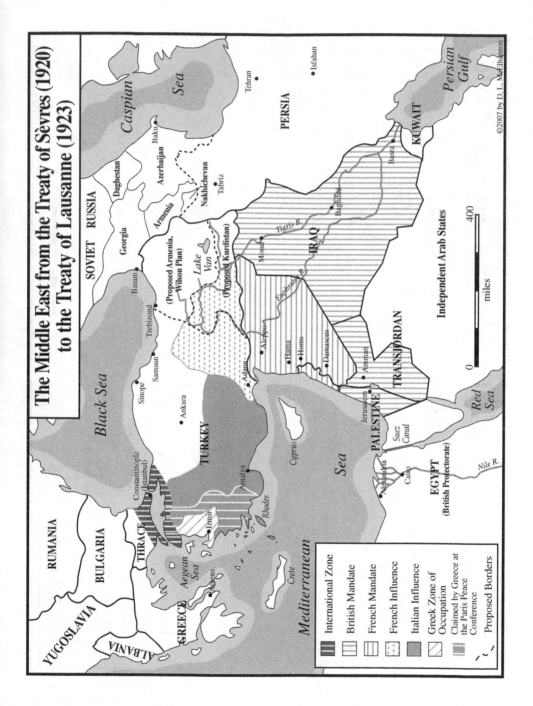

The Middle East from the Treaty of Sèvres (1920)
to the Treaty of Lausanne (1923)

©2007 by D. L. McElhannon

Independent Arab States

International Zone
British Mandate
French Mandate
French Influence
Italian Influence
Greek Zone of Occupation
Claimed by Greece at the Paris Peace Conference
Proposed Borders

0   400
miles

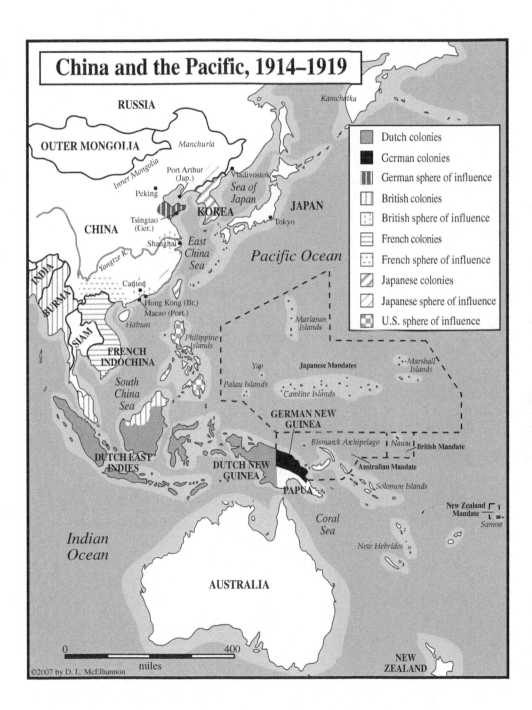

China and the Pacific, 1914–1919

RUSSIA

OUTER MONGOLIA

Manchuria

Inner Mongolia

Port Arthur
(Jap.)

Peking

Vladivostok

Sea of
Japan

JAPAN

CHINA

Tsingtao
(Ger.)

KOREA

Tokyo

Shanghai

East
China
Sea

Pacific Ocean

INDIA

Yangtze R.

Canton

Hong Kong (Br.)

Macao (Port.)

Hainan

BURMA

SIAM

FRENCH
INDOCHINA

Philippine
Islands

Marianas
Islands

Yap

Japanese Mandates

Marshall
Islands

Palau Islands

Caroline Islands

South
China
Sea

DUTCH EAST
INDIES

DUTCH NEW
GUINEA

GERMAN NEW
GUINEA

Bismarck Archipelago

Nauru

British Mandate

Australian Mandate

PAPUA

Solomon Islands

New Zealand
Mandate

Samoa

Indian
Ocean

Coral
Sea

New Hebrides

AUSTRALIA

Kamchatka

	Dutch colonies
	German colonies
	German sphere of influence
	British colonies
	British sphere of influence
	French colonies
	French sphere of influence
	Japanese colonies
	Japanese sphere of influence
	U.S. sphere of influence

0   400

miles

©2007 by D. L. McElhannon

NEW
ZEALAND

BIBLIOGRAPHY

The purpose of this volume is to point the way toward a number of issues about which I have thought deeply since my days as an undergraduate at Harvard and in my travels as a journalist. In that sense, therefore, it combines both research and commentary. More than two hundred sources were consulted in the course of its preparation; since I have elected to omit detailed footnotes, this bibliography may serve to help those interested in retracing my steps. My senior honors thesis, *Massachusetts Public Opinion and the Ratification of the Treaty of Versailles*, was for me a starting point in 1965 and was itself an intensively researched and footnoted work, which may still be consulted in the Harvard University library.

Throughout my writing, Margaret MacMillan's exhaustive *Paris 1919* (New York: Random House, 2001), was a valuable road map and helped spark my interest in taking the study of this period several steps further—particularly in dealing with many of the secondary individuals and smaller nations that played such an integral behind-the-scenes role in Paris, while at the same time examining their legacy. As a journalist I have lived through many consequences of the actions of the peacemakers decades hence. Richard Holbrooke's insightful preface I cited in chapter 8, a tribute to his brilliant diplomatic resolution of the deadly Balkan wars.

In terms of primary sources, there were a number whose value extended across many chapters. The fifteen-volume series *Foreign Relations of the United States: Paris Peace Conference* (Washington: U.S. Government Printing Office), published between 1942 and 1947, is the ultimate documentary source on the conference from the U.S. side. When it was first published in 1942, in the midst of World War II, the preface observed:

Whether a more effective peace settlement in 1919 or a more effective execution of that settlement would have saved us from the devastating war in which we are now engaged is a question which it may not be possible even for the historians of later generations to settle beyond a doubt. But irrespective of the verdict of history it is imperative that we make every effort to avoid the pitfalls of the period following the last war.

A two-volume series of *FRUS: The Lansing Papers 1914–1920* previously had been published by the GPO in 1939 and 1940. The brilliant French historian Paul Mantoux served as the French-English interpreter for the Council of Four during the critical period of March 24 through June 28, 1919. One copy of his complete notes survived the German occupation of Paris and was subsequently published in 1992 in a masterful translation by the historian Arthur S. Link, *The Deliberations of the Council of Four* (Princeton, NJ: Princeton Univ. Press, 1992).

Fortunately, 1919 was a time when participants and observers at all levels of historical events kept detailed memoirs of their thoughts and actions—some published, others unpublished but retained today in archives, often in their original typescripts. Those that covered issues raised in a number of chapters included from the U.S. side: *The Intimate Papers of Colonel House* (New York: Houghton Mifflin), edited by the Inquiry's Charles Seymour and published in four volumes from 1926 through 1928; and two diary-style works by House's aide Stephen Bonsal, *Suitors and Suppliants: The Little Nations at Versailles* (New York: Prentice-Hall, 1946) and *Unfinished Business* (Garden City, NY: Doubleday, Doran, 1944). Others from important members of the United States delegation included *The Memoirs of Herbert Hoover, Years of Adventure: 1874–1920* (New York: Macmillan, 1951); *Citizen Extraordinaire: The Diplomatic Diaries of Vance McCormick in London and Paris, 1917–1919*, edited by Michael Barton (Mechanicsburg, PA: Stackpole Books, 2004); and Edward Mandell House and Charles Seymour, *What Really Happened at Paris: The Story of the Peace Conference 1918–1919* (New York: Charles Scribner's Sons, 1921).

There were useful, published works from two Inquiry members: Yale historian, subsequently Yale president (and Skull and Bones member) Charles Seymour, *Letters from the Paris Peace Conference*, edited by Harold B. Whiteman Jr. (New Haven, CT: Yale Univ. Press, 1965); and Columbia historian, Professor James T. Shotwell, *At the Paris Peace Conference* (New York: Macmillan, 1937).

Of the unpublished diaries of Inquiry members, two of the best are on deposit in their original typescripts in Columbia University's Rare Book and Manuscript Library. George Louis Beer's 144-page diary covers the period from December 9, 1918, through August 11, 1919, in colorful and opinionated detail. The 102-page *Personal Diary of William Linn Westermann*, one of the Inquiry's Middle East experts, covers the period from December 4, 1918, through July 4, 1919. Another unpublished diary was kept by Hugh Gibson, a young American diplomat who was a close friend of Herbert Hoover and was the first postwar United States minister to Poland, of which 340 pages cover the period from September 11, 1918, through August 31, 1919, in Paris and Warsaw. They are all on deposit with the Hugh Gibson Papers at the Herbert Hoover Presidential Library in West Branch, Iowa.

From the French side, perhaps the most valuable single work was the diary kept with what for a French aide, and particularly a military officer, is unusual frankness and detail: that of Général Jean Jules Henri Mordacq, *Le Ministère Clemenceau: Journal d'un Témoin, Tome III, Novembre 1918–Juin 1919* (Paris: Librairie Plon, 1931).

From Britain, the greatest single and most colorful chronicler of all those present at the Peace Conference was without question the young diplomat Harold Nicolson, whose *Peacemaking 1919: Being Reminiscences of the Paris Peace Conference* (New York: Houghton Mifflin, 1933) all but stands alone in its candor, brilliance of perception, and attention to the epiphanal detail. Nicolson also published *Curzon: The Last Phase, 1919–1925: A Study in Post-War Diplomacy* (London: Constable & Company, 1934), about British Foreign Secretary Lord George Curzon (who, before his second marriage to an American widow, had a long affair with the romance novelist Elinor Glyn, also a figure in Paris during the peace talks). Also from the British side: press baron George Allardice Riddell, *Lord Riddell's Intimate Diary of the Peace Conference and After, 1918–1923* (New York: Reynal & Hitchcock, 1934); the memoirs of Sir Robert Vansittart, *The Mist Procession: The Autobiography of Lord Vansittart* (Hutchinson of London, 1958); and from David Lloyd George's longtime confidential secretary and publicly admitted mistress, *Lloyd George: A Diary by Frances Stevenson*, edited by A. J. P. Taylor (New York: Harper & Row, 1971).

Several other observers also produced useful works. From the U.S. side: E. J. Dillon, *The Inside Story of the Peace Conference* (New York: Harper & Brothers, 1920); and Charles T. Thompson, *The Peace Conference Day by Day: A Presidential Pilgrimage Leading to the Discovery of Europe* (New York: Brentano's, 1920), from the Associated Press correspondent who was among the better connected American reporters in Paris. Another journalist who found his way to Paris was Oswald Harrison Villard, son of the wealthy railroad magnate Henry Villard, who took over The Nation magazine that his father had owned, and left us *Fighting Years: Memoirs of a Liberal Editor* (New York: Harcourt, Brace & Company, 1939).

From the European side, Marcel Cachin, a founder of the French Communist Party and editor of its newspaper, *L'Humanité*, has left us his *Carnets, Tome II: 1917–1920* (Paris: CNRS Editions, 1993). And perhaps the most comprehensive journalistic memoir was from Henry Wickham Steed, editor of the *Times* of London, who often fancied himself a top negotiator before, during, and after the Peace Conference, as he detailed remarkably in his diary, *Through Thirty*

Years: 1892–1922, A Personal Narrative (Garden City, NY: Doubleday, Page & Company, 1925).

Another volume of enormous use throughout was Lawrence E. Gelfand's saga, *The Inquiry: American Preparations for Peace, 1917–1919* (New Haven, CT: Yale Univ. Press, 1963), which plumbed archives of the Inquiry and its members. Also, Georgetown diplomacy professor Seth P. Tillman published his doctoral thesis at the Fletcher School of Law and Diplomacy: *Anglo-American Relations at the Paris Peace Conference of 1919* (Princeton, NJ: Princeton Univ. Press, 1961).

Prologue

1. Onward to Paris

2. Le Début

Many of the diaries and memoirs mentioned above were especially useful in filling in the details for these chapters. Beyond that, there were several books by or about Allen Dulles and his years involved with the peace talks, of which the best is without question Peter Grose's *Gentleman Spy: The Life of Allen Dulles* (London: André Deutsch, 1994) by the distinguished former *New York Times* foreign and diplomatic correspondent and *Foreign Affairs* executive editor. Another biography is James Srodes, *Allen Dulles: Master of Spies* (Washington: Regnery Publishing, 1999). Two years after his retirement as director of Central Intelligence, Dulles published his own look back, *The Craft of Intelligence* (New York: Harper & Row, 1963). Major General Ralph H. Van Deman, in charge of security and intelligence for the U.S. delegation, produced a number of extraordinary memoranda, which were collected by Ralph E. Weber of Marquette University in *The Final Memoranda* (Wilmington, DE: Scholarly Resources, 1988). Hugh Wilson, a U.S. diplomat in Berlin, Bern, and Vienna, was a close friend of U.S. delegates Allen Dulles and Joseph Grew, as he mentions in his *Education of a Diplomat* (London: Longmans, Green & Company, 1938).

Setting the scene in Paris most effectively, in addition to Harold Nicolson, were Elsa Maxwell, in *R.S.V.P.: Elsa Maxwell's Own Story* (Boston: Little, Brown & Company, 1954), and Anthony Glyn, writing about his extraordinary grandmother, the "It" girl, romance novelist, lover of Lord Curzon, and "Queen of Romance," in his *Elinor Glyn: A Biography* (Garden City, NY: Doubleday & Company, 1955). Hamilton Fish Armstrong first became a Wilsonian in 1912 as a Princeton undergraduate, then detailed his travels through Paris and much of the Europe that the Peace Conference remade in his memoir, *Peace and Counterpeace: From Wilson to Hitler* (New York: Harper & Row, 1971). French historian Pierre Miquel examines the media context in which the peace talks unfolded in *La Paix de Versailles et l'Opinion Publique Française* (Paris: Flammarion, 1972).

3. Le Mistral

The single most comprehensive history of the decline and fall of the Ottoman Empire and the emergence of the modern Middle East is David Fromkin's exhaustively researched *A Peace to End All Peace: The Fall of the Ottoman Empire and the Creation of the Modern Middle East* (New York: Henry Holt, 1989). Broadening the periods on both ends of Fromkin is William L. Cleveland, *A History of the Modern Middle East* (Boulder, CO: Westview Press, 2000). A number of biographies of T. E. Lawrence have been produced, including Lawrence James, *The Golden Warrior: The Life and Legend of Lawrence of Arabia* (New York: Paragon House, 1993), which seeks to debunk some of the more outrageous tales of Lawrence, many of them encouraged, or at a minimum not discouraged, by himself. Not surprisingly, Lawrence has left behind a considerable body of work, notably his *Seven Pillars of Wisdom: A Triumph* (London: Jonathan Cape, 1935). *The Home Letters of T. E. Lawrence and His Brothers* (New York: Macmillan, 1954), assembled by his brother, M. R. Lawrence, provides many compelling insights, as does *T. E. Lawrence: The Selected Letters*, edited by Malcolm Brown (New York: Paragon House, 1992). Lawrence's Middle East intelligence colleague, erstwhile friend, and sometime Paris companion, Colonel Richard Meinertzhagen, kept a *Middle East Diary: 1917–1956* (London: Cresset Press, 1959). Another British Middle East intelligence specialist, Sir Compton MacKenzie, produced a multivolume diary, of which one deals with the period that most concerns us, *My Life and Times, Octave Five 1915–1923* (London: Chatto & Windus, 1966). He also authored a wonderful novel of the times, *Extremes Meet* (London: Chatto & Windus: 1928). Two excellent works on Lawrence's colleague and sometimes rival, the extraordinary Gertrude Bell, are Janet Wallach, *Desert Queen* (New York: Doubleday, 1996), and the earlier H. V. F. Winstone, *Gertrude Bell* (New York: Quartet Books, 1978). Anthony Cave Brown, *Treason in the Blood: H. St. John Philby, Kim Philby and the Spy Case of the Century* (New York: Houghton Mifflin, 1994) delves deeply into the life of Kim Philby's father and explores some of the personal and psychological roots of St. John's traitorous son, with some useful background of the origins of the supremacy of Ibn Saud in Arabia.

A brilliant study, essential to an understanding of the lead-up to the Sykes-Picot Agreement, the context in which Lawrence and all the peacemakers in Paris operated, is Elie Kedourie's exhaustive *In the Anglo-Arab Labyrinth: The McMahon-Husayn Correspondence and Its Interpretations 1914–1939* (London: Frank Cass, 1976), which includes extensive material from the exchanges of letters and cables. Finally, the early history of the U.S. entry into the Arabian oil regions is contained in *Out in the Blue: Letters from Arabia 1937–1940* (Vista, CA: Selwa Press, 2000) by Thomas C. Barger, the former CEO of Aramco. The book was given to me by a senior Saudi official in the interest of helping me to understand the extraordinary obstacles that were overcome in the deserts of the Arabian Peninsula. And of course, the previously cited unpublished diary of William Westermann, the Inquiry expert on the Middle East, is invaluable in providing insight into the Paris discussions, particularly within the U.S. delegation.

4. The State of the Jews

We are fortunate that Chaim Weizmann left behind a vivid two-volume autobiography. The first volume, *Trial and Error* (Philadelphia: Jewish Publication Society of America, 1949), deals with his early life through the conclusion of the San Remo Conference. It's worth cross-referencing this in parts with the biography by Jehuda Reinharz, *Chaim Weizmann: The Making of a Statesman* (Oxford: Oxford Univ. Press, 1993). Reinharz, professor of modern Jewish history and provost at Brandeis University, has consulted a number of other contemporary sources for a different version of some events. Oscar S. Straus, the member of the distinguished New York Jewish family who served a succession of presidents and did considerable behind-the-scenes work at the Peace Conference, left his compelling memoir, *Under Four Administrations* (New York: Houghton Mifflin, 1922). Noah Lucas, *The Modern History of Israel* (New York: Praeger, 1975), was useful in tracing the story of Palestine and Israel since the San Remo Conference.

5. A Wicked Wind from the East

The encyclopedic biography by William J. Duiker, *Ho Chi Minh* (New York: Hyperion, 2000), traces the life of the father of communist Vietnam from his earliest days, including his peripatetic wanderings, in exquisite detail. What Duiker omits on Ho's early days in Paris is more than made up for by Thu Trang-Gaspard, *Ho Chi Minh à Paris* (1917–1923) (Paris: Editions L'Harmattan, 1992). Mme. Thu, born into an ancient family of intellectuals from northern Vietnam, came to France in 1961. She managed to obtain access to the most closely held archives of the Sûreté Générale, Ministère des Colonies, and Ministère des Affaires Etrangères on deposit in Paris and at the Archives Nationales in Aix-en-Provence. These included the detailed reports of agents who followed Nguyen Ai Quoc (later known as Ho Chi Minh) throughout his daily rounds and transcripts of overheard conversations. Two other interesting biographies are Yevgeny Kobelev, *Ho Chi Minh* (Moscow: Progress Publishers, 1989), a Soviet account that details Quoc's earliest days in Moscow; and a rare, and anonymous, North Vietnamese biography, *Avec L'Oncle Ho* (Hanoi: Editions en Langues Etrangères, 1972), which mentions the two-way exchange between Quoc and the U.S. delegation. This first set me on the track of the actual correspondence, which was uncovered in Box 162, Folder 8060 of the Colonel Edward House papers at the Manuscripts & Archives division of the Yale University Library.

Also useful for an understanding of those who served as mentors or friends of Quoc were Jacques Duclos, *Mémoires: 1896–1934: Le Chemin que J'ai Choisi de Verdun au Parti Communiste* (Paris: Fayard, 1968); Juliette Goublet, *Léo Poldès 'Le Faubourg'* (Aurillac, France: Editions du Centre, 1965); and Ernest Lavisse et al., *Lettres à Tous Les Français* (Paris: Comité de Publication, 1916); as well as the diary (cited above) of early French Communist Party leader and *L'Humanité* editor Marcel Cachin, who published some of Quoc's works.

6. A Pair of Princes

It was inevitable that Tomáš Masaryk, a distinguished scholar, would produce a comprehensive memoir, *The Making of a State: Memories and Observations 1914–1918* (New York: Frederick A. Stokes, 1927), with, of course, a preface by the ubiquitous Wickham Steed. More useful in understanding the sweep of Masaryk's life and career, and that of his son Jan, is Zbynek Zeman, *The Masaryks: The Making of Czechoslovakia* (London: Weidenfeld & Nicholson, 1976). The close Masaryk friend, the British historian and government advisor R. W. Seton-Watson, produced a personal memoir, *Masaryk in England* (New York: Macmillan, 1943). A detailed study of Czechoslovakia in the peace process is David Perman, *The Shaping of the Czechoslovak State* (Leiden, The Netherlands: E. J. Brill, 1962), which, the author points out, was prepared when "the archives of Great Britain, France and Italy [were] largely closed to a great extent." From the Polish side, the most useful work is the quasi-authorized biography by Rom Landau, *Ignace Paderewski: Musician and Statesman* (New York: Thomas Y. Crowell, 1934). Heading the British military mission to Poland, and a confidant of Pilsudski, Lieutenant-General Sir Adrian Carton de Wiart produced his memoir, *Happy Odyssey* (London: Jonathan Cape, 1950). The previously cited memoir of Wickham Steed was also useful.

7. All Aboard the Orient Express

The most detailed account of the issue of Russia and Bolshevism at the Peace Conference is John M. Thompson, *Russia, Bolshevism, and the Versailles Peace* (Princeton, NJ: Princeton Univ. Press, 1966), an outgrowth of his Columbia doctoral dissertation in 1960. The critical Bullitt mission to Moscow is especially well chronicled in two places: Beatrice C. Farnsworth, *William C. Bullitt and the Soviet Union* (Bloomington: Indiana Univ. Press, 1967), which also goes on to discuss the evolution in Bullitt's thinking about the Soviet Union in later years; and *The Bullitt Mission to Russia: Testimony before the Committee on Foreign Relations United States Senate of William C. Bullitt* (New York: B.W. Huebsch, November 1919), which contains much of the wonderful repartee between Bullitt and his Senate inquisitors. The views of Lincoln Steffens are detailed in *The Autobiography of Lincoln Steffens* (New York: Harcourt, Brace, 1931). The

Nansen episode is discussed in Herbert Hoover, *The Ordeal of Woodrow Wilson* (New York: McGraw-Hill, 1958); Roland Huntford, *Nansen: The Explorer as Hero* (London: Gerald Duckworth & Company, 1997); and the explorer's own version, Dr. Fridtjof Nansen, *Russia & Peace* (London: George Allen & Unwin, 1923). An early contemporary view of Soviet foreign policy is Alfred L. P. Dennis, *The Foreign Policies of Soviet Russia* (New York: E.P. Dutton, 1924). British historian David Mitchell provides some color and insight on the years around 1919 in Russia in his *1919 Red Mirage* (New York: Macmillan, 1970).

Harold Nicolson's memoir/diary, cited above, details the Smuts/Nicolson mission to Budapest. Nicholas Roosevelt's *A Front Row Seat* (Norman: Univ. of Oklahoma Press, 1953) describes in vivid detail what he calls "the Red Revolution in Hungary, from his arrival in Budapest on March 17, 1919, as a twenty-six-year-old army officer and member of the armistice commission in Central Europe, whose views were sought by the Allies in Paris."

8. Into the Balkan Soup

The most comprehensive history of the Balkans, providing an overview of the domestic and foreign policies of the various Balkan nations and territories, is the two-volume Barbara Jelavich, *History of the Balkans* (Cambridge, England: Cambridge Univ. Press, 1983). The second volume deals with the twentieth century. With respect to the formation of Yugoslavia, the most comprehensive work is from Croatian-born (December 11, 1929) Yale historian Ivo J. Lederer, *Yugoslavia at the Paris Peace Conference: A Study in Frontiermaking* (New Haven, CT: Yale Univ. Press, 1963), which appeared three years after his *The Versailles Settlement—Was It Foredoomed to Failure?* (New York: D.C. Heath, 1960) and says a lot as to this historian's view of the whole process. The memoir of Michael Pupin, *From Immigrant to Inventor* (New York: Charles Scribner's Sons, 1924), is from the Columbia scientist and member of the Serbian delegation in Paris. Dalmatia's Count Louis Voinovitch offers *Dalmatia and the Jugoslav Movement* (New York: Charles Scribner's Sons, 1917). A member of the Yugoslav Committee, Bogumil Vosnjak, weighs in with a Slovene perspective, *A Bulwark against Germany: The Fight of the Slovenes, the Western Branch of the Jugoslavs, for National Existence* (New York: Fleming H. Revell, 1919).

For Rumania, there is Hannah Pakula's *The Last Romantic: A Biography of Queen Marie of Roumania* (New York: Simon & Schuster, 1984). Queen Marie herself produced two somewhat overlapping autobiographies: *The Story of My Life* (New York: Charles Scribner's Sons, 1934) and *Ordeal: The Story of My Life* (New York: Charles Scribner's Sons, 1935). Princess Anne-Marie Callimachi, *Yesterday Was Mine* (New York: McGraw-Hill, 1949), is another self-told tale of a Rumanian princess in Paris. The First Lady, Edith Bolling Wilson, who accompanied her husband to Paris, gives an entertaining account of her meetings with Queen Marie in *My Memoir* (New York: Bobbs-Merrill, 1938). For Bulgaria, there's Stephane Groueff, *Crown of Thorns: The Reign of King Boris III of Bulgaria 1918–1943* (Lanham, MD: Madison Books, 1987).

9. Greater Asian Insecurity

Several excellent studies of the Far East and the U.S. role include Roy Watson Curry's *Woodrow Wilson and Far Eastern Policy 1913–1921* (New York: Twayne Publishers, 1957). The definitive biography of the leading Chinese negotiator, Pao-chin Chu's *V. K. Wellington Koo: A Case Study of China's Diplomat and Diplomacy of Nationalism 1912–1966* (Hong Kong: Chinese Univ. Press/Hong Kong, 1981), is an invaluable study of this extraordinary man with color and anecdote. Stephen Bonsal's *Suitors and Suppliants*, cited above, was valuable in describing some of the U.S. delegation's dealing with the Chinese, Koreans, and Japanese, while Mantoux's notes on the Council of Four provided detailed accounts of the debates between the parties in the later stages of the Peace Conference. Paul S. Reinsch, Wilson's ambassador to China and a distinguished political scientist from the University of Wisconsin who helped found the American Political Science Association, produced two monumental works: *An American Diplomat in China* (London: George Allen & Unwin, 1922), and *Secret Diplomacy: How Far Can It Be Eliminated?* (New York: Harcourt Brace, 1921), from which I also quoted in chapter 10.

10. Setting Up a Global Economy

Not surprisingly, John Maynard Keynes himself is the greatest single source not only on his own thoughts but on the entire issue of reparations and the economic future of Europe—particularly is two masterful works, *The Economic Consequences of the Peace* (New York: Harper & Row, 1971, with Robert Lekachman's valuable preface) and *Two Memoirs: Dr. Melchior: A Defeated Enemy; and My Early Beliefs* (London: Rupert Hart-Davis, 1949), the former written with the detail only a brilliant economist could muster, the latter with the sensitivity of an embedded member of the Bloomsbury Group. For a more dispassionate and comprehensive examination of Keynes and his times, University of Warwick economist/historian Lord Robert Skidelsky's two-volume biography is without peer—*John Maynard Keynes: Hopes Betrayed 1883–1920* (New York: Macmillan, 1983) and *John Maynard Keynes: The Economist as Saviour 1920–1937* (New York: Macmillan, 1992). The entire issue of reparations in their economic and historic contexts is provided by University of Pennsylvania historian Marc Trachtenberg, *Reparations in World Politics: France and European Economic Diplomacy, 1916–1923* (New York: Columbia Univ. Press, 1980). Most of the key documents connected with reparations were assembled for the Carnegie Endowment for International Peace by Philip Mason Burnett,

Reparation at the Paris Peace Conference [2 volumes] (New York: Columbia Univ. Press, 1940).

Several of the key participants or observers have weighed in with their views including Bernard M. Baruch, *The Making of the Reparations and Economic Sections of the Treaty* (New York: Harper & Brothers Publishers, 1920); the British diplomat, politician and peer (Edgar Vincent) Viscount D'Abernon's *The Diary of an Ambassador – Versailles to Rapallo 1920–1922* (New York: Doubleday, Doran, 1929); and *The Diary of an Ambassador: Rapallo to Dawes 1922–1924* (New York: Doubleday, Doran, 1930). From the French perspective there is Jacques Seydoux, *De Versailles au Plan Young: Réparations – Dettes Interalliées, Reconstruction Européenne* (Paris: Librairie Plon, 1932). Etienne Mantoux, the brilliant economist son of Paul Mantoux, was determined to debunk Keynes' view of reparations and produced, *The Carthaginian Peace, or The Economic Consequences of Mr. Keynes* (Univ. Pittsburgh Press, 1952), or as Mantoux puts it in a preface: "It is hard to see why anyone should be denied a sporting chance of hitting back on the pretext that the first blow was delivered a quarter century ago." David Lloyd George did not wait as long to deliver his riposte in *The Truth About Reparations and War Debts* (New York: Doubleday, 1932). Other useful works include Yale historian Robert E. Bunselmeyer, *The Cost of the War 1914–1919: British Economic War Aims and the Origins of Reparation* (Archon, 1975); Edgar Ansel Meyer, *Germany Puts the Clock Back* (New York: William Morrow, 1933); and Ron Chernow, *The Warburgs* (New York: Random House, 1993).

11. Where Did They All Go?

The observations in this epilogue are entirely my own, though the context—including my readings in the thoughts of contemporary observers and participants, including Harold Nicolson, Charles Seymour, William Westermann, George Louis Beer, and a host of others—certainly helped shape my thinking. Moreover, as indicated in the prologue, my travels in more than fifty nations over the past forty years, where I encountered extraordinary individuals far too numerous to name, have in scores of languages and at times heart-stopping circumstances also played an important role in developing my views.

INDEX

NOTE: Page numbers in *italics* refer to illustrations and maps.